DATE DUE

DEC 3 '02			

GREAT LIVES FROM HISTORY

GREAT LIVES FROM HISTORY

American Women Series

Volume 4
Lyn-Rot

Edited by

FRANK N. MAGILL

SALEM PRESS

Pasadena, California   Englewood Cliffs, New Jersey

∞ The paper used in these volumes conforms to the American National Standard for Permanence of Paper for Printed Library Materials, Z39.48-1984.

Library of Congress Cataloging-in-Publication Data
Great lives from history. American women series / edited by Frank N. Magill.
p. cm.
Includes bibliographical references and index.
1. Women—United States—Biography. 2. Women—Canada—Biography. 3. Women—United States—History. 4. Women—Canada—History. I. Magill, Frank Northen, 1907- . II. Title: American women series.
HQ1412.G74 1995
305.4′0973—dc20
ISBN 0-89356-892-9 (set) 94-38308
ISBN 0-89356-896-1 (volume 4) CIP

PRINTED IN THE UNITED STATES OF AMERICA

LIST OF BIOGRAPHIES IN VOLUME FOUR

LIST OF BIOGRAPHIES IN VOLUME FOUR

GREAT LIVES FROM HISTORY

HELEN MERRELL LYND

Born: March 17, 1896; La Grange, Illinois
Died: January 30, 1982; Warren, Ohio
Areas of Achievement: Sociology and education
Contribution: Helen Merrell Lynd is best known for her collaboration with her husband, Robert S. Lynd, in writing the classic studies *Middletown: A Study in Contemporary American Culture* (1929) and *Middletown in Transition: A Study in Cultural Conflicts* (1937). She also made her mark as an innovator in higher education for women, as a historian, and as a social psychologist.

Early Life

Helen Merrell was born on March 17, 1896, in La Grange, Illinois, one of three daughters of Edward Tracy Merrell and Mabel Waite Merrell. Her paternal grandfather had been one of the founders of Ripon College in Wisconsin; her father was editor of the Congregationalist Church magazine *The Advance*. Helen grew up in a strongly religious atmosphere permeated with a commitment to improve human life, establish social justice, and live according to an egalitarian ethos.

Helen attended primary and secondary school in La Grange. When her father moved the family to Framingham, Massachusetts, because of a new job, she attended nearby Wellesley College. Her major interest as an undergraduate was philosophy, especially Hegelianism, and she was elected to the Phi Beta Kappa society in her senior year. After being graduated from Wellesley in 1919, she taught for one year at the Ossining School for Girls at Ossining, New York, and at Miss Master's School in Dobbs Ferry, New York.

She met Robert S. Lynd, a 1914 Princeton graduate then working in publishing, while mountain climbing in 1919. They were married on September 3, 1922. By that time, Robert had left publishing to enroll in Union Theological Seminary, from which institution he received his D.D. degree in 1923, while Helen had begun graduate work in history at Columbia University. Robert's exposure to poor working conditions at the oil drilling camp owned by a Rockefeller-controlled firm in Elk Basin, Wyoming, where he had gone as a missionary preacher, led to his being hired by the Rockefeller-financed Institute of Social and Religious Research to study the religious life of a typical small industrial city.

Life's Work

After Robert S. Lynd picked as the site for the study Muncie, Indiana (which he renamed Middletown), he and Helen Merrill Lynd spent a year and a half living there to gain firsthand knowledge of the city and its people. Going beyond the limited aim of the institute, the Lynds wrote a comprehensive account of all aspects of daily life—describing not only religious practices and organizations but also how Muncie's people made and spent their money; family structure and child rearing practices; leisure-time activities; and attitudes, values, and beliefs. The officers of the institute were so unhappy with the result that they balked at its publication. Only after much difficulty were the Lynds able to arrange for the publication of *Middletown: A Study in Contemporary American Culture* in 1929 by the publishing firm of Harcourt, Brace.

The work was an immediate success, winning popular and academic plaudits. In 1935, the Lynds returned to Muncie to study the impact of the Great Depression upon the community. The result was *Middletown in Transition: A Study in Cultural Conflicts*. The new work's most apparent difference from the first study was in its emphasis on the domination of the city by the economic power of the "X" family (the Ball brothers, who had become rich manufacturing glass jars for preserves). To their disappointment, however, the Lynds found that the Depression had failed to dislodge the popular faith in the traditional American myth of success through hard work.

Although Helen was listed as coauthor of the Middletown studies, the gender bias permeating university life meant that Robert was the major beneficiary of the works' success. He was appointed Giddings Professor of Sociology at Columbia University in 1931. In order to gain the requisite Ph.D. status, he went through what Helen termed in her recollections the "fake process" of submitting as his dissertation a copy of the first Middletown book with her contribution supposedly removed. Helen taught social philosophy at Sarah Lawrence College from its founding in 1928 as an experimental liberal arts college for women located in the New York City suburb of Bronxville. She remained a full-time faculty member at Sarah Lawrence until her retirement in 1964; she continued teaching there on a reduced-load basis until shortly before her death in 1982.

Helen enjoyed teaching the bright and often unconventional young women who were attracted to Sarah Lawrence. She was instrumental in the adoption of the college's flexible interdisciplinary curriculum featuring individually tailored programs and detailed evaluations instead of number or letter grades. Her thoughts on reshaping the educational process were most fully elaborated in her books *Field Work in College Education* (1945) and *Toward Discovery* (1965). The first gives examples of teaching sociology via student projects in the community; the pieces on education in the second—a collection of her articles and speeches—are more philosophical in their approach.

Helen received a combined Ph.D. in history and philosophy from Columbia University in 1944 with a dissertation that was published the following year under the title *England in the Eighteen-Eighties: Toward a Social Basis for Freedom*. Highly praised for its stylistic elegance, the book was a landmark study of the interaction of economic changes, ideas, and social movements. The work's first theme was the contradiction between material progress and the continued poverty of the masses; the second, the accompanying tension between authority and freedom. The result, Lynd found, was that "[b]etween the late 'seventies and the end of the 'eighties the gradual whittling away of economic individualism that had been going on in practice was suddenly recognized in theory. . . . England in the 'eighties found articulate expression for new norms, new criteria of social values, new conceptions of freedom."

During the 1930's and 1940's, Helen and Robert were active in a wide range of liberal and left-wing causes. Although they kept their distance from the Communist Party, they were naïvely sympathetic to the Soviet Union and thus prone to place major blame for the Cold War upon the United States. Helen was even more publicly outspoken than Robert in her attacks on what she saw as a hysterical, reactionary-inspired, anti-Communist witch hunt. As a result, she was called before a hostile Senate investigating committee.

In her later years, the major focus of Helen's interest was the role of the social environment in shaping personality in the contemporary world. She was extraordinarily well read, familiar with the work of the major figures of British and European literature, and she utilized those authors' insights for her psychological analysis of the sources of human identity in her book *On Shame and the Search for Identity* (1958). Her core thesis was the distinction between guilt—the result of the breaking of society's external code—and shame, or the betrayal of a personal sense of self. At one level, the work was an attack on psychotherapist Sigmund Freud and sociologist Talcott Parsons for their failure to appreciate the historical bases of social group membership and their neglect of the role of social values in shaping the individual self. On the positive side, she appealed to the creative individual to transcend socially prescribed limits. The book was favorably received by many psychologists and psychiatrists, and it was reprinted in a paperback edition in 1970.

Helen and Robert Lynd had a son, Staughton, born in 1929, and a daughter, Andrea Merrell, born in 1934. Helen died on January 30, 1982, in Warren, Ohio.

Summary

Helen Merrell Lynd's most important legacy was her collaboration with Robert Lynd in writing the two Middletown studies. The works, which set the standard for community studies in the United States, constitute a major source for historians of American values and behavior between the two world wars. In his appraisal for the *International Encyclopedia of the Social Sciences*, Irving Louis Horowitz concludes that the works "illumined for a generation of social science the essence of the American way of life. . . . [T]aken together the *Middletown* studies remain a most significant record of this period in American social life."

Helen Lynd also made significant intellectual contributions on her own. She was an important figure in efforts to reform higher education. Her *England in the Eighteen-Eighties* remains "must" reading for students of the late nineteenth century transformation of English society and politics, and the leading historians of the study of the identity-formation process praise her "creative argument" in *On Shame* "as an important transition piece from psychoanalytic writings to work more central to sociological psychology."

Bibliography

Deegan, Mary Jo., ed. *Women in Sociology: A Bio-Bibliographical Sourcebook*. New York: Greenwood Press, 1991. The entry on Lynd contains the fullest available account of her life and work outside her collaboration on the Middletown studies.

The piece is, however, based primarily upon published materials; the author did not examine Lynd's papers in the Library of Congress and at Sarah Lawrence College.

Fox, Richard Wightman. "Epitaph for Middletown: Robert S. Lynd and the Analyses of Consumer Culture." In *The Culture of Consumption: Critical Essays in American History, 1880-1980*, edited by Richard Wightman Fox and T. J. Jackson Lears. New York: Pantheon Books, 1983. A provocative interpretation of the Middletown studies that sees the works as an analysis, and an indictment, of the rise to dominance of the consumer culture in American life.

Horowitz, Irving Louis. "Robert S. and Helen Merrell Lynd." In *International Encyclopedia of the Social Sciences: Biographical Supplement*, edited by David L. Sills. New York: Free Press, 1979. An excellent perceptive analysis/appraisal of the work of both Lynds by one of the leading historians of sociology. The best available introduction to the couple's significance in American social science.

Lynd, Helen Merrell. *Toward Discovery*. Bronxville, N.Y.: Sarah Lawrence College, 1965. The introduction ("Curved and Rendered by Reason") to this collection of Helen Lynd's articles and speeches, written by Bert James Loewenberg, an intellectual historian who was a longtime colleague of Lynd's at Sarah Lawrence College, emphasizes as her dominant concern "the context of discovery: the environment of ideas; education in contemporary society; the nature of historical objectivity."

Stein, Maurice R. *The Eclipse of Community: An Interpretation of American Studies*. Princeton, N.J.: Princeton University Press, 1960. Includes an in-depth analysis of the two Middletown studies and their role in shaping the future direction of community studies in the United States.

Weigert, Andrew J., J. Smith Teitge, and Dennis W. Teitge. *Society and Identity: Toward a Sociological Psychology*. New York: Cambridge University Press, 1986. Includes a history of the investigation by social and psychological analysts of the process of identity formation that appraises the contribution of Lynd's *On Shame*.

John Braeman

LORETTA LYNN

Born: April 14, 1935; Butcher Hollow, Kentucky

Area of Achievement: Music
Contribution: This "Queen of Country Music" was the first woman to be named Entertainer of the Year by the Country Music Association in 1972. Her popularity and productivity remain unmatched; writing and recording more than fifty records, while achieving sales exceeding twenty million albums.

Early Life

Loretta Webb was born on April 14, 1935, in a small town in the hills of eastern Kentucky called Butcher Hollow. She was the second oldest of eight children, four boys and four girls, and was descended from two great-grandmothers who were full-blooded Cherokee. When Loretta was born, her mother tried to keep the wind from coming through the cracks in their one-room cabin by covering the walls with pictures from old film magazines. Her particular favorites were Claudette Colbert and Loretta Young; the latter providing the inspiration for her baby daughter's name. When little Loretta was eleven months old, she suffered a severe ear infection called mastoiditis. Lacking access to modern medical treatment, Loretta nearly lost her life, but she was able to survive with minimal scarring.

Born during the Great Depression, Loretta at first was largely unaware of her family's poverty; she recalled later that what was most important was that her family provided plenty of love. Loretta Lynn credits those early days of hunger and survival with giving her strength and courage in her later life. The Webbs' house had no indoor plumbing, running water, or electricity; there were no paved roads in the whole town. The lumber mills and the coal mines provided employment for the area, and the coal company also furnished a post office, a company store, and a recreation hall in the "big city" located five miles from Butcher Hollow. About once a month, Loretta and her family would venture into the town to shop and occasionally see a motion picture. Being poor meant sharing shoes, wearing flour sack dresses, being educated in a one-room schoolhouse, and leaving school at the end of the eighth grade (with the equivalent of a fourth-grade education). While the men worked in the mines, the women and children were expected to tend to the farm. Loretta was eleven years old when her father bought their first radio (a battery-operated model); she was twelve years old before she had her first ride in an automobile.

Life's Work

When Loretta Webb was only thirteen years old, she met the man who was to change her life. Oliver Vanetta Lynn, more commonly known as "Mooney" Lynn from his moonshine days and "Doolittle" Lynn by his family, was to be Loretta's first and only boyfriend and husband. Although at nineteen he was older and "more worldly" (he had been away in the service), Oliver courted Loretta and asked her to marry him before her fourteenth birthday. Before he would give consent to their marriage, Loretta's father made Oliver Lynn promise "not to whip her or take her too far from home." In her later songs, Loretta modeled her perception of how a husband should act on her father's respectful treatment of her mother, including references to the "right" and "proper" way to treat a wife and consistently rejecting the use of whipping as a way to "handle" a woman.

As a young wife, Loretta knew little about living away from her family, marriage, or even cooking. The Lynns' early years were fraught with conflicts and difficulties, but their marriage survived. After only four months of marriage, Loretta was expecting their first child. She eventually had three more children, all before she turned eighteen. It was several years, however, before she had her last two children (twins) in 1964. Loretta's experiences with these early pregnancies, which included several miscarriages, led her to write one of her most controversial and best-selling songs, "The Pill" (1975). This song was controversial within the conservative world of country music because its lyrics spoke of women putting an end to being constantly "barefoot and pregnant."

Loretta enjoyed singing around the house, so her husband bought her her first guitar for her eighteenth birthday. She taught herself to play and soon progressed from playing other people's music to writing her own songs. Eventually, her husband told Loretta that she was good enough to sing in public, and he provided her with an opportunity to do so by arranging for her to perform in a local club. Loretta began singing with the club band and then went on to form her own group. Her later singing engagements included appearances at fairs, amateur contests, and even on a local television show. The Lynns were using their last pennies to finance these trips with no prospect of receiving any money in return. They were fortunate when a wealthy businessman offered to assist them with the money to make a recording. That first record, privately produced and distributed, made its way onto the *Billboard* country music charts. It was called "Honky Tonk Girl."

With much additional self promotion, Loretta finally made fulfilled her dream of appearing on The Grand Ole Opry in Nashville, Tennessee. The full range of country music performers—from legends to novices—had their moment of glory on the stage at the Opry. In addition to being seen and heard by the studio audience, their music was broadcast live over the radio. Their appearances on the show could potentially generate many other opportunities to perform; such was the case for Loretta Lynn. After appearing on the Opry stage, she moved on to a new major recording contract and a new life in Nashville.

It was at this time, during Loretta's rise in popularity, that she first encountered some of the jealousy that is so prevalent in all facets of the entertainment field. Nevertheless, Lynn's staunchest supporter, other than her husband, was Patsy Cline. Cline was already a number one artist who had also struggled to make her way to the top. She welcomed Loretta's friendship and helped her join the elite group of top female country singers. On March 6, 1963, Patsy Cline was killed in a plane crash on her way home from a benefit concert. Loretta was devastated by Cline's death. She named one of her twins Patsy in honor of her friend.

As Loretta Lynn became more popular, it became necessary for her to spend more time away from her family in order to please her fans. At times she was gone for several weeks on the road, and the children were left to babysitters or their father. Loretta regretted the time she missed rearing her family and later admitted that she was a little jealous of her husband's close relationship with their children.

Although Loretta Lynn was named "Most Promising Newcomer" in 1960 by *Billboard* magazine, her first album hit the top of the country music charts in 1963. She quickly captured the title of "Top Female Vocalist" in 1964. Invited to sing at the Grand Ole Opry for a record seventeen straight shows, Lynn was then honored by being asked to join their membership. The Grand Ole Opry eventually was expanded to include television as well as radio broadcasts.

Lynn's celebrity brought new opportunities and new pressures. In order to satisfy the demands of her audiences, she had to increase her repertoire of songs, the majority of which she wrote herself. She believes her songs are most significant because they are written from a woman's point of view, while most early country music songs were written by and directed at men. Her songs came from her heart and from her life. Despite her newfound wealth, she never forgot the country values she learned as a child. Aware of the poverty she once suffered and fearful of being poor again, she chose to spend her money frugally and continued to can her own meat and vegetables even after she became wealthy. In 1967, Loretta and her family moved into their dream house, a 1,450-acre ranch in Hurricane Mills, Tennessee, some sixty-five miles southwest of Nashville. In the years that followed, the Lynns bought additional land and developed new properties in the area, eventually owning the entire town.

Loretta Lynn continued to tour and work into the early 1990's. In addition to advancing her own career, she has written and recorded with some of country's greatest stars, including a long partnership with Conway Twitty. She has had some health problems which included chest surgery and blood poisoning which nearly took her life. The migraine headaches she has had since she was seventeen began to improve when she stopped taking aspirin for them (she found she was allergic to aspirin) and changed her eating habits to control her high blood pressure. She has also started taking better care of herself by taking some time off each month and spending long holidays in her vacation home in Mexico. Despite various difficulties that have placed a strain on their marriage, and his ill health in recent years, Oliver Lynn continues to be involved with managing their ranch and Loretta's business affairs.

Summary

Loretta Lynn believes in being herself. She says what she thinks in her words as well as her music. Though she has never considered herself to be a feminist, she has always believed that many problems could be solved if all people were more respectful of each other. She is not afraid to let both men and women know what she expects from them in terms of appropriate behavior and responsibility. Her songs have focused on real life—particularly the experiences of women such as herself—and many of her songs are about women's issues. As expressed in her lyrics, Lynn believes that "a man doesn't have the right to tell a woman what to do"; but she also expects women to take responsibility for their own lives. Her song "Two Steps Forward" talks about relationships. In "I Only See the Things I Wanna See" and in one of her most famous songs "Don't Come Home A-Drinkin' (With Lovin' on Your Mind)" she continues to relate her life to other women's problems in their marriages. Two other songs which are popular with women are "You Ain't Woman Enough to Take My Man" and "Fist City," which describes what other women will encounter if they try to take her man. As with much of country music, the titles of Lynn's songs create vivid stories in the minds of her listeners.

Loretta Lynn has appeared in countless benefit concerts on behalf of children and has championed American Indian causes. Through it all, she has continued to affirm her proud heritage as a "coal miner's daughter"—the title of one of Lynn's most popular hits as well as the 1980 film biography based on her life. Proud of her gift for dealing with others, she has said, "When I die, I want God to put me in charge of all the people that nobody loves."

Bibliography

Busnar, Gene. *Superstars of Country Music*. New York: Julian Messner, 1984. This book details the lives of nine popular country artists including Loretta Lynn. It includes a complete listing of each artist's recordings.

Green, Douglas B. *Country Roots: The Origins of Country Music*. New York: Hawthorn Books, 1976. This book provides a detailed history of America's musical background with specific reference to the origins of country music. Especially useful is the indexed information which includes noted artists, chronology, discography, and a bibliography.

Krishef, Robert K. *Loretta Lynn*. Minneapolis, Minn.: Lerner Publications, 1978. Aimed at juvenile readers, this clearly written biography of the star provides a useful introduction to her life and career. Illustrated with many photographs not seen in other publications. Contains an index of Lynn's recordings.

Lynn, Loretta, with George Vecsey. *Loretta Lynn: Coal Miner's Daughter*. Chicago: Henry Regnery, 1976. This autobiography provides the most comprehensive source of information on Lynn. In addition to providing insights into Lynn's life, this book includes a behind-the-scenes look at the country music business.

Malone, Bill C. *Country Music, U.S.A.* Rev. ed. Austin: University of Texas Press, 1985. The most complete reference on the history and present state of country music. It contains biographical information on country music artists and their recordings including an index of song titles.

Mason, Michael. *The Country Music Book*. New York: Charles Scribner's Sons, 1985. A well organized and comprehensive look at the past and present of country music and its stars. It contains several different types of useful bibliographic indexes of written and recorded materials.

Laurie Schwartz Guttenberg

MARY LYON

Born: February 28, 1797; Buckland, Massachusetts
Died: March 5, 1849; South Hadley, Massachusetts
Area of Achievement: Education
Contribution: A lifelong teacher and advocate of education for women, Mary Lyon founded what was to become Mount Holyoke College, the first permanent institution of higher learning designed exclusively for women.

Early Life

It is sometimes said that hardship early in life builds strength that carries on throughout adulthood. This is certainly true of Mary Lyon's life. Born on February 28, 1797, on a small farm in Buckland, Franklin County, in the hills of northwest Massachusetts, Mary Lyon never had an easy life. The sixth of eight children born to Aaron Lyon and Jemima Shepard (one boy died before Mary was born), Mary started school as soon as she could make the mile-long walk to the school in Hog Hollow, when she was about four years old. Shortly before Christmas the following year, 1802, her father died, leaving his widow and his thirteen-year-old son Aaron to run the farm, helped by Mary's oldest sister Electa, who at seventeen was teaching school in Buckland. The family managed to eke out an existence on the farm for several years, but when Mary was thirteen, her mother accepted a proposal of marriage from Jonathan Taylor and moved to Ashfield with Mary's two younger sisters. Because Mary's three older sisters were either married or "boarding out" and teaching, this left only Mary and Aaron, now twenty-one, to run the farm.

Mary had stayed in school for a couple of years after her father's death, but when she was six or seven, the school in Hog Hollow moved farther away, making the walk more difficult. As she grew older and had to assume more responsibility on the farm, her attendance at school became less and less frequent until it stopped altogether. She attended terms of school sporadically before her mother's marriage by living with a family who lived near a school and doing housework to pay for her keep. Anything beyond a minimal education was expensive and hard to find for girls in that era; such education was mostly the prerogative of the daughters of the wealthy. Still, Mary continued to dream.

When her mother remarried, Mary saw no chance of realizing this dream, but her brother Aaron, who strongly supported Mary's ambitions, offered to pay her one dollar a week for her services on the farm for her to save toward an education. This was a good wage for the day, when female teachers were only paid about three dollars per month. (Men were paid ten to twelve dollars per month.) Aaron soon married, however, and when Mary was seventeen, she went to teach in nearby Shelbourne Falls. She spoke later of her problems with discipline in this first job, saying that her sense of humor and propensity to laughter sometimes made it difficult to keep order.

It was not until she was twenty that Mary managed to pursue her education on a formal basis again. In 1817, using her savings, she enrolled for the fall term at

Ashfield's Sanderson Academy. During this time, she lived with the Whites, establishing close, enduring friendships with the daughters of the family. "Squire" White, their father, was so impressed with Mary's abilities that he asked the trustees of the academy to allow her to attend another term free of tuition, since her savings were exhausted. During this time, the Whites also helped to develop Mary's social graces, hitherto rough at best, which were necessary to a person wishing to associate on equal terms with educated society. When Amanda White decided to attend Amherst Academy in 1818, Mary went with her, borrowing money from Squire White to do so.

For the next few years, Mary alternated between teaching terms of school and attending them at various academies, finally becoming a teaching assistant at Sanderson Academy. She was the first woman to teach there. Her scholarship was amazing. A story is recorded in several places of a time at Sanderson when, partly in order to give Mary something to occupy her so that she would not get too far ahead of the rest of the class, the instructor assigned Mary a book on Latin grammar to learn. When she came to school after the weekend, she had learned the entire book, and could recite it verbatim almost flawlessly. It had taken her three days. When questioned, she admitted that she had broken the Sabbath by studying on Sunday because she had found the book too fascinating to stop. With this drive, she attained a level of education rarely achieved by anyone, especially any woman, of her day.

Life's Work

As Mary Lyon's fame grew, she was in increasing demand as a teacher, and in 1826 she was appointed preceptress at Sanderson Academy. Sanderson only maintained classes in the winter, which made it possible for her to teach elsewhere the rest of the year. When her friend Zilpah Grant, for whom she had taught at Adams Female Academy in Londonderry (later Derry), New Hampshire, asked her in 1828 to teach at Ipswich Seminary near Boston, she accepted. In 1830, she decided to devote her whole year to Ipswich, and she became assistant principal under Grant. It was during her time at Ipswich that Lyon became convinced of the need for an endowed, permanent institution of higher learning for women.

Opportunities for women's education in the nineteenth century were oases in a desert. Beyond the district schools, many schools were not open to women, and those that were tended to be expensive. Even Oberlin College, founded in 1833 and open to women, did not allow its female students to attend the same regimen of classes as male students, providing instead a "ladies' course" of study. There were other schools for girls: Catharine Beecher's Hartford Female Seminary, Emma Willard's Troy Female Seminary, and others. These were expensive, however, and they followed the current trend of providing "finishing" in feminine accomplishments, such as French, music, and painting. Lyon wanted to found an institution that would provide a solid classical education at as low a cost as possible. To do this, funds would have to be found to provide buildings, equipment, books, and faculty.

Lyon was above all a realist. She knew that without male support, she could not raise the money needed to establish a new seminary. Enlisting the services of several prominent clergymen, academics, and businessmen, in 1834 she began a campaign to find money, support, and future pupils for what has become Mount Holyoke College. One of these men, Edward Hitchcock, later became president of Amherst College and Lyon's first biographer after her death.

For almost four years, from early 1834 to November of 1837, Lyon stopped teaching to build foundations of her new seminary. Traveling from place to place to solicit funds, she slowly established the base on which a secure institution could be grounded. In January of 1835, the trustees chose (after much debate) South Hadley, Massachusetts, as the site of the seminary. In April of the same year, the name Mount Holyoke Female Seminary was chosen, after the mountain in South Hadley of the same name. Professor Hitchcock's suggestion of Pangynaskean Academy (derived from the Greek and meant to convey the concept of the education of the whole woman) was much ridiculed and was decisively voted down. In October, 1836, the cornerstone was laid for the building of Mount Holyoke. Finally, on November 8, 1837, the first pupils came to South Hadley to start their three-year course of studies toward graduation.

All of this did not go without a hitch. Because Lyon's aim was to provide quality education at a low cost, she decided that the housework should be done by the students and faculty themselves. This was unheard of in a time when seminaries were places where wealthy families sent their daughters to prepare them for lives of relative ease. Accusations that Lyon was trying to establish a "manual-labor school" and "a Protestant nunnery" followed. Funds were still short, also, and the students were asked to bring with them what they could in the way of linens, blankets, pillows, and silverwear. The students arrived, bringing what they could, and Mount Holyoke grew and flourished.

Mary Lyon presided over her seminary, referring to her students as her "daughters," for twelve years. Those years saw an increase in the size of the student body, from the initial number of seventy-nine to more than two hundred in 1849, and an increase of faculty from three (besides Lyon) to eleven. Student applications were so numerous that many were turned down. Lyon tried to make the admission process more selective each year, raising the caliber of the students along with the difficulty of the curriculum. Despite the strict rules and hard work, both academic and manual, attendance at Mount Holyoke continued to be the goal of a growing number of women.

In 1849, a case of the disease erysipelas occurred in the student body. Because there had been fatal epidemics in some parts of the country, panic spread. Lyon marshaled her students, telling them that those who wished to go home could do so. Few did. Lyon nursed the student, overtiring herself in the process. The girl died. Soon afterward, Lyon learned that a nephew of hers had committed suicide. The combination of the news and her fatigue resulted in a collapse. Mary Lyon died within a short time, on March 5, 1849.

Summary

The legacy that Mary Lyon has left continues to provide motivation and opportunity for the thousands of women who attend Mount Holyoke College each year. Her strength and determination formed the basis for a movement in education that started with Mount Holyoke and continued with the establishment of other women's colleges, among them Vassar, Smith, Radcliffe, and Barnard. Mary Lyon's example as a scholar, which moved her own teachers to wish that she could have the opportunity to attend college, convinced many people that women were worth educating, that they had the ability to learn and the motivation to use their knowledge.

Mount Holyoke College still stands out as an institution dedicated to widening horizons for young women in all areas. Known among other things for its excellence in chemistry, Lyon's first academic love, it carries on her work in its adherence to the high standards set at its conception.

Mary Lyon broke ground in a field full of sexism, convincing people through her faith in herself and others that women were valuable enough to teach, and able enough to learn.

Bibliography

Banning, Evelyn I. *Mary Lyon of Putnam's Hill*. New York: Vanguard Press, 1965. An easy-to-read, lightly fictionalized account of Mary Lyon's life. Much space is devoted to personal incidents, with little given to the years after the founding of the college.

Gilchrist, Beth Bradford. *The Life of Mary Lyon*. Boston: Houghton Mifflin, 1910. A florid, pleonastic biography, complete in detail but dated in assessment. Includes an extensive bibliography and a chronology.

Green, Elizabeth Alden. *Mary Lyon and Mount Holyoke: Opening the Gates*. Hanover, N.H.: University Press of New England, 1979. A comprehensive, exhaustively researched biography that focuses primarily on the college years. Includes many reproductions of daguerreotypes not found elsewhere. Extensive bibliography and notes.

Hitchcock, Edward. *The Power of Christian Benevolence Illustrated in the Life and Labors of Mary Lyon*. 3d ed. Northampton, Mass.: Hopkins, Bridgman, 1852. A thorough, clear biography, written by people who knew Mary Lyon personally. Includes correspondence and memories not found in other publications.

Howe, M. A. De Wolfe. *Classic Shades: Five Leaders of Learning and Their Colleges*. Boston: Little, Brown, 1928. Mary Lyon is the only woman included in this volume, and the work gives an interesting comparison of Lyon and the male founders of Yale, Williams, Princeton, and Harvard.

Margaret Hawthorne

MARY McCARTHY

Born: June 21, 1912; Seattle, Washington
Died: October 25, 1989; New York, New York
Areas of Achievement: Journalism and literature
Contribution: The most prominent woman among what came to be called the New York intellectuals, notorious for her acerbic tongue and for rather stormy relations with her male colleagues, McCarthy brought great vigor and insight and an uncompromising set of standards to American criticism and fiction.

Early Life

Mary Therese McCarthy's earliest years took their color from her charming alcoholic father and her devoted, beautiful mother. Her secure childhood in Seattle, in the home of a father who had apparently reformed for love of his wife, and within the environs of an influential, wealthy family, graced by the rather romantic figure of her vibrant Jewish grandmother, was shattered during the flu epidemic of World War I. McCarthy lost both of her parents at the age of six and was wrenched from the comfort of Seattle to live in Minneapolis, taken care of by relatives who apparently pocketed most of the funds intended for the support of Mary and her brother Kevin. She describes this period with chilling effectiveness in *Memories of a Catholic Girlhood* (1957).

In her memories of her earliest years, McCarthy would often put a high gloss on her father's figure, refusing to see the flaws that were painfully apparent to family members who had had to support him during his drinking bouts. Something of a loner, McCarthy demonstrated an intense interest in literature at Vassar College (she was graduated in 1933) but no remarkable talent. She first found work as a book reviewer for *The Nation* and *The New Republic*, but it was not until the mid-1930's, after a series of affairs which culminated in a short marriage to theater director Harold Johnsrud and a liaison with the critic Philip Rahv, that she began to develop her own literary style and point of view.

These male figures served as mentors, especially the truculent Rahv, one of the editors of *The Partisan Review*, which was arguably the most influential intellectual journal of its time. The journal had begun as a Marxist, pro-Soviet organ, but by the late 1930's it had adopted an anti-Stalinist position and championed the work of the great modernist writers. In this feisty, combative milieu, McCarthy honed her skills as drama editor and critic, exciting the interest of Edmund Wilson, the dean of American literary critics. McCarthy's stormy marriage to Wilson lasted eight years (1938-1946). With his encouragement, she wrote her first fiction, *The Company She Keeps* (1942), an incisive portrayal of a bohemian, intellectual young woman.

Rahv, McCarthy later admitted, would never have encouraged her to write novels, and he was incapable of removing her from the intense but curiously provincial milieu of New York intellectuals who spent too much of their time in sectarian fights among liberals, Stalinists, anti-Stalinists, Trotskyites, and so on. Yet Rahv seemed to love

McCarthy for herself, a quality she evidently found rare in the men who were attracted to her.

Life's Work

Mary McCarthy is best known for her astringent critical writing and her best-selling novel *The Group* (1963), which details the lives and sexual affairs of eight Vassar College graduates. She often reviewed films and plays and was notorious for her negative reviews. In private life, she had an equally sharp tongue that made her a fearsome presence on the New York literary scene. She was also a much-admired debunker of the fashionable and facile products of American culture.

McCarthy began to hit her stride in the late 1940's and the 1950's. She married Bowden Broadwater, who catered to her love of gossip, often supplying the background for scenes that would become a part of *The Group*. During her marriage to Broadwater (1946-1961), she published three novels that reflect her critical and imaginative grasp of the canvas of American Life. *The Oasis* (1949) is a sharp, satiric portrayal of a utopia established by a group of intellectuals on a mountaintop. It reveals her witty grasp of group dynamics, of the way intellectuals feed upon and destroy one another as ideas are perverted by warring personalities. *The Groves of Academe* (1952) is another satire set in her favorite territory, a liberal arts college for women. Similarly, *A Charmed Life* (1955) takes place in an artist's colony in which the putative creators become destroyers. In much of her fiction, McCarthy dramatizes the inability of intellectuals to sustain a cohesive community; the acid of their intellectuality seems to corrode their humanity.

The Group exemplifies McCarthy's expertise at delineating social manners and the ideas of her time. It is perhaps her most ambitious work because it essays an interpretation of a whole generation. Yet it has also been faulted for its shallow characterizations. One of her biographers, Carol Brightman, contends that only in memoirs such as *Memories of a Catholic Girlhood* was McCarthy able to concentrate on a character (herself) who grew over time and developed in depth and complexity.

Brightman also suggests that McCarthy was adept at fastening on real-life characters, exaggerating and combining the aspects of several personalities, dressing them up in fiction, so to speak, but ultimately proving unable to transcend her real-life models, who often recognized themselves and were hurt by her biting sarcasm. McCarthy thus failed the test of the greatest novelists: She could not create transcendent characters, selves independent of their creator and their roots in reality. Yet the fact that McCarthy stayed close to her real-life models also made the novels extraordinarily authentic as documents of their age, and her fiction remains valid as a brand of social history.

Perhaps because criticism by its nature does not demand warmth and charity (although some critics have been known to be kind), McCarthy's scathing attacks have been accepted more readily in her criticism than in her fiction, where her assaults on intellectuals and opinion makers wear thin because human character seems to be manipulated merely to serve the points she wants to make. What the novels lack is psychological profundity, a certain mystery or ambiguity that would enliven and complicate her characters. Instead, too many of those characters are contemptible.

As a cultural and political critic, however, critics agree that McCarthy deserves a very high place in America literature. Her theater reviews, collected in *Sights and Spectacles, 1937-1956* (1956) and in *Mary McCarthy's Theatre Chronicles 1937-1962* (1963), demonstrate a discriminating, if severe, standard for American drama. They are often characterized as witty, a quality that often makes them more interesting than the plays they criticized.

McCarthy's later works—particularly *Vietnam* (1967), *Hanoi* (1968), and *The Mask of State: Watergate Portraits* (1974)—show her courage in taking on controversial political events. She was a fierce critic of the American government, and she opposed the Vietnam War and the policies created in its aftermath as steadfastly as she had castigated the hypocrisy of intellectuals. She also turned to fiction again in *Cannibals and Missionaries* (1979), an uneven novel about the hijacking of a plane carrying a motley group to the Shah's Iran. Once again, McCarthy was focusing on the dynamics of group behavior, seeing in the group a metaphor for the politics that she saw pervading human interaction. Similarly, she continued to examine generational conflicts in her novel *Birds of America* (1971), which depicts the strained relations between a mother and her son.

Almost all of McCarthy's writing has been about a clarification of values and an exposure of those who purvey false precepts. By the mid-1930's, McCarthy had jettisoned a brief fascination with Marxism, realizing that Stalin's Moscow trials (in which the founders of the Soviet state were accused of treason) were a sham and that the communists would not be able to deliver on their promise of a new and democratic free world based on human equality. When many writers of her generation persisted in their Stalinism, they confirmed her skeptical view of intellectuals and the dishonest uses to which they put their dialectical skills.

Less important are her travel books, *Venice Observed* (1956) and *The Stones of Florence* (1959), which show a more relaxed, appreciative side of McCarthy's character. They are a product of her extensive travels, continued during her last and enduring marriage in 1961 to the diplomat James West. It was a happy union, but McCarthy was restless, constantly on the move from New York to Paris to Castine, Maine (where she and West had a summer home), to various parts of Italy, and to Saigon and Hanoi during the Vietnam War, when she made herself extremely unpopular with the U.S. government.

Her last autobiographical books, *How I Grew* (1987) and *Intellectual Memories* (1993), continue the story of *Memoirs of a Catholic Girlhood*, but they do not have that volume's verve and do not rank with it as classics of American autobiography. *Ideas and the Novel* (1980) is an impressive recapitulation of her long-held views on the nature of fiction and its potential as an intellectual instrument.

Summary

Mary McCarthy was not a standard-definition feminist. She belonged to a generation growing up in the 1920's and 1930's that took for granted and ignored the advances achieved by late nineteenth and twentieth century feminists. As she moved beyond the college campus and the boundaries of conventional marriage, McCarthy sought her freedom in the city among intellectuals and bohemians. She was influenced by powerful male mentors, but she soon developed an independent viewpoint and outspoken positions on literary and political matters.

McCarthy would have disliked the tag woman writer, for like many of her generation she wanted to be considered a writer first and to be judged by her work, not by her sex. Yet her very ability to compete with and often surpass her male colleagues made an impact on other women, showing them what could be accomplished even in the fiercely competitive milieu of New York male intellectuals. She was an outsider, by virtue of her sex and her sharp tongue, yet she was a part of this group. This simultaneous inside/outside perspective of hers gave her great insight into how groups define themselves and choose their members. By virtue of her sex, she was a minority member, yet her superiority as a critic gave her an edge in assessing the peculiar characteristics of the group she had joined. Perhaps her greatest gift to women was to show that they could be thoroughly absorbed in the culture of their times and yet remain intact and independent.

Bibliography

Brightman, Carol. *Writing Dangerously: Mary McCarthy and Her World*. New York: Clarkson Potter, 1992. A full-length, sensitive, well-balanced account of McCarthy's life and work. A friend of McCarthy, Brightman is very sympathetic toward her subject, but she does not overlook the faults of her work and her character. A biographical glossary, extensive notes, and an index are included.

Gelderman, Carol. *Mary McCarthy: A Life*. New York: St. Martin's Press, 1988. Written with McCarthy's cooperation, this is a solid and reliable full-length biography. Includes extensive notes and a bibliography.

Hardwick, Elizabeth. *A View of My Own: Essays in Literature and Society*. New York: Noonday Press, 1963. Contains a chapter on McCarthy which is an excellent, succinct appraisal of her character and her work by a close friend.

McKenzie, Barbara. *Mary McCarthy*. New York: Twayne, 1966. An introductory study with chapters on McCarthy's life, intellectual development, fiction, and nonfiction. Includes a chronology, notes, an annotated bibliography, and an index.

Stock, Irvin. *Mary McCarthy*. Minneapolis, Minn.: University of Minnesota Press, 1968. A long biographical and critical essay emphasizing McCarthy's fiction. A selected bibliography is included.

Carl Rollyson

BARBARA McCLINTOCK

Born: June 16, 1902; Hartford, Connecticut
Died: September 2, 1992; Huntington, Long Island, New York
Area of Achievement: Genetics
Contribution: A pioneer in both classical genetics and molecular genetics, McClintock won the Nobel Prize in Physiology or Medicine in 1983.

Early Life

Barbara McClintock was the third daughter born to Sara Handy and Thomas Henry McClintock. Shortly after the marriage, Thomas McClintock finished medical school at Boston University, and, after a few short stays elsewhere, the couple moved to Hartford, Connecticut, where Barbara was born on June 16, 1902. Much later in her life, she said that her father, disappointed at having another girl, tried in many ways to raise her as a boy, buying her boxing gloves and tools and spending more time with her than with her older sisters. Relations with her mother were always strained, possibly for this reason. Less than two years after Barbara's birth, her younger brother Malcolm was born. Barbara's mother, unable to cope with four small children and very little money, decided to send Barbara to live with her aunt and uncle in Massachusetts. Rather than resenting this, Barbara said later that she "enjoyed herself immensely."

Barbara came back to her parents' house when it was time for her to start school. In the interim, the McClintocks had moved to the Flatbush section of Brooklyn, New York, which in those days was a semirural area. Barbara spent her time playing games with the neighborhood boys, ice-skating, and spending large amounts of time alone, "thinking about things." Her father, believing that the hours spent in school were enough for a growing child, informed his children's teachers that they were not to assign the McClintock children homework. Childhood was to be a time of freedom, and if Barbara did not want to go to school, she stayed home—sometimes for weeks.

In high school, Barbara discovered science. She "loved information" and loved to solve problems. Her mother began to worry that Barbara would pursue knowledge to the detriment of her "feminine development," and tried to dissuade her, but Barbara was set on attending Cornell University, known for accepting and supporting the education of women. After being graduated from high school at sixteen, Barbara took a job at an employment agency but continued to study, persisting in her requests to be allowed to go to Cornell. Her mother eventually relented, probably because Barbara's father, who had recently returned home from overseas army duty, supported Barbara.

At Cornell, Barbara blossomed both intellectually and socially. Elected president of the women's freshman class, she began to date, played banjo in local cafes, and managed a heavy class schedule. After a couple of years, however, she began to be disillusioned with the social whirl. Devoting more and more time to academics, she was allowed to take a graduate class in genetics during her junior year, and her lifelong fascination began.

Life's Work

At the time of Barbara McClintock's matriculation at Cornell, genetics was a new science, scarcely older than she. Cytology was relatively new, and many cellular structures were still a mystery. Thomas Hunt Morgan, working with *Drosophila* (fruit flies) at Columbia, had proposed that genes were located on the chromosomes "like beads on a string," but many scientists did not accept that idea.

McClintock managed to start her career by succeeding in a few days at something her adviser had been trying (and failing) to do for some time: identifying maize (Indian corn) chromosomes and distinguishing among the ten individual chromosomes in each kernel. After completing her B.S. degree, McClintock entered the botany department, because the plant-breeding department, which included genetics, did not accept women as graduate students. She registered a major in cytology and a minor in genetics, setting the course for her future work. She received her doctorate in 1927, when she was twenty-four. Fascinated by the work being done by Morgan and others, she stayed on at Cornell to try to parallel Morgan's *Drosophila* work with maize. Two other researchers came to Cornell at this time, Marcus Rhodes and George Beadle, both of whom later became prominent geneticists. The three formed a core around which other scientists moved, establishing friendships that would prove to be life-long. In this environment, McClintock's research thrived. She published nine papers on maize chromosomal morphology by 1931 and began to be widely recognized in her field.

During these years, a new graduate student arrived at Cornell: Harriet Creighton. On her first day she met Barbara, who convinced her to enroll as a cytology and genetics major. Creighton began her studies by working as McClintock's assistant. Toward the end of the first year, McClintock suggested that Creighton attack the problem of proving the common assumption that there was a correlation between chromosomal crossover (an actual physical exchange of chromatids during meiosis) and genetic crossover (the display by an organism of a combination of parental traits that are normally linked). McClintock believed that this could be proved through a series of experiments involving a particular maize chromosome, and she had identified and isolated kernels that involved the traits needed. Creighton agreed, and the two worked on the problem until the spring of 1931, when, at the urging of Morgan himself, they published their successful results. It became a landmark essay in classical genetics.

Very soon afterward, McClintock decided to leave Cornell. Positions on the faculty were simply not open to women, and they would not be for many years. Resenting the lack of opportunity and wishing to continue her research, McClintock refused to take a job at one of the women's colleges that would have gladly hired her. She was not particularly fond of teaching, and these institutions were not equipped to support extensive research.

For a couple of years, McClintock wandered between her cornfield at Cornell, the California Institute of Technology, where Morgan now worked, and Columbia, Missouri, where with Lewis Stadler she was researching the existence of ring chromosomes. In 1933, McClintock received a fellowship to go to Germany and work with Richard B. Goldschmidt, a famous geneticist. She found the reality of Nazi Germany unbearable and returned, very depressed, within the year. Back at Cornell, friends appealed to the Rockefeller Foundation to support her and her research for a time. Eventually, in 1935, Stadler convinced the University of Missouri to offer McClintock a position as assistant professor, which she accepted. Her unconventional ways and her outspokenness did not fit in well at Missouri. Neither she nor the university was happy with the situation. Her research went well, but she was isolated and was passed over for promotion in favor of men whose credentials were far less impressive. In 1941, she left, finally landing at the Carnegie Institute of Washington at Cold Spring Harbor, New York, where she remained for the rest of her life.

Cold Spring Harbor was, and is, a research facility that hosts summertime gatherings of biologists and other scientists. In 1944, soon after her arrival, the National Academy of Sciences elected Barbara McClintock to its membership. She was only the third woman to receive this honor. This seems to be the validation she needed to pursue the research that was to be pivotal in the field of genetics. Between 1944 and 1951, McClintock studied patterns of genetic traits caused by mutations that did not seem to follow the accepted rules of genetics. These traits did seem to occur with some regularity, however, implying some sort of control. McClintock proposed that at some point during development, sections of chromosomes actually detached and moved to a new location, contrary to Morgan's "beads on a string" concept. Furthermore, these transpositions seemed to be controlled by a factor on the chromosome itself. In 1951, she presented her findings at the annual Cold Spring Harbor Symposium. She was met with silence. Almost no one understood what she proposed. Many scientists admired her work but could not fit it into their framework of knowledge. Used to being believed, McClintock was shocked. She found herself professionally isolated, and, although she continued her research, she stopped publishing. During the next decade, while the field of molecular genetics was growing rapidly, McClintock kept to herself, listening to the new research but never sharing her own. In 1961, Jacques Monod and François Jacob published a paper that confirmed some of her findings. She immediately submitted an article for publication and presented another at Cold Spring Harbor, but still her work was not accepted.

In the mid-1960's, her situation began to improve. She received the Kimber Genetics Award in 1967 and the National Medal of Science in 1970. More and more of her findings were being confirmed by other researchers. People again started citing her work. This trend continued in the 1970's, and McClintock started publishing again. She gained new prominence, winning awards and prizes that brought her prestige and money. She won the Nobel Prize in Physiology or Medicine in 1983, becoming the first woman to win an unshared Nobel Prize in this category and the third woman to do so in any science category.

McClintock continued her research, staying at Cold Spring Harbor, maintaining her independence and isolation despite her belated acceptance. In later years, she studied Tibetan Buddhism and biofeedback techniques, which fascinated her in their incorporation of the same holistic approach to the study of the organism that she had brought to maize for so many years. Barbara McClintock died on September 2, 1992, at the age of ninety.

Summary

The influence of Barbara McClintock's work on the field of genetics simply cannot be overstated. Much of her work is still unconfirmed, although few believe that it will remain so.

Throughout her life, McClintock tried to achieve a gender-free science. She wanted to be accepted and respected on her own merit, as a researcher and expert in her field. Faced with many barriers because of her sex, she moved around them. Others followed her example. Evelyn Witkin, later the holder of the Barbara McClintock Chair at Rutgers University, named the chair to acknowledge the enormous debt she owed McClintock for her inspiration and encouragement in their ten years together at Cold Spring Harbor. Harriet Creighton, who owed the inception of her career to McClintock, said later, "It was the best steering anyone could have given me."

The goal of a gender-free assessment of a person's worth as a scientist is still elusive in the scientific community. Barbara McClintock paved a rocky road in one area, and this continues to be a path followed by many scientists, male and female. Her complete dedication and unique vision serve as an example to women in every field, proof that barriers can be overcome by one who is willing to strive for the life she wants.

Bibliography

Dash, Joan. *The Triumph of Discovery*. New York: Simon & Schuster, 1990. A high-school-level set of biographies, slightly romanticized, giving good outlines of the lives of the four women of whom McClintock is one. A short bibliography and an index are included.

Fedoroff, Nina, and David Botstein, eds. *The Dynamic Genome*. Cold Spring Harbor, N.Y.: Cold Spring Harbor Laboratory Press, 1992. A collection of essays written as tributes and remembrances for McClintock's ninetieth birthday, this work includes some very technical articles on genetics and McClintock's impact on the field and the authors. Also included are reprints of four of McClintock's most influential articles, as well as some personal recollections by friends and colleagues. Name and subject indexes are provided for the collection.

Hammond, Allen L., ed. *A Passion to Know: Twenty Profiles in Science*. New York: Charles Scribner's Son's, 1984. This brief biography of McClintock, written shortly after she received the Nobel Prize, puts her in the context of the scientific community. An index and recommended reading lists are provided.

Keller, Evelyn Fox. *A Feeling for the Organism: The Life and Work of Barbara McClintock*. San Francisco: W. H. Freeman, 1983. A must-read, this is the source that all others cite. The only full-length biography of McClintock that has been written, this work is based on extensive interviews with McClintock and her family, friends, and colleagues. Comprehensive in its coverage of her pre-Nobel Prize life, it is easy to read and includes an index and a particularly helpful glossary of genetics terms as well as eleven pages of notes.

Lewin, Roger. "A Naturalist of the Genome." *Science* 222, no. 4622 (October 28, 1983): 402-405. This biography, published shortly after McClintock received the Nobel Prize, includes a concise and clear overview of the work for which the prize was awarded as well as some discussion of where McClintock's discoveries have led since.

Margaret Hawthorne

CARSON McCULLERS

Born: February 19, 1917; Columbus, Georgia
Died: September 29, 1967; Nyack, New York
Area of Achievement: Literature
Contribution: A Southern novelist and short-story writer, Carson McCullers presented in her fiction a world of alienated adolescents, misfits, and outcasts, treating themes of human isolation with great sensitivity.

Early Life

Carson McCullers was born Lula Carson Smith, the daughter of Lamar Smith, a watchmaker, and Marguerite Waters Smith. For generations, Smith's family had been Southerners, so her family history, as well as her own childhood and adolescence, deepened her relationship with the South. It was in ramblings through Columbus' streets and the disparate quarters of African Americans, millworkers, and the wealthy that she gained the many impressions that enrich her fictional world. Carson was recognized as an odd, lively girl with artistic talents, and her passion for music and writing was encouraged. She studied the piano assiduously and as an adolescent wrote some violence-filled plays (patterned after those of Eugene O'Neill), a novel, and some poetry. An early short story, "Sucker," about a sixteen-year-old boy whose first friendship causes him to reject the affection of a younger brother, demonstrates her precocity. She changed her name, read voraciously, and earned a reputation for having a phenomenal memory. Although in all her work Carson McCullers focuses on alienated individuals, she herself grew up in a harmonious family that accepted her eccentricities and extended her their affection.

At eighteen, Carson traveled to New York, purportedly to attend the Juilliard School of Music, but she lost the tuition and was forced to work at several jobs. She did, however, register for creative writing courses at Columbia University and New York University. One of her teachers, Whit Burnett, liked one of her stories, "Wunderkind" (1936), about a self-critical child musical prodigy who abandons her music, and he had it published in *Story Magazine*. Because of frail health resulting from childhood illnesses, Carson took trips home to Georgia for recuperative purposes. On one such trip, she met a Georgia soldier named Reeves McCullers, and in 1938 she was married to him. For two years, they lived happily in Charlotte, North Carolina, where she wrote a novel outline called "The Mute," earning a Houghton Mifflin Fiction Fellowship and a book contract. The editor changed the title to *The Heart Is a Lonely Hunter*, and the book appeared in 1940 to generally enthusiastic reviews. For a twenty-two-year-old writer to probe so perceptively into adult characters was a startling achievement.

Life's Work

Characteristically, *The Heart Is a Lonely Hunter* is set in Georgia. Filled with impressions of Carson McCullers' childhood, it creates a richly detailed view of a

Southern mill town. At the center of the novel is a deaf-mute surrounded by four lonely characters who are unable to connect with the world. One is a thirteen-year-old girl who is burdened with frustrated musical ambitions. Through her, McCullers deals with the individual's compulsion to revolt against enforced isolation, and she presents love as the only anodyne.

When her first novel was published, the author and her husband settled in New York, where she was lauded as the literary discovery of the year. She was invited to be a Fellow at the Bread Loaf Writers Conference in Vermont. That fall, *Reflections in a Golden Eye*, a hastily written story of infidelity, murder, and perversion at a Southern army base, appeared in installments in *Harper's Bazaar* before it was published as a book in 1941. Although it may have contributed to McCullers' image as a writer of Southern gothic fiction, it disappointed serious readers who were expecting as careful and sympathetic a delineation of character and situation as that contained in her first novel. The critical response was unenthusiastic.

McCullers' disappointment at the second novel's reception was matched by domestic misfortune and divorce. For the next five years, McCullers lived sporadically in Columbus and at Yaddo, an artists' colony in Saratoga, New York, but mostly amid a legendary gathering of artists and writers at February House, in Brooklyn Heights. The old brownstone rented jointly by McCullers and George Davis, editor of *Harper's Bazaar*, harbored celebrated artists and writers, including Christopher Isherwood, W. H. Auden, Richard Wright, Oliver Smith, Benjamin Britten, and Gypsy Rose Lee. Many famous guests dropped by. February House provided spirited company and singular material for novels and stories. The irregular life did exhaust McCullers, however, and she returned to Columbus to recuperate. While there, she suffered the first in a series of strokes that were to plague her the rest of her life. On regaining her health, she composed the short story "A Tree, a Rock, a Cloud," which was published in *Harper's Bazaar* (1942) and selected for the anthology *O. Henry Prize Stories of 1942*. She also received a Guggenheim Fellowship that year.

After her father's death in 1944, she moved with her mother and sister to Nyack, New York. She resumed a correspondence with her former husband after his reenlistment, and they remarried after his discharge in 1945 for war wounds.

The early 1940's were McCullers' most productive period. Her third major work, a novella, *The Ballad of the Sad Café*, the story of a grotesque love affair between a giantess and a hunchback, appeared in *Harper's Bazaar* in 1943. A thousand-dollar grant from the American Academy of Arts and Letters, along with various other grants and fellowships, encouraged her. *The Member of the Wedding* (1946), the most directly autobiographical of all her works, which explores a teenage girl's feelings of isolation and longing, was immediately both popular and critically successful. Playwright Tennessee Williams was so impressed by its remembrance of childhood memories that he persuaded McCullers to rework it into a play. Spending some weeks at Williams' cottage on Nantucket, she finished the play by the end of the summer of 1946. A second Guggenheim Fellowship was given to her that same year.

For the next three years, McCullers fought failing health and tried to find a producer for *The Member of the Wedding*. In 1947, she experienced two serious strokes that impaired her vision and partially paralyzed her. Her recuperation was slow. At the same time, her husband underwent treatment for acute alcoholism. The decade, however, ended triumphantly: In 1950, *The Member of the Wedding*, starring Julie Harris and Ethel Waters, opened in New York to the praise of audience and critics. It won three awards, including the New York Drama Critics' Circle Award, and after it had received 501 performances, it was made into a film by Stanley Kramer. The successful Broadway production, together with the enthusiastically received collected edition of her work by Houghton Mifflin in 1951, established her literary reputation in America and Europe.

If her literary reputation was secure, her health and domestic security were not. In 1951, she and her husband bought a house near Paris, where they lived on and off for two years. He drank heavily and had fits of depression. She returned alone to Nyack by 1953, planning a divorce. He committed suicide in France. Between 1952 and 1953, McCullers published two short stories in *Mademoiselle* and some of her poems in *Botteghe Oscure*. In 1954, she made lecture appearances with Tennessee Williams and worked at Yaddo. Her mother, who had been a great help to her, died suddenly in 1955.

The play McCullers produced in 1957 and the novel she published in 1961 were triumphs of will but artistic failures. The play *The Square Root of Wonderful*, an autobiographical attempt to re-create and understand her mother and her husband, closed after forty-five Broadway performances. It lacks the dramatic purpose and compelling characterizations necessary to make it work on stage. Discouraged by its failure, she returned to the unfinished manuscript of *Clock Without Hands*, which she completed for publication in 1961. An uneven work treating a central character's preparations for death and unsuccessfully attempting a comic allegory of the ways in which the 1950's had changed the South, it was her last novel.

Despite her illness, McCullers achieved remarkable success between the ages twenty-three and thirty. Although she continued writing as an invalid until her death at fifty of a massive cerebral hemorrhage, her creative activity between 1958 and 1962 was necessarily lessened. She underwent surgery for breast cancer and for an atrophied hand muscle, and psychiatric care for depression. In 1964, she underwent hip surgery, and a long critical illness in 1965 led to her death in 1967. Despite her later artistic disappointments, McCullers' early work continued to be widely read and appreciated. Adapters were eager to translate her work into other media. Edward Albee dramatized *The Ballad of the Sad Café* in 1963, and the play ran for 123 performances on Broadway. John Huston cast Marlon Brando and Elizabeth Taylor in a film version of *Reflections in a Golden Eye* in 1967, and a film version of *The Heart Is a Lonely Hunter*, with Alan Arkin, appeared in 1968.

McCullers' sister, Margarita C. Smith, published *The Mortgaged Heart* (1971), a posthumous collection of McCullers' short stories, essays, and poems. In several essays, McCullers discusses the methods and concerns of her own writing. She states her belief that good prose must be both realistic and poetic, and admits her reliance on the South of her childhood for locales. Furthermore, she reports that her technique of creating characters involves getting entirely within those characters so that their motives become her own: "I become the characters I write about," she wrote. If her vision is one of alienation, it is a vision that is imbued with sympathy; her isolated eccentrics and disturbed children are portrayed as human beings who are not, in the final analysis, extremely different from the rest of humanity.

Summary

Although frail health plagued Carson McCullers throughout her life and limited her productivity, she achieved critical and popular success in four genres in her twenties. Her first three novels, all of which were best-sellers, appeared within a six-year period, and her award-winning play *The Member of the Wedding* appeared four years later.

McCullers is an accomplished portrayer of character who presents in her novels a richly detailed world of lonely and often unlovable misfits with a need for love that they find difficult to satisfy. They embody such major themes of the author as human isolation and loneliness caused by inability to love, communicate deep feeling, or find one's identity. Although her works are outwardly realistic, they often move into a symbolic or allegorical dimension without allowing their characters to lose their humanity. Commonly rendering fiction as parable, McCullers accents truths about human nature. She displays virtuosity in her language, mixing the poetic and the prosaic to her advantage. Musical and metaphysical perspectives blend, for example, with ordinary sounds of life in a Southern town. Music pervades her work, sometimes lending it structure, as in *The Member of the Wedding*, in which the themes are suggested, stated, and restated, sonata fashion, throughout the three distinct parts of the story.

That McCullers has become a significant figure in the study of women's literature is no surprise. Her compelling portraits of women and adolescents such as Frankie Adams in *The Member of the Wedding* are memorable, and they reflect an uncommon compassion for hidden suffering. In her brief lifetime, this richly talented and diversely gifted writer left a distinctive legacy to American fiction.

Bibliography

Bloom, Harold, ed. *Carson McCullers*. New York: Chelsea House, 1986. An excellent collection of criticism encompassing all of McCullers' fiction. Essay authors include Marguerite Young, Tennessee Williams, Gore Vidal, Oliver Evans, Richard M. Cook, Lawrence Graver, and Margaret B. McDowell. Includes a bibliography, a chronology, and an index. Gives readers a helpful perspective on critical writing about McCullers.

Cook, Richard M. *Carson McCullers*. New York: Frederick Ungar, 1975. This biography also contains insightful writing about McCullers' five novels. Included are a chronology, a bibliography, and an index. Cook considers McCullers' compassionate insight into hidden suffering her greatest achievement.

Evans, Oliver. *The Ballad of Carson McCullers: A Biography*. New York: Coward-

McCann, 1966. A biography that includes incisive comments on McCullers' work, emphasizing its allegorical aspect. Includes eight photographs, index, and McCullers' outline of "The Mute," later published in book form as *The Heart Is a Lonely Hunter*. Valuable for detailing connections between McCullers' life and fiction.

Graver, Lawrence. *Carson McCullers*. Minneapolis: University of Minnesota Press, 1969. A forty-eight-page biography with an interesting discussion of each major work. Offers a helpfully condensed yet substantial view of the author's life and work. Graver places McCullers in a quartet of accomplished Southern women writers consisting of McCullers, Eudora Welty, Katherine Anne Porter, and Flannery O'Connor.

McDowell, Margaret. *Carson McCullers*. Boston: Twayne, 1980. A comprehensive study that contains summaries and well-detailed analyses of her major works, including short stories, poems, and her second play, *The Square Root of Wonderful*. Included are a chronology, the author's photograph, and a bibliography of primary sources and annotated secondary sources.

Christian H. Moe

CATHARINE A. MacKINNON

Born: 1946; Minneapolis, Minnesota

Areas of Achievement: Law and women's rights
Contribution: A pioneer in the development of feminist legal theory, MacKinnon formulated the argument that sexual harassment should be viewed as a form of sex discrimination—an argument that later became embedded in law.

Early Life

Catharine Alice MacKinnon was born in Minneapolis, Minnesota, in 1946, the daughter of George E. and Elizabeth V. (Davis) MacKinnon. George MacKinnon was a leading figure in Minnesota politics during Catharine's childhood; he was an adviser to the Eisenhower and Nixon presidential campaigns, served as a U.S. congressman from Minnesota and as Republican nominee for governor, and was appointed by President Richard M. Nixon to serve on the U.S. Court of Appeals for the District of Columbia.

Like her mother and her maternal grandmother, Catharine MacKinnon attended Smith College. She graduated magna cum laude in 1969 with a bachelor of arts degree in government. She went on to study at Yale University, where she did graduate work in political science before being accepted at Yale Law School, where she received her law degree in 1977. (She was awarded the Ph.D. in political science from Yale in 1987.) While at Yale, MacKinnon created the first course in the university's women's studies program, and was active in radical politics, working with the Black Panthers and in the campaign against the Vietnam War.

It was while still a law student that she conceived her now-famous argument that sexual harassment is a form of sex discrimination. Since its initial publication, her book *Sexual Harassment of Working Women* (1979) has been considered to be the definitive work on the subject.

While feminist legal theory has become a firmly established part of the curriculum at most American law schools, this was not the case when MacKinnon first set out; indeed, her pathbreaking work was one of the main influences on the development of this new discipline. The basic premise of feminist legal theory, as advanced by MacKinnon and others, is that the law, as a social institution in a male-dominated (patriarchal) society, reflects the viewpoints, and represents the interests, of men rather than women. According to MacKinnon and other feminist legal scholars, laws against rape are based on men's conceptions of what constitutes nonconsensual sex, obscenity laws reflect men's conceptions of offensiveness, and so forth.

During the 1980's, MacKinnon was a guest lecturer at a number of leading universities, including Chicago, Harvard, Stanford, and Yale. Despite widespread acknowledgment of the significance of her work, however, MacKinnon was not offered a full-time teaching position until 1990, when she obtained a position as tenured professor at the University of Michigan Law School.

Life's Work

Catharine MacKinnon's first book was the pioneering study, *Sexual Harassment of Working Women*. The book contains her analysis of harassment, which was taken up by a U.S. Court of Appeals in *Barnes v. Costle* (1977), and thus provided the theoretical basis for viewing harassment as an offense that transgresses the law. Her basic idea was simple: Sexual harassment is a kind of behavior to which a person is subject because of her sex, and therefore it can be seen as a form of discrimination under Title VII of the Civil Rights Act of 1964, which forbids differential treatment in the workplace on the basis of group membership (race, sex, religion, or other classification).

Barnes was a landmark decision: for the first time, a high-level court went on record as opposing the popular notion that harassment is an inevitable fact of life and that for the law to try to protect against such treatment is equivalent to tampering with the laws of nature. A typical feature of pre-*Barnes* cases as documented by MacKinnon was the courts' insistence that what plaintiffs had argued was abusive treatment was merely a normal expression of male sexuality ("boys will be boys," in effect), where "normal" is assumed to mean something like "natural." Another typical feature of such cases was the courts' assumption that harassing behavior was a feature of the unique dynamics of the relationship between two individuals, rather than as a pattern that was made possible by the fact that the harasser is in a position of power vis-à-vis the harassed and so should be seen as an expression of that power.

Thus MacKinnon's argument, basically endorsed by *Barnes*, involved two steps: recognizing that certain typical expressions of male sexuality may be abusive despite their being typical; and recognizing the workplace as an environment in which men will tend to harass women because they have the power to do so.

While *Barnes* was significant, feminists such as MacKinnon considered that its definition of what constituted harassment—basically, "sleep with me or you're fired" or variations of this sort of quid pro quo—was too narrow. Then, in 1986, the U.S. Supreme Court unanimously decided, in *Meritor Savings Bank v. Vinson*, that harassment as a legal offense is committed whenever unwanted sexual remarks or behaviors create a "hostile environment" for workers. MacKinnon was part of the plaintiff's legal team in this case. She wrote Vinson's brief to the Court, helped her attorney prepare for oral argument, and appeared as co-counsel before the Court. What was at issue was whether Title VII covered only tangible losses—such as if an employee were fired for not sleeping with the boss—or whether psychological damage was also covered. Vinson's employer conceded that her supervisor harassed her—by fondling her, for example—but that such behavior was not illegal. MacKinnon's argument was again quite simple: Does the court require that a person "bring intensified injury upon herself"—quit or be fired—"in order to demonstrate that she is injured at all?" The Court responded unanimously: No!

In *Harris v. Forklift Systems* (1993), the Supreme Court took a further step along the course charted by *Vinson*, when it decided unanimously that the criteria for deciding whether a hostile environment exists should depend on the quality of the environment—specifically, on whether it could be reasonably perceived as hostile or abusive—and not on the psychological or other effects it has on its victims. Otherwise, a harassed individual who did not break down under the pressure of harassment would, in effect, be punished for having summoned the emotional resources to survive the experience. This argument is basically the same as the "intensified injury" argument MacKinnon made in the *Vinson* case.

Since the early 1980's, MacKinnon has been involved in a campaign against another normal expression of male-dominant sexuality that she perceives as harmful to women: pornography. She notes that in the video age the harm done is direct and immediate: What is depicted in visual pornography as rape, coercion, and torture, actually occur as rape, coercion, and torture in the making of the pornography. MacKinnon implies that there are at least two reasons why most people fail to recognize this obvious fact about pornography (and why, as a result, her views on the subject are considered outrageous by many commentators). First of all, pornography depicts women as enjoying what is done to them. Second, even if they are not enjoying themselves, it is assumed that these women are participating voluntarily. To take the second assumption first: MacKinnon argues that women are in most cases coerced into making pornography by their boyfriends or pimps or drug suppliers (who may, of course, be the same person). Once this coercion becomes apparent, the first defense of pornography falls by the wayside: If you can be forced to make pornography, you can be forced to appear to enjoy it. Furthermore, MacKinnon argues that pornography is an indirect cause of tangible harms to women in the sense that abusers and rapists are often inspired to abuse and rape by the scenes of abuse and rape they have seen, and been turned on by, in pornography.

In the mid-1980's, MacKinnon and feminist writer and activist Andrea Dworkin embarked on a campaign to make it possible for victims of pornography to sue their victimizers. In the fall of 1983, MacKinnon and Dworkin framed a civil antipornography ordinance for the city of Minneapolis; it was passed by the city council, but was vetoed by the mayor before being passed and vetoed again. In 1984, a similar law was passed by the city of Indianapolis and was signed by Mayor William Hudnut. This ordinance was struck down by a district court shortly thereafter; and the district court's decision was upheld by a federal court of appeals in 1986. It agreed with the lower court that the ordinance violated the First Amendment guarantee of free speech—even while conceding, for the most part, the harms pornography does to women.

Despite these legal setbacks, MacKinnon has continued to campaign tirelessly against the pornography industry. Over the years, she has further refined her argument against pornography. In her 1993 book, *Only Words*, she continues to treat pornography, like harassment, as sex discrimination, and points out the tension between the First Amendment guarantee of free speech, which has so far protected the pornography industry, and the Fourteenth Amendment guarantee of equal protection of the laws, which MacKinnon believes ought to apply to victims of pornography. But then she adds a new argument, which would, if accepted, resolve this tension, at least in the case of pornography: While the defenders of pornography assume that pornography is "merely speech," the reality of pornography is what it does.

MacKinnon's views on pornography have made her a frequent target of attacks in the press; reviews of *Only Words* in major publications ranged from the politely dismissive to the crude and badgering. The review that appeared in *The Nation* was so abusive that it elicited a written protest from her publisher. She has been ridiculed by Katie Roiphe, in her book *The Morning After*, as an "anti-porn queen." Many feminists oppose MacKinnon's "obsession" with pornography, which they claim diverts attention from more significant issues of economic and political equality (though MacKinnon believes these issues are all related) and depicts women as helpless victims in need of protection by the state (as if demanding equality does not normally involve seeking protection from the state, as in the case of civil rights legislation).

Despite these criticisms, MacKinnon has become a popular speaker on college campuses and at academic conferences, and is widely regarded as a charismatic teacher who has profoundly influenced an entire generation of law students—not to mention influencing the law itself.

Since 1993, MacKinnon has been involved in publicizing the sexual atrocities perpetrated by the Bosnian Serbs as part of their ethnic cleansing campaign, and providing legal assistance for the victims.

MacKinnon's other books include *Feminism Unmodified* (1987) and *Toward a Feminist Theory of the State* (1989), both published by Harvard University Press.

Summary

There is perhaps no other feminist of her generation who has had as direct and profound an impact on society as Catharine MacKinnon. Her views on sexual harassment have become the law of the land; she continues to struggle, however, to achieve the same recognition for her views on pornography. That the law has begun to recognize certain normal expressions of male sexuality as violative of women's dignity and women's rights is an astonishing development—as astonishing as court decisions striking down segregation must have seemed in their day. Her crusade against the victimization of women raises the same painful question: Is society ready for equality? The development of case law in the areas of sexual harassment and pornography is largely the result of the influence of feminist legal theory, of which MacKinnon is widely acknowledged to be the foremost representative.

Bibliography

Cornell, Drucilla. *Transformations: Recollective Imagination and Sexual Difference*. New York: Routledge, 1993. A respectful yet critical assessment of MacKinnon's analysis of sex inequality. Situates MacKinnon's views within the context of contemporary feminist theory.

Fineman, Martha A., and Nancy S. Thomadsen, eds. *At the Boundaries of Law*. New York: Routledge, 1991. This collection of essays in feminist legal theory includes detailed analysis of MacKinnon's work.

Lacayo, Richard. "Assault by Paragraph." *Time* 143 (January 17, 1994): 62. Provides an account of MacKinnon's war of words with book critic Carlin Romano, whose review of *Only Words* opened with a provocative statement about rape that offended MacKinnon deeply. Although brief, this article does provide insight into MacKinnon's thesis concerning the representation of an assault as inciting real acts of discrimination and rape.

Rhode, Deborah L. *Justice and Gender*. Cambridge, Mass.: Harvard University Press, 1989. A prominent law professor at Stanford University, Rhode surveys a wide range of issues bearing on women and the law. Includes pertinent discussion of MacKinnon's views on harassment and pornography.

Stoltenberg, John. *Refusing to Be a Man: Essays on Sex and Justice*. New York: Penguin, 1990. A collection of essays by a leading antipornography activist. Stoltenberg's detailed discussion of the Minneapolis civil rights ordinance drafted by MacKinnon and Andrea Dworkin provides insights into how the ordinance came to be written, how its provisions were expected to be implemented, and why the issues raised by this ordinance are central to the struggle for gender equality.

Sunstein, Cass R. *Democracy and the Problem of Free Speech*. New York: Free Press, 1993. A professor at the University of Chicago, Sunstein is a widely respected expert on constitutional law. Because it contains a detailed argument that is in close accord with MacKinnon's position on pornography, Sunstein's work provides a noteworthy signal of the gradual mainstream acceptance of MacKinnon's views.

Jay Mullin

ANNE SULLIVAN MACY

Born: April 14, 1866; Feeding Hills, Massachusetts
Died: October 20, 1936; Forest Hills, Long Island
Area of Achievement: Education
Contribution: Macy was Helen Keller's teacher and lifelong companion until Macy's death.

Early Life

Anne Mansfield Sullivan was born on April 14, 1866, in Feeding Hills, Massachusetts, to Thomas Sullivan and Alice Cloesy Sullivan. The Sullivans had fled Ireland along with many of their compatriots because of famine. Anne's father was illiterate, unskilled, and given to drinking and brawling. Alice Sullivan was tubercular; nevertheless, she gave birth to five children, of whom Anne was the oldest.

When Anne was five, she contracted trachoma, which gradually destroyed her vision. When she was eight, her mother died and Anne began to keep house for her father. He could not maintain the shack in which they lived, however, so Anne and her brother Jimmie went to live with their uncle and aunt. Their uncle was more prosperous than their father, but he also found it difficult to support them, so they were then sent to Tewksbury Almshouse in February of 1876. This was the state poorhouse, where conditions were truly terrible. Jimmie died there in May of 1876. Anne was ten years old and grief-stricken. She lived at Tewksbury for several years before she was able to leave.

She had heard from one of the other residents that there were special schools for the blind, and she began to desire an education. She might never have left Tewksbury except that one day a state commission headed by Frank B. Sanborn came to inspect the almshouse. Anne followed them around, finally calling out to Sanborn, whom she could not see, begging for the chance to go to school. As a result, in 1880, at age fourteen, she was admitted to the Perkins Institution for the Blind in Boston. She was unkempt, willful, ignorant, and capricious because of the circumstances of her life. Under the care of the Perkins staff, especially Sophia Hopkins, the matron in the cottage where Anne lived, she matured into a responsible young woman. Hopkins was a widow whose only daughter had died. She had come to Perkins looking for a place to be of service.

While at Perkins, Anne also came under the influence of Samuel Gridley Howe, who was no longer alive but whose spirit lived on. He had previously worked with Laura Bridgman, who was blind and deaf. He used a manual alphabet that had originally been developed by Spanish monks who had taken vows of silence. The manual alphabet allowed one to communicate using only the sense of touch. While at Perkins, Anne underwent two eye operations that partially restored her sight, so that she could read. She was graduated from Perkins in 1886 and was the valedictorian of her class.

Life's Work

In 1880, the same year Anne Sullivan had entered the Perkins Institution, Helen Keller was born in Tuscumbia, Alabama. Nineteen months later, she became ill with a disease that left her blind, deaf, and dumb. In 1887, Anne Sullivan was hired by the Kellers to teach Helen. She had hoped for more exciting work, but this was the only job offered her and she was in no position to turn it down. No one expected great results. Fifty years had passed since Howe had worked with Laura Bridgman. Many talented teachers had tried to do for other deaf and blind children what Howe had done with Laura Bridgman, but with little success.

To prepare for her task, Anne Sullivan spent several months reading Howe's reports on his work with Laura Bridgman, a painful task because of her eyes. She already knew the manual alphabet. She and her classmates at Perkins had learned it in order to communicate with Laura Bridgman, who was still cloistered there, having never been able to adapt to any other kind of life.

On March 3, 1887, Anne Sullivan arrived in Tuscumbia and immediately began spelling into Helen's hand. Helen responded by imitating the finger motions. Sullivan could tell that Helen was bright, which was encouraging. Helen also was as willful as Sullivan herself had been. Helen's family had not tried to discipline her. On one occasion, Helen knocked out Sullivan's two front teeth.

Realizing that she could never teach Helen until she brought her under control, Sullivan asked permission to take Helen out of her family surroundings for a couple of weeks. Reluctantly, the Kellers agreed. They had a little garden house not far from the main house where Helen and Sullivan could stay and the Kellers could look in on them without Helen being aware of it. There, Helen learned to depend on Sullivan, and her willfulness came under control.

On April 5, as Sullivan pumped water over Helen's hand, Helen finally realized that the finger motions she had felt in her hands stood for water. From that day on, Helen's progress was rapid. Although Sullivan began with lesson plans that included crocheting and sewing at certain times of the day, she quickly abandoned these formal plans and in their place constantly spelled sentences into Helen's hand. She wanted Helen to learn language the way normal children do, by constantly "hearing" normal speech. Within two months of Sullivan's arrival, Helen was forming coherent sentences that were appropriate to her age.

When Sullivan decided it was time to teach Helen to read, she used the raised alphabet that was favored at Perkins. Helen learned the alphabet in a single day. Not wanting to bore her with the inane readers through which children often learn to read, Sullivan developed her own method. She put a mouse in a box and a cat over the box. She had Helen read sentences about the situation which she then showed Helen tactually. Helen quickly grasped the problem and was quite concerned that the cat not eat the mouse. At the end of the lesson, she fed the mouse and the cat and was quite pleased. Although she did not know all the words in the story, she knew enough of the words to figure out what was happening. This is the way sighted children develop vocabulary.

Helen also learned how to print in letters that sighted people could read so that she could write letters to people who did not know the special alphabets developed for the blind.

At the end of 1887, Sullivan was encouraged to write a report of her work for the Perkins Institute's Annual Report. Although she was reluctant to do this, finding it hard to spare time from her work with Helen, she did write the report, portions of which were reprinted and reviewed in nearly every newspaper and magazine in the country.

At age ten, Helen decided that she wanted to learn to talk like hearing people. She did learn to do this, but never as perfectly as she or Sullivan wanted. Educators realized that a great teacher, greater even than Howe had been, was working with Helen. After a time, however, public opinion was divided. Some called Helen a miracle. Others gave Sullivan all the credit and called Helen an automaton. A few, such as the inventor Alexander Graham Bell, understood that it was the combination of a gifted teacher and intelligent student that produced such incredible results.

In 1900, Helen Keller, accompanied by Anne Sullivan, went to Radcliffe College and was graduated *cum laude* four years later. Then the two women bought a farm on seven acres in Wrentham, Massachusetts. A year later, Anne Sullivan became Anne Sullivan Macy when she married John Macy, a literary critic. John helped Helen with *The Story of My Life*, which was published in 1904. This was followed by *The World I Live In* (1908) and *Out of the Dark* (1913), a book of socialist writings. This last book was not received well by the public.

Hard times were coming for Anne Sullivan Macy and Helen Keller. Macy's sight was becoming increasingly undependable, her marriage was failing, and Keller's writing career seemed to be at an end. In 1913, the two women began to lecture. Keller spoke and Macy interpreted. After three months, they admitted that they could not survive in this way. Keller wrote to Andrew Carnegie and accepted a pension that she would not have considered in earlier years. The pension would have been enough for one person, but it was not adequate for two disabled women. Therefore, they went back out on the lecture circuit again, this time with Keller's mother to help them.

This was not a permanent solution, however, and in 1914, Polly Thomson joined them to do all the things they could not do. They continued lecturing until 1916, when Keller's concern with the war in Europe, the possibility of American involvement in it, and her disapproval of such involvement because of her pacifistic tendencies were received badly by audiences.

Macy was not well, so she and Thomson went to Puerto Rico for a rest and Keller went to be with her mother. After Macy recuperated, she, Thomson, and Keller were reunited. They had not been able to keep the farm in Wrentham because of financial difficulties, so they bought a cottage in Forest Hills, Long Island.

Keller was concerned that, if she died before Macy, her pension would die with her and leave her beloved teacher penniless. As a remedy to this problem, she decided to try Hollywood. A movie of her life (*Deliverance, Deliverance*) was made, but it was not a financial success. Then Keller and Macy tried vaudeville. They developed a twenty-minute act in which they demonstrated how Macy had taught Keller. This lasted on and off for several years and made enough money so that a little could be saved for the future.

In 1924, Keller began her work with the American Foundation for the Blind. During this period she was anxious about Macy's health. In 1930, Macy became quite ill. Macy, Keller, and Thomson went to Scotland, England, and Ireland to help Macy recover.

During the period from 1931 to 1932, both Keller and Sullivan received honorary degrees from Temple University. They also visited France, Yugoslavia, England, and Scotland.

In 1933, they made another trip to England and Scotland. In 1934, Nella Braddy Henney published a biography of Macy. On October 20, 1936, Anne Sullivan Macy died. Years later, in 1955, Keller published a tribute to her teacher, *Teacher: Anne Sullivan Macy*.

Summary

Anne Sullivan Macy's impact on Helen Keller was immeasurable. The day she arrived in Tuscumbia was the day that Keller called her soul's birthday. Macy made contact with Keller in her dark, silent world and taught her how to communicate with the rest of humanity using only the sense of touch. Macy's impact was not limited to Helen Keller. Her insistence that Keller live as normal a life as possible was a precursor of contemporary approaches to the problems of the disabled.

Although Macy's name is not as well known as Keller's, a fact that disturbed Keller throughout her life, Macy has been honored for her work in a number of ways. The Anne Sullivan Macy Service for Deaf-Blind Persons was set up. A residential cottage at the Perkins Institute was named the Keller-Macy cottage in honor of both women. In 1966, a year-long Anne Sullivan Centennial Commemoration was sponsored jointly by the Industrial Home for the Blind and the Perkins School for the Blind. This observance of the anniversary of Macy's birth culminated in a memorial service at the National Cathedral in Washington, D.C., in which gold medals were presented to eight outstanding deaf-blind men and women.

Bibliography

Henney, Nella Braddy. *Anne Sullivan Macy: The Story Behind Helen Keller*. Garden City, N.Y.: Doubleday, Doran, 1934. This work, the first biography of Anne Sullivan Macy, was published while its subject was still alive.

Keller, Helen. *The Story of My Life*. New York: Bantam Books, 1904. Keller's first published description of her early years through her graduation from Radcliffe College includes much information about Anne Sullivan.

__________. *Teacher: Anne Sullivan Macy*. Garden City, N.Y.: Doubleday, 1955. This work is Keller's tribute to Macy, whom she called Teacher.

Lash, Joseph P. *Helen and Teacher: The Story of Helen Keller and Anne Sullivan Macy*. Radcliffe Biography Series. New York: Delacorte Press, 1980. This is the definitive modern biography of Macy and Keller. It is a lengthy work that draws on all previous material.

Waite, Helen Elmir. *Valiant Companions: Helen Keller and Anne Sullivan Macy*. Philadelphia: Macrae Smith, 1950. This is a moving account of Keller and Macy's life together.

Alice Ogden Bellis

WILMA P. MANKILLER

Born: November 18, 1945; Tahlequah, Oklahoma

Area of Achievement: Government and politics

Contribution: By becoming the first woman to be the principal chief of the Cherokee Nation, or of any major American Indian tribe, Wilma Mankiller renewed a long tradition of female leadership in Cherokee affairs.

Early Life

Wilma Pearl Mankiller was born on November 18, 1945, in the W. W. Hastings Indian Hospital in Tahlequah, Oklahoma. Her father, Charley Mankiller, a full-blooded Cherokee, married her mother, Clara Irene Sitton, of Dutch-Irish descent, in 1937. Wilma was the sixth of their eleven children. The family lived on Mankiller Flats in Adair County, northeastern Oklahoma. Mankiller Flats was an allotment of 160 acres that had been given to John Mankiller, Charley's father, in 1907, when Oklahoma became a state. The name "Mankiller" was the Cherokee military title of Wilma's great-great-great grandfather, Mankiller of Tellico, in the eighteenth century. Tellico, in eastern Tennessee, was part of the original Cherokee Nation. The Mankillers and most other Cherokee were forcibly moved to the Indian Territory, later the state of Oklahoma, on the infamous Trail of Tears in 1838 and 1839.

The first eleven years of Wilma's life were spent on Mankiller Flats and in traditional Cherokee culture. In 1956, however, the Mankiller family moved to San Francisco, California, as part of a government relocation plan to move American Indians to large cities and into mainstream American life. Life in San Francisco was a culture shock, especially for the Mankiller children, but they soon adjusted to their new life.

On November 13, 1963, Wilma Mankiller was married to Hugo Olaya, a member of a wealthy Ecuadorian family, who was then a student in San Francisco. Two daughters, Felicia and Gina, were born to the couple before differences in lifestyles led to a divorce in 1975. During the years of her first marriage, Wilma earned a degree from San Francisco State College.

Wilma's Cherokee background was revived, and her activist work was initiated, in 1969, when a group of American Indians occupied Alcatraz Island, in San Francisco Bay, to gain support for American Indian rights. Wilma and many others in her family participated in that occupation.

Charley Mankiller, who had become a longshoreman and a union organizer in California, died in 1971. His body was returned to his native Adair County, Oklahoma, for burial. That burial seemed to be a signal for the Mankillers to return, one by one, to Oklahoma. Wilma returned after her divorce in 1975. Only two older brothers remained in California.

After living in two worlds, Wilma Mankiller was able to emulate Nancy Ward, an eighteenth century Cherokee woman who had also lived in both worlds. Like Ward, Wilma was able to combine the best of Cherokee tradition with the best of European-

American civilization. Her balanced philosophy enabled Wilma to contribute greatly to the welfare of the Cherokee Nation.

Life's Work

Wilma Mankiller began her work to improve American Indian life before she left California. In 1974, with Bill Wahpapah, she cofounded the American Indian Community School in Oakland. Her return to Oklahoma in 1975, however, marked the beginning of her full-time service to the Cherokee Nation.

The Cherokee Nation, with 55,000 acres of northeastern Oklahoma and a population of about 67,000 people, ranks second only to the Navajo in size among American Indian tribes in the United States. When Oklahoma became a state in 1907, the traditional tribal government of the Cherokee was dissolved. This created a unique political organization, neither a reservation nor an autonomous government, with unique political and social problems. Wilma Mankiller now began directing her energy toward solving those problems.

Wilma's first regular job with the Cherokee Nation began in 1977, when she was hired as an economic-stimulus coordinator. Her job was to guide as many people as possible toward university training in such fields as environmental science and health, and then to integrate them back into their communities. Wilma soon became frustrated with the slow-moving male-dominated bureaucracy of the Cherokee Nation.

Before Europeans came to North America, Cherokee women such as Nancy Ward occupied leadership roles in tribal affairs. The title of Beloved Woman was given to those who performed extraordinary service. The first Europeans to contact the Cherokee accused them of having a "petticoat government." After this contact, the influence of Cherokee women began to decrease. In her autobiography *Mankiller: A Chief and Her People* (1993), Wilma Mankiller declared her belief that the Trail of Tears in 1838 and 1839, combined with the tremendous strain of relocation in the West, was the final step in the development of a more subservient position for women.

A very significant development in 1971 helped to open the way for a return to more female participation in Cherokee affairs. A revision of the tribal constitution provided that, for the first time since Oklahoma statehood in 1907, the principal chief would be elected by the people of the tribe rather than be appointed by the president of the United States. An entirely new constitution in 1976 solidified that change and provided for the election of a new fifteen-member tribal council.

In 1979, after working for two years as an economic-stimulus coordinator, Wilma Mankiller was made a program-development specialist and grant writer. Her immediate success in this position, especially in writing grant proposals, brought her to the attention of the tribal council and Principal Chief Ross Swimmer. This phase of Wilma's work was soon interrupted by tragedy. On November 9, 1979, she was seriously injured in a head-on collision on a country road. The driver of the other car was Sherry Morris, a white woman who was a very close friend of Wilma Mankiller. Morris was killed. In *Mankiller: A Chief and Her People*, Wilma gives an extremely moving account of that tragedy.

Within a year of the accident, Wilma was afflicted with a rare form of muscular dystrophy. These back-to-back experiences caused her to reach more deeply into her Cherokee background and led to a change in her philosophy of life.

In 1981, although still undergoing physical therapy, Wilma was able to return to her work with the Cherokee Nation, and she did so with her old energy. In that year, she helped to establish the Cherokee Nation Community Development Department and became its first director.

The next step in Wilma's career came in 1983, when Chief Ross Swimmer asked her to join his reelection ticket as his deputy chief. This request, by which Chief Swimmer recognized Wilma's potential, was very unusual because Swimmer was a conservative Republican and Wilma Mankiller was a liberal Democrat. After first declining, Wilma accepted the offer as a way to help her people.

One of Wilma's opponents for deputy chief was Agnes Cowan, the first woman to serve on the tribal council. Wilma was surprised when gender became an immediate issue in the campaign. The hostility toward Wilma ranged from having her car tires slashed to death threats. She fought that negative campaigning by conducting a very positive and cheerful campaign based primarily on her past service to the Cherokee people. The victory for the Swimmer-Mankiller ticket meant that, on August 14, 1983, Wilma Mankiller became the first female deputy chief in Cherokee history.

In 1984, Deputy Chief Mankiller participated in a very significant meeting—a reunion between the Cherokee Nation of Oklahoma and the Eastern Band of the Cherokee from North Carolina. The Eastern Band had descended from those who escaped the Trail of Tears by hiding in the mountains. This meeting, the first full tribal council since 1838, was held at Red Clay in Tennessee, the last capital of the original Cherokee Nation. In her autobiography, Wilma emphasized the tremendous historical impact that this event had on the Cherokee people.

A major career surprise for Wilma Mankiller came in 1985, when President Ronald Reagan nominated Chief Swimmer as Assistant Secretary of the Interior for Indian Affairs. This meant that, on December 14, 1985, Wilma Mankiller was inaugurated as the first woman principal chief of the Cherokee Nation.

Chief Mankiller immediately declared that economic growth would be the primary goal of her administration. She described her guiding theory as bubble-up economics, in which the people would plan and implement projects that would benefit the tribe in future years, even though the present generation might not benefit. Until the next scheduled election in 1987, however, Chief Mankiller had to govern without a mandate from the people. She faced strong opposition that limited her real power.

In October of 1986, while considering whether to run for a full term, Chief Mankiller married Charlie Soap, a full-blooded Cherokee whom she had first met in 1977. She described her new husband as the most well-adjusted male she had ever known. It was Charlie Soap who persuaded her to run in 1987, and she won in a runoff election. Because the Cherokee had now returned to the strong female leadership of their past, Chief Mankiller described her election as a step forward and a step backward at the same time.

Although Chief Mankiller's first full term was successful in terms of economic progress, her level of personal involvement was influenced by a resurgence of kidney disease, from which she had suffered for many years. This difficulty led to a kidney transplant in June, 1990. The donor was Wilma's older brother Don.

Summary

The early years of Principal Chief Wilma P. Mankiller produced many significant results, both tangible and intangible. The most important of the former is the Department of Commerce, which was created soon after Mankiller's 1987 victory. This department coordinates the business enterprises of the tribe and tries to balance tribal income with the needs of tribal members, creating jobs and producing a profit. The intangible results include a renewed spirit of independence for all Cherokee and a renewed confidence that Cherokee women can once again influence the destiny of the tribe.

In 1990, Chief Mankiller signed a historic self-governance agreement that authorized the Cherokee Nation to administer federal funds that previously had been administered by the Bureau of Indian Affairs in Washington. The same year saw a revitalizing of tribal courts and tribal police as well as the establishment of a Cherokee Nation tax commission.

The impact of Chief Mankiller was soon recognized far beyond the borders of the Cherokee Nation. In 1988, she was named Alumnus of the Year at San Francisco State College. This was followed, in 1990, by an honorary doctorate from Yale University.

The most outstanding proof of Chief Wilma Mankiller's impact on the Cherokee Nation was her reelection victory in 1991, one year after her kidney transplant, with more than 82 percent of the votes. The same election put six women on the fifteen-member tribal council. The Cherokee Nation, with a resounding voice, had returned to its past.

Bibliography

Mankiller, Wilma. *Mankiller: A Chief and Her People*. New York: St. Martin's Press, 1993. This autobiography is by far the best source available for the life, career, and philosophy of Mankiller. Includes many excellent photographs of the Mankiller family, other key individuals, and major events in Wilma Mankiller's life.

Nabokov, Peter, ed. *Native American Testimony: A Chronicle of Indian-White Relations from Prophecy to the Present, 1492-1992*. New York: Viking, 1991. A collection of essays and personal accounts. Gives an emotional vision of the sufferings and the sacrifices of American Indians, including the Cherokee. No reference to Wilma Mankiller.

Van Viema, David. "Activist Wilma Mankiller Is Set to Become the First Female Chief of the Cherokee Nation." *People Weekly* 24 (December 2, 1985): 91-92. Based on an interview with Mankiller by Michael Wallis, this article conveys the initial impression she had of her new job as chief. Reveals Mankiller's identification with her Cherokee roots.

Wallace, Michele. "Wilma Mankiller." *Ms.* 16 (January, 1988): 68-69. Wallace emphasizes the role of women in Cherokee history. Also covered is Mankiller's philosophy of leadership and her influence on women's rights in general. Includes Mankiller's plans for future Cherokee progress.

Woodward, Grace Steele. *The Cherokees*. Norman: University of Oklahoma Press, 1963. This author presents a close look at the Cherokee tradition to which Mankiller sought to return. Covers Nancy Ward and refers to Mankiller of Tellico but makes no reference to Wilma Mankiller.

Glenn L. Swygart

ALICE MARBLE

Born: September 28, 1913; Beckwourth, California
Died: December 13, 1990; Palm Springs, California
Area of Achievement: Sports
Contribution: Alice Marble was the foremost woman tennis player in the United States between 1936 and 1945. Her style of play and her lifestyle helped change the image of the female sports star.

Early Life

The fourth of five children and the younger of two girls, Alice Marble was born on September 28, 1913, in Beckwourth, California. Her mother, Jessie Wood, was a nurse, and her father, Harry Marble, was a logger and a farmer. Alice's father died when she was seven years old, and Dan, her oldest brother, who was only thirteen years old at the time of her father's death, became a major influence in her life. Alice came from an athletic family: Her father was a "high climber," the most dangerous job in the logging business; her brother Dan was a champion handball player.

After her father's death, Alice and her family moved to San Francisco. There she displayed excellent athletic skills in various sports, but her special love was baseball. She and her brother Tim would often watch the local minor league team practice, and one day when she was only thirteen years old she was allowed to shag flies in the San Francisco Seals' outfield with Lefty O'Doul and Joe Dimaggio. She became the mascot of the Seals, and on one occasion, after Babe Ruth gave her a tip about throwing a baseball, she won a contest among women for the longest baseball throw. Years later, she learned that the great athlete Babe Didrikson Zaharias was one of the women whom she defeated in that contest.

Her brother Dan, believing that she should act more like a girl, gave her a tennis racquet and told her that she would have to give up baseball. Although she was disappointed and worried about the teasing she would receive because she was playing a "sissy's" game, she soon became fascinated with the sport and took every opportunity to play on the public courts at Golden State Park in San Francisco. She played tennis in the same aggressive manner that had earlier earned for her the nickname in baseball the "Little Queen of Swat," and she quickly began to win a few local tournaments. She played at the California Tennis Club after her brother Dan purchased a junior membership for her, but she never felt as comfortable at the private club as she had on the public courts at Golden Gate Park.

Life's Work

By the time she was twenty years old, Alice Marble was ranked seventh in the United States, but tennis experts agreed that she could win only on the asphalt courts of California. She made the decision to take lessons from the teacher of some of the players who had been defeating her, Eleanor "Teach" Tennant, a woman who by 1930 had not only developed an excellent reputation as a tennis instructor of clinics for novices but also had proved that she could take a promising individual and turn her into a champion.

"Teach" taught many film stars, and she introduced Marble to the Hollywood tennis crowd and the social set that frequented La Cuesta Encantada, the San Simeon estate of millionaire publisher William Randolph Hearst. The young lady who had learned her tennis on the public courts of San Francisco was dazzled but not overwhelmed by the opulence of the Hearst estate. She won immediate acceptance by Hearst, helping him defeat Charlie Chaplin and Teach Tennant in an exhibition doubles match, and she was described in a syndicated article by Arthur Brisbane of the Hearst newspaper chain as having everything that Venus de Milo had plus two "marvelously efficient" arms.

Relearning tennis under Teach Tennant, however, was more difficult than winning the support and admiration of California high society had been. Teach, a domineering individual, nevertheless had the ability to recognize when she needed the help of an expert. The expert she needed to change Marble's game was Harwood "Beese" White, a millionaire who had become interested in tennis after an injury had forced him to retire from his career as a gymnast. Considered brilliant but eccentric, White, after initial resistance by Alice, helped to remake her style and technique. Alice Marble appeared to be well on her way to accomplishing her goals of winning on the grass surfaces that dominated the summer tennis circuit and culminated in the Wimbledon and U.S. National championships.

A series of events occurred in 1933, however, which not only would challenge her career as a tennis player but also would threaten her life. Eager to qualify for the prestigious Wightman Cup team, Marble acquiesced to the demands of an East Hampton, New York, tournament official who was a powerful man in the United States Lawn Tennis Association, and, playing both singles and doubles in the three-day affair, played 108 games in temperatures higher than 100 degrees on the last day of the tournament. She collapsed that evening and was diagnosed by a doctor as suffering from sunstroke and mild anemia. Marble suffered dizziness and loss of stamina for the next few months, although she continued to play in tournaments. While she was playing for the American team against the French team in an expanded Wightman Cup contest in Paris, Marble once again collapsed. She was hospitalized and had to return to the United States. In her twenty-first year, Alice Marble was told that she had chronic anemia and tuberculosis and would never play competitive tennis again.

Teach Tennant stood beside her player. She helped place her in a sanatorium and shared the burden of the medical bills. When Alice rebelled after five months and decided to leave the sanatorium against the advice of her doctors, Teach took her into her home, placed her on a high-protein diet, and began an initially mild but increasingly demanding physical exercise regimen. Encouraged by film actress Carole Lombard, who was credited with giving "Teach" her nickname, Alice steadily began to improve. By the time Tennant took a teaching position at the Palm Springs Racquet Club in 1935, Alice was strong enough to join her mentor and to play in local tennis tournaments. Two years after she had been told that she would never play competitive tennis again, Alice Marble began one of the most remarkable comebacks in sports history.

She became a dominant woman tennis player in the United States and the world. Ranked number one in the United States from 1936 through 1940, Alice Marble won the U.S. National Singles Championship, the U.S. National Doubles Championship, and the U.S. National Mixed Doubles Championship in 1936, 1938, 1939, and 1940. She also won the U.S. National Clay Court Singles and Doubles Championships in 1940. She was also successful in achieving her other goal, the Wimbledon Singles Championship, which she won in 1939. Her success at Wimbledon in doubles in those years was remarkable: she was a Doubles Champion in 1938 and 1939 and a Mixed Doubles Champion in 1937, 1938, and 1939. Her dominance was recognized when she was voted Woman Athlete of the Year in 1939 and 1940.

She was also successful off the tennis courts. She designed sportswear, under the logo "Tom Boy," for Best and Company, she was in constant demand to give exhibitions featuring Wilson Sporting Goods equipment, and she became an associate editor of the Wonder Woman series for Max Gaines's All-American Comics. With Carole Lombard and Clark Gable as her friends and William Randolph Hearst and Will du Pont, Jr., as her friends and patrons, she had easy access to the elite social circles of the nation. Blessed with remarkable athletic talent, a good singing voice, and photogenic looks, she was even given a screen test, but as she tells in her autobiography *Courting Danger* (1991), she, Clark Gable, and Carole Lombard would often play the screen test when they needed a few good laughs. Alice, however, might have developed a successful singing career; in fact, she first performed professionally in 1937 and sang as well as played exhibition tennis for the armed services during the World War II.

By 1940, however, her amateur tennis career appeared to have ended. The Wimbledon championships were canceled for the duration of the war, and the amateur tennis circuit was seriously curtailed in the United States. She decided to turn professional and went on a tour with Don Budge, Bill Tilden, and Mary Hare. When she discovered after her second match that she was receiving one-third the amount that Budge was receiving for the seventy-five-match tour, Alice Marble threatened to withdraw from the tour unless she was paid the same amount as Budge. The promoter of the tour, which was sponsored by the Wilson Company, capitulated. The tour was a success, but Alice was exhausted from the grueling schedule. She was unwilling, however, to turn down the offer, once the war had begun, to continue the tour for the United States. Soon, she, Budge, Tilden, and Hare were touring military bases and introducing tennis to young men and women who had never before seen the game.

Alice Marble met Joe Crowley while she was entertaining the troops at the Stage Door Canteen in New York City, and soon a friendship blossomed into romance and a secret marriage. She was pregnant and considering curtailing her tennis career when two tragedies nearly ended her life. The first was an automobile accident that caused her to miscarry, a fact that she decided to keep from her husband until he returned to the States. Soon after that tragedy, Alice learned that Captain Joe Crowley had been killed on a mission for Army Intelligence. Distraught, Alice Marble, for the first time in her life, surrendered; she attempted suicide.

After her recovery, Alice was contacted by Army Intelligence and asked to spy on Hans Steinmetz, a man who was her former lover and who, as a Swiss banker, had financial contacts with several German Nazis. Using tennis as her cover, she was partially successful in her mission but was wounded in her attempt to escape.

Following the war and a break with Tennant, her longtime coach, Alice gave tennis exhibitions, delivered lectures, and taught tennis. She gave up exhibitions and teaching for eight years until she came out of semiretirement to teach Darlene Hard, a young woman who won the U.S. Nationals in 1960 and 1961. For a brief period of time, she also served as the tennis coach to Billie Jean Moffitt (later King). Alice Marble remained active throughout the 1960's and 1970's as a tennis teacher. She also established the first Motion Picture Tournament in twenty-five years, was inducted in 1964 into the Tennis Hall of Fame, and was considered by many the grand dame of tennis. Diagnosed with colon cancer in 1981, Alice Marble responded as always with fight and determination, and she remained active in tennis in California. She died in Palm Springs, California, on December 13, 1990.

Summary

Jack Kramer once described Alice Marble as the forerunner of modern women's tennis. She played an aggressive serve-and-volley game and was known for her athletic ability. Just as important was the fact that she served as a role model for female athletes in the years between 1935 and 1960. She fought against adversity and won, never forgot her common public court origins, spoke for both female and racial equality in the sport at a time when such candor was not fashionable, and demonstrated that tennis and glamour could certainly be combined.

Bibliography

Himber, Charlotte. *Famous in Their Twenties*. New York: Association Press, 1942. This is a collection of ten essays on famous personalities such as Lowell Thomas, Margaret Bourke-White, and Paul Robeson. It contains a brief biographical essay on Alice Marble.

Jacobs, Helen Hull. *Gallery of Champions*. New York: A. S. Barnes, 1949. This is a collection of essays about some of the champion women tennis players during the period 1920 to 1940, including Suzanne Lenglen, Helen Wills Moody, and Alice Marble.

Marble, Alice. *The Road to Wimbledon*. New York: Charles Scribner's Sons, 1946. Alice Marble claimed that she wrote this book because so many of her fans had asked her to tell the secret of her success. It is an account of the events in her life which led to the winning of the singles championship at Wimbledon in 1939, but it does not reveal either the secret of her success or many of her other secrets.

Marble, Alice, and Dale Leatherman. *Courting Danger*. New York: St. Martin's Press,

1991. Alice Marble told her story to Dale Leatherman but died before the book went to print. Unlike her other autobiographical work, *The Road to Wimbledon*, this book is extremely candid in its description of Alice Marble's life.

Robert L. Patterson

FRANCES MARION

Born: November 18, 1887; San Francisco, California
Died: May 12, 1973; Los Angeles, California
Area of Achievement: Film
Contribution: Described by *The New York Times* as "the dean of Hollywood screenwriters," Frances Marion helped forge the narrative conventions of the classic American cinema.

Early Life

Frances Marion Owens was born in San Francisco on November 18, 1887. She attended Hamilton Grammar School, St. Margaret's Hall, and the University of California, Berkeley. Although the facts of her early years are sketchy, by the time she arrived in Los Angeles from San Francisco in 1913 at age twenty-three, she had been twice married and divorced. She had worked as an artist's and photographer's model, and as a commercial illustrator. Marion was also an experienced writer with published poetry and short stories to her name. In addition, like later screenwriting greats Ben Hecht and Charles MacArthur, she had been a journalist, a nineteen-year-old cub reporter with the *San Francisco Reporter*, where she had honed a keen sense of the human drama pulsing beneath the facts of a story.

Marion's first job in Los Angeles was as a designer of theatrical posters for impresario Oliver Morosco. As she recounts in her autobiography *Off with Their Heads!* (1972), the Los Angeles of 1913 was an essentially rural and provincial community where the first waves of fair-weather filmmakers escaping wintry climes in the East were regarded as hoards of invading locusts. Indeed, her friends at Morosco's sneered at motion pictures as "trotting tintypes." With the film debuts of theatrical personages such as Sarah Bernhardt, Lillie Langtry, and Minnie Maddern Fiske, it became clear that the tide was turning.

Although at first skeptical, Marion was persuaded of the film medium's bright future by her close friend, journalist Adela Rogers St. Johns. Through an introduction by St. Johns, Marion landed a job with Lois Weber, then the only woman director in the film business. Weber hired Marion as a jill-of-all-trades at Bosworth Studios where the neophyte apprenticed in acting, stuntwork (she was an excellent equestrian), film editing, publicity work, and scenario writing.

Life's Work

Frances Marion, along with her other talents, had a considerable gift for friendship. Indeed, she soon became acquainted not only with Hollywood's elite but also with the esoteric literary circle that called New York's Algonquin Hotel home. During this period, films were produced in New York as well as Hollywood, thus accounting for the frequent transcontinental shuttlings of film people such as Marion. Although Marion's own intimate circle included Anita Loos, Dorothy Parker, and Hedda Hopper, it was her close relationship with Mary Pickford that proved pivotal in launching her career as one of the silent era's top scenarists.

Marion's first important writing assignment was *The Foundling* (1916), a Pickford feature produced by Adolph Zukor's Famous Players-Paramount. Originally scheduled for release in September of 1915, the film was severely damaged in a laboratory fire. Pickford and Marion were dismayed at this destruction of their work, but the star promised they soon would collaborate again. Determined to see the project through, Pickford reshot the ruined scenes. The reedited film successfully debuted in January of 1916, and Marion was suddenly in demand as a Hollywood writer.

The notoriety of Marion's first credited feature with no less a star than Mary Pickford provided a glittering calling card for the ambitious screenwriter. In 1916, she scripted eighteen features, including *The Feast of Life* with Clara Kimball Young and *Bought and Paid For* with Alice Brady. The year 1917 was equally successful with eighteen additional scripts produced. Marion's output in 1917 was highlighted by two well-received Pickford projects—*A Poor Little Rich Girl*, directed by Maurice Tourneur, and an adaptation of *Rebecca of Sunnybrook Farm*, helmed by Marshall "Mickey" Neilan. In each, Marion helped fashion characters and plots that framed Pickford at her scrappy, spunky best. In 1920, Marion's adaptation of *Pollyanna* solidified Pickford's persona as a spirited underdog whose hard work, honesty, and indomitable pluck were the true essence of well-being rather than wealth and privilege. As the embodiment of the Pollyanna ideal, Pickford was christened in 1920 as "America's Sweetheart," a tag that perfectly encapsulated Pickford's unique position in American culture.

With America's entry into World War I in 1917, Marion interrupted her career to serve as the first woman war correspondent through a commission as a first lieutenant issued by General John Pershing. Sobered by the harsh realities of war, Marion yearned for an opportunity to deal with serious issues. The industry's moguls, however, wanted pictures with happy endings. So, too, apparently, did the public. Although Marion delivered such frothy fare with style and dispatch, her characters, when permitted, often had a hard, gritty realistic edge. Such was the case with two films she wrote for Lillian Gish, *The Scarlet Letter* (1926) and *The Wind* (1928), both of which became classics.

Marion was a perceptive judge of acting talent. When she was hired by William Randolph Hearst in 1920, at the then extraordinary salary of $2,000 a week, she risked her new position by refusing to work on Marion Davies' projects unless the actress' comedic abilities were tapped. Hearst, who wanted to transform his mistress into a "serious" actress was initially reluctant. Eventually taking Marion's advice, Davies won a new lease on her screen career as one of the period's great comediennes. Hearst, perhaps in appreciation, permitted Marion to direct her first film, *Just Around the Corner* (1921). Marion also wrote and directed *The Love Light* (1921), which featured good friend Mary Pickford and Marion's new husband Fred Thomson, who became a popular cowboy star. While her few directorial efforts garnered mostly favorable reviews, Marion preferred writing to the grueling pace of directing during the silent era.

Marion worked with the brightest stars of the Hollywood firmament. Along with Pickford, Gish, and Davies, there was Greta Garbo in *Love* (1927), *Anna Christie* (1930), and *Camille* (1937); Marie Dressler in *Tillie Wakes Up* (1917) and in her Oscar-winning role in *Min and Bill* (1930); Norma Talmadge in *He Comes up Smiling* (1918); Anna May Wong in *The Toll of the Sea* (1922); Rudolph Valentino in *Son of the Sheik* (1926); Ronald Colman in *A Thief in Paradise* (1925); Lionel Barrymore in *Paris at Midnight* (1926); Wallace Beery in *Min and Bill, The Secret Six* (1931), and, with Jackie Cooper, in *The Champ* (1931); and Jean Harlow in *Dinner at Eight* (1933).

In contrast to the stereotypical view of the Hollywood writer as an alienated, marginalized worker toiling in isolation, Marion, like good friend and fellow scenarist Anita Loos, moved freely among Hollywood's elite. Her favorite producer, Samuel Goldwyn, returned the compliment by calling her his favorite scriptwriter. Irving Thalberg, the boy-wonder executive producer who helped turn the fortunes of Metro-Goldwyn-Mayer (MGM) around, sought her counsel. She was an intimate as well as a collaborator to the industry's movers and shakers be they stars, directors, producers, or fellow writers.

Unlike many of her silent era colleagues, Marion was notable for having made a smooth transition from the silent to the sound film. In fact, Marion won the second and third Academy Awards for screenwriting with *The Big House* (1930) and *The Champ*, both of which featured Wallace Beery, who won an Oscar as best actor for his role in the latter film. Nevertheless, although Marion signed a $3,500 a week contract with MGM in 1930, the nature of film writing was shifting from an individual to a team or "assembly line" approach. Wanting to retain as much control over her scripts as possible, Marion decided to become a producer-writer. Her efforts in this direction in the late 1930's and early 1940's went unrewarded prompting her to turn to magazine stories and serials. She also became involved in studying and making sculpture.

In 1928, her happy personal life took a tragic turn with the loss of her beloved husband, Fred Thomson, who died suddenly of tetanus. Later, a short-lived marriage in 1930 to director George W. Hill was followed by his suicide in 1933, two years after their divorce. Frances Marion died in Los Angeles in 1973.

Summary

In a film career spanning some forty years, Frances Marion is credited with more than 130 produced screenplays, a remarkable accomplishment. Her work is highlighted by two Oscars and a handful of beloved films that in their lean narrative structure are representative of the best in the classic Hollywood tradition. Insight into her no-nonsense, action-oriented approach emerges from her still useful book, *How to Write and Sell Motion Picture Stories* (1937), which emphasizes visual over aural means of communication, simplicity and detail, colorful personalities, and common emotions. Her autobiographical collection of reminiscences, *Off with Their Heads!*, though telling more about her glittering friends than herself, is a witty memoir chronicling Hollywood's golden years. In summing up Marion's style, however, critic

Marjorie Rosen observed that at their best, Marion's scripts were fast-paced, action-oriented, without romance, naturalistic and "exactly the antithesis of . . . the archetypical 'women's pictures' "—a final testament, perhaps, to Marion's background as a journalist and war correspondent.

During Hollywood's difficult transition out of the silent era to the age when films seemed to prattle nonstop under the spell of the novelty of synchronized sound, Marion was one a handful of film artists who recognized that cinema was an inherently eye-oriented rather than ear-oriented medium. In fact, the lasting allure of Marion's greatest sound films rests largely on their nondialogue passages where the faces of Garbo, Dressler, and Beery "speak" more eloquently than words.

Bibliography

Acker, Ally. *Reel Women: Pioneers of the Cinema, 1896 to the Present*. New York: Continuum, 1991. Acker correctly brackets her useful essay on Francis Marion under the heading "From the Silents to the Sound Era" in a chapter devoted to "Reel Women Writers." Filmography of Marion's screenwriting credits included.

Marion, Frances. *How to Write and Sell Film Stories*. New York: Covici, Friede, 1937. Dedicated to the memory of Irving Thalberg "as a tribute to his vision and genius," Marion's guide is still highly useful for aspiring writers or anyone wishing a more refined understanding of film's unique narrative powers. Includes chapters on such story elements as characterization, plot, motivation, theme, and emotions, along with the shooting script for *Marco Polo* by Robert E. Sherwood.

____________. *Off with Their Heads!: A Serio-Comic Tale of Hollywood*. New York: Macmillan, 1972. This vibrantly witty recounting of Marion's life among Hollywood's elite at the height of their youth and newfound power and influence is highly informative, but falters when Marion turns her gaze on herself. A complete filmography of Marion's work is included.

Rosen, Marjorie. *Popcorn Venus: Women, Movies and the American Dream*. New York: Coward, McCann & Geoghegan, 1973. A pioneering survey of the singular contributions made by women to the Hollywood film industry. Includes Rosen's thoughtful consideration of Marion.

Slide, Anthony. *Early Women Directors*. New York: A. S. Barnes, 1977. Slide's informative essay on Marion focuses on the three feature-length silent films she directed, *Just Around the Corner*, *The Love Light*, and *The Song of Love* (1923).

Starr, Cecile. "Francis Marion." In *The International Dictionary of Films and Filmmakers: Volume IV, Writers and Production Artists*, edited by James Vinson. Chicago: St. James Press, 1984. A compact yet solid overview of Marion's career and personal life. Filmography and bibliography included.

Charles Merrell Berg

PENNY MARSHALL

Born: October 15, 1942; Bronx, New York

Areas of Achievement: Film and television

Contribution: Achieving fame as a television actress, Penny Marshall made a successful transition to feature film direction with critically acclaimed hits such as *Big* (1988), *Awakenings* (1990), and *A League of Their Own* (1992).

Early Life

Carole Penny Marshall, named for actress Carole Lombard, was born on October 15, 1942, in New York City, the third child of Marjorie Marshall, a dance instructor, and Tony Marshall (formerly Tony Masciarelli), an industrial filmmaker. Marshall's brother Garry is a prominent writer-director; her sister Ronny Hallin is a successful television producer. Show business was a leitmotif threading its way through the family's life. Marshall's mother ran a dancing school, the Ballroom, in the basement of the family's apartment building. At age three, with prodding from her mother, Penny began to take dance lessons. Soon she was performing with the Marshallettes, a precision dance team of sixteen young girls organized by her mother who were novel enough to win spots on *Ted Mack's Original Amateur Hour* and *The Jackie Gleason Show*. Claiming she hated it, Penny continued dancing under the threat of having to do Saturday chores.

Marshall's birthplace, the Bronx, was another formative influence. In the mid-1950's, the Mosholu Parkway, a patch of green in the middle of the neighborhood's concrete contours, was a favorite meeting place of Marshall and such future successes as comedian Robert Klein and fashion designer Ralph Lauren. In recalling her teen years, Marshall describes herself as a tomboy who made fun of herself before anyone else did. Insecure about her appearance because she had braces, she remembers being heartbroken when boys she fell for did not reciprocate her interest. Though she does not remember being funny, her friends do. Marshall was well known for being a loyal friend and having a ready shoulder to share. Marshall's introspective yet humorous self-deprecation seems to have given her insights into the human condition that have been important in delineating her fictive characters as both an actress and director.

After her graduation from Walton High School in the Bronx, Marshall was sent to the University of New Mexico at her mother's insistence so that the awkward teen might lose her New York accent. As Marshall tells it, her mother also thought Albuquerque was nearby, assuming that all the "News"—New York, New Jersey, New Hampshire, and New Mexico—were bunched together. Majoring in psychology, an academically unfocused Marshall dropped out of classes at the end of her sophomore year to marry a football player, have a daughter, Tracy, and then divorce. Discontent with life in Albuquerque, Marshall moved to Los Angeles in 1967, where her brother Garry, who was active in television as a writer and aspiring producer, urged her to study acting at night while working as a secretary during the day.

Life's Work

Penny Marshall's first national exposure as an actress came in a 1967 shampoo commercial in which her "stringy hair" was contrasted with actress Farrah Fawcett's "beautiful hair." It was, in a case of art imitating life, a microcosmic representation of Marshall's insecurity and self-doubt. In addition to making commercials, Marshall had bit parts in films such as the comedy *How Sweet It Is!* (1968), the motorcycle exploitation film *The Savage Seven* (1968), and the melodramatic *The Grasshopper* (1970), a Jacqueline Bisset vehicle coproduced and cowritten by Garry Marshall. Penny Marshall's television debut, aside from commercials, came in a 1968 episode of *The Danny Thomas Show*. In 1971, she married a former colleague from the Los Angeles comedy troupe The Committee, actor and director-to-be Rob Reiner. In the same year, her brother Garry, then coproducing and cowriting the ABC comedy *The Odd Couple*, based on Neil Simon's Broadway hit, cast Penny as Myrna Turner, Oscar Madison's screwball secretary. She also had roles in television sitcoms such as *The Bob Newhart Show* and made-for-television pictures, the first being *The Feminist and the Fuzz* (1971).

In 1975, after ABC had canceled *The Odd Couple*, Marshall and Cindy Williams appeared in an episode of Garry Marshall's *Happy Days*, a comic glimpse into high-school life during the late 1950's. The chemistry between the actresses was immediate. Only months later, with the blessings of ABC programming chief Fred Silverman, Garry Marshall introduced *Laverne and Shirley*. Within a year of its debut in January of 1976, the spinoff was television's top-rated show and Marshall and Williams were stars. During its seven-year run, which ended in May of 1983, Marshall directed four episodes, her first professional directing assignments. She also appeared in the 1978 television picture *More than Friends*, a romantic comedy cowritten by and costarring Rob Reiner based loosely on the couple's courtship. She also appeared in Steven Spielberg's feature film *1941* (1979), which, though a flop, gained for her in Spielberg an important ally and friend.

In 1981, after divorcing Reiner, Marshall fell into what she describes as her "doormat years." Wrestling with self-doubt, she experimented with psychedelic drugs and partied with acting friends such as James Belushi and Joe Pesci, who rented rooms in a large home Marshall had bought for tax purposes after her split from Reiner. Soon, however, she regained her equilibrium.

After *Laverne and Shirley* ended, Marshall received good notices for starring performances in the television pictures *Love Thy Neighbor* (1984) and *Challenge of a Lifetime* (1985). She made her stage debut in *Eden Court* (1985), an Off-Broadway play in which she played the alcoholic best friend of Ellen Barkin. Although the show was panned, the critics praised Marshall for her impeccable comic timing, which she had sharpened during her television sitcom days.

Though Marshall had directed four episodes of *Laverne and Shirley* and a sitcom pilot called *Working Stiffs* with Michael Keaton and James Belushi, she never really intended to make directing, a mostly male preserve, a career objective. As had been the case with so many other events in her life, however, serendipity played a role. Her first big-screen assignment might have been *Peggy Sue Got Married* (1986). At the onset of the project, Jonathan Demme had been signed to direct Debra Winger. Winger, however, wanted Marshall, who then replaced Demme. When Winger withdrew after a back injury and Kathleen Turner was hired to take her place, Marshall was dismissed in favor of the high-profile Francis Ford Coppola.

Hollywood's version of musical chairs worked to Marhsall's advantage when she was picked, because of her friendship with star Whoopi Goldberg, to replace Howard Zieff for an action-comedy about spies called *Jumpin' Jack Flash* (1986). The film's weak script and tight shooting schedule conspired to make it unpopular with critics and audiences alike. Nevertheless, industry insiders who were aware of the film's production problems gave Marshall high marks for bringing the project in with some semblance of coherence and style.

With a simple title and an understated star turn by Tom Hanks, who received an Oscar nomination for his role as a twelve-year-old boy displaced into the body of a thirty-five-year-old man, Marshall had a success with *Big* (1988). It was the first film by a woman director to gross more than $100 million. On the strength of *Big*'s financial and critical success, Marshall became a sought-after director. Deluged with scripts from the major studios, she selected Steven Zaillian's adaptation *Awakenings* (1990), which was based on a 1973 book by neurologist Oliver Sacks about a man rendered mute and immobile by encephalitis who emerges from his catatonia thanks to an experimental drug, L-dopa. Starring Robin Williams as the introverted Malcolm Sayer, a physician willing to take a last chance on "a hopeless case," and Robert DeNiro as the erudite patient, *Awakenings* received Oscar nominations for best picture, best actor, and best screenplay. The Academy of Motion Picture Arts and Sciences' failure to nominate Marshall in the best director category prompted some insiders to complain that she was the victim of sex discrimination. When she was informed that "she had been robbed," Marshall thought that someone had broken into her house. Marshall noted that in 1986, Steven Spielberg had had a similar experience when *The Color Purple* had been nominated for eleven other Oscars, but not for best director. Although *Awakenings* was a departure in terms of its serious theme, it reflected an unabashed sentimentality and humanistic warmth reminiscent of one of Marshall's favorite directors and fellow Italian American, the legendary Frank Capra.

In 1992, Marshall directed *A League of Their Own*, a poignant and comedic telling of the story of the All-American Girls Professional Baseball League, which thrived during World War II. Bolstered by an all-star cast headed by Tom Hanks, Geena Davis, Lori Petty, Rosie O'Donnell, Jon Lovitz, and Madonna, *A League of Their Own* was a major hit during the summer of 1992. (It also inspired a television spinoff of the same title, which, though coproduced and initially directed by Marshall, failed to connect with viewers during its short run on CBS during the spring of 1993.) The 1992 film, with its theme and its cast of some thirty-six women, provoked questions about its being inspired by feminism. Marshall disavows such interpretations, arguing that the film's problems apply equally to men and women. Marshall says that the film is about not being ashamed of one's talents, "a universal thing."

Summary

Penny Marshall is destined to remain visible to television viewers because of her memorable portrayal of the blue-collar Laverne DeFazio in the syndicated television series *Laverne and Shirley*. Marshall has already won a place in the pantheon of cinematic auteurs with her entertaining and engaging *Big*, *Awakenings*, and *A League of Their Own*. For feminist critics and commentators, Penny Marshall, in spite of distancing herself from the movement and its ideology, still occupies an important place by virtue of being one of a handful of women to prove that women can successfully direct big-budget Hollywood films. For this reason, Marshall, like Barbra Streisand, should be viewed as an important influence in helping to increase opportunities for women who aspire to direct feature narrative films.

Part of Marshall's directing success can be explained by her extensive experience in television, where communicating clearly is a "must" for broad audience appeal. Her sense of timing is also a major factor. Most important, however, is her compassion for her characters and the quixotic nature of their predicaments. Like Frank Capra, Marshall is an unabashed sentimentalist who has given audiences a gallery of unforgettable men and women who do their best to sort through and make sense of life's vicissitudes.

Bibliography

Acker, Ally. *Reel Women: Pioneers of the Cinema, 1896 to the Present*. New York: Continuum, 1991. Acker's invaluable compendium includes a thoughtful essay on Marshall that focuses on her career as a film director up to and including *Awakenings* (1991). Includes a filmography.

Morgenstern, Joe. "Penny from Heaven." *Playboy* 38, no. 1 (January, 1991): 144-145. Morgenstern's interesting article examines Marshall's personality and personal problems as well as her career as a director.

Orenstein, Peggy. "Making It in the Majors." *The New York Times Magazine* 141 (May 24, 1992): 18. This incisive interview, conducted while Marshall was directing *A League of Their Own*, reveals much about the director's view of feminist issues and about her family and personal background.

Waters, Harry F., and Charles Fleming. "TV Sheds Its Stigma: Top Film Directors Are Turning to the Small Screen—And Both Are Better for It." *Newsweek* 121 (April 26, 1993): 70-71. A probing discussion of the tendency of major networks to hire name film directors such as Penny Marshall and Steven Spielberg to produce for television; for the networks, that action is a response to shrinking markets, while for directors, it provides an opportunity to reach vast audiences and have increased creative freedom.

Charles Merrell Berg

AGNES MARTIN

Born: March 22, 1912; Maklin, Saskatchewan, Canada

Area of Achievement: Art
Contribution: A leading American artist of the style of minimalism in the 1960's and 1970's, Agnes Martin persevered in her commitment to art as a means of spiritual expression to become one of the few women artists of the twentieth century to achieve recognition and success.

Early Life

Born on a farm in Maklin, Saskatchewan, Canada, on March 22, 1912, Agnes Bernice Martin grew up in a pioneer family in Vancouver, British Columbia, and moved to Bellingham, Washington, in 1919, where she attended high school and college. She went on to receive a degree from the Teachers College of Columbia University in New York City, majoring in fine arts and art education. After working for four years as an art teacher, she moved to New Mexico looking for new opportunities and the environment to pursue her own work, away from the complexities of city life. She taught in a number of art programs in high schools and colleges in New Mexico and received early recognition for her own work with the receipt of scholarships and awards. In 1950, Agnes Martin became a United States citizen.

The experience of living in the beauty and open spaces of the West would always be inspirational to her work, despite a number of return trips to New York to complete her education and earn a Masters of Arts degree in 1952. Although her early work was dominated by landscapes and floating abstract shapes, in the period of postgraduate study, she was finally ready to understand and accept the stylistic achievements of the avante-garde painters working in New York. Finding it too difficult and expensive to live in New York, she returned to Taos, New Mexico, for five years. Beginning in 1957, Agnes Martin lived and worked in New York City. It was a dynamic period for art, dominated by the New York school of abstract expressionists and action painters. For the next ten years, a critical phase of development in her early life as an artist, she would become part of the movement of many of her contemporaries to respond to the painterly aggression of the abstract expressionists. Seeking new solutions to the pictorial problems inherent in painting, she would progress from painting simple biomorphic shapes in open spaces to the tranquil geometric canvases of her own personal and mature vision of art.

In December of 1958, Agnes Martin had her first one-artist exhibition at the Betty Parsons Gallery in New York City and received critical acclaim for her work, a significant accomplishment for a woman artist at that time.

Life's Work

The decade of the 1960's in New York was definitive in the formulation of Agnes Martin's personal aesthetic. Based on the total distillation of geometric forms to pure translucent surfaces, this aesthetic was quiet and simple. It appeared to be totally contrary to the brash and gestural painting techniques practiced by the abstract expressionists beginning in the 1940's and much more structured than those of their followers, the color field painters, who reduced their canvases to freely formed areas of color. After many years of working with abstract shapes floating in space, Martin realized that geometry was the most appropriate vehicle for her to express the spiritual content that was implicit in her paintings. Taking the "expressionist" definition of modern painting seriously, she sought the means to express the inspirational views of nature that had so affected her for many years in the West. Inspired by the Greeks, who had also used the perfection of mathematical geometric forms as the basis of Classical art, her canvases used mathematics in their underlying organizational structure. In the middle of the twentieth century, however, the representational subject matter that was so important to the Greeks was no longer necessary; it had been rejected in favor of the purity of mathematical forms. Over monochromatic color surfaces painted in thin washes of oils, Agnes Martin penciled in geometrics as a series of grids of different sizes and arrangements within the rectangle of the picture frame.

In 1964, Agnes Martin changed her technique from oils to acrylics painted in a limited palette on white-gessoed canvases. With the graphite grids dematerializing beneath the muted colors, the paintings were simplified to the bare minimum. Acrylics also allowed her to create misty background effects that would enhance the spiritual and emotional content of her works. Requiring the utmost concentration, these canvases lured the viewer into their very being and acted as meditational devices. They created a transcendental reality in paint. With nature as the source of inspiration, the paintings of Agnes Martin went beyond the simple forms favored by other artists of the 1960's known as minimalists.

Although hailed as a minimalist artist during her entire career, Agnes Martin was inspired to produce simple geometric shapes for reasons that were quite different in concept from the minimalist school. Minimalism, with Agnes Martin in its midst, was introduced to the American public in 1966 at an exhibition at the Guggenheim Museum in New York titled "Systemic Painting." True minimalist artists avoid expressive painting devices and representational subjects and concentrate on the repetition of simple shapes and forms which can be extended indefinitely. The repetitive grids played out in infinite series of variations by Agnes Martin appear to reflect such ideas. Nevertheless, her work was full of personal meaning and human expression, while minimalism was purely objective and lacking in sentimentality. Actually, Martin was far more of an abstract expressionist according to its true definition and saw herself as such, rather than as a minimalist totally devoid of expressive feeling. Abstract expressionism embraces a number of styles that reveal emotional content, its "expression" revealed through "abstract" means. Agnes Martin also expresses herself, but with quiet sublime means based on the reductive abstract principles of geometry. These principles are closer to abstract expressionism than minimalism.

Agnes Martin's personal philosophy emerged from a number of sources which were popular in the intellectual communities of the 1950's and 1960's. The teachings of Taoism and Zen Buddhism joined those of the Bible as inspiration for artists looking beyond mundane earthly reality for their subject matter. Asserting that enlightenment could be attained through self-contemplation and inner awareness, these Asian philosophies directed an entire generation to participate in the tranquillity of meditation. The paintings of Agnes Martin assist in the meditative process, affecting the viewer with the chant of their subliminal atmospheric vibrations.

The personal content of Agnes Martin's work demanded spiritual isolation and a level of quietude that was impossible in the vibrant life of the New York art world. In 1967, she announced her retirement from painting and left the constant interruptions of the city to find solitude in New Mexico. She settled on an isolated mesa near the village of Cuba, built an adobe and log house, and abandoned the distractions of the world for an existence without even a telephone. It was not until 1974, after several offers by gallery dealers and museum directors to organize exhibitions of her work, that she built a studio adjacent to her home and resumed painting.

At the age of sixty-two, Agnes Martin began another phase of her painting career. The translucent canvases with their wide variety of pencil grids barely visible through the dominantly white color field were replaced by paintings featuring broad stripes of lightly modulated colors. As if merely washed with bands of pale colors, her canvases of the late 1970's and 1980's are as luminous as the perfect harmony found in nature. The graphite markings are less conspicuous and washes of color are dominant. Still contained within the geometric construction of the canvas and defined by ordered and ruled markings, the broad color bands shimmer and tremble as if induced by a meditative state.

In the early 1990's, Agnes Martin has continued to work in solitude, surrounded by the desert beauty of the American West. True to her belief that art involves an awareness of perfection to achieve beauty and happiness, she has maintained a personal and unique vision during a lifetime of work. In a field of achievement where many women have failed to receive proper recognition, Agnes Martin deserves a place as a major figure in the history of American art.

Summary

The history of modern art follows two major paths of artistic stylization: expressionism and abstractionism. Beginning at the end of the nineteenth century, artists have followed these paths in an effort to create a visual language significant to modern life. Agnes Martin determined that she could do both: express her own personal concepts about art and its meaning as a universal phenomenon created by human beings from their own instincts and formalize these concepts within the perfect structures of geometry. As a woman working outside of the commercial environment and demands of the New York art world, she was prevented from receiving the popular acclaim and recognition given to so many of her male contemporaries, despite critical praise from writers. The highly personal and intellectual nature of her art often demanded more than the ordinary art viewer was willing to invest in order to comprehend its meaning fully. Agnes Martin determined her own path as an artist and maintained her vision throughout her long career. It was a vision of sublime perfection incorporating deceptively simple imagery and the tenets of modernism as understood and successfully executed by very few artists. For this perfect association of personal expression and abstraction, Agnes Martin stands as one of the masters of twentieth century modern art.

Bibliography

Arnason, H. H. *History of Modern Art*. 3d ed. Englewood Cliffs, N.J.: Prentice-Hall, 1986. History of modern art includes section on minimal art and the work of Agnes Martin. Excellent basic survey of modern art.

Gruen, John. "Agnes Martin: 'Everything, Everything Is About Feeling . . . Feeling and Recognition.'" *ARTnews* 75 (September, 1976): 91-94. Review of exhibition of Agnes Martin's paintings at The Pace Gallery and Robert Elkon Gallery.

Haskell, Barbara. *Agnes Martin*. New York: Whitney Museum of American Art, 1992. The catalog for the major retrospective exhibition of Agnes Martin's works organized by the Whitney Museum in 1993. Includes essays by Barbara Haskell, Rosalind Krauss and Anna C. Chave and quotations from writings by the artist. It is the only monograph to date on the artist.

Hunter, Sam, and John Jacobus. *Modern Art*. Englewood Cliffs, N.J.: Prentice-Hall, 1992. Overview of modern painting, sculpture, and architecture that includes chapter on minimalism and brief commentary on works of Agnes Martin.

Carol Damian

ANTONIA MAURY

Born: March 21, 1866; Cold Spring, New York
Died: January 8, 1952; Dobbs Ferry, New York
Area of Achievement: Astronomy
Contribution: Maury's spectroscopic analysis of star systems contributed to the discovery and confirmation of a variety of astronomical phenomena.

Early Life

Antonia Caetana De Paiva Pereira Maury was born on March 21, 1866, in Cold Spring, New York, the eldest of three children. Maury's scientific career to a significant degree was a continuation of the intellectual genealogy already well established within her family. Her father, Mytton Maury, though professionally an Episcopalian minister, was both a naturalist and editor of a geographical magazine. The Reverend Maury's cousin, Matthew Maury, was a noted oceanographer. Antonia's great grandfather had been the British physician to Dom Pedro I, emperor of Brazil; he subsequently married into the de Paiva Pereira family, a prominent Portuguese clan. Antonia's mother, Virginia Draper Maury, was herself the daughter of John William Draper, who was among the first astronomers to apply photography to that field. Antonia's uncle, Henry Draper, was also a noted astronomer and Harvard benefactor. This rich scientific background contributed significantly to Antonia's interests in nature. In addition to receiving acclaim in her chosen profession, Antonia also became a noted ornithologist and naturalist. In the family tradition, her sister, Carlotta Joaquina Maury, later became a prominent South American paleontologist.

The Reverend Maury strongly encouraged intellectual pursuits among his children, often to the extent of actively guiding (or interfering) in their early lives. Indeed, it was through the intervention of her father that she was launched on her scientific career. In 1877, Antonia received a Bachelor of Arts degree from Vassar College, where she had trained in the teaching of physics and chemistry and had come under tutelage of astronomer Maria Mitchell. Following her graduation, her father planned a move for his family from New York to the Boston area. At the same time, he made a number of contacts that eventually landed his daughter a job at the Harvard Observatory.

The Henry Draper Memorial program was begun at Harvard in 1886, under the direction of Edward Pickering, director of the Harvard College Observatory. The Reverend Maury contacted Pickering on the pretext of inquiring into the memorial named for his brother-in-law, but steered the conversation in order to discuss a job for his daughter. Pickering was at first reluctant; the job only paid twenty-five cents an hour, and he questioned whether a Vassar graduate would even be interested. After consulting with Anna Draper, Henry's widow and current benefactor of the observatory, Pickering offered Antonia a position as computer for his studies of astronomical spectra. Although Antonia's father had apparently contacted Pickering without her knowledge, she nevertheless accepted the offer, beginning her work at Harvard in 1888.

Life's Work

Edward Pickering, with whom Antonia Maury would work during her most productive years in astronomy, was among the most important of the nineteenth century investigators in stellar spectroscopy. A professor of physics at the Massachusetts Institute of Technology at the age of twenty-two, Pickering was appointed director of the Harvard College Observatory in 1877. He had an almost unmatched ability to carry out mundane projects involving observations and data collection on an unprecedented scale; in his lifetime, Pickering personally recorded nearly 1.5 million observations of stellar magnitudes, in addition to his development of new innovations for wide-angle stellar photography.

Pickering's colleague, and Maury's uncle, Henry Draper, was equally as well known in the field of stellar spectroscopy. Upon Draper's death in 1882, his widow, Anna Palmer Draper, wished to establish a memorial to honor her husband, and to enable his work to continue. In 1886, she established an endowment program at Harvard, the Henry Draper Memorial, with Pickering as its director. Under Pickering, the spectroscopic program began an extensive cataloging of stars on the basis of various astronomical criteria (published in 1890). The Draper Memorial Catalogue would be the basis for all future spectral classifications.

Although it was a milestone in the field, the classification scheme as first devised quickly proved less than ideal. Quantifications for specific classifications were inadequate, and more detailed study of observations was badly needed. It was here that Maury was given her task, an examination of nearly 5,000 photographic plates of brighter stars within the northern sky.

Maury's background in physics and chemistry made her an ideal choice for the work. Although Pickering closely supervised the work of his staff, a characteristic which Maury found irritating, he recognized Maury's abilities in the area and gave her freedom to develop her own classification system. Maury found the observatory's system for spectral analysis, recently established by another of Pickering's female assistants, Williamina Fleming, to be grossly inadequate. Spectral analysis involved passage of light from the star under observation through a prism, presenting a series of spectral lines on a photographic plate (in some respects analogous to a rainbow). Analysis of these lines could yield information on size, brightness, and composition of the star. Maury noted that spectral lines often differed in width, and her "collateral divisions" which took these into account provided a significant clarification of the Fleming system. By developing a two-dimensional system based on both arrangements of spectral lines and their relative width and clarity, Maury opened the door to a more efficient means of stellar analysis. Indeed, it was a direct result of Maury's subdivisions that Danish astronomer Ejnar Hertzsprung in 1905 verified his discovery, within the same spectral-temperature class, of distinct varieties of stars: dwarfs and giants. In 1897, Maury's work on spectral classification was published in the *Annals of the Harvard College Observatory* (the first work in the *Annals* with a woman listed on the title page).

While her work on the star catalog was underway, Maury was also assigned to study the spectrum of the star Sirius, eventually noting the presence of more than five hundred spectral lines. This work was instrumental in confirming Pickering's 1889 discovery of the first spectroscopic binary, a star which looks single through the telescope, but proves to be a binary system through doubling of spectroscopic lines as the two stars move in different directions; Maury herself later discovered the second such binary, Beta Aurigae. Study of such spectroscopic binary systems later became the focus of her career.

Maury remained at the observatory through 1891. Personality conflicts between Pickering and Maury, coupled with the tedium of an admittedly boring type of analysis, influenced her decision to leave. She returned periodically over the next five years to complete her work on the star catalog, but effectively cut her direct ties to the observatory for several decades after 1896.

The conflict between Pickering and Maury stemmed primarily from his impatience to publish their findings. In part, their differences also resulted from distinct types of personalities: Maury was highly systematic in her work and developed her own classification scheme, while Pickering became incensed when she failed to follow his established system and schedule. Maury's departure placed a particular strain on their relationship. Pickering was scrupulously fair in assigning credit to his colleague's work. Nevertheless, in the interest of completing the star catalog, he wished to assign the task to somebody else in her absence. This decision Maury would not accept. Pickering's habit of daily observations of his assistants' progress was also annoying to Maury. A letter from Maury's father, accusing Pickering of mistreating Antonia, only complicated matters even further. Despite continual prodding on the part of Pickering, it was not until 1897 that the work was finished.

Maury did not return to the Harvard Observatory until 1908. After a year at Vassar in 1896 studying spectra, she spent much of her time teaching high school, lecturing at colleges and to the general public, and teaching private students.

Despite their differences, Pickering and Maury retained a strong professional relationship. In 1908, she was highly recommended by Pickering for an adjunct professorship at a little-known university, but chose to return to Harvard as a research associate. She spent most of the remainder of her career in the study of another spectroscopic binary, Beta Lyrae. Much of this work was published in the *Harvard Annals* in 1933, along with her analysis of other spectroscopic binaries.

Maury retired from Harvard in 1935, but she continued to make yearly visits to the observatory until 1948 in order to examine photographs of the spectrum generated by Beta Lyrae and test her theories on spectral changes. The major instrument for this work, an eleven-inch Draper refractory telescope, originally belonged to Henry Draper; Maury's yearly observations represented its last scientific use at Harvard. After her retirement, Maury became curator for three years of the Henry Draper Memorial Museum, the original Draper Observatory built in 1860 on the Draper estates in Hastings-on-Hudson. She also continued with her interests in natural history, ornithology, and conservation. Maury died at the age of eighty-five on January 8, 1952.

Summary

Without question, Antonia Maury's most productive years at the Harvard Observatory were hindered by continual conflicts with her director, Edward Pickering. To what extent this was related to her role as a woman, and how much was "simply" a result of personality differences, is difficult to judge. Pickering closely supervised the work carried out under his direction, to an extent many of the women found irritating. This situation, however, was far from unusual in any field of science whether staff were men or women, and, to his credit, Pickering never failed to acknowledge the work carried out by others. For example, in his reports to the observatory benefactor, Anna Draper, Pickering often praised the work carried out by Maury. Her confirmation of his discovery of a spectroscopic binary was a "discovery of no little importance."

More important, and arguably her most significant contribution to the field of astronomy, was Maury's development of the star catalog. Maury's classification method, based on line widths, formed the basis for the modern luminosity classification scheme. Hers was the first genuine two-dimensional approach to the classification of stellar spectra.

That Maury obviously was more of a "free spirit" than most was a source of conflict. Exacerbating the problem was the routine and tedious nature of the work, not least of which involved mathematical calculations carried out by hand in that precomputer age. Yet, Pickering was willing to allow Maury a free hand in her systematic approach to the work, though it was some time before he fully accepted her system as being far superior to those it replaced. Other peers had no such problem. Hertzsprung continually praised Maury's system to others, even including Pickering. In 1943, Maury was awarded the Annie J. Cannon prize (named for another of Pickering's associates) for her system of spectral classification. By the time of her death, Maury's career had become almost legendary at the Harvard Observatory.

Bibliography

Hearnshaw, John B. *The Analysis of Starlight*. New York: Cambridge University Press, 1986. An outstanding book on the history of spectroscopic analysis of starlight. The text covers both concepts and development of methodology. An extensive discussion of Maury's contributions is included. Some knowledge of astronomy is helpful, but not necessary for enjoyment of the reading.

Jones, Bessie, and Lyle Boyd. *The Harvard College Observatory*. Cambridge, Mass.: Harvard University Press, 1971. An excellent history of the first eighty years (1839-1919) of the Harvard Observatory. Particularly relevant is a discussion of the role played by women in the field of astronomy. An extensive analysis of Maury's work is included within the topic.

Kass-Simon, G., and Patricia Farnes, eds. *Women of Science: Righting the Record*. Bloomington: Indiana University Press, 1990. An extensive discussion of the often unacknowledged important roles played by women in numerous fields of science. The text consists of excellent biographical overviews of the subjects, including that of Maury.

Ogilvie, Marilyn Bailey. *Women in Science—Antiquity Through the Nineteenth Century: A Biographical Dictionary with Annotated Bibliography*. Cambridge, Mass.: MIT Press, 1986. Short biographies of prominent women in major fields of science. Little specific detail is provided on Maury's life, but highlights of Maury's career are provided, along with references of major works.

Struve, Otto, and Velta Zebergs. *Astronomy of the Twentieth Century*. New York: Macmillan, 1962. A different methodology than that of Hearnshaw in the history of astronomy. The authors provide a topical approach which highlights technical advances in the field. A significant discussion is provided of Maury and the importance of her work.

Richard Adler

MARIA GOEPPERT MAYER

Born: June 28, 1906; Kattowitz, Upper Silesia, Germany
Died: February 20, 1972; San Diego, California
Area of Achievement: Physics
Contribution: Mayer developed the shell model of the atomic nucleus for which, with Hans Jensen, she won the Nobel Prize in Physics in 1963.

Early Life

Maria Gertrude Goeppert was born on June 28, 1906, in Kattowitz, Upper Silesia, then a part of Germany (later Poland). Her father, Friedrich Goeppert, was a pediatrician and professor—the sixth generation of a line of university professors in which Maria was to become the seventh. To be a professor in Germany at that time was to hold a position of high social standing and income. Maria's mother was from a working-class family, but she rose to the status demanded of her by her marriage and became a renowned hostess. When Maria was four years old, she moved with her parents to the town of Göttingen. Friedrich Goeppert joined the medical faculty at the Georgia Augusta University (commonly referred to merely as Göttingen, like the town) and established a children's clinic there. It was in this rarefied atmosphere of a world-famous institution of learning that Maria grew up.

As an only child, Maria enjoyed the devoted attention of both of her parents. A frail child, she was often ill, suffering from severe headaches that often kept her home from school. Her father, although sympathetic, admonished her not to become an invalid but to ignore the headaches as much as possible and concentrate on other things. He often took her on science walks, answering her questions and encouraging her curiosity and exploration. It was his steadfast belief in her potential as a student and a person that left Maria in no doubt of her future at the university, although not even 10 percent of German university students at the time were female.

Maria's eighth birthday marked the beginning of World War I. Food became scarce and the social scene of Göttingen faded, but Maria's academic pursuits continued. She attended the Höhere Töchterschule, a public elementary school for girls, until she was about fifteen. She then transferred to the Frauenstudium, a private school, to prepare for the rigorous university entrance examination, the Abitur. The Frauenstudium was the only school in Göttingen that was equipped to prepare girls for the Abitur. By the end of Maria's second year there, the school had run out of money and been forced to close. Maria decided to attempt the Abitur a year early, despite dire warnings from her teachers and friends. She passed and then entered Göttingen in 1924 as a mathematics student.

Life's Work

The Göttingen Maria Goeppert attended in the 1920's was world renowned for its mathematics department, and this fame attracted scholars in other disciplines, most notably theoretical physics. As both a student and a member of Göttingen's social set,

Goeppert met all of those scholars. Max Born, who became Goeppert's mentor, encouraged her to transfer into physics, where she could study under him as well as such eminent physicists as James Franck and Werner Heisenberg, and have as fellow students Enrico Fermi, Max Delbrück, Paul Dirac, and Eugene Wigner.

During Maria Goeppert's years as a university student, two events shaped her life. In 1927, Friedrich Goeppert unexpectedly died. Maria's mother decided to take in boarders, a common decision for widows in Göttingen. One of these boarders was a flashy, boisterous postgraduate student from California named Joseph E. Mayer, with whom Maria fell in love. They were married on January 18, 1930. Within months, Maria Mayer had completed her thesis and examinations and received her doctorate in theoretical physics.

Joseph Mayer had been offered a teaching position at The Johns Hopkins University in Baltimore, Maryland, and the couple moved there almost immediately. Maria had reservations about leaving her mother and her homeland but had high hopes of being accepted as a physicist at Johns Hopkins as she had been at Göttingen. American universities had a better record than German universities in hiring women professors. Yet the United States was in the midst of the Depression, and no university would give a family a second paycheck, no matter how well-qualified the applicant. There were also antinepotism rules governing hiring. Maria spent her first years in Baltimore homesick, writing her mother constantly, and spending her summers either in Germany or with her friends from Göttingen. By pulling strings, she secured a position handling the German correspondence for a member of the physics department. Here, at least, she could converse on her own level with people who recognized and appreciated her abilities. She and Joe spent many hours teaching each other their subjects: She studied quantum mechanics; he, physical chemistry. This study gave Maria much of the knowledge upon which she later drew to construct the nuclear model that made her famous.

In 1933, Maria gave birth to her first child, Marianne. By this time, she had been forced to recognize what was happening politically in Germany, and she became an American citizen just before her daughter was born. In 1938, her son Peter was born. Soon after Peter's birth, Johns Hopkins fired Joseph Mayer, an event that Maria Mayer believed occurred because of her. Columbia University immediately offered him a position at twice his previous salary, so the family moved to Leonia, New Jersey, a New York City suburb. Columbia was just as unwilling to give Maria a job as Johns Hopkins had been, although Harold Urey, who was her husband's boss, asked her to give some lectures in chemistry. In December, 1941, Sarah Lawrence College offered Maria a part-time teaching position, which she accepted. By this time, Joe was doing wartime work in conventional weapons research in Maryland as well as teaching at Columbia and was rarely home.

In the spring of 1942, Urey extended another job offer—this time for Maria. He wanted her to join the Substitute Alloy Materials project, which was trying to develop the enriched uranium needed for nuclear fission. Although Maria was nervous about leaving the children when Joe was already gone so much, the temptation was too great. Leaving Marianne and Peter in the care of an English nanny, she embarked on a stressful schedule of top-secret research. Although she worked on a side-line project, trying to separate uranium isotopes by means of photochemical reactions (ultimately unsuccessfully), her dedication quickly caused her to be put in charge of twenty other scientists, finally working at a paying job where people valued her skills and knowledge. Although the science was fascinating, the schedule and secrecy—even from Joe—were hard to bear. Maria Mayer endured a series of illnesses during this time, including pneumonia, a gallbladder operation, and a thyroid operation. When the first nuclear bomb was dropped on Hiroshima in August, 1945, her relief at finally being able to tell Joe was great.

After the war, Maria returned to half-time teaching at Sarah Lawrence, again able to spend time with her children. Almost immediately Joe, Urey, Fermi, and Maria's good friend Edward Teller were all offered jobs by the University of Chicago, where Fermi and his team had achieved the first nuclear chain reaction. For the first time, there was a university post for Maria, although it was unpaid. Nevertheless, Chicago was the first university that did not consider her an annoying appendage to her husband, and she threw herself into the academic world there with gusto. She was soon offered a paid part-time appointment at the Argonne National Laboratory as well. Maria Mayer was in her element. She had a supportive group of fellow scientists who would respond to her ideas and with whom she could work and socialize. She began to consider, with Teller, the odd set of numbers that seemed to be popping up in particularly stable atomic nuclei. She called these "magic numbers," and she found that they seemed to correspond with the number of neutrons or protons in atoms with unusually large numbers of stable isotopes. Teller soon lost interest in the subject, but Maria continued to study it, and in 1948 she published a short paper on the topic in *Physical Review*. She had seven magic numbers by this point: 2, 8, 20, 28, 50, 82, and 126. Elements that had one of these numbers of protons or neutrons maintained isotopes that were more stable than those of other elements.

It was well accepted that electrons orbit the nucleus of an atom in particular shells, or energy levels, which correspond to quantized angular momentum values. Certain elements, the noble gases, are particularly stable because their outer shells are full. Mayer proposed that the nucleus had a similar shell structure, in which the magic numbers of nucleons correspond to full shells. For atoms, this stability can be tested by measuring ionization energies—energies needed to remove an electron from the atom. Analogous tests of energies of alpha and beta decay from the nucleus showed analogous results. Mayer correlated these results with the atomic electron spins and hypothesized a nucleon spin-orbit coupling—slight variations in energy based on the direction in which a nucleon is spinning. Her theory, well backed by experimental results and mathematical facts, left some skeptical, but it immediately convinced Joseph Mayer and Fermi, who urged her to publish at once. She procrastinated, however, and a group of German scientists, led by Hans Jensen, published the same theory almost simultaneously.

Surprisingly, instead of allowing a rivalry to develop, Maria Mayer and Jensen decided to collaborate. After corresponding for a year, they met and began to write a book together. As it turned out, Mayer wrote most of it, Jensen was incurably easygoing and lazy. It took them four years to finish, and by the time it was published, the nuclear shell model was well established.

It was some time before the decision makers on the Nobel Prize committee in Sweden caught up with the scientific community's acceptance of the shell model theory. In the meantime, the Mayers had moved to California, where both Maria and Joe were offered full professorships at the University of California at San Diego. (Interestingly, University of Chicago officials suddenly found a way to bend their nepotism rules and offered Maria a salary when they learned of the California offer, but it was too late.) Shortly after the move, Maria Mayer had a stroke. By the morning the phone rang at 4:00 A.M., announcing a call from Stockholm for Maria Mayer, she had stopped hoping for recognition of her work. When Jensen received a similar call, he thought it was a practical joke. It was no joke: Mayer and Jensen were awarded the Nobel Prize in Physics in 1963, sharing it with Mayer's Göttingen classmate Eugene Wigner, who had proposed a different nuclear model. Maria was the first woman to receive the Nobel Prize for theoretical physics, the second to receive the Nobel Prize for physics, and at the time the only living woman with a Nobel Prize in science.

Maria's last years were spent in California, where she worked when she could in spite of her ill health. She died on February 20, 1972.

Summary

Maria Goeppert Mayer's contributions to science were many. Her shell model provided fodder for a multitude of researchers. She also did significant work in the fields of spectroscopy and quantum electrodynamics. She was awarded honorary degrees from such notable institutions as Mount Holyoke and Smith College, honoring the example she set for future women in science and the path she helped to clear for them.

When she was young, Mayer's father said to her, "never be a woman," meaning only a housewife, without her own interests. Yet she did become a woman—a brilliant, multifaceted individual who was fully capable of competing in the male-dominated world of science and achieving the highest honor possible.

Bibliography

Dash, Joan. *A Life of One's Own*. New York: Harper & Row, 1973. This extremely valuable work is the biography on which all biographies of Mayer are based.

McGrayne, Sharon Bertsch. *Nobel Prize Women in Science*. Secaucus, N.J.: Carol, 1993. A concise biography with interesting comments on the atmosphere and social standards of the circles in which the Mayers moved, as well as illuminating quotations from Mayer.

Mayer, Maria Goeppert. "The Shell Model." *Science* 145 (September, 1964): 999-1006. Mayer's Nobel lecture, this article gives an amazingly lucid explanation of the shell model, as well as an account of its development and a short autobiography.

Opfell, Olga S. *The Lady Laureates*. Metuchen, N.J.: Scarecrow Press, 1978. A rather romanticized version of Mayer's biography is included in this volume.

Shepherd, Linda Jean. *Lifting the Veil: The Feminine Face of Science*. Boston: Shambhala, 1993. Although it only uses Mayer as an example a few times, this work provides excellent insight into the roles of women in science and the particular strengths women bring to their scientific disciplines.

Margaret Hawthorne

MARGARET MEAD

Born: December 16, 1901; Philadelphia, Pennsylvania
Died: November 15, 1978; New York, New York
Area of Achievement: Anthropology
Contribution: Through her best-selling books, her public lecturing, and her column in *Redbook* magazine, Mead popularized anthropology in the United States. She also provided American women with a role model, encouraging them to pursue professions while simultaneously championing their roles as mothers.

Early Life

Margaret Mead credited her parents, Emily Fogg and Edward Sherwood Mead, and her paternal grandmother, Martha Ramsay Mead, as her primary childhood influences. They were all educators; her mother was a teacher and sociologist who was pursuing graduate work when Margaret was born, her father was a professor of economics at the University of Pennsylvania, and her grandmother, who was primarily responsible for teaching Margaret, was a retired school principal. As a child, Margaret received only sporadic formal education, attending two years of kindergarten, one year of half days in fourth grade, and six years at a variety of high schools during which she was given supplemental instruction by her grandmother. Her inherent love of ritual found expression in religion when, at the age of eleven, Mead joined the Episcopalian church. She sustained her faith throughout her life.

Her mother and grandmother were the principal role models for Mead. Both were able women who had married and borne children but also had attended college and pursued careers. From them she learned to enjoy reading and to observe and record the world around her.

Mead anticipated finding a rich intellectual and social life in college. Instead, she suffered isolation during her freshman year at DePauw University in the Midwest, where she experienced the trauma of exclusion by college sororities. She was also profoundly affected by her discovery that "bright girls could do better than bright boys" but "would suffer for it." She departed after one year, convinced that coeducation disadvantaged women, and subsequently entered Barnard College, where she found intellectual stimulation in the company of several intelligent young women. Her ordeal shaped her preference for her life's work: She decided "not to compete with men in male fields, but instead to concentrate on the kinds of work that are better done by women." In anthropology, Mead found such a niche investigating families and child-rearing practices.

Initially, Mead studied psychology, but in her senior year she was influenced by the Columbia University anthropologist Franz Boas and his graduate student Ruth Benedict, who inspired her by the urgency with which they pursued their work. Boas, the founder of modern American anthropology, recognized that cultures rapidly were being corrupted by world contact and was busily orchestrating the ethnographic description of as many cultures as possible with the limited number of field workers available to him. Both Boas and Benedict were responsible for convincing Mead that she could make a contribution in anthropology.

Life's Work

Margaret Mead first traveled to the field in 1925, when Boas dispatched her to American Samoa, where she was to observe adolescence as an aid in determining whether it was universally a time of stress. The science of anthropology was in its infancy when Mead departed for Samoa. Methods for gathering and deciphering information were yet to be defined, and Mead invented techniques while in the field. She lived with adolescent girls in a Samoan village, becoming the first American to use the participant observer method developed by the British anthropologist Stanislaw Malinowski.

Upon returning to the United States, Mead earned her Ph.D. and simultaneously achieved fame by publishing *Coming of Age in Samoa* (1928). In her work, she described a culture that was free of the *Sturm und Drang* of American adolescence and in which girls as well as boys were taught to value and cherish their sexuality.

Between 1925 and 1939, Mead zealously performed field work, observing seven Pacific cultures as well as the American Omaha Indians. After her initial trip to Samoa, she never again worked alone, choosing instead to collaborate with others, thereby making possible a more thorough analysis of cultures. She focused on women and children who were inaccessible to her male colleagues. Throughout her career, she was concerned with character formation and the influence of cultural and biological determinants of behavior.

During three months of intensive discussion among Mead, her husband and collaborator Reo Fortune, and the British anthropologist Gregory Bateson, with whom they lived in New Guinea, Mead developed her theories of character formation. In *Sex and Temperament in Three Primitive Societies* (1935), she formalized her inferences regarding the process by which cultures established behavioral norms for men and women. She also provided explanations for deviance. Mead observed among the Iatmul, Arapesh, and Mundugumor peoples widely diverging behavioral patterns for men and women which she determined were culturally defined rather than biologically mandated. Traits that were considered feminine in one culture—the nurturing of children, for example—could as easily be considered masculine in another. In 1949, Mead explored more fully the interactive nature of cultural and biological determinants of gender in *In Male and Female: A Study of the Sexes in a Changing World*.

In 1935, Mead and Fortune divorced, and Mead married Bateson, with whom she also collaborated. In two exceptionally productive years during which the pair worked in Bali, Mead pursued her work on character formation while Bateson continued his theorizing regarding the nature of human nonverbal communications. Together, they pioneered the use of photographs and films as tools for anthropological research. Whereas previously anthropologists had taken still photographs for the purpose of illustrating their books, Mead and Bateson used film as a technique for studying nonverbal behavior. They shot an unprecedented 22,000 feet of film and 25,000 still photographs and edited and released several films, including *Balinese Character* and *Trance and Dance in Bali*. Their use of photography was a major innovation in anthropological methodology.

During World War II, Mead, along with other social scientists throughout the country, contributed her expertise to the war effort through work in government intelligence agencies. Some efforts were destructive in nature. Gregory Bateson, for example, at the Office of Strategic Services, forerunner to the CIA, developed methods of psychological warfare and ways of using propaganda to unnerve the Japanese. For her part, Mead lectured in England for the Office of War Information in 1943, attempting to facilitate relations between American troops and wartime Britons. She also served as the executive secretary of the Committee on Food Habits and in 1942 joined the National Research Council. Her principal contribution, however, occurred in the development of national character studies that provided techniques for analyzing the cultural characteristics of nations that could not be directly studied, such as Japan and Germany. Techniques for studying "culture at a distance" in which numerous sources, including movies, fiction, and interviews with immigrants, were employed to determine the nature of complex cultures in which the war inhibited fieldwork but which were strategically significant. In her 1942 book *And Keep Your Powder Dry*, Mead utilized her skills to analyze American society. At war's end, Mead continued to work as a Cold War intellectual at Columbia University's Research in Contemporary Cultures (RCC), which was funded by the Office of Navy Research. Initially the director of research, Mead replaced Ruth Benedict as director of the council after Benedict's sudden death.

Mead never, except peripherally, entered the male bastion of academe, choosing instead to work for the American Museum of Natural History in New York City. There she was appointed assistant curator of ethnology in 1926, promoted to associate curator in 1942, and promoted to curator in 1964. She retired from the museum in 1969 as curator emeritus.

In the last twenty-five years of her life, Mead focused extensively on teaching, becoming an adjunct professor at Columbia in 1954. She also served in a variety of visiting professorships. Among other positions she held were the presidencies of the World Federation of Mental Health (1956-1957), the American Anthropological Association (1960), and the American Association for the Advancement of Science (1975). She received several honorary degrees and was awarded posthumously the Presidential Medal of Freedom.

In 1962, Mead was invited to contribute a monthly column to *Redbook* magazine, and through it she developed a vast popular readership. She wrote to women about social problems, the future of the family, and child-rearing practices. In return, she used the letters she received from her readers as a source of information regarding the concerns of American women.

Summary

For American women, one of Mead's most salient achievements was her reevaluation of gender roles while she simultaneously championed tradition and ritual. She wrote and worried about the future of the American family, condemning the isolation imposed on women in modern suburbia and mourning the loss of the community of extended families. Mead envisioned a world in which women's and men's unique skills and contributions would be valued equally. Women would have options for contributions outside the traditional domestic sphere, but maternal and domestic roles also would be valued.

Mead's numerous contributions to the field of anthropology included her field work in seven Oceania cultures, her innovations in the use of film, and the development of national character studies. Mead also was instrumental in popularizing anthropology through her best-selling books, which were written for a public as well as for a scholarly audience, and through her column in *Redbook*. She provided insights and advice to women in her roles as anthropologist and mother.

To her lengthy list of achievements may also be added that of role model for American women. She was a successful and famous professional in an era in which the professions were virtually closed to women.

Bibliography

Bateson, Mary Catherine. *With a Daughter's Eye: A Memoir of Margaret Mead and Gregory Bateson*. New York: William Morrow, 1984. Bateson, who is also an anthropologist, provides her own intimate recollections of her parents' lives. Illustrated.

Cassidy, Robert. *Margaret Mead: A Voice for the Century*. New York: Universe Books, 1982. Because of its brevity (156 pages) and lack of obvious footnotes (there are synopses for all chapters at the end) this book may seem appealing. It should, however, be viewed with caution, because it is uncritical and often simplistic. It does provide a useful chapter on Mead's views and contributions to feminism.

Foerstel, Lenora, and Angela Gilliam, eds. *Confronting the Margaret Mead Legacy: Scholarship, Empire, and the South Pacific*. Philadelphia: Temple University Press, 1992. This is a compilation of ten articles critiquing Mead's anthropological achievements. Foerstel and Gilliam's "Margaret Mead's Contradictory Legacy" is particularly useful in its discussion of her entire career, including her long service in American intelligence agencies.

Holmes, Lowell D. *Quest for the* Real *Samoa: The Mead/Freeman Controversy and Beyond*. South Hadley, Mass.: Bergin & Garvey, 1987. In 1954, anthropologist Holmes traveled to Samoa to re-create the conditions and reexamine the conclusions of Mead's Samoan research. He challenged Derek Freeman, whose scathing and well-publicized critique of Mead, *Margaret Mead and Samoa: The Making and Unmaking of an Anthropological Myth* (1983), engendered fierce debate regarding the value of her work. While Holmes's conclusions differ in several details from Mead's, he finds that the validity of her research is "remarkably high" but that it was prone to such exaggerations as are commonly found in the work of novice fieldworkers.

Howard, Jane. *Margaret Mead: A Life*. New York: Simon & Schuster, 1984. Although Howard uses numerous interviews with people who knew Mead, she is uncritical in her sources. Mead's former husbands are quoted extensively along with colleagues, friends, and critics. The author's frequently florid language and her inclusion of gratuitous observations are disconcerting. Contains an extensive bibliography.

Mead, Margaret. *An Anthropologist at Work: Writings of Ruth Benedict*. Boston: Houghton Mifflin, 1959. Because their professional lives were intertwined, Mead's collection of Benedict's papers, in which she includes five biographical essays, provides invaluable biographical data on Mead's own career, including, notably, her training with Franz Boas and her World War II intelligence work.

__________. *Blackberry Winter: My Earlier Years*. New York: Pocket Books, 1972. In many ways the most useful work on Mead's life, this book contains three parts detailing her early personal life, professional work, and experiences as a mother and grandmother. Illustrated with photographs.

Metraux, Rhoda. "Margaret Mead: A Biographical Sketch," *American Anthropologist* 82 (June, 1980): 262-269. Metraux, Mead's friend and collaborator from the American Museum of Natural History, provides a concise but detailed biography of Mead which organizes her contributions into four distinct periods.

Mary E. Virginia

DOROTHY REED MENDENHALL

Born: September 22, 1874; Columbus, Ohio
Died: July 31, 1964; Chester, Connecticut
Area of Achievement: Medicine
Contribution: Best known for her medical research identifying the cell responsible for Hodgkin's disease, Mendenhall spent most of her career as a physician interested in maternal and child health. As one of the first doctors employed by the U.S. Children's Bureau, she merged social welfare and preventive health strategies as the best approach for reducing maternal and infant mortality and morbidity.

Early Life

Dorothy Reed was born on September 22, 1874, in Columbus, Ohio. She was the youngest of three children, two girls and a boy, born to Grace Kimball and William Pratt Reed. Her mother, described by a family chronicler as a woman who had something of the air of a grande dame, was a descendant of the Talcott and Kimball families, seventeenth century English immigrants to New England. Dorothy's father, a successful Columbus shoe manufacturer, was also descended from a prominent New England family. He died in 1880 when Dorothy was only six. Following her father's death, Dorothy, her mother, and her sister Elizabeth ("Bessie") spent summers at a family residence in Talcottville, New York. As did many young men of the time, the Reeds' only son went West and was never heard from again. From 1887 to 1890, Grace Reed lived in the winters with her daughters in Berlin, Germany, while Bessie studied music. Although William Reed had provided well for his widow and children, Grace's lifestyle threatened to deplete the family funds. Dorothy eventually relinquished her own inheritance to her mother and in 1894 took over the management of her mother's financial affairs, which she continued to manage until Grace's death in 1912. In 1903, Bessie died of spinal meningitis, leaving behind a distraught husband, two daughters, and a son. The children's father had little money. Consequently, Dorothy also accepted the financial responsibility for the education of her nieces and nephew. These experiences taught Dorothy to be a skillful investor and an independent wage earner.

Life's Work

In 1891, eighteen-year-old Dorothy Reed entered Smith College. Educated as a child by her maternal grandmother and later by a hired governess, Reed was graduated from Smith in 1895 with a B.L. degree. At first she was interested in journalism, but she changed her mind and entered The Johns Hopkins University Medical School in the fall of 1896. There she achieved two important firsts. In 1898, she and another student, Margaret Long, became the first women to be employed by the United States Navy when they spent a summer assisting in the operating room and bacteriological laboratories at the Brooklyn Navy Yard Hospital. Earning her M.D. in 1900, Reed then served an internship at The Johns Hopkins University Hospital and received a fellowship in pathology. This position enabled her to teach at the medical school and conduct research on Hodgkin's disease. As part of her work, she became the first researcher to identify a peculiar blood cell, thereafter called the Reed cell (or sometimes the Sternberg-Reed or Reed-Sternberg cell), present in every Hodgkin's disease victim. This was a significant finding because it contradicted the scientific thought of the time, which assumed that Hodgkin's disease resulted from a bacterial infection similar to tuberculosis.

Although she was at one of the few medical schools in the United States that accepted women, Reed refused an extension of her fellowship at the end of the academic year because she believed that there were limited opportunities for women at Johns Hopkins. This proved to be a significant career choice because it changed Reed from a medical researcher to a health care practitioner. Beginning in June, 1902, she worked as a resident at the New York Infirmary for Women and Children. This led to a job as the first resident physician at the newly organized New York Babies' Hospital. In this position, Reed became involved in the popular Progressive Era infant welfare movement. Like many female physicians of the era, Reed found that pediatrics and obstetrics were fields in which women doctors could practice with greater autonomy and respect than they could in the more traditional medical specialties.

Unlike many other professional women of her generation, Reed was able to combine career and marriage. A woman who described herself as good looking and was identified by her colleagues as strikingly beautiful, Dorothy Reed married Charles Elwood Mendenhall, a professor of physics at the University of Wisconsin, on February 14, 1906. The couple had four children. Their firstborn, Margaret, died only a few hours after her birth in 1907. Margaret's death resulted primarily from poor obstetric care, which also left Dorothy with permanent injuries and puerperal fever. This unhappy experience furthered Mendenhall's interest in child and maternal health care. The couple's second child, Richard (b. 1908), died in 1910 from fatal injuries received in a fall. Thomas (b. 1910), their third child, lived to adulthood and served for a time as president of Smith College. The family's last born, John (b. 1912) became a professor surgery at the University of Wisconsin, Madison.

After spending eight years as a full-time wife and mother, Mendenhall returned to her professional career as a field lecturer on infant and maternal care for the University of Wisconsin's home economics department. Besides providing needed and desired information to women throughout Wisconsin, her work also led to the collection of statewide data on infant and maternal mortality rates. In 1915, working with the U.S. Department of Agriculture and a variety of women's volunteer associations, she organized the state's first infant welfare clinic in Madison. Part of the larger national baby-saving movement, Mendenhall's work served as an example for other cities to copy. By 1937, Madison had the nation's lowest infant mortality rate.

In 1917, Mendenhall and her children moved to Washington, D.C., where her husband Charles was already involved in war work. Retaining her position at the University of Wisconsin and developing a correspondence course for the Department of Agriculture entitled the "Nutrition Series for Mothers," Mendenhall also accepted a job as a U.S. Children's Bureau physician. The Children's Bureau, established in 1912 in the Department of Commerce and Labor as a part of Progressive Era reform, was headed by Julia C. Lathrop, an Illinois social worker and the first woman to head a federal agency. Lathrop welcomed Mendenhall because her medical credentials and international reputation as a researcher lent credibility to the largely female-led and social work-oriented Children's Bureau. Infant mortality was the first field study undertaken by the agency. The work of Mendenhall and another female doctor, Grace L. Meigs, highlighted the need for good medical care as well as social welfare reform as the best means to reduce the nation's high infant mortality rate. The Children's Bureau had found that the 1913 U.S. rate of 132 deaths per 1,000 live births ranked behind seven comparable nations. Mendenhall's 1918 Children's Bureau publication "Milk, the Indispensible Food for Children" was a widely read and significant contribution in the effort to save babies' lives. Informational bulletins such as Mendenhall's and those produced by other Children's Bureau employees, such as Mary Mills Wests's "Prenatal Care" (1913) and "Infant Care" (1914), served as how-to books for many American women who were anxious about the inadequate medical care then available for themselves and their children.

During the agency's Children's Year (1918-1919), Mendenhall was instrumental in the preventive health care effort, setting standards of height and weight for every American child. In 1919, also as part of her responsibilities for the Children's Bureau, Mendenhall represented the United States at an International Child Welfare Conference and conducted a survey of war orphanages in Belgium and France. She also examined the nutritional levels of children in England. These studies served twenty years later as models for work completed by the Children's Bureau on English and French refugee children fleeing Nazi aggression. In 1921, Mendenhall coauthored with other Bureau staff members the agency's seminal publication "Child Care and Child Welfare: Outlines for Study." Another of her most influential publications appeared as the Bureau's 1929 "Midwifery in Denmark," which compared infant and maternal mortality rates in the United States and that European country. Mendenhall's research proved to be controversial with the American Medical Association because she concluded that higher mortality rates in the United States were partly the result of unnecessary intervention by doctors during delivery. She also observed a lack of affordable and accessible medical care for many American mothers and babies. Acknowledging the successful use of professional midwives in Denmark, Mendenhall recommended the training of midwives to serve in remote and poor American communities. The American Medical Association also condemned this suggestion. In addition, Mendenhall wrote the useful "What Builds Better Babies" (1925).

During the 1920's, Mendenhall also became active in the Social Hygiene movement, an effort to reduce high rates of venereal disease, which often contributed to infant and maternal mortality and morbidity. For example, infants born to mothers with syphilis risked blindness unless silver nitrate was administered to the babies' eyes immediately after birth. Mendenhall continued her association with the Children's Bureau until 1936. After her husband's death in 1935, she spent some time traveling in Central America and Mexico, and "retired" in Tyron, North Carolina. She eventually moved to Chester, Connecticut, where she died in 1964 of heart disease.

Summary

In her unpublished autobiography and her cousin's published memoirs, Dorothy Reed Mendenhall reveals the many obstacles facing women who sought a professional medical career in the late nineteenth century and early twentieth century. Even members of her own family believed that such activity was inappropriate. Attending medical school also involved other challenges for women. For example, during Mendenhall's second year at Johns Hopkins, a throat and nose specialist gave a lecture on some disease of the nose. Apparently trying to offend her, from the beginning he included the "dirtiest stories" as part of his presentation. Women students were also subjected to "unpleasant practical jokes." As evidence of her strong-willed determination, Mendenhall reported that she dealt with such harassment by deciding that she "would never object to anything that a fellow student or doctor did to me in my presence if he would act or speak the same way to a man." Regarding anyone who discriminated against her because of her gender, she "would crack down on him by myself or take it up with the authorities if he proved too much for me alone."

Such was the impact Mendenhall had throughout her life. She was a dedicated professional who combined career and family at a time when most Americans believed that such behavior was unacceptable. She is best known for her discovery of the blood cell indicating Hodgkin's disease but her significant contributions to the development of preventive maternal and infant health care policy should not be overlooked. Mendenhall's work at the Children's Bureau helped to pioneer the notion that both good medical care and social welfare reforms are needed to help save the lives of mothers and babies.

Bibliography

Ladd-Taylor, Molly. *Mother-Work: Women, Child Welfare, and the State, 1890-1930.* Urbana: University of Illinois Press, 1994. An informative overview of the effort by social workers and doctors, including those in the Children's Bureau, to train mothers on how to care for their babies.

Meckel, Richard A. *"Save the Babies": American Public Health Reform and the Prevention of Infant Mortality, 1850-1929.* Baltimore, Md.: The Johns Hopkins University Press, 1990. Although this work contains nothing specific to Mendenhall, it offers a good overview of the Progressive Era infant and maternal welfare movement.

Mendenhall, Dorothy Reed. "A Case of Acute Lymphatic Leukaemia Without Enlargement of the Lymph Glands." *American Journal of Medical Science* (October, 1902). Another seminal report on Mendenhall's Hodgkin's disease research.

———. "Milk: The Indispensible Food for Children." Washington, D.C.: Government Printing Office, 1918. Probably the most widely distributed informational pamphlet written by Mendenhall.

————. "On the Pathological Changes in Hodgkin's Disease with Especial Reference to Its Relation to Tuberculosis." *Johns Hopkins Hospital, Reports* 10 no. 3 (1902): 133-196. A technical report on Reed's research on Hodgkin's disease conducted at Johns Hopkins.

Wilson, Edmund. *Upstate: Records and Recollections of Northern New York.* New York: Farrar, Straus and Giroux, 1971. These memoirs of Mendenhall's mother's cousin include information on Dorothy in the fifth and sixth chapters.

Kriste Lindenmeyer

ETHEL MERMAN

Born: January 16, 1908; Astoria, New York
Died: February 15, 1984; New York, New York
Area of Achievement: Theatre and drama
Contribution: A leading actor of musical comedies on stage in the United States, Merman defined that theatrical form. She was known for her clarity of diction and strong vocal projection.

Early Life

Ethel Agnes Zimmerman was born on January 16, 1908, in the third-floor bedroom of her maternal grandmother's home in Astoria, New York. Ethel's father, Edward Zimmerman, was an accountant for a wholesale dry-goods company. Her mother was Agnes Gardner Zimmerman.

Ethel and her parents occupied the third floor of Grandmother Gardner's home in Astoria, where Ethel had a fairly untroubled childhood. During Ethel's early childhood, her grandmother and her mother took her to stage performances. She admired the singers and actors and dreamed of becoming an "actress." Her mother disapproved of a career in entertainment, since the family had no history in the theater, and encouraged her daughter to become a teacher instead. Ethel, however, had no interest in teaching. As a compromise, Ethel agreed to study stenography, so that she would have stenography to support herself should she need an income.

Ethel loved to sing and could sing whole songs before she was two. Throughout her youth, she performed at churches, clubs, and charities, and her father bragged of her perfect pitch. In 1917, when Ethel was nine, she had a sort of debut when she sang for soldiers at the Army base at Camp Mills. She was received enthusiastically and continued to perform at other bases.

Until 1930, when Ethel adopted the stage name of Merman and began her career in Broadway musicals, she earned her way by doing secretarial work and singing at nightclubs. During these years, she was signed on by Warner Bros.; she received $200 per week but had little work. The contract, fortunately, provided a stable income for Merman when she had to have a tonsillectomy. Merman worried that the surgery would ruin her voice, but to her delight, her voice was even louder after the surgery.

In the late 1920's, Merman connected with Al Siegel, who was instrumental in getting Merman into her first Broadway musical, *Girl Crazy* (1930), in which Merman sang the songs of George and Ira Gershwin. The friendship between Merman and Siegel was short-lived, but on October 14, 1930, opening night, Siegel left his hospital bed to accompany Merman on piano during the first act. Merman, playing Kate Fothergill, the daughter of the saloonkeeper, was called back for repeated encores of "I Got Rhythm." She was a sensation. Al Siegel left the theater on a stretcher after the first act. After the performance, George Gershwin went to Merman's dressing room, where he made his often-quoted comment to Merman, "Never, but never go near a singing teacher." Merman's career was launched.

Life's Work

Ethel Merman is best known for her stage and screen career, particularly for her thirty-year participation in the development of the musical comedy. During these years, she worked with the major composers of the time—the Gershwins, Cole Porter, Irving Berlin, and Stephen Sondheim—and, together, they produced musical hit after musical hit. Merman combined her long stage career with marriages (four in all) and parenting, and without formal training, she developed a singing and acting style that made her the leading lady of the Broadway musical for three decades.

After twenty-one-year-old Merman had established her place on Broadway with the Gershwins' songs in *Girl Crazy*, she played in a series of Broadway musical comedies, including four Depression-era hits: *Take a Chance* (1932), *Anything Goes* (1934), *Red, Hot, and Blue* (1936), and *DuBarry Was a Lady* (1939). Merman's roles in these hits marked a striking change in leading ladies. The fragile heroines of the 1920's were replaced by the brash, brassy, and good-hearted women that Merman played. In *Take a Chance*, Merman played Wanda Brill, a part of the nightlife scene in Arizona, where playboy Danny Churchill immersed himself in the seamy life he was supposed to be avoiding. The show ran for 243 performances. In *Anything Goes*, the first of Merman's five Cole Porter musicals, she played a nightclub singer. The play ran for 420 performances. In *Red, Hot, and Blue*, Merman played Nails O'Reilley Duquesne, in the story of a search to locate a young woman who was branded when she accidentally sat on a hot waffle iron. The play ran for 183 performances. In *DuBarry Was a Lady*, Merman played both May Daley and DuBarry. May Daley, a floor-show performer, is pursued by Louis Blore, the nightclub's men's room attendant. Knocked out by a Mickey Finn, Blore dreams that he is Louis XIV and Daley is Mme DuBarry. The show, the biggest hit of Cole Porter's career, ran for 408 performances.

In 1940, improving economic times allowed Porter and Merman's *Panama Hattie* to run for more than 500 performances. In this culmination of the parts that Merman played in the 1930's, she starred as Hattie Maloney, one of the "friendly girls of the canal zone." Hattie reforms to earn the affection of the daughter of the man she hopes to marry. Hattie, like Merman's women of the 1930's, was worldly, brassy, and good-hearted.

As Merman's career in musical comedy continued full-blast into the 1940's, her roles were written specifically for her. Cole Porter called her his favorite singer, and, like the Gershwins and Irving Berlin, he wrote his music so that Merman's strongest notes—A, B-flat, and C—would be accentuated. As critic Gerald Mast contends, the songs Porter wrote for Merman combined "the classy and the brassy," "the chic and the tough, the lady and the dame." Merman's voice and character determined the music and the productions. Composers counted on and respected Merman's impeccable diction. Alan Jay Lerner, in *The Musical Theatre: A Celebration* (1986), quotes an Irving Berlin comment about Merman's voice: "If you ever write lyrics for Ethel Merman, they had better be good, because *everybody* is going to hear them." Arturo Toscanini said of Merman's voice that it was "like another instrument in the band."

In 1946, Merman received a Donaldson Award for her performance as Annie Oakley in *Annie Get Your Gun*. The musical, produced by Richard Rodgers and Oscar Hammerstein, was sharply criticized for being "devoid of novelty" and "aesthetic risks," but the audiences were not concerned with such shortcomings. In the play, Annie learns that to win a husband she will have to lose a shooting contest. She deliberately loses the contest and wins the man. One of the show's hit songs, "There's No Business Like Show Business," became a sort of anthem for Broadway. The show ran for 1,147 performances, and on June 7, 1947, it opened in London.

The 1940's were active personal, as well as public, years for Merman. After a brief marriage to agent William R. Smith (1940-1941), Merman married Robert D. Levitt, a newspaperman. Their marriage lasted from 1941 until 1952. During those years, Merman had a daughter, Ethel Merman Levitt (July 20, 1942), and a son, Robert D. Levitt, Jr. (August 11, 1945). In addition, in the late 1940's, Merman appeared frequently on *The Big Show* on radio with Tallulah Bankhead and remained involved in film.

In 1951, Merman won an American Theatre Wing Antoinette Perry (Tony) Award for her performance as Sally Adams in *Call Me Madam* (1950). The play, in which Merman played an exuberant, socialite American ambassador, was a spinoff on the 1949 appointment of Washington hostess Perle Mesta as ambassador to Luxembourg. According to critic Robert Coleman of the *Daily Mirror*, by curtain time on opening night, "would-be first-nighters" offered as much as $400 a pair for any tickets (top box-office price was $7.50) but could find no sellers. The play was an instant sensation. Critic William Hawkins of the *World Telegram & Sun* reported the next day that Irving Berlin had "officially nominated Eisenhower for the presidency in a song called 'They Like Ike.'" The play ran for more than a year and a half, 644 performances.

During the 1950's, Merman married Robert F. Six, president of Continental Airlines, a marriage that lasted from 1953 until 1960. At the end of the 1950's, Merman played the role that she called her favorite, that of Mama Rose, the stage mother in Stephen Sondheim's *Gypsy*, the story of Gypsy Rose Lee. Merman's part could easily have become a stereotype, but Merman developed Mama Rose so well that in "Rose's Turn," Rose's last soliloquy, critics and general audiences alike responded to what has been called "one of the most moving scenes ever performed in a musical." Many critics regard *Gypsy* as a turning point in musicals, putting a new emphasis on the drama itself. The show ran for 702 performances.

In the 1960's, Merman was less active on Broadway. Her final Broadway appearances came in a revival of *Annie Get Your Gun* (1966) and *Dolly!* (1970). In Merman's personal life, the 1960's were difficult years. She was briefly and unhappily married to actor Ernest Borgnine (1964-1965), and her daughter died in 1967. Though *The New York Times* called the death a suicide, the coroner's report called it an accidental overdose.

Merman's film career, between 1930 and 1965, did little more than reinforce her success on Broadway. She appeared in more than a dozen films, but none of them received the recognition of her Broadway performances.

Even when Merman left Broadway and film, she continued to receive recognition. In 1972, she received a second Tony Award, this one for career achievement. In 1982, in a touching performance for the *Night of 100 Stars*, Merman sang "There's No Business Like Show Business."

In April of 1983, Merman had surgery for a brain tumor. Less than a year later, she was found dead, of natural causes, in her Manhattan apartment. Her memorial service was held on March 1, 1984, at the Huntington Hartford Theater in Hollywood, where friends viewed a screening of a 1963 Merman performance beginning with "Alexander's Ragtime Band" and ending with "There's No Business Like Show Business."

Summary

Ethel Merman was a star on Broadway, in films, and on radio. Her greatest impact, however, was in her role in the development of musical comedy, leading the way for women to assume important roles on the musical stage. In her early Broadway roles, Merman displaced one stereotype only to come dangerously close to creating another, as roles and music were increasingly written with her in mind. Particularly in her portrayal of Mama Rose in *Gypsy*, however, Merman demonstrated that she could avoid the stereotype by infusing sensitivity and complexity into the role of the stage mother. Part of Merman's appeal, nevertheless, was that personal signature—the leading lady that critic Gerald Bordman described as "tougher, more knowing, and cynical."

At the very least, Merman extended the range of parts available to women. She also lived out a new American myth of the self-made woman. Without benefit of formal education, drama and singing lessons, or wealth, she rose to the top of the profession in Broadway musicals. She remained there in person for more than thirty years and remains there still as a symbol and a model for new performers to emulate.

Bibliography

Bordman, Gerald. *American Musical Comedy: From "Adonis" to "Dreamgirls."* New York: Oxford University Press, 1982. Bordman explores the development of American musical comedy and contends that it "borrowed haphazardly" from both operetta and revue, and responded to multiple influences outside the theater. Bordman's 250-page book includes illustrations, an index, and appendices with data about productions.

Lerner, Alan Jay. *The Musical Theatre: A Celebration*. New York: McGraw-Hill, 1986. Lerner explores development and change in the musical. Loosely chronological, this 240-page book begins with a historical overview and then explores the musical by topic and decade. The book contains illustrations (some in color), a bibliography, and an index.

Merman, Ethel, with George Eells. *Merman*. New York: Simon & Schuster, 1978. Dedicated to her parents and children, Merman's 320-page autobiography, written in collaboration with George Eells, includes appendices with stage and film information and an index. In the book, Merman candidly discusses her career and her personal life.

Merman, Ethel, with Pete Martin. *Who Could Ask for Anything More*. Garden City, N.Y.: Doubleday, 1955. Dedicated to her parents, Merman's first autobiography tells stories of her experiences on Broadway. The book contains no index or illustrations, but it is good reading for Merman fans.

Thomas, Bob. *I Got Rhythm!: The Ethel Merman Story*. New York: G. P. Putnam's Sons, 1985. Thomas's 239-page biography of Merman integrates Merman's life on and off stage. Readable and well researched, the book is organized by topic and, somewhat, by chronology. It includes an index, illustrations, and two appendices of stage and film information.

Carol Franks

PERLE MESTA

Born: October 12, 1889; Sturgis, Michigan
Died: March 16, 1975; Oklahoma City, Oklahoma
Area of Achievement: Government and politics
Contribution: Perle Mesta, one of Washington's most celebrated hostesses, spent her life involved in politics. In 1949, Harry Truman appointed her to a diplomatic post in Luxembourg, where she served until 1953.

Early Life

Pearl Reid Skirvin (she changed the spelling of her first name to Perle in 1944) was born in Sturgis, Michigan, in 1889. Her father, William Balser Skirvin, the seller of farm implements when Perle was born, became highly successful in the Texas and Oklahoma oil fields, accumulating considerable real estate with the profits he made from his oil enterprises. His wife, the former Harriet Elizabeth Reid, was a good mother, renowned for her wit and hospitality.

The Skirvins moved to Oklahoma City in 1906. That year Perle's father built the Skirvin Hotel there, fourteen stories high. It was one of the finest hotels in that part of the country. Perle received the genteel education appropriate to young ladies of her class. She attended private schools in Oklahoma City and in Galveston, Texas, and was intent on being a singer. She studied voice and piano at the Sherwood Music School in Chicago and had, if not overwhelming talent, certainly considerable musical ability.

Her ambition for a musical career ended in 1915, when the twenty-six-year-old Pearl met George Mesta, president of the Mesta Machine Company in Pittsburgh. He was twenty years her senior. In 1917, the couple was married. George Mesta soon became a one-dollar-a-year consultant in steel for the government in Washington, D.C., during World War I.

Maintaining their home in Pittsburgh, the Mestas also maintained a residence in Washington, where they met President Woodrow Wilson and such political luminaries as Herbert Hoover and Calvin Coolidge. Perle had the opportunity during this period to meet some of Washington's most renowned hostesses—Alice Roosevelt Longworth, Evelyn Walsh McLean, Eleanor Patterson—who had become legendary party-givers. She also became active in directing the Washington Stage Door Canteen to entertain servicemen.

If George Mesta's bride arrived in Washington with some rough edges, they were soon smoothed by the company the couple kept. The newlyweds traveled extensively in Europe after the war, making some twenty trips abroad between their marriage in 1917 and George Mesta's death in 1925. These trips added considerably to Perle's sophistication, which, although it developed apace, never eclipsed the warm, down-home humanity that made people gravitate to her.

Upon George's death, Perle inherited his substantial holdings in company stock. Her father's death shortly thereafter resulted in her inheriting another fortune. She served on the board of directors of the Mesta Machine Company, where she learned about the steel industry. She later owned an 18,000-acre cattle ranch in Arizona, which she managed actively for some years.

Life's Work

The phase of Perle Mesta's life for which she is best known began in earnest when, in 1929, she bought Mid-Cliffe, a large, formal mansion in Newport, Rhode Island. In this summer residence, misleadingly referred to as her cottage, she began to entertain extensively, inviting all the influential people she knew.

As the reputation of her parties grew, Mesta, who had been a frequent guest at the White House during Calvin Coolidge's presidency, was able to attract an ever-widening circle of noted Washington politicians to these social events. Her parties were generally orchestrated so that guests entertained guests and everyone had a good time. The atmosphere was warm and relaxed, the food excellent. Expensive wines flowed from seemingly inexhaustible stores, although Mesta, a Christian Scientist, did not drink. It has been said that even if Mesta had served five-cent beer, people would have enjoyed themselves; she was a born hostess.

Early in Mesta's life in Newport, Vice President Charles Curtis attended one of her parties. This contact resulted in Curtis's arranging for her to be presented at Britain's Court of St. James. This honor marked a significant step in Mesta's development as a socialite.

By 1935, Mesta had become interested in women's rights. She became a member of the National Woman's Party, in which she soon held office. In 1938, Mesta was among the founders of the World Woman's Party and served as publicity chairperson in charge of publicizing the party's first meeting in Geneva, Switzerland.

In the mid-1930's, Mesta became an articulate proponent of the Equal Rights Amendment, frequently lobbying for it on Capitol Hill. She managed to make a women's rights amendment part of the Republican Party's 1940 platform, then, having switched parties, part of the Democratic Party's 1944 platform. These efforts gave her considerable visibility among the nation's most powerful politicians.

Until 1940, Mesta was a staunch Republican. She and her husband contributed monetarily to Calvin Coolidge's presidential campaign, and, upon George Mesta's death, Perle continued to be a loyal and generous party supporter. She strongly endorsed Wendell Willkie during his 1940 bid for the presidency and was distressed that his party did not offer him more strenuous assistance during his campaign. Disillusioned by how the party treated Willkie, Mesta began to swerve from her Republican loyalties.

During Franklin Roosevelt's third term from 1941 to 1945, Mesta, who lived part of each year at Washington's Sulgrave Club, spent considerable time in Arizona, where she managed the working cattle ranch she owned. Having almost doubled in acreage, it had at that time more than three thousand head of cattle and was turning a handsome profit. She was politically enamored of neither Franklin Roosevelt nor his vice president, Henry Wallace, but she remained active in Washington society during her sojourns in town.

In the 1944 election, Roosevelt was nominated for a fourth time, and a little-known Missouri senator named Harry S Truman, a frequent guest at Mesta's parties, was selected as his running mate. Mesta knew Truman well, having first met him during her lobbying efforts and having then established a social bond with him and his family. She appreciated his homey ways and forthrightness. She also admired his wife and felt a special affinity for his daughter, Margaret, then trying to establish a career in music, as Mesta herself had hoped to do some thirty years earlier.

When the Roosevelt-Truman ticket won, Mesta gave the first Washington party to honor the new vice president who, within a few months, became president of the United States. During the Truman presidency, when the Trumans were living in Blair House during the renovation of the White House, Mesta became the president's unofficial hostess.

When Truman ran for reelection in 1948, his chances of victory seemed slim. Nevertheless, Mesta, a loyal friend, generated more than $300,000 in campaign contributions by presiding over fund-raising dinners held on Truman's behalf. When Truman defeated Thomas Dewey, the favored candidate, Perle Mesta was appointed cochair of the inaugural ball scheduled for January 20, 1949.

Soon afterwards, Truman created a diplomatic post in Luxembourg, which had previously fallen under the aegis of the American ambassador to Belgium. Appreciating Mesta's expertise in steel production, he nominated her for the post with the title of Envoy Extraordinary and Minister Plenipotentiary. The Grand Duchy of Luxembourg, about 1,000 square miles in size and with a population of 300,000, enjoyed one of the highest per capita incomes in Europe and was the world's seventh largest producer of steel.

The Senate confirmed Mesta in July, 1949, making her the third American woman to hold such a diplomatic post. The following month, she assumed her post for what was to be a four-year tenure. Mesta took her job seriously. She used her extensive contacts to attract dignitaries to the Duchy and entertained lavishly for orphans, for the mayors of Luxembourg's communities, for foreign visitors, and for fellow diplomats. Immediately after she left her diplomatic post, Mesta spent three months in the Soviet Union, traveling some twelve thousand miles or more to survey the country's steel facilities.

The year after Mesta went to Luxembourg, Russel Crouse and Howard Lindsay wrote *Call Me Madame* (1950), with lyrics by Irving Berlin. The musical was about Mesta and her transformation from party-giver to diplomat. Berlin's song, "The Hostess with the Mostes' on the Ball," inspired the designation by which Mesta is most often identified: The hostess with the mostest.

In addition to her political activities, Perle Mesta contributed large sums of money to help finance the educations of American and foreign students at the secondary and university levels. She was awarded an honorary doctorate by Fairleigh Dickinson University in 1952, partly in recognition of what she had done for students. Korea's Ehwa University bestowed a similar honor upon her in 1955 for helping Korean students come to the United States to study.

Mesta was the only woman to receive Luxembourg's Grand Cross of the Oak Crown and Cross of War. In 1950, she was named "Woman of the Year" by a poll of women newspaper editors. In 1953, the National Press Club accorded her the same honor.

On her return to Washington in 1953, Mesta resumed strenuous entertaining. In 1960, although she supported Richard Nixon for the presidency, she hosted an orange juice and coffee party in Los Angeles for more than 7,000 guests to celebrate Lyndon Johnson's nomination as John F. Kennedy's running mate.

Mesta remained active in Washington society until 1972, when, at age eighty-two, she gave her last party. She remained in the capital until early 1974, when a broken hip forced her to enter a convalescent facility in Oklahoma City. She died there slightly more than a year later.

Summary

People who recognize Perle Mesta's name usually think of her as a party-giver. Actually, her party-giving overshadowed the fact that she was a strong, down-to-earth person who espoused important causes and took significant stands. She worked tirelessly to force the federal government to recognize the equality of women through enactment of an Equal Rights Amendment to the Constitution, an end many feminists continued to work toward in the 1990's.

Besides her efforts for women's rights, Perle Mesta had substantial impact as a tough and knowledgeable business person who, while expending huge amounts of energy giving parties, did not neglect her corporate responsibilities to the Mesta Machine Company or to her cattle ranch. Mesta brought to her diplomatic post the same energy, intelligence, and enthusiasm she had consistently brought to her other endeavors, and her legendary party-giving merely paved the way for her social and political activities.

Bibliography

Conkin, Paul K. *Big Daddy from the Pedernales: Lyndon Baines Johnson*. Boston: Twayne, 1986. Conkin reveals that when Lyndon Johnson became vice president, he and Lady Bird purchased Mesta's house, The Elms, to use as their official Washington residence. Mesta, although a Nixon supporter, felt a special bond to Johnson because she had grown up in his part of the country.

Lester, David, and Irene Lester. *Ike and Mamie: The Story of the General and His Lady*. New York: G. P. Putnam's Sons, 1981. The Lesters tell about Mamie Eisenhower's confiding to Mesta the deep uncertainties she and her husband had about the D-Day invasion of Normandy. They also write about Mesta's attendance at the state dinner the Eisenhowers gave for Nikita Khrushchev during his 1959 visit to Washington.

McCullough, David. *Truman*. New York: Simon & Schuster, 1992. In his exhaustive biography of Truman, McCullough tells about Mesta's help in raising campaign funds for the presidential candidate. He also tells about her diplomatic appointment, and relates a little-known story of how Harry Truman, weeks before his death, made a surprise appearance at a Kansas City performance of *Call Me Madame* and appeared briefly on stage as himself.

Mesta, Perle, with Robert Cahn. *Perle: My Story*. New York: McGraw-Hill, 1960. Although Mesta does not tell all in this book, she provides fascinating insights into her political relationships. Fine illustrations, including many of her interacting with students whose educations she helped finance.

Miller, Merle. *Lyndon: An Oral Biography*. New York: G. P. Putnam's Sons, 1980. Among other anecdotes in this biography, Miller relates how Mesta hosted an orange juice and coffee party in Los Angeles for Johnson when he was nominated to be Kennedy's running mate.

Truman, Margaret. *Harry S. Truman*. New York: William Morrow, 1973. Truman illustrates Mesta's loyalty by telling of how she flew to Pittsburgh for a concert at which Truman was trying to reestablish her musical career. Mesta was ever the loyal family friend of the Trumans.

R. Baird Shuman

BARBARA MIKULSKI

Born: July 20, 1936; Baltimore, Maryland

Area of Achievement: Government and politics

Contribution: The first Democratic woman elected to the U.S. Senate on her own (in 1986), Mikulski is dedicated to the achievement of social and economic equity for working-class Americans.

Early Life

Barbara Ann Mikulski was born on July 20, 1936, in an ethnic, working-class neighborhood of East Baltimore, Maryland. Her parents, William Mikulski and Christina Eleanor Kutz Mikulski, were second-generation Polish Americans who ran a grocery store across the street from their house. Her paternal grandfather, who had emigrated from Poland, worked in a Baltimore licorice factory, while her grandmother baked pies and cakes for extra money. Later, the couple opened a bakery with a loan from an ethnic savings and loan. The entrepreneurial spirit exhibited by her grandmother and others like her made a lasting impression on Mikulski, and she often refers to the contribution that women make at the neighborhood economic level.

Another important influence was Eleanore Kurek, Barbara Mikulski's great grandmother, who took care of her while both of her parents worked in the grocery. Kurek had come to America at the age of sixteen for a prearranged marriage with little more than the clothes on her back and a few dollars. Mikulski admired the strength and tenacity of her great grandmother, who represented the hard work and hope of ethnic America. Mikulski spoke Polish with her great grandmother, went to Mass with her, and followed her through the markets of East Baltimore.

Catholicism also played an important role in shaping Barbara Mikulski's ideas and values. She received a Catholic education, attending Sacred Heart Elementary School and the Academy of Notre Dame High School. She received a bachelor's degree in social work from Mount St. Agnes College and a master's degree in social work from the University of Maryland.

As an undergraduate at Mount St. Agnes, she considered joining a religious order but later remarked that she could accept the vows of poverty and chastity but not that of obedience. Instead, she went to work for a number of social work agencies, including Associated Catholic Charities (1958-1961), the Department of Social Services (1961-1963, 1966-1970), and the York Family Agency (1964). Working with people on a one-to-one basis led Mikulski to the realization that governments needed to do more to help people—especially working-class people.

Mikulski's ethnic upbringing and religious education had its impact. She became an ardent activist on behalf of the poor. She challenged absentee landlords and unscrupulous storeowners on behalf of her clients. In 1966, she met Sister Mary Elizabeth, a former member of the Little Sisters of the Poor, who ran a halfway house in Baltimore. Sister Mary Elizabeth introduced Mikulski to the Catholic Worker movement and the teachings of religious activist Dorothy Day. Mikulski's own developing political philosophy, as well as her religious commitments, were influenced further by two other reformers: Father Geno Baroni and Saul Alinsky.

From Day, Mikulski learned that successful change begins not by setting elaborate goals but by creating the conditions for change. From Baroni, a priest from the coalfields of Pennsylvania who moved to Washington in the early 1960's and became an assistant secretary of Housing and Urban Development, Mikulski learned how to build coalitions among minorities to create a force as powerful as the forces oppressing them. From Alinsky, a Chicago writer and community organizer, she learned that power is not only what one has but what the enemy thinks one has. The lessons provided by these three mentors have inspired and guided Mikulski throughout her life.

Barbara Mikulski's political involvement began in 1968, when she became an organizer of a community group called the Southeast Council Against the Road (SCAR). The primary objective of the group was to stop a proposed eight-lane expressway connecting three major interstate highways in the center of Baltimore's ethnic and black neighborhoods. The idea that the city would destroy these neighborhoods so distressed Mikulski that she moved back to her old East Baltimore neighborhood and bought a house at 802 South Ann Street, right in the path of the planned highway. Along with other supporters, she waged a tireless battle to stop the road. The SCAR built alliances with groups in the black community. The fight took years to resolve and laid the foundation for Mikulski's political career.

During the long fight to stop the road, Mikulski founded the Southeast Community Organization to fight for better services for the neglected ethnic communities. Mikulski's concern for the forgotten ethnics was voiced in an article published in *The New York Times* in 1970. She criticized government for pitting the African American and ethnic communities against each other.

In 1971, Mikulski decided to take her fight against the road and for the forgotten to City Hall. There, she won a seat on the Baltimore City Council. Although she ultimately lost the vote to stop the road, her skill at coalition building caught the eye of the new mayor, William Donald Schaefer, who found a new location for the interstate connector. Mikulski's tenacity and perseverance saved the neighborhoods. Mikulski's involvement with the Southeast Community Organization was a turning point in her career. She left the world of social work and community organizing for elected office.

Life's Work

Barbara Mikulski's election to the Baltimore City Council was the beginning of her political career. While on the Council, she was instrumental in the creation of the Commission on Aging and Retirement Education. She also worked to reduce bus fares for senior citizens and to improve treatment of and services to rape victims. She also became the champion of the ethnic and working classes. An article written for *The New York Times* in 1970 set the stage for her enduring concern. In "Who Speaks for

Ethnic America?" Mikulski criticized elitist and phony liberals for the slick, patronizing labels they apply to ethnic Americans and for creating divisions between ethnics and African Americans. She wrote that government was polarizing people by creating the myth that the needs of African Americans are met at the expense of ethnic Americans. Mikulski believed that the pitting of one working group against another was destroying communities.

It was her advocacy of ethnic Americans that brought her to the attention of the national Democratic Party. In 1972, she was appointed cochair of the Democratic Party's Commission on Delegate Selection and Party Structure. In 1973, she replaced Leonard Woodcock, President of the United Auto Workers, as chairperson of the Commission. Mikulski succeeded in mediating between reformers and conservatives, both of whom wanted to control the future direction of the Democratic Party. She was successful in expanding the delegate selection process, replacing the strict quota system with a more flexible affirmative action rule that was sensitive to the inclusion of women, minorities, American Indians, and young people in the process.

Her delegate selection rules were successful. They helped the Democratic convention nominate Jimmy Carter in 1977. In addition, Barbara played a prominent role in party politics in subsequent elections. She headed Senator Edward Kennedy's Maryland campaign when he ran for president in 1980, she played a key role in the 1984 presidential campaign of Walter Mondale, and she advocated putting a woman on the ticket in the vice presidential slot. In 1992, she was instrumental in promoting the election of four more Democratic women to the U.S. Senate.

In 1974, the year after the Mikulski commission made the delegate selection rules, Mikulski made her first run for the Senate. She ran against a popular liberal Republican incumbent, Charles MacMathias. Although few expected her to win, she did better than expected, polling a respectable 43 percent of the vote. She gained statewide name recognition and was well positioned to run for Congress two years later.

In 1976, Barbara Mikulski was elected to the U.S. House of Representatives from Maryland's Third Congressional District, which included her old neighborhood. She served in the House for ten years. She was given seats on the Energy and Commerce Committee and the Merchant Marine and Fisheries Committee. Eventually, she chaired the subcommittee on Oceanography of the Merchant Marine and Fisheries Committee. Although she chaired no high profile committees, Mikulski spent her first years in the House learning the system—a strategy she would use again.

In 1986 she was elected to the U.S. Senate. She became the first female Democrat to win election to the Senate on her own—without a famous husband or father—and one of only two women in the Senate. Mikulski defeated two formidable opponents in the Democratic primary, Congressman Michael Barnes and former Maryland Governor Harry Hughes. The general election pitted Mikulski against Republican Linda Chavez, a former Reagan appointee, in what became a nasty, negative campaign. Mikulski won with 61 percent of the vote. In 1986, *Ms.* magazine voted her one of its Women of the Year.

In the Senate, Mikulski followed a similar tactic—learn the ropes. Senate Majority

Leader Robert Byrd took Mikulski under his wing, shocking colleagues by giving the freshman senator a seat on his Appropriations Committee. In 1989, by muffling her punches with a velvet glove, Mikulski became chair of one of the thirteen Appropriations Subcommittees on the Veterans Administration, Housing and Urban Development, and Independent Agencies. She also chairs the Committee on Labor and Human Resources' subcommittee on Aging. Mikulski is part of the Senate's Democratic leadership, serving as an assistant floor leader. She also serves on the Senate Ethics Committee.

As a senator, Barbara Mikulski remains committed to social and economic equity. She is a national leader on the issue of women's health care and a cosponsor of the Women's Health Equity Act, which included the establishment of an Office of Research on Women's Health at the National Institutes of Health. She authored the Spousal Anti-Impoverishment Act, the American Automobile Labeling Act, and the National and Community Service Act.

Mikulski's background in social work has been a driving force in her political life. She has been an outspoken champion of equal rights, health care, and economic development. She has also been an ardent proponent of women's issues and a supporter of women in politics.

Summary

Barbara Mikulski is a pioneer and a role model for women seeking political careers. As the first female Democratic senator elected on her own, and one of only twenty-one women to serve in the U.S. Senate, Mikulski has worked hard to promote social and economic equity. The empowerment of women, older Americans, ethnic Americans, and the working class are given high priority by Mikulski. She has used her skills as a social worker and community organizer to turn people's needs into public policy.

Not surprisingly, Mikulski continues to live in her Baltimore neighborhood and commutes to her Washington, D.C., office daily. In order to meet with her constituents, Mikulski spends at least one full working day in Maryland each week. She has been a spokesperson for the ethnic working class and has demonstrated that organizing, coalition building, and perseverance bring results. She stopped the highway in the 1970's and continues to fight for social and economic equity.

Bibliography

Boxer, Barbara. *Strangers in the Senate: Politics and the New Revolution of Women in America*. Washington, D.C.: National Press Books, 1994. A chapter is devoted to Barbara Mikulski and her efforts on behalf of women. The focus is on Mikulski's years in the Senate, with some reference to early political activities.

Edmunds, Lavinia. "Barbara Mikulski." *Ms.* 15 (January, 1987): 63. A short, informative article on Mikulski, who was selected as one of *Ms.* magazine's Women of the Year for 1986. Focuses on women's issues promoted by Mikulski.

Le Veness, Frank P., and Jane P. Sweeney, eds. *Women Leaders in Contemporary U.S. Politics*. Boulder, Colo.: L. Rienner, 1987. A chapter on Barbara Mikulski focuses on her background and political development. Emphasizes her role in the U.S. House of Representatives.

Mikulski, Barbara. "Who Speaks for Ethnic America?" *The New York Times*, September 29, 1970, p. 43. This article brought Mikulski to national attention. In it, she outlines her views about government and the forgotten ethnic Americans.

Toni Marzotto

EDNA ST. VINCENT MILLAY

Born: February 22, 1892; Rockland, Maine
Died: October 19, 1950; Austerlitz, New York
Area of Achievement: Literature
Contribution: Edna St. Vincent Millay was a symbol and spokeswoman for women's sexual liberation, particularly during the Roaring Twenties, and continues to be regarded as a pioneering American feminist.

Early Life

Edna St. Vincent Millay was born in Rockland, Maine, on February 22, 1892. Her parents were divorced in 1900, and her strong-minded mother reared her three girls by working as a practical nurse. Cora Millay encouraged her daughters to be independent individualists like herself and supported any intellectual or artistic interest they displayed. Her mother's example was the most important influence in Millay's childhood; it was largely responsible for her uninhibited behavior and the autonomous attitude expressed in her writing.

Millay displayed musical talent at an early age. She took piano lessons for several years and planned on a musical career, but decided in favor of becoming a writer when her poem "Renaissance" was published in *Lyric Year* in 1912 and received enthusiastic praise. Her musical talent and musical education contributed to her remarkable sense of harmony and rhythm, which were the features of her poetry that made her celebrated during the 1920's and 1930's. She was also interested in drama as a young girl; this interest continued throughout her life and led to her writing a total of six dramatic works.

Millay was educated at Vassar College, one of the leading American institutions of higher education for women. She studied Latin, French, Greek, Italian, Spanish, and German while continuing to write poetry and to act in amateur theatrical productions. When she was only twenty years old, she was already establishing a reputation as a writer. She experimented with all the literary forms she would work in for the rest of her life. Her first collection of poetry, *Renascence and Other Poems*, was published in the fall of 1917.

The most significant event in Millay's early life came when she moved to Greenwich Village in New York City. The Village was considered by many to be the center of American intellectual and cultural life, and Millay responded to life there with enthusiasm. She met people whose names would become famous in American art and literature, including Theodore Dreiser, Dorothy Day, Paul Robeson, E. E. Cummings, Hart Crane, Wallace Stevens, Susan Glaspell, Eugene O'Neill, and Edmund Wilson.

For many years, Millay had a hard time surviving financially. Despite these challenges, she was sustained by a zest for life, for nature, for beauty, for love, and for art that was expressed in all of her writing. She supported herself by turning out stories, light verse, and personal articles under the pen name of Nancy Boyd. She also did some professional acting, but received little pay.

The year 1923 was a turning point in her life. That year she became the first woman ever to receive the Pulitzer Prize for Poetry. In 1923, Millay also was married to Eugen Jan Boissevain, a wealthy importer who adored her and was willing to provide her with financial security for the rest of her life.

Life's Work

Edna St. Vincent Millay will always be identified with the rebellious, hedonistic, iconoclastic, crusading, and often self-destructive spirit of the Roaring Twenties, the era when America came of age as a world power and a unique cultural force with its jazz, uninhibited dances, motion pictures, comic strips, bizarre slang, shocking feminine fashions, cheap mass-produced consumer goods, awesome skyscrapers, gaudy automobiles, potent cocktails made from bootleg gin and whiskey, and sometimes shocking plays and novels.

Millay was popular with men because of her beauty, wit, talent, and vivacious spirit. She had many love affairs, even after her marriage to the tolerant Boissevain, and wrote about them candidly in her poetry. She shared the hedonism of the 1920's, believing that life is a short, essentially meaningless but endlessly fascinating phenomenon that should be lived to the fullest. Her most often-quoted lines are:

> My candle burns at both ends;
> It will not last the night;
> But ah, my foes, and oh, my friends—
> It gives a lovely light.

In contrast to the flippant attitude Millay affected in much of her poetry, she was actually a studious and hard-working person. During her lifetime, she turned out an impressive body of work. In addition to her many volumes of poetry, she wrote six plays, including the widely popular *Aria da Capo* (1919) and the highly original *Conversation at Midnight* (1937), a great many short stories, essays and sketches, and collaborated on *Flowers of Evil* (1936), an English translation of Charles Baudelaire's *Les Fleurs du mal* (1857). She also carried on an extensive correspondence and was always in demand for readings and lectures all over the United States. She frequently complained that importunate strangers made such demands on her time with requests for advice and criticism that they prevented her from turning out even more original work.

Millay was one of the most popular American poets of all time. Critic Louis Untermeyer explained the reason for the success of her poetry as follows: "Plain and rhetorical, traditional in form and unorthodox in spirit, it satisfied the reader's dual desire for familiarity and surprise."

Millay received an honorary doctorate from New York University and another from Colby College in 1937, and in 1940 she was elected to the American Academy of Arts and Letters. After the 1930's, however, her reputation faded because literary tastes were changing. The Great Depression of the 1930's, World War II in the 1940's, and the Cold War which followed all made the cavalier tone of much of the art of the

1920's seem hopelessly trivial and irrelevant.

Highly influential Modernist critics and poets such as T. S. Eliot were totally out of sympathy with romanticists such as Millay, who wrote personal, lyrical poetry addressed to the general reader. Modernists generally felt that poetry should sound almost like conversation. Hostile critics pointed out that Millay often used unnatural constructions purely for the sake of rhyme or meter. An example can be drawn from the opening lines of one of her most famous poems:

What lips my lips have kissed, and where, and why,
I have forgotten, and what arms have lain
Under my head till morning; but the rain
Is full of ghosts tonight, that tap and sigh
Upon the glass and listen for reply,
And in my heart there stirs a quiet pain
For unremembered lads that not again
Will turn to me at midnight with a cry.

The natural way of expressing the thought contained in the last three lines might be: "A quiet pain stirs in my heart for forgotten lads who will never turn to me again at midnight with a cry." This change, however, would destroy the rhyme and meter entirely.

After her husband's death in 1949, Millay continued living at their rural retreat in upstate New York and went on working in increasing loneliness and solitude until her death of a heart attack on October 19, 1950.

Summary

Edna St. Vincent Millay's greatest impact came as a result of her outspoken advocacy of sexual freedom for women. She shocked American by repudiating the so-called "double standard" both in her writings and in her personal life. The double standard, which had existed since time immemorial, was tolerant of men's sexual experimentation, but expected women to be chaste, monogamous, and virtually asexual. Millay was responsible for challenging social restrictions and prejudices against women's freedom of self-expression. She ignored the boundaries of conventional subject matter for women writers, and revealed the range of depth of the feminine character.

As a poet, Millay was influenced by the style and subject matter found in works by the English Cavalier poets of the seventeenth century, particularly by Andrew Marvell. Yet sexual freedom was only one part of the total freedom that women of Millay's generation were demanding. Millay's flippant, sophisticated poetry—so modern and yet so reminiscent of the Cavaliers—conveyed the implicit message that the subject of sex could be amusing and was not necessarily the fire-and-brimstone affair that had been traditionally made of it. The rigid self-censorship that had always existed in the publishing world began to relax with the evolution of public opinion.

Millay, although never a militant feminist, was in wholehearted sympathy with the women's rights movement. She belonged to Alice Paul's National Woman's Party, which agitated for woman suffrage and later for an Equal Rights Amendment, but Millay did not participate in demonstrations. Her unique contribution to feminism was in assuming she already possessed the rights other women were fighting to obtain.

Millay was not cut out to be a follower or crusader; when she tried writing propaganda poems during World War II, she was unsuccessful and injured her literary reputation. She will always be remembered as a courageous individualist; she contributed more by her personal example than by marching or passing out leaflets. Writing about her shortly after her death, John Ciardi summarized her career in the following words: "It was not as a craftsman nor as an influence, but as the creator of her own legend that she was most alive for us. Her success was as a figure of passionate living."

Bibliography

Brittin, Norman A. *Edna St. Vincent Millay*. Rev. ed. New York: Twayne, 1982. An excellent study of Millay full of valuable reference material. Discusses some of her most important works in a scholarly but not overly difficult manner. Part of Twayne's excellent United States Authors series. Contains many pages of endnotes, a chronology, and an annotated bibliography.

Cheney, Anne. *Millay in Greenwich Village*. University: University of Alabama Press, 1975. A psychological biography of Millay focusing on her liberated lifestyle and relationships with men during her days of experimentation with free love in Greenwich Village. Contains a good bibliography of books, articles, and interviews.

Daffron, Carolyn. *Edna St. Vincent Millay*. New York: Chelsea House, 1989. This short biographical and critical study, part of the American Women of Achievement series, was written especially for young readers. Contains many photographs and direct quotations from Millay's poetry. Daffron does a good job of making younger readers appreciate the political and intellectual climate of Millay's time.

Gurko, Miriam. *Restless Spirit: The Life of Edna St. Vincent Millay*. New York: Thomas Y. Crowell, 1962. This biography is addressed to readers of high school age. It does an effective job of bringing Millay to life as a real person—idealistic, contradictory, romantic, rebellious. Analyzes the role she played in the intellectual and cultural life of the early twentieth century. Contains excellent bibliography.

Millay, Edna St. Vincent. *Collected Poems*. Edited by Norma Millay. New York: Harper & Bros., 1956. This large volume contains a selection of poems representing Millay's range of subject matter and technical versatility, drawn from many of her previously published volumes.

———. *Letters of Edna St. Vincent Millay*. Edited by Allan Ross Macdougall. New York: Harper & Bros., 1952. Reprint. Westport, Conn.: Greenwood Press, 1972. A generous selection of letters written to Millay's many friends, acquaintances and admirers from earliest childhood until the last days of her life. Extensively footnoted.

Sheean, Vincent. *The Indigo Bunting: A Memoir of Edna St. Vincent Millay*. New York: Harper & Bros., 1951. Written by a personal friend who was himself a noted journalist, biographer, and novelist, this sensitively written memoir focuses on Millay's life at Steepletop during the 1940's and her long interest in birds and bird imagery.

Bill Delaney

KATE MILLETT

Born: September 14, 1934; St. Paul, Minnesota

Area of Achievement: Women's rights
Contribution: Since the 1970 publication of her book *Sexual Politics*, a manifesto of the feminist movement, Millett has been an acknowledged leader of the modern women's movement.

Early Life

Katherine Murray Millett was born on September 14, 1934, in St. Paul, Minnesota. Her father, James Albert Millett, was an engineer, and her mother, Helen Feely Millett, was a teacher. The family's background was Irish Catholic, and Kate attended several parochial schools. When Kate was fourteen, her father deserted the family. After attending parochial schools with dwindling faith and increasing rebelliousness, Kate Millett attended the University of Minnesota, where she received her bachelor's degree in English, magna cum laude and Phi Beta Kappa, in 1956. A rich aunt, who was disturbed by Kate's increasing tendency to defy convention, offered to send her to Oxford University for graduate study. For two years, Kate Millett studied English literature at Oxford, and she received first-class honors in 1958. Returning to the United States, she obtained her first job, teaching English at the University of North Carolina. In mid-semester, she quit her position and moved to New York City to paint and sculpt. In New York, she rented a loft to serve as her studio and living quarters, and to support herself she worked as a file clerk in a bank and as a kindergarten teacher in Harlem.

From 1961 to 1963, Kate Millett sculpted and taught English at Waseda University in Tokyo, Japan. She had her first one-woman show at the Minami Gallery in Tokyo. While in Japan, she met her future husband, Fumio Yoshimura, also a sculptor. In 1968, she returned to academic life, working for her Ph.D. degree in English and comparative literature at Columbia University while teaching English in the university's undergraduate school for women, Barnard College.

Life's Work

At Columbia University, Kate Millett's concern with politics and women's rights began to develop and deepen. After returning from Japan, she joined the Congress of Racial Equality (CORE) and the peace movement. In 1965, the campaign for women's liberation attracted her attention and energies. At Columbia, she was a vocal organizer for women's liberation and a militant champion of other progressive causes, including abortion reform and student rights. On December 23, 1968, because her activism made her unpopular with the Barnard College administration, she was relieved of her teaching position.

In its original form, *Sexual Politics* was a short manifesto that Millett read to a women's liberation meeting at Cornell University in November of 1968. In February of 1969, however, Millett began to develop the manifesto into her doctoral dissertation. Working on it with undivided attention, Kate Millett finished it in September of 1969 and successfully defended it to receive her doctorate in March of 1970. She was awarded the degree "with distinction."

Few doctoral dissertations are published outside the academic community, and fewer still become bestsellers, but Millett's *Sexual Politics* (1970) was a huge success, going through seven printings and selling 80,000 copies in its first year on the market. Although some reviews of *Sexual Politics* were decidedly hostile, most critics have judged the book to be a reasonable and scholarly political analysis of gender tensions.

Sexual Politics is divided into three sections. The first, which deals with theories and examples of sexual politics, establishes the fundamental thesis that sex is a political category with status implications. Millett argues that what is largely unexamined in the social order is an automatically assumed priority whereby males rule females as a birthright. In monogamous marriage and the nuclear family, women and children are treated primarily as property belonging to the male. Lower-class women are exploited and reduced to a source of cheap labor, while middle-class and upper-class women are forced into a parasitical existence, dependent for food and favor upon the ruling males. When the system is most successful, Millett says, it results in an interior colonization—the creation of a slavelike mentality in which women are devoted to their masters and the institutions that keep them in bondage.

The second part of *Sexual Politics* discusses the historical background of the subjugation and liberation of women. The section begins with an account of the first phase of the sexual revolution, which started about 1830 and ended, abortively, in reform rather than revolution, when women in the United States gained suffrage. Going on to analyze the counterrevolution, Millett identifies Sigmund Freud as its archvillain. She dismisses as a male supremacist bias Freud's theory that "penis envy" is the basis for women's masochism and passivity and that fear of castration is the basis for men's greater success at repressing instinctual drives and therefore attaining higher cultural achievement. She also examines and rejects Erik Erickson's theory of womb envy, among other versions of anatomy-is-destiny thought.

In the third and final section, Millett examines four major modern writers insofar as they reflect the sexual politics of our society. D. H. Lawrence sees women at their most womanly as willing subjects and sacrifices to male creative power. Henry Miller sees women only as sexual partners and sees the ideal sexual partner not as a person but as an object, a genital playground designed solely to fulfill male needs. Norman Mailer is a prisoner of the cult of virility, to whom sexuality means sadism, violence, and usually sodomy as well. Only in Jean Genet, the French chronicler of the homosexual underworld, does Millett find a sympathetic understanding of the position of women. She sees in Genet's portrayal of the hatred and hostility directed at homosexual "queens" a mirror image and intentional parody of relations between the sexes in heterosexual society.

Since the publication of her book, Kate Millett has been involved in a wide range of feminist activities. In 1970, she partially financed and directed an all-woman crew in the production of a low-budget documentary film about the lives of three women. Although *Three Lives* was intended for college and other noncommercial audiences, it was premiered at a commercial New York City theater late in 1971 and received generally excellent reviews. Millett then taught a course on the sociology of women once a week at Bryn Mawr College.

Kate Millett is an activist and supporter of a full range of women's liberation groups, from the National Organization for Women to the Radical Lesbians. She has been involved in attempts to organize prostitutes, and in August of 1970 she took part in the symbolic seizing of the Statue of Liberty in celebration of the passage of the Equal Rights Amendment, prohibiting discrimination because of sex, by the House of Representatives. (The amendment ultimately failed to be ratified by enough states to become law.)

Sexual Politics removed Millett from the anonymity of the New York art world and established her as a widely interviewed spokesperson for the women's movement. Within months, however, the author realized that she could not control the image of herself that was projected by the press and on television. In the midst of her excessive celebrity, Millett found herself unsuited to life as a talk-show exhibit, but she did not quit the scene. Once recognized as an articulate member of the women's movement, she had somehow ceased to be a free agent. In her uncomfortable new spokeswoman status, she was urged by other women to do her duty in speaking out on their behalf, while, at the same time, being browbeaten and harassed for her arrogance and elitism in presuming to do so. Millett's book *Flying* (1974) details her struggle to remain self-aware, personally happy, and productive in the face of all the publicity she was receiving as a result of *Sexual Politics*. The central theme of *Flying*, as well as that of her 1977 memoir *Sita*, is her avowed lesbianism and the effect that her honest admission of lesbianism had on her public and private life. The extent of the publicity attached to Millett was so intense that her greatest desire after the publication of *Sexual Politics* was to reconstruct some sort of private personality for herself after the glare of the cameras had begun to fade.

With her two autobiographical works finished, Millett turned to a topic that had haunted her for more than ten years—the brutal torture and murder of an Indianapolis teenager named Sylvia Likens. *The Basement*, released in 1980, offers a chilling chronology of Sylvia's last months, from her point of view as well as her killers'. The book combined reporting, the various consciousnesses of those involved in the crime, and a feminist analysis of power to follow human realities wherever they might lead. What emerges is not only the story of an isolated incident but also that of the powerlessness of children, the imposition of sexual shame on adolescent girls, and the ways in which a woman is used to break the spirit and body of younger women. Clearly, the fourteen years that Millett spent pondering Sylvia's fate and how to detail it enhance the book's value. Quite apart from any feminist polemics, *The Basement* can stand alone as an intensely felt and movingly written study of the problems of cruelty and submission. *The Loony-Bin Trip* (1990) recounts the ordeals Millett experienced after her involuntary hospitalizations in psychiatric wards for manic-depression, her divorce from sculptor Fumio Yoshimura, and the painful efforts she made to reconstruct her personal and public identities despite her illness. Millett now spends most of her time at a farm she owns where an art colony of other like-minded artists and activists reside.

Summary

Kate Millett will be remembered primarily as the author of *Sexual Politics*. *Sexual Politics* is an impressively informed, controlled analysis of the patriarchal order by a young radical sensibility that is challenging the confinements of cultural stereotypes and institutions in order to envision possibilities for refashioning power relationships between the sexes. With its phenomenal success, *Sexual Politics* provided the women's movement with a theoretical background for its struggles against male domination. It also pioneered academic feminist literary criticism, which has since influenced heavily the teaching and research on literature in many American colleges and universities. In addition, by avowing and celebrating first her bisexuality and later her lesbianism, Kate Millett has become an articulate and influential spokesperson in the struggle for gay and lesbian rights. Combining feminist ideals with careful and controlled analyses of the limitations and abuses of patriarchal social control, she has emerged as a champion of human rights.

Bibliography

Charvet, John. *Feminism*. London: J. M. Dent and Sons, 1982. Traces the evolution of feminism from its beginnings in eighteenth century thought to the twentieth century. The chapter "Radical Feminism" includes a summary of the major arguments of *Sexual Politics*.

Donovan, Josephine, ed. *Feminist Literary Criticism*. 2d ed. Lexington: University of Kentucky Press, 1989. A series of essays examining the impact of feminist literary criticism on the academy. The first essay places *Sexual Politics* in the context of other works that analyze images of women created by male authors.

Millett, Kate. *Flying*. New York: Simon & Schuster, 1974. After the phenomenal success of *Sexual Politics*, Kate Millett found herself both canonized and reviled as the near-mythical leader of the women's movement. This book recounts the relationship between a writer's life and her art, and her attempts to salvage a believable, productive woman out of the uproar surrounding the publication of her first book.

__________. *The Loony-Bin Trip*. New York: Simon & Schuster, 1990. An autobiographical account of Millett's thirteen-year struggle with manic-depression, her treatment with the drug lithium, and her decision in 1980 to stop taking the drug. Her account is an indictment of psychiatric treatment as a form of social control that she resolutely challenges and opposes.

__________. *Sita*. New York: Simon & Schuster, 1977. Millett's autobiographical account of her first diagnosis as a manic-depressive, her divorce from her husband, and the road to recovery she journeyed when she met and fell in love with Sita, a woman ten years older than Millett, artistic, witty, seductive, and strong. The memoir recounts the successes and despairs of a deeply felt lesbian relationship.

Roberta M. Hooks

JONI MITCHELL

Born: November 7, 1943; Ft. Macleod, Alberta, Canada

Area of Achievement: Music

Contribution: Mitchell has been an influential figure in American folk and popular music since the release of her first album in 1968. She is an original and innovative songwriter who has enjoyed a distinguished recording career. Her songs have been widely recorded by other artists as well.

Early Life

Joni Mitchell was born Roberta Joan Anderson on November 7, 1943, at Ft. Macleod, Alberta, Canada, the only daughter of William Anderson, a former officer in the Royal Canadian Air Force and merchandising manager for a grocery store chain, and Myrtle McKee Anderson, a schoolteacher. Roberta spent her earliest years in Ft. Macleod and then moved with her family as a young child to Saskatchewan, where she attended public schools in Saskatoon.

Her mother and maternal grandmother instilled in Roberta a love of poetry and literature, and her father, an amateur trumpeter, encouraged her budding interest in music. She took piano lessons for a few years and taught herself to play guitar. She also cultivated an interest in art and taught herself to paint. By the time she was graduated from high school in Saskatoon, she was a competent painter, and she moved to Calgary to enter the Alberta College of Art, where she hoped to study to become a commercial artist.

Roberta had not, however, abandoned her interest in music, and in spare moments at the art college, she sang folk songs, accompanying herself with a bass ukelele. Encouraged by friends, she began to perform at local Calgary coffeehouses, and music soon became her main focus. Disillusioned with her art courses, she gave up on the idea of a career in commercial art and concentrated instead on singing and performing. She soon made a name for herself in Calgary, and it was not long before she was performing in other cities.

When she was nineteen, she traveled to Toronto to the Mariposa Folk Festival, where the debut of a song she had composed on the train trip there caused a minor sensation. Encouraged, she decided to stay in Toronto, where she worked as a department store clerk to pay the rent and musicians' union dues while she sang at Toronto coffeehouses and clubs.

It was while she was in Toronto that she met Chuck Mitchell, a singer and performer from Detroit, Michigan. The two were married in 1965, and the next year they moved to Detroit, taking up residence near the campus of Wayne State University. It was at this point that Roberta Joan Anderson took the stage name Joni Mitchell. Mitchell and her husband performed as a folk duo in Toronto and Detroit coffeehouses and clubs, but their marriage (and their act) broke up after about a year. Mitchell, determined to strike out on her own, moved to New York City in 1967 to pursue a solo career.

Life's Work

When Joni Mitchell arrived in New York, the acoustic folk of the early and mid-1960's was on the wane as folk-rock gained in popularity. She was able to perform in small clubs, singing her own songs and playing acoustic guitar, but record companies were reluctant to sign someone who, to them, represented a dying trend. She did not find recording success immediately, but she did make some important contacts, among them the musician David Crosby, who agreed to produce her first album, *Song to a Seagull* (later retitled *Joni Mitchell*), which appeared in March, 1968.

Critics praised *Song to a Seagull* for its lyric insights and songwriting, and for Mitchell's unique voice, with a range of two and a half octaves, but the album was not a commercial success. Other artists, however, did have success with Mitchell's compositions. Judy Collins' versions of "Both Sides Now" and "Chelsea Morning" were popular chart hits. Both songs appeared on Mitchell's second album, *Clouds* (1969), and Mitchell received the 1970 Grammy award for best folk performance for her rendition of "Both Sides Now."

Tiring of New York, Mitchell moved to Los Angeles after her second album was released, accompanied by her agent, David Geffen, and her manager, Elliot Roberts. She took up residence in Laurel Canyon, and with *Ladies of the Canyon* (1970), *Blue* (1971), and *For the Roses* (1972), she made a name for herself as a "confessional" singer-songwriter, chronicling the details of love relationships gone wrong. On the basis of clues taken from her songs, speculation abounded in the music press about her private life. She had been romantically involved with such well-known musicians as Graham Nash and James Taylor, and *Rolling Stone* magazine went so far as to print a chart that mapped out her liaisons with Nash, Taylor, and others. Stung by the intrusion into her privacy, Mitchell purchased an isolated piece of land in British Columbia, which she used as an occasional retreat from the pressures of the music industry and Southern California.

By 1973, she was at the peak of her popularity and had toured extensively, selling out halls throughout the United States, Canada, and Great Britain. She was not content to settle into a single musical style, however, and her next album, *Court and Spark* (1974), moved away from the spare, acoustic folk flavor of her earlier albums, and instead featured more jazz-influenced pop arrangements. Saxophonist Tom Scott and his jazz-pop ensemble, the L.A. Express, worked with Mitchell on *Court and Spark*, which was generally well received, and Mitchell and the group toured together after its release.

Her next studio album, *The Hissing of Summer Lawns* (1975), was even more musically experimental, utilizing synthesizers and featuring African warrior drums from Burundi. With *The Hissing of Summer Lawns*, Mitchell's lyric themes changed as well. They were less personal and confessional, and instead became more critical of contemporary American social values. When first released, the album was a critical and commercial disaster. Fans accustomed to the confessional folksinger were unhappy with the album, and many critics were less than kind about her musical experimentation—*Rolling Stone* named it worst album of the year.

Having fallen from the heights of pop acclaim, Mitchell felt free to forge ahead on new musical paths. Although her music received less and less radio play, she continued to experiment musically on *Hejira* (1976), a flowing guitar-based album whose songs were written on a solo cross-country car trip, and on *Don Juan's Reckless Daughter* (1977), which contained more jazz and world-music influences. Excellent musicianship was important to Mitchell, and she sought out the best young jazz musicians to play on her records. Thematically, she balanced personal with broader social themes on these albums.

Mitchell's jazz experimentation culminated with her 1979 album *Mingus*, a collaboration with legendary jazz bassist Charles Mingus. Mingus had admired her music, and he wrote several new songs for her, in hopes that she would write lyrics for them. By the time Mingus was able to contact Mitchell about the project, he was gravely ill with Lou Gehrig's disease, and though they were able to begin the collaboration, he died before they could complete the project together. In the end, the album contained the Mingus-composed songs with Mitchell's lyrics, an original Mitchell song, and a version of Mingus' jazz standard "Goodbye Porkpie Hat," for which Mitchell also wrote lyrics. Neither pop nor mainstream jazz, *Mingus* was difficult to categorize, and it took a beating from both fans and critics. Even Mitchell admits that some of the pieces from *Mingus* were not completely successful, but the project was an important milestone in her development.

Mitchell's post-*Mingus* work has been less experimental. *Wild Things Run Fast* (1982), an album of celebratory love songs, coincided with her marriage to producer and bassist Larry Klein. Still anchored by the guitar and piano, *Dog Eat Dog* (1985) featured more synthesizers and social commentary. *Chalk Mark in a Rainstorm* (1988) and *Night Ride Home* (1991), while firmly in the pop genre, featured Mitchell's unique brand of fluid guitar and vivid and well-crafted observational lyrics on topics ranging from love to money to growing older to the environment and materialism.

Throughout her career, painting has remained a passion for Mitchell. She is said to paint as often as she writes, and her paintings and photos have appeared on the sleeves and liners of most of her albums. She even spent time in New Mexico studying with the artist Georgia O'Keeffe. Mitchell will not sell her paintings and has been reluctant to exhibit her work, but she has occasionally had shows at galleries such as the James Corcoran Gallery in Los Angeles.

Mitchell splits her time between Southern California and British Columbia, and she continues to write and produce finely crafted, innovative music that encompasses a number of genres but is uniquely her own. She tours infrequently, but she occasionally appears at benefit concerts for such causes as Amnesty International.

Summary

Although she is a talented painter, photographer, singer, and musician, Joni Mitchell's greatest impact has been as a songwriter of considerable skill and innovation. Her lyrics, always rich with many layers of images, have moved away from the personal, confessional descriptions of relationships found in her early albums. Her later work celebrates the joy of mature relationships and chronicles the process of growing older; it also comments on such topics as consumerism, materialism, world hunger, Indian rights, and televangelism. Regardless of the subject, Mitchell's lyrics usually express a definite female point of view.

Similarly, Mitchell's musical style has moved from the fairly structured folk idiom to the freer forms of jazz, jazz fusion, rock, and pop. Throughout her stylistic evolution, Mitchell has maintained her particular personal vision, making each genre uniquely her own.

Although her musical style has undergone considerable stylistic change in the course of her career, it has always been influential, particularly among her fellow musicians. Her contemporaries in the 1960's and 1970's folk scene frequently performed and recorded her songs, while younger pop stars such as Prince, Thomas Dolby, Annie Lennox, and Ric Ocasek have cited Mitchell albums as various as *The Hissing of Summer Lawns*, *Hejira*, *Ladies of the Canyon*, and *Blue* as influential in their own musical development. Artists as diverse as Frank Sinatra, Willie Nelson, and the group Nazareth have recorded her songs.

Bibliography

Collins, Judy. *Trust Your Heart: An Autobiography*. Boston: Houghton Mifflin, 1987. Collins was the first major artist to record and popularize Mitchell's early songs "Both Sides Now" and "Chelsea Morning." In this autobiography, Collins discusses Mitchell's musical influence on her early career and describes their friendship in the early 1970's.

Hood, Phil, ed. *Artists of American Folk Music*. New York: Quill, 1986. Although Mitchell is only briefly mentioned in this volume, the book does provide a valuable introduction to the beginnings of American folk music, and it profiles many of Mitchell's contemporaries on the folk scene of the 1960's and 1970's.

Pendle, Karin, ed. *Women and Music: A History*. Bloomington: Indiana University Press, 1991. In this comprehensive history of women and music, Joni Mitchell and Joan Baez are mentioned as representatives of the 1960's urban folk revival. The discussion of Mitchell includes biographical information as well as critical evaluation of her work.

Simon, George T. *The Best of the Music Makers*. Garden City, N.Y.: Doubleday, 1979. Simon profiles a number of popular musicians from the 1950's onward, and he includes a biographical sketch of Mitchell. In it, Mitchell discusses her feelings about her art, and the pressures that fame and recognition place upon the creative process.

Wild, David. "A Conversation with Joni Mitchell." *Rolling Stone* 605 (May 30, 1991): 63-67. In this wide-ranging conversation with David Wild, Mitchell reflects on her early folk career and the reception of her musical experiments with jazz and other styles; she also discusses her heroes, painting, changes in the music industry, and the current state of pop music.

Catherine Udall Turley

MARIA MITCHELL

Born: August 1, 1818; Nantucket, Massachusetts
Died: June 28, 1889; Lynn, Massachusetts
Area of Achievement: Astronomy
Contribution: A dedicated and meticulous observer of the sky, Mitchell discovered the comet that bears her name and trained future women astronomers in her position as professor of astronomy and director of the observatory at Vassar College.

Early Life

Maria Mitchell was born August 1, 1818, on Nantucket Island, the second daughter and third of ten children born to William and Lydia (Coleman) Mitchell. Lydia Mitchell, remembered as a stern and hard-working woman, was an eager reader and had been a librarian prior to her marriage. William Mitchell, mild of manner but resolute of purpose, was originally a cooper, but, in 1827, opened his own school. Later, in 1836, he became principal officer of the local Pacific Bank. Most important, however, for Maria's future, he was a highly respected amateur astronomer.

Maria was a bright child who enjoyed joining her father at the telescope he had set up, first on the roof of their house and later in an observatory established on the roof of the bank building. She learned how to adjust the chronometers that the seafaring men of Nantucket brought to her father to be recalibrated upon their return to land. In 1831, she was deeply moved by experiencing her first solar eclipse. By that time she was already keeping a journal of her observations.

The Mitchells were part of the Quaker community that dominated life on Nantucket at that time. Maria was drawn to the Quaker doctrines of love and peace, but chafed at the confining discipline inherent in their teaching. She exhibited at an early age her lifelong characteristic of independence and questioning of authority. As an adult she severed her Quaker membership and attended, but never joined, the Unitarian Church.

As an island thirty miles off the coast of Massachusetts, the Nantucket of Maria's childhood was isolated in many ways, especially during bad weather. Nevertheless, it was a center for the whaling industry. Whalers brought back many objects and wondrous tales of faraway places. Maria's older brother Andrew, to whom she was very close, ran away to sea. She accompanied him early one morning to the ship on which he departed, wishing that she were free to go with him.

Maria's education took place in private schools run by individual schoolmasters. As a student at her father's school, she was educated by him to the age of fourteen in a rather unorthodox manner involving observation and experience rather than rote learning. Later, she attended a school "for young ladies" run by Cyrus Peirce, who subsequently founded the first Normal School in the United States. Peirce was impressed by her ability and encouraged Maria's interest in mathematics. Her formal education ended when she was sixteen, but, for a time, she served as Peirce's assistant. In 1835, at the age of seventeen, she opened her own school, which operated with an unconventional curriculum.

In 1836, a new Atheneum was established on Nantucket Island. The Atheneum was an intellectual center for the population and it sponsored visiting lecturers as well as vocal and dramatic presentations; it also had a library with limited open hours. Maria was hired to become its librarian. In this position, she embarked on a program of self-education, especially in the mathematics related to astronomy. She also taught herself to read both French and Latin in order to have access to the mathematical volumes she wished to study.

Life's Work

Maria Mitchell, continuing in the position as the Atheneum's librarian for twenty years, lived at home with her family and maintained a busy schedule, assuming her full share of domestic chores. She continued to assist her father with his astronomical work as part of a network of astronomers involved with the United States Coastal Survey. On her own, she became a "sweeper of the sky," continually watching for any astronomical changes that might occur.

On October 1, 1847, she spotted a new comet and immediately shared the information with her father. He, in turn, mailed news of his daughter's discovery to his friends and colleagues at the Harvard College Observatory. This was a time when there was widespread interest, especially in Europe, in such discoveries. The king of Denmark had announced that he would give a gold medal to the first person to discover a comet through the use of a telescope. Within a few days of Mitchell's sighting, other astronomers in Europe also saw her comet. Their reports were received before that of Mitchell. It took many months for her priority to be established—recognition that was only made possible by the intervention of officials at Harvard. Instantly Mitchell achieved worldwide fame, not only among astronomers but also as a marvel in the growing women's movement of the mid-nineteenth century.

In 1849, she received an appointment as a "computer" (person making mathematical computations) for the *American Ephemeris and Nautical Almanac*, the first woman to be so designated. This position paid $300 per year, augmenting her $600 annual salary as Atheneum librarian, and involved work that she could do at home.

Mitchell had always been eager for travel beyond the occasional trip to the mainland. An opportunity to do so came in 1857, when a wealthy Chicago banker engaged her services as chaperone for his young daughter during a tour of the United States and Europe. In those pre-Civil War years Mitchell's eyes were opened to the vastness of the United States and the plight of black slaves living in the South. In Europe, Mitchell's reputation as comet discoverer gave her access to many scientific figures, such as the astronomer John Herschel and the science writer Mary Somerville. Well read as she was, Mitchell reveled in visiting famous sites in England and on the Continent.

Upon her return to the United States in 1858, Maria Mitchell was honored with the presentation of a five-inch telescope, made by the foremost telescope maker of the time, Alvan Clark. The money for its purchase had been raised by a group of American women led by educator Elizabeth Peabody. This telescope was much better than any

Mitchell had available on Nantucket and remained a prized possession for the rest of her life.

When Mitchell returned to Nantucket, she found that her mother's health had greatly deteriorated in her absence; Lydia Mitchell died three years later. In 1863, Maria and her father moved to Lynn, Massachusetts, to be near the home of her married sister, Kate.

A few years after settling in Lynn, a new vista opened for Mitchell. She was invited to become professor of astronomy and director of the observatory at Vassar College in Poughkeepsie, New York, the first American college established exclusively for women. Reluctant at first to accept the post since she had never been to college herself, Mitchell was persuaded by the founder, Matthew Vassar, to make the move in 1865. The college provided a house for Mitchell and her father on campus near the observatory.

For the next twenty-three years, Maria Mitchell served Vassar College well. An excellent and dedicated teacher, she inspired all her students, several of whom became astronomers themselves. Rather than lecturing, she preferred to work with small groups of students to give them individual attention, emphasizing the mathematical aspects of astronomy. The students also participated with her in pioneering the daily photographing of sunspots. Twice, in 1869 and 1878, she led groups of students to observe solar eclipses in Burlington, Iowa, and Denver, Colorado.

Mitchell traveled again to Europe in 1873 in the company of her sister Phebe and family, most notably to Russia, where she was cordially received by the director of the Pulkova Observatory, whom she had met in England on her previous trip to Europe.

Mitchell received much recognition and many honors in her lifetime, such as honorary doctoral degrees and membership in prestigious societies. She was a founder of the Association for the Advancement of Women (AAW) and served as its president from 1875 to 1876.

Recognizing that her health was failing, she retired from Vassar College in 1888 and returned to Lynn. For a while she was able to continue her astronomical work in a small observatory built for her by a nephew. Realizing that her days were numbered, she remarked, "Well, if this is dying, there is nothing very unpleasant about it." Mitchell died on June 28, 1889, and was buried on Nantucket Island, where an observatory, museum, and library were later established as a memorial to her.

Summary

Maria Mitchell's achievements and outlook exerted wide influence on her own and subsequent generations. As America's first woman astronomer she paved the way for the acceptance of women working in observatories. The gold medal that she won for her comet discovery brought worldwide recognition of American scientific activity in general as well as her unique role as a woman.

In her position at Vassar College she not only provided professional training to her own young students but also influenced the entire Vassar community by her unusual methods and questioning attitude. She retained her distrust of organized religion and attended compulsory chapel services reluctantly. Her sole creed was "there is a God and he is good." She was passionately dedicated to higher education for women as a means of increasing the opportunities available to them, believing education to be more important than the question of access to the ballot box that occupied many nineteenth century feminists.

As one of the founders of the Association for the Advancement of Women, she joined with other moderate feminists from various backgrounds, holding annual congresses to exchange views and argue for recognition of women's potential. In addition to serving as president of this organization, she was permanent chairman of the AAW Science Committee. She not only argued for women in science but also for a scientific outlook in other professions, resulting in her being elected vice president of the American Social Science Association.

Many magazine articles for the general reader were written about her. Some of her own speeches were published, and she edited, for many years, the astronomical column of the *Scientific American*. Joseph Henry, director of the Smithsonian Institution in Washington, was among her lifelong friends, as was Louis Agassiz, who sponsored her election to membership in the American Association for the Advancement of Science. Unconventional in her outlook and ways for a nineteenth century woman, Mitchell has achieved respected status as an individual as well as a woman astronomer.

Bibliography

Drake, Thomas E. *A Scientific Outpost: The First Half Century of the Nantucket Maria Mitchell Association*. Nantucket, Mass.: Nantucket Maria Mitchell Association, 1968. Describes the work of the association, founded in 1902 by relatives, friends, and Vassar College associates, to establish a museum, library, and observatory as a memorial on Nantucket Island to Maria Mitchell. Illustrated.

Jones, Bessie Z., and Lyle Gifford Boyd. *The Harvard College Observatory: The First Four Directorships, 1839-1919*. Cambridge, Mass.: Harvard University Press, 1971. Contains a three-page discussion of the role played by Harvard officials in assuring Mitchell's receiving the gold medal for her comet discovery.

Mack, Pamela E. "Straying from Their Orbits: Women in Astronomy in America." In *Women of Science: Righting the Record*, edited by G. Kass-Simon and Patricia Farnes. Bloomington: Indiana University Press, 1990. Contains a section on Maria Mitchell with emphasis on her training of younger women astronomers at Vassar College.

Mitchell, Maria. *Maria Mitchell: Life, Letters and Journals*. Compiled by Phebe Mitchell Kendall. Boston: Lee and Shepard, 1896. Reprint. Freeport, N.Y.: Books for Libraries Press, 1971. Compiled by a sister of Maria Mitchell, this volume provides access to the text of many original documents associated with Mitchell. Also includes some commentary on life in the Mitchell household.

Ogilvie, Marilyn Bailey. *Women in Science—Antiquity Through the Nineteenth Cen-*

tury: A Biographical Dictionary with Annotated Bibliography. Cambridge, Mass.: MIT Press, 1986. Includes a comprehensive and critical essay summarizing Mitchell's career and achievements, followed by a list of sources including articles written by Mitchell.

Wright, Helen. *Sweeper in the Sky: The Life of Maria Mitchell, First Woman Astronomer in America*. New York: Macmillan, 1949. A somewhat dated yet complete biography of Mitchell written by a science writer, trained in astronomy at Vassar College. Written for the general reader, this work provides a sympathetic portrait of Mitchell as a female scientist and role model.

Katherine R. Sopka

MEREDITH MONK

Born: November 20, 1942; Lima, Peru

Areas of Achievement: Dance, music, and theater and drama
Contribution: A composer, choreographer, singer, and multimedia performance artist, Monk expands in her work the boundaries of dance performance by juxtaposing movement, sound, and theatrical images.

Early Life

Meredith Jane Monk was born in Lima, Peru, where her mother, a singer, was on tour. She grew up in Connecticut and studied Dalcroze eurythmics as a child, learning to sing before she could talk, reading music before she read words. Monk is the descendant of European Jews, and her genealogy includes several generations of musicians and singers: Her grandfather founded the Harlem School of Music. She also studied music theory and harmony; modern dance with Ernestine Stodelle, a former Humphrey-Weidman dancer; and ballet and character dance with Olga Tarassova as a teenager. Monk cites these early experiences as influences on her later choreographic style. As an adjunct to her more formal training, Monk performed with an Israeli folk dance ensemble before attending college.

At Sarah Lawrence College, Monk majored in performing arts. There she studied with Bessie Schonberg, Judith Dunn, and Beverly Schmidt, each of whom had a profound impact on her. Monk credits Schonberg with teaching her the craft and discipline of choreography without imposing a particular style on her work. Schonberg's inspirational teaching methods and high standards allowed Monk to discover her own movement integrity and choreographic identity. Monk states that from Beverly Schmidt, a former Alwin Nikolais dancer, she developed an interest in the articulated body, which moves with attention to detail, especially isolated gestural movements. Judith Dunn's fascination with primal movement qualities awoke Monk's interest in the initiation of movement and is still apparent in her work decades later.

Monk moved to New York City in 1964, embracing the avant-garde arts world and a dance community in the throes of revolution. It was an environment of experimentation and radical creativity. Young choreographers in an informal workshop run by composer Robert Dunn and his wife Judith formed the nucleus of the Judson Church Group, in which dancers Yvonne Rainer, Steve Paxton, and others declared war on the conventions of dance performance. Arriving on the heels of the Judson rebels, Monk slipped easily into the avant-garde environment created by them. Although her aesthetic vision was singular, Monk shared their concern for making movement that was expressive of new ideas and for creating work that was a radical departure from the established dance tradition.

Although in her early work, movement played a more significant role than did music, her *16 Millimeter Earrings* (1966) was a seminal piece, for she wrote her first score for the dance and sang. With this piece, she began to discover the mosaic integration of forms that was to become her signature. She began to concentrate on the voice as an instrument of expression, and she incorporated a complex combination of elements into the work: film, layers of sound, movement images, costumes, and props. Monk views *16 Millimeter Earrings* as a breakthrough piece that provided her with an understanding of her life's work as a choreographer, composer, and singer.

Life's Work

Meredith Monk's choreographic productions are a natural consequence of her eclectic interests and training. She insists on finding a new movement vocabulary and formal structure for each piece she choreographs, and she organizes the space as carefully as she organizes the movement. She prefers to have each work grow out of the location for which it is designed and to create a separate world of images for each piece as it evolves.

With *Blueprint* (1967) and *Juice: A Theater Cantata* (1969), Monk began designing her pieces for specific environments, either nontheatrical sites or distinct architectural sites such as the Guggenheim Museum. Whereas earlier Judson Church choreographers experimented with works performed in nontraditional spaces, Monk radically redefined presentational space and time. In *Blueprint*, the first section was performed outdoors in Woodstock, New York. The audience changed locations as the action shifted from place to place. The second part of *Blueprint* occurred a month later in New York City.

Juice was even more unconventional: The first section included three separate events at the Guggenheim, beginning with dancers traveling the spiral stairway while the audience watched from below; the second involved the audience walking past tableaux of dancers with Roy Lichtenstein's paintings in the background; and the third featured dancers running past the audience, down to the ground floor.

Three weeks later, the second installment of *Juice* was performed at Barnard College. Elements of the first production were present in minimized form and new arrangements. The piece concluded a week later at Monk's loft with artifacts from the previous two sections on view for the audience.

Having the audience travel through space and time was a deliberate component of Monk's choreographic design. Monk's description of *Vessel: An Opera Epic* (1971) affords an explanation of her use of multiple locations: "I called *Vessel* an epic because of the sense of journeying . . . the point of having the audience move from one place to another . . . is that [they] are also on an epic . . . traveling." Monk stretches, compresses, and manipulates time and space in the same way that she manipulates sound: The voice dances and the dance speaks.

Monk expects audience members to be actively engaged participants in the performance; although her later works relied less on nontraditional theater spaces, the nonlinearity of Monk's productions challenges the viewer's perceptions and assumptions about performance.

Monk's music is integral to her compositions. Referring to herself as a composer of music, of movement, of images, she delights in breaking apart the boundaries that exist between the categories. The Meredith Monk Vocal Ensemble, created in 1978, performs her compositions all over the world. Often labeled a minimalist because of her use of rhythmic repetition, Monk has created music that is too full of emotional content to be truly classified as "minimalist." Monk's compositions are rich, multilayered pieces that attempt to "create a world with layers of perceptual situations where people see and hear things in a new, fresh way."

Monk's music incorporates Asian, Middle Eastern, Western, and Eastern European influences, and it combines elements from folk, classical, and popular music. The vocal language Monk creates provides a challenge for classically trained singers and often for her audience as well: Performers sing, chant, yodel, and emit chirps, grunts, and guttural noises. Monk's interest in the expressive possibilities of the voice echoes choreographer Merce Cunningham's use of all movement, from the pedestrian to highly technical dance phrases. For Cunningham and Monk, the traditional boundaries of dancing and singing are meaningless.

The House, Monk's interdisciplinary company, was founded in 1968 and is emblematic of her dedication to the concept of community in both literal and philosophical terms. Members of The House share personal as well as professional ties, and many have been associated with Monk since the 1960's. The theme of community features strongly in Monk's work: a global community that transcends boundaries of history, locale, and culture. Her communities are nontraditional and sometimes utopian, composed of individuals who support and care for each other. Monk thinks in terms of society, geography, and "the wholeness of the human organism"; she offers her work as a visual, aural, and sensory communal experience.

Monk's work is metaphoric and ambiguous. The images presented are nonlinear, fragmented, and dreamlike: Characters perform mysterious rituals and everyday activities; words (if present) in the text are fragmented and provocative. In *Quarry: An Opera* (1976), a young child wakes, complaining, "I don't feel well. I don't feel well. I don't feel well." Each complaint and subsequent explanation—"It's my eyes," "It's my hand," "It's my skin"—is repeated as a chant, and the audience is drawn into the world of the child and her fevered perception of World War II. The images in *Quarry* and Monk's other works are grounded in reality but appear surrealistic. Monk speaks of wanting to create "simultaneous realities" that evoke multiple layers of meaning.

A recurrent theme in Monk's work is the spiritual journey of an individual through a symbolic landscape, supported by a community of diverse individuals. Concepts of home and childhood permeate the narratives, and the journeys are opportunities for transformation and education. Highly allegorical, her work suggests personal and cultural archetypes that the audience is free to interpret.

Education of the Girlchild (1972-1973) remains one of Monk's masterpieces. In the first part, women dressed in white sit around a kitchen table, performing ritual actions, eating, interacting with one another. Odd monklike figures announce changes in the action with signboards; the women travel, dance, and vocalize. The second part is a solo for Monk, an eerie, reverse-order journey from old age to youth. The vocal score with which Monk accompanies her movement is hauntingly lyrical, and the piece has an emotional resonance that is deeply moving.

Images of history and geography are also prevalent in Monk's work. References to multiple historical, cultural, and geographic eras exist simultaneously within a single piece. The nonlinear juxtaposition of time, location, and relationships is often bewildering but emotionally compelling—an imagistic collage.

Monk organizes theatrical elements as a film director would, achieving on stage cinematic cuts, dissolves, washes, flashbacks, and foreshadowing: The chorus in *Quarry* washes away the previous scene by moving horizontally across the stage; *Vessel* incorporates a flash-forward section. Her interest in cinematic techniques has led her to create two films—*Ellis Island* (1979) and *Book of Days* (1988)—that have won critical acclaim.

Monk is an artist who is concerned with the healing potentialities of performance, and her political convictions and artistic vision merge seamlessly. In describing *Atlas: An Opera in Three Parts* (1992), Monk said, "In a way, what I am trying to do in this piece—and I say it with humility—is an attempt at healing . . . There's a place for idealism now, a hunger for it . . . I hope *Atlas* will provide an alternative reality in a sophisticated way." Under her direction, the classical art of opera is undergoing radical transformation. Monk acknowledges that her unique approach to opera may alienate traditionalists, yet she views her productions as integrating the elements of opera completely.

Summary

Meredith Monk is world renowned as a composer, singer, and choreographer. Her idiosyncratic approach to interdisciplinary performance is revolutionizing traditional concepts of dance, music, theater, and opera. Monk has received numerous awards in recognition of her creativity, including two Guggenheim Fellowships, six ASCAP awards, two Obies, a Brandeis Creative Arts Award, and various film festival prizes.

Monk is a Renaissance woman whose success is especially inspiring for young women. In the traditionally male-dominated fields of music composition, cinema, and opera, Monk's success is unparalleled. Cited as one of the most versatile creative artists in the United States, she is renowned as a musical pioneer along with such luminaries as John Cage, Philip Glass, and Robert Ashley. Her contributions to the field of dance/theater performance reflect many of the social issues of her time: feminism, multicultural fusion, concern for the global environment, and the search for community.

Meredith Monk has firmly established herself as an artist of exceptional talent by creating more than fifty multidisciplinary works incorporating music, dance, and theater that transcend traditional categories in a way that is uniquely her own.

Bibliography

Banes, Sally. *Terpsichore in Sneakers: Post-Modern Dance*. Middletown, Conn.: Wesleyan University Press, 1987. An exploration of choreographers influenced by the Judson Church Group. Banes's analysis of Monk is insightful and thought provoking.

Cohen, Selma Jeanne. *Dance as a Theatre Art.* 2d ed. Princeton, N.J.: Princeton Book, 1992. Source readings in dance history from 1581 to the 1980's provide an overview of the changing aesthetics of dance performance. The chapter on Monk features Monk's explanation of her juxtaposition of cinematic and choreographic styles in creating *Vessel.*

Kreemer, Connie. *Further Steps: Fifteen Choreographers on Modern Dance.* New York: Harper and Row, 1987. An anthology of essays by and about choreographers in the 1970's and 1980's. Kreemer's focus is how life and art changed after the 1960's. She interviews sixteen choreographers about their creative process, their influences, and what is important to them as artists.

McDonagh, Don. *The Rise and Fall and Rise of Modern Dance.* 2d ed. Pennington, N.J.: A Capella Books, 1990. McDonagh presents a history of modern dance in the 1950's and 1960's, a period of choreographic revitalization and rebellion. The book attempts to connect trends in all the arts with innovations in dance. The chapter on Monk covers her work from 1963 through 1970.

Mazo, Joseph. *Prime Movers: The Makers of Modern Dance in America.* Princeton, N.J.: Princeton Book, 1977. A concise history of modern dance, with an emphasis on the early founders of the art. Mazo's section on Monk is brief but helps contextualize her accomplishments.

Cynthia J. Williams

HELEN WILLS MOODY

Born: October 6, 1905; Centerville, California

Area of Achievement: Sports

Contribution: Helen Wills Moody established a remarkable record in women's tennis in the Golden Age of Sports in the 1920's, one that might never be equaled in the sport. Her skills, determination, and record have remained as a model for women's tennis.

Early Life

Helen Newington Wills was born in Centerville, California, on October 6, 1905. Her father Clarence, a surgeon and an average tennis player, encouraged Helen to play tennis near their new home in Berkeley at an early age. On her fourteenth birthday, she was given a membership to the Berkeley Tennis Club. Helen went on to become the best player in California while she was a student in high school. Although Helen's mother had earned a bachelor's degree in education, she decided to remain home to support and help her daughter in both her tennis and educational endeavors.

Avid to learn more about the sport, Helen began receiving help from William Fuller, a volunteer coach at the Berkeley Tennis Club. Soon, she was playing daily and began competing in local tournaments with the encouragement of Fuller and her parents. In 1919, she won the Pacific Coast Juniors championship, and went on to capture her first national juniors title in 1921 at the age of fifteen. In 1922, she won the National Junior Singles title and went on to sweep the doubles title with her partner Helen Hooker. That same year, she reached the finals of the U.S. women's national championships, but was beaten by eight-time winner and defending champion Molla B. Mallory in straight sets. Disappointed by this defeat, Helen nevertheless managed to win the national championship doubles title with Marion Z. Jessup. Helen's impressive record at the tender age of seventeen rocketed her to third place among the top ten U.S. women tennis players in 1922.

Life's Work

Helen Wills quickly emerged as a dominant figure in the sport of women's tennis and achieved a remarkable record between 1923 and 1939. Seven times she was the U.S. National Singles champion (1923, 1924, 1925, 1927, 1928, 1929, and 1931), in addition to earning three more titles as U.S. National Doubles champion (1924, 1925, and 1928) and two titles as U.S. National Mixed Doubles champion (1924 and 1928).

Wills's success at Wimbledon, which at the time was considered the world championship, was even more remarkable. She won the singles championships at Wimbledon eight times (1927, 1928, 1929, 1930, 1932, 1933, 1935, and 1938), and the doubles championship three times (1924, 1927, and 1930). It has been remarked that, had Wimbledon offered a mixed doubles championship in the interwar years, Wills would have won her share of those championships as well.

Although she developed her tennis game on the asphalt courts of California and perfected it on the grass courts of Forest Hills and Wimbledon, Helen Wills also demonstrated her talents on the slow French clay courts. She won the French singles championship four times (1928, 1929, 1930, and 1932) and the doubles championship two times (1930 and 1932). At the 1924 Olympic Games in Paris, Wills won the gold medal in singles, defeating Julie Vlasto of France, and also teamed with Hazel Wightman to win a second gold medal in doubles competition. Few doubted that had tennis been offered as an Olympic sport in 1928, the year that she won the French, English, and American championships, Helen Wills would have repeated her 1924 triumphs.

In fact, Wills was incomparable and apparently unbeatable in the years between 1927 and 1932: During that time she did not lose a set in competition and she lost only one match (by default to Helen Jacobs) in the almost nine-year period between August, 1926, and January, 1935. Wills, however, never received the adulation that was given to the other female sports stars of that era, such as Americans Gertrude Ederle and Alice Marble and French tennis star Suzanne Lenglen. Labeled "Little Miss Poker Face," a term coined by the press to describe her steely concentration and lack of emotion on the court, Helen Wills apparently cultivated the image that sportswriter Paul Gallico captured in his description of her in the 1920's—"regally beautiful, efficient, calm, cold, ruthless, implacable, dignified, aloof, ambitious, imperious, successful."

Ironically, Helen Wills Moody has been remembered by sports historians as much for two matches in her career in which she was defeated as she has been praised for her remarkable lifetime record.

The first defeat came at the hands of a talented, eccentric, and charismatic French tennis star of the 1920's, Suzanne Lenglen. Lenglen was the favorite of the sports writers because she provided them with "good copy." She engaged in theatrics, scandalized proper society and even more proper tennis patrons by her attire on the courts (she actually revealed the calves of her legs) and by her behavior off the courts: she danced until all hours, smoked in public, did not keep a training schedule, and she openly flaunted her much publicized romances.

The French and American press publicized the match between the two women as the match of the decade if not the century. Helen Wills, in addition to her Olympic triumphs, had won three consecutive United States National Singles Championships. Lenglen had captured six of the last seven Wimbledon Singles Championships. Wills, at twenty, was described by the French press as the pretty young girl from the provinces, while Lenglen, at twenty-six, was considered the grand dame of European tennis. They had never met in competition and oddly enough would never test each other again after their classic confrontation.

The match, which took place at the Carlton Hotel in Cannes in February of 1926, became *the* social event of the tennis season: Special grandstands were created for the crowd of 6,000 spectators, and celebrities checked into the hotel days in advance in order to catch the ambience of the event. James Thurber, whose knowledge of tennis was miniscule, was commissioned to write an article for the European edition of the

Chicago Tribune, and Vicente Blasco Ibáñez, the famous Spanish novelist, was paid 40,000 francs to write about the event even though he had never seen a tennis match. Even Max Eastman, the editor of the radical magazine *The Masses*, stopped off on his way from the Soviet Union to catch the match. It proved to be everything the press had claimed it would be. The French cheered their favorite daughter, who won the first set, and one bystander became so excited that on match point he shouted "out" on a shot by Wills, thus causing crowd to flow onto the court. When order was restored Lenglen lost the next game but regained her composure, winning the second set (8-6) and the match. Later in the day, after defeating Helen Wills in doubles, Lenglen collapsed in the arms of her supporters.

In the midst of her tennis fame, Wills found time for other pursuits. She proved that she was capable of serious scholarly study, earning a Phi Beta Kappa key when she graduated from the University of California, Berkeley, with a degree in fine arts in 1928. In 1929, Helen Wills was married to Frederick S. Moody, a stockbroker from San Francisco who purportedly had proposed to her in the wake of her 1926 defeat by Lenglen at the French Open. She continued to compete after her marriage and retained her national and international ranking as the top female player in the world from 1927 through 1933, the year of her second embarrassing defeat.

The second celebrated match was less dramatic and certainly more damaging to the image Helen Wills Moody hoped to project. Six years after the Lenglen-Wills event, Helen Wills Moody faced her arch rival Helen Hull Jacobs in the singles finals of the United States Nationals. She had not lost a match since 1926, but inspired play by Jacobs, combined with her own fatigue, forced Moody to default in the third set when she was trailing 3-0. The press mercilessly argued that her default was an unsportsmanlike attempt to avoid outright defeat. She later admitted that she should have completed the match, but the damage was done.

Although she played without apparent emotion, and her famous concentration during matches gave the impression that tennis was her only interest, Helen Wills Moody's life was not one-dimensional. She wrote in 1937 that she always viewed tennis as a "diversion" and not a career and her activities outside the confines of the tennis court attest that statement. She was an accomplished painter and artist: Several of her drawings were featured in *Vanity Fair* and other publications, and she had numerous public showings of her work as an artist. She attempted a career in 1927 as a film actress, but Hollywood producers believed that her legs and arms were "too developed" in comparison to the images which appeared on the screen at that time. She did, however, make a short film for Herbert Hoover's 1928 presidential campaign. Her talents were also put to use by the newspaper wire services, which enlisted her to do feature articles while she was visiting Europe and Britain during her tennis competitions. She even tried her hand, admittedly not too successfully, at writing a detective novel.

After she and her first husband were divorced in 1937, Helen married Aidan Roark, a writer and polo player. She retired from tennis in 1938, choosing to live a private life in California.

Summary

Although she had significant achievements off the tennis courts, Helen Wills Moody's influence upon the development of women's tennis was her most noteworthy accomplishment. While her demeanor on the court and the machinelike quality in which she dispatched her opponents did not win her either the adulation of a Lenglen or the strong fan support of a Jacobs, she was admired and respected by American sportswriters, as evidenced by the Associated Press naming her the Female Athlete of the Year in 1935. She also was embraced by the British press, which gave her the title of "Queen Helen" for her accomplishments both on and off the court during her numerous appearances at the Wimbledon championships. In her quiet way she became the heroine for women tennis players in the years between World War I and World War II. Moody's skills on the court were recognized in 1959 when she was inducted into the International Tennis Hall of Fame. Her accomplishments off the court in art and in the promotion of dress emancipation for women tennis players won the respect of the young players of the 1950's and 1960's. During the 1970's and 1980's, Billie Jean King, Martina Navratilova, and Chris Evert often cited her as the model they looked to for skill, grace, and talent in women's tennis. She was, in brief, a champion among champions.

Bibliography

Condon, Robert J. *Great Women Athletes of the Twentieth Century*. Jefferson, N.C.: McFarland, 1991. In his collection of profiles on top women athletes of the twentieth century, Condon places Helen Wills Moody among the top five athletes to achieve distinction and praises her accomplishment in raising the competitive level of women's tennis to a point where it garnered equal attention with men's tennis among sports fans and sportswriters.

Engelmann, Larry. *The Goddess and the American Girl: The Story of Suzanne Lenglen and Helen Wills*. New York: Oxford University Press, 1988. Engelmann's book is a lengthy and often detailed account of the famous match between Lenglen and Wills. It also describes the general environment of women's tennis in the 1920's.

Jacobs, Helen Hull. *Gallery of Champions*. New York: A. S. Barnes, 1949. A collection of essays about the pre-World War II tennis champions written by Moody's last rival, Jacobs. Many of the individuals included were players against whom Jacobs competed. The essay on Helen Wills is even-handed and makes little note of the famous defaulted match of 1933.

Wills, Helen. *Fifteen-Thirty: The Story of a Tennis Player*. New York: Charles Scribner's Sons, 1937. In twenty-five brief chapters, Wills describes her life as a tennis player and an aspiring artist. The reader will have to look elsewhere to discover the inner dimensions of Helen Wills's life.

————————. *Tennis*. London: Charles Scribner's Sons, 1928. A tennis instructional book which, while not providing much insight to Helen Wills the individual, provides a good indication of Wills's technique and tennis philosophy.

Wills, Helen, and Robert W. Murphy. *Death Serves an Ace*. New York: Charles

Scribner's Sons, 1938. Written in collaboration with Robert W. Murphy, this book is a detective novel about the experiences of a "poker-faced" tennis player. One reviewer noted that in Helen Wills's hand, the racket certainly proved to be "mightier than the pen."

Woolum, Janet. *Outstanding Women Athletes: Who They Are and How They Influenced Sports in America*. Phoenix, Ariz.: Oryx Press, 1992. This collection of biographical profiles includes an essay on Helen Wills Moody which emphasizes in addition to her championship play the impact that she had on the sport of tennis.

Robert L. Patterson

MARIANNE MOORE

Born: November 15, 1887; Kirkwood, Missouri
Died: February 5, 1972; New York, New York
Area of Achievement: Literature
Contribution: An early leader in Modernist poetry, Moore eventually gained recognition as one of the half-dozen major poets in English of the middle twentieth century.

Early Life

Marianne Craig Moore was born on November 15, 1887, in Kirkwood, Missouri, near St. Louis, where her mother had moved after a breakdown had permanently institutionalized her father. Her mother's brother, pastor of the Presbyterian Church, provided all Marianne knew of a father during her first years. Upon his death in 1894, Marianne, an older brother, and her mother moved to be with friends at Carlisle, Pennsylvania. Here Marianne attended the Metzger Institute, where her mother took a part-time teaching position. Another Presbyterian pastor, George Norcross, involved young Marianne in the life of the mind and the spirit.

Marianne next enrolled at Bryn Mawr College, where she struggled, especially during the first two years, gradually finding a home in the biology laboratory and at the literary magazine, although literature courses daunted her. To contribute to the household income after receiving her degree in 1909, she took a business and secretarial course at Carlisle Commercial College. This gained her a job at the Carlisle Indian School, at the time a center for assimilating American Indians into the common culture. Here she taught classes in English and business skills, maintained the typewriters and stenographic equipment, and coached both boys and girls in field sports for four years. She also sent out poems for publication, placing pieces in the most prestigious and progressive journals of the time: *Egoist* (London) and *Poetry* (Chicago).

In 1916, mother and daughter moved first to Chatham, New Jersey, and then two years later to New York, where Marianne lived for the rest of her life. At first supporting herself by tutoring, Moore eventually obtained a part-time position with the New York Public Library, but she quickly decided to devote her life to literature. Without her knowledge, some of her editors and readers at *Egoist* published her first book, *Poems*, in 1921. Her subsequent volume *Observations* (1924), however, proclaimed her entry into the literary lists. Besides containing some of her finest and most reprinted poems, it declared her dedication to the literary life. Editing *Dial*, another pioneering journal, from 1925 to 1929 confirmed her decision. When that journal ceased publication, Moore resolved to devote the rest of her life solely to writing.

Life's Work

For the next forty years, Marianne Moore supported herself as a freelance reviewer, essayist, and poet, proving it possible to make money by writing: By the time she "retired," she had put enough away so that she could live comfortably on the interest, even in a sickbed. She also gained recognition, though quietly. Throughout her publishing career, every new work earned both acclaim and merit; her list of literary prizes was longer, the weight of her medals heavier, than those of her more celebrated colleagues. She may look at first like a token "female representative" among the writers, but a second look reveals that if there was prejudice against women writers, Moore deserves more credit for having broken through the barriers. Besides, her male peers were the first to acknowledge her eminence.

At least some of her lack of celebrity stems from her own withdrawn habits, her failure to promote herself. Still, within her own limits, she outperformed all of her rivals. She alone succeeded at supporting herself entirely by writing—the only professional among amateurs. Moreover, she is the only world-class poet to have thrown out the first pitch of the season for both the Brooklyn Dodgers and New York Yankees, just as she is the only one to have held a conference on poetry with then-heavyweight boxing champion Muhammad Ali. Late in life, she even gained a semipopular following, especially after being seen about New York conspicuously garbed in billowing cape and tricorn hat. In the 1960's, the picture magazines made regular copy of her. Yet she never found the audience she deserved.

What is called her early work was hardly early; she was in her mid-thirties before her publications gained much currency. Still, many of her best-known poems and several signature techniques appeared in her first two books. Her fascination with animals, especially with exotic and bizarre forms, stands out, as do her jagged lines, quirky rhythms, and metaphorical tangents. Still, although she gained positive reviews, she had not yet found herself. Editing *The Dial*, however, introduced her to the leading writers of the time, and she made much of her contacts. Several of those writers urged her to publish more widely, and her *Selected Poems* (1936) was introduced by T. S. Eliot (1888-1965). From that point on she did not lack readers.

Selected Poems did not so much break new ground as expand established colonies. It also demonstrated one of Moore's most ingrained habits, variously considered irritating or refreshing. Several touchstone poems reappeared here in altered form; the poet had improved them, even after publication. Such constant tinkering is typical of Moore. For her a poem is constantly in process, in the act of being brought about, rather than a product fixed and definite. In her final volume, *The Complete Poems of Marianne Moore* (1967), she perfected this process, paring down her best-known poem, "Poetry," to a three-line distillation of the original thirty-four. In doing so, she deprived many readers of lines they cherished. At the same time, again typically, she made amends by reprinting the original version in the notes appended to the text of the poems—another characteristic gesture of playfulness.

That habit of concentration, of reducing poems to their metaphorical essence, is at the core of Moore's poetic practice, although this was not at first recognized. Partly because of her fascination with depicting unusual animals in minute detail, partly because her second book was titled *Observations*, she was long considered a visual poet, distinguished as much by what she saw as by her techniques of reporting and reconstructing. Thus a catalog of typical titles reads much like the roster of a peculiar zoo: "The Fish," "No Swan So Fine," "The Frigate Pelican," "The Pangolin," "The Jerboa," "To a Snail," "Sojourn in the Whale," "The Basilisk," "Elephants," "Peter" (about a cat), and many more. Even poems ostensibly dealing with unrelated topics regularly modulate—by Moore's methods—to images of animal behavior. Furthermore, this pseudopictorial mode carries the animal images over into other scenes, so that reading Moore often seems like touring a splendid museum.

Ultimately, however, Moore's work strikes home because of technique, structure, and imaginative wit, qualities that rule her major publications: *The Pangolin and Other Verse* (1936), *What Are Years?* (1941), and *Nevertheless* (1944). Although Moore had experimented early with free verse and Imagist formulas, in these works she developed her idiosyncratic forms and verbal techniques. She derived these from the wordplay of certain sixteenth and seventeenth century English prose masters: Lancelot Andrewes, John Donne, Francis Bacon, and Sir Thomas Browne. Her poetry begins, as her contemporary and friend Ezra Pound had prescribed, as good prose—that is, it exemplifies precision, conciseness, weight, poise, and exactness. This gives her work hard edges, definite lines, a felt presence; her poems display rather than decorate. Often they seem to be sculpted.

Moore developed poetic forms and techniques to complement these prose-based virtues. Although her metrics are basically conventional, she considered the stanza rather than the line as the formal center of the poem. Her poems began with an individuating stanzaic form, chosen ordinarily by working with a found or invented verbal pattern—more often than not a quotation from something essentially prosaic: a guidebook, a review, a memo. Completing the poem meant fashioning further stanzas on identical linear patterns, so that the rhymes and line divisions all occurred at precise points and each poem had a unique pattern. Furthermore, because the line divisions do not control the shapings of the phrase, Moore was free within the formal strictures to exploit the phrase rhythms characteristic of prose. The cross-patterns thus generated often seem abrupt and jagged, even crude, at first, but they allow her wit and playfulness to sport within them, and occasionally break free. An early poem, "The Past Is the Present," established this aesthetic objective for all of her work: "Ecstasy affords/ the occasion and expediency determines the form."

Summary

Despite making a living out of writing and gaining some late recognition, Marianne Moore cannot be termed a female pioneer or even a successful role model in a conventional sense. She lived almost as a recluse, acquiring fame only as a caricature of the female poet, grotesquely caped, bonneted, and caparisoned. Far from asserting her sexual independence, she spent most of her life caring for her increasingly infirm mother and her minister brother; clearly, she was the hero in the family. She carried Victorian reticence about sexuality around with her as if it were a veil. As the editor of *The Dial*, she rejected some overt sexual references in a submission by Hart Crane, prompting him to call her a hysterical virgin; and, asked late in life for her opinion about current poets, she complained about their sexual frankness.

Nevertheless, she deserves credit as the truest liberator. At a time when almost no one in a remarkable generation of poetic genius could make literature pay, she did. Furthermore, she showed that women could compete on equal terms with men in one of the most intensely combative arenas anywhere: that of professional literature. What better demonstration could anyone ask of the potential of women? As daringly as any explorer into uncharted regions, she blazed her own trails, established her own range, and gained the respect and admiration of the men who walked beside—but never before—her. She continues to hold the territory she staked out.

Bibliography

Goodrich, Celeste. *Marianne Moore and Her Contemporaries*. Iowa City: University of Iowa Press, 1989. In some respects a study for specialists, this work does document the interactions between Moore and her more conspicuous male colleagues T. S. Eliot, Wallace Stevens, Ezra Pound, and William Carlos Williams. It is fully documented and indexed, and contains a selected bibliography.

Holley, Margaret. *The Poetry of Marianne Moore: A Study in Voice and Value*. New York: Cambridge University Press, 1987. This mainstay standard scholarly commentary on Moore's poetry is more readable and useful than most. It provides insights and persuasive interpretations. The biographical sketch is separate and concise, and the text also includes a chronology of publication, notes, an accurate bibliography, and an index.

Martin, Taffy. *Marianne Moore: Subversive Modernist*. Austin: University of Texas Press, 1986. Martin attempts to integrate Moore into the women's movement, with some success but also some strain. The study combines biography and commentary, and includes notes and an index.

Molesworth, Charles. *Marianne Moore: A Literary Life*. New York: Atheneum, 1990. Molesworth's work is the major literary biography, massive in scholarship and compiled from total immersion in all available sources. Meticulous in its detailed reconstruction of Moore's life, it has been criticized for failing to bring its subject to life. It includes full scholarly apparatus.

Phillips, Elizabeth. *Marianne Moore*. Modern Literature Series. New York: Frederick Ungar, 1982. Intended as an introduction to the poet and woman for the general reader, this work achieves its objectives. Although the biographical material is dated and superficial, Phillips' work remains the first reference of choice. It is fully noted and indexed.

Tomlinson, Charles, ed. *Marianne Moore: A Collection of Critical Essays*. Englewood Cliffs, N.J.: Prentice-Hall, 1969. Although it is badly dated, this work contains indispensable material not readily available elsewhere: letters, an interview, early reviews about and by Moore, and particularly essays by leading critics of the mid-century: Kenneth Burke, John Crowe Ransom, Stevens, Williams, Randall Jarrell, and various major scholars.

Willis, Patricia C., ed. *Marianne Moore: Woman and Poet*. Orono, Maine: National Poetry Foundation, University of Maine, 1990. This major work is invaluable for making possible an uncluttered view of the poet. It collects essays about Moore's life and writings from a kaleidoscopic array of perspectives and by a formidable battery of scholars. It also contains a complete and useful annotated bibliography.

James Livingston

JULIA MORGAN

Born: January 26, 1872; San Francisco, California
Died: February 2, 1957; San Francisco, California
Area of Achievement: Architecture
Contribution: One of the first female architects in the United States, Morgan designed nearly eight hundred buildings, including the magnificent Hearst Castle.

Early Life

Julia Morgan was born on January 26, 1872, in San Francisco. She grew up in her parents' stylish Victorian house in a wealthy Oakland neighborhood, along with her one sister, Emma, and three brothers, Parmalee, Avery, and Sam. The Morgan family was quite wealthy and employed several servants. Julia was a frail and sickly child who often suffered from chronic ear infections. These painful infections would force her to remain in bed for several days at a time. Despite her illnesses, Julia was lively and very strong-willed. Julia's personality development was influenced by her mother, Eliza Morgan, who was, for her time, a very independent woman.

Eliza dominated the Morgan household. It was necessary for Eliza to be self-sufficient because her husband, Charles Bill Morgan, was often away from home prospecting for gold. Eliza single-handedly supervised the servants, managed the family funds, and raised the children. Although it was unconventional to assign household tasks to well-to-do children, Eliza insisted that her children do common household chores. One of Julia's tasks, for example, was to wax and polish a three-story banister. Eliza believed that these duties taught her children how to accept responsibility.

When Julia attended grammar school, she liked to associate with her brothers. She preferred their active games to the quiet ones that the girls always played. Julia especially enjoyed vigorous exercise in her brothers' gymnasium, where she would hang fearlessly from the rope swing and glide across the balance beam. Julia's father had created the gymnasium exclusively for her brothers, and he forbade her to play there. He thought it was improper behavior for a young girl. Julia defied her father, however, and continued to make full use of the gymnasium until she entered high school.

When Julia attended high school, she forgot all about her athletic interests and became more intellectual. Many of Julia's girlfriends were interested in pretty clothes and parties, but she spent much of her time studying. Julia learned math, physics, German, and Latin. Much to her pleasure, she won an award in mathematics. Julia often achieved high marks in all her subjects. This prompted people to comment that she was unusually smart "for a girl."

During Julia's last year of high school, she began to think about her future. At first, she considered a career in medicine. She was especially attracted to medical research. Julia finally decided on architecture as a profession, however, because it combined the scientific, the mathematical, and the artistic. Julia received her high-school diploma in 1890, a noteworthy accomplishment in its own right, since not many girls completed high school during that era.

After Julia was graduated from high school, her mother planned to have a large party for her and then find her a suitable husband, but Julia disapproved of that idea. She asked her parents to send her to college so that she could fulfill her dream of having a career. Julia's father was astounded at her request. Women did not have careers. Julia's mother, however, recognized her daughter's determination in this matter and agreed to help her with her college plans. Julia's father never completely accepted the idea. Julia applied to the University of California at Berkeley and was admitted. Only about one hundred women were enrolled there at the time.

Life's Work

In 1894, Julia Morgan completed her studies at Berkeley and was graduated with a degree in engineering. The school did not offer a degree in architecture at that time. Morgan was the first woman ever to receive a degree in engineering at the University of California. In order to fulfill her hopes of becoming an architect, she needed specialized training. Following her graduation, Morgan studied with Bernard Maybeck, a prominent California architect noted for his eccentric style. He encouraged Julia to go to Paris to attend the École des Beaux-Arts. At first, her mother refused to give Morgan the money to study in Paris, but she later changed her mind and supported her daughter in this venture. Although it took Julia Morgan nearly two years to gain entrance to the previously all-male school, she ultimately completed her studies in 1902, becoming the first woman to receive a degree in architecture from the esteemed institution.

After earning her degree, Morgan was eager to find work. She stayed in Paris for a while to fulfill her first commission: Harriet Fearing, an American from Newport, Rhode Island, employed Morgan to design a room for her. Fearing wanted to add a large salon for parties and concerts to her seventeenth century home in Fontainebleau. Morgan created a rectangular, thirty-four-foot room with four tall arched French windows. The walls were pale pink decorated with dark pink flowers. Fearing was pleased with Morgan's work, and her first commission was a complete success.

Not long after she completed this first commission, Julia Morgan returned to California, where she quickly contacted her old instructor Bernard Maybeck. She hoped that he would offer her a position in his firm. Maybeck did not have a place for Morgan, but he referred her to John Galen Howard, a famous New York architect. Howard was impressed with Morgan's European education. He hired her and assigned her the task of drafting designs for the Hearst Mining Building on the Berkeley campus.

This building had been commissioned by Phoebe Hearst as a memorial to her late husband. Pleased with Morgan's designs, Howard gave her a more challenging project, the Greek Theater at the university. This vast outdoor amphitheater had been commissioned by Phoebe Hearst's son, William Randolph Hearst, the wealthy newspaper publisher. Hearst later became Morgan's foremost client. She designed the amphitheater to be constructed in reinforced concrete, a sturdy building material rarely used in the United States at that time. Reinforced concrete is concrete that has been made stronger by the placement of steel rods or bars within the concrete itself. During the early 1900's, reinforced concrete was a revolutionary new building material. She had studied how to use reinforced concrete when she was in Paris. She liked this new building material because, in addition to being strong, it was easy to shape. Although the theater has needed minor repairs, it is still in use.

In 1904, Morgan left Howard's office to establish her own business. She desperately wanted her own office but did not have the necessary funds. Fortunately, her parents allowed her to set up a studio in their carriage house in Oakland. At first, she received very few commissions, but after a few months, her old college friends began hiring her to design their homes. One important commission that Morgan acquired at that time was to design the bell tower at Mills College, in Oakland. Completed in 1904, the tower, like the Berkeley amphitheater, is composed entirely of reinforced concrete, with smooth gray walls that rise seventy-two feet into the air. Because it is so beautiful, the students refer to it as "the gem." On April 18, 1906, an earthquake struck San Francisco, destroying much of the city. The terrible earthquake demolished many of the city's buildings. Some structures withstood the jolt, however, and remained standing. Among those that survived were several buildings designed by Morgan, including the Mills College Bell Tower. Her bell tower survived the quake largely because it was made of reinforced concrete. The tower is still standing today, nestled among the eucalyptus trees.

Following the earthquake, Julia Morgan received many commissions. Her most important project, however, was the restoration of the Fairmont Hotel. This San Francisco landmark was once the most exquisite hotel in the city. Guests would gather in its magnificent dining room with walls of gold and ivory. The quake had destroyed the hotel's gleaming interior, leaving only the stone pillars standing. She restored the Fairmont by strengthening its stone pillars and walls with the same reinforced concrete that had preserved the Mills College Bell Tower. Her restoration of the Fairmont helped her to gain still more clients.

In 1912, Morgan was commissioned by the Young Women's Christian Association (YWCA) to design several buildings for their newly acquired land in Asilomar, near Monterey, California. The word "asilomar" is Spanish for refuge by the sea. Phoebe Hearst had donated thirty acres near the ocean for the members to have a place where they could hold conferences and retreats. Morgan designed several buildings for Asilomar, but the most impressive structure was Merrill Hall. Completed in 1928, Merrill Hall could seat a thousand spectators. Constructed of local stone and wood, the structure was intended by Morgan to blend in with the natural pines and redwoods on the site. Inside the hall, she had seashells and seahorses painted on the auditorium's walls to suggest the nearby ocean. She also designed a chapel, a lodge, a dining facility, and a swimming pool for Asilomar. The Asilomar Complex was still in active use through the early 1990's and was designated a California State Monument.

After Asilomar, Julia Morgan received many commissions from the YWCA. She designed twenty-three YWCA facilities, most located in California. Her trademark in these buildings was her abundant use of light. The Oakland and San Jose YWCAs, for example, had long skylights over their pools which allowed the sun to shine in. The Oakland YWCA also had an open courtyard in the center of the building. This design provided the tenants with both ample sunlight and a view of the outdoors. Morgan wanted the young residents to feel as comfortable as possible in their limited quarters.

By 1917, Morgan's business was flourishing. She was wealthy and well-respected in her field. She had a spacious office in the prestigious Fairmont Hotel. Julia Morgan had not forgotten, however, how difficult it had been for her to succeed in a profession dominated by men. She helped other women who wanted to become architects by training them in her own office. In fact, nearly half of her office staff were women. Employing so many women was very unusual during that era. Not many woman had a career outside the home. Some of her trainees attended college while working at her office, and she generously paid their tuition. A few of these young hopefuls completed their degrees and established offices of their own.

In 1919, Phoebe Hearst died, leaving her entire estate to her son, William Randolph Hearst. Hearst wanted to build a memorial to his mother and fill it with precious artworks that he had collected from all over the world. He chose a rocky hilltop site with a magnificent view of the Pacific Ocean, about two hundred miles from San Francisco. Hearst commissioned Julia Morgan to design the memorial. Morgan began her task by building a five-mile road up to the estate, which was named San Simeon. The road was needed to transport water and supplies. She then designed and constructed small homes for the workers. Finally, she presented a completed plan for the structure to Hearst, and he approved it. In 1922, however, before the structure was completed, Hearst presented Morgan with a new plan. He wanted her to design three small guest houses, one large building, a swimming pool, and a rose garden. Excited by the architectural challenge, she accepted Hearst's plan.

Julia Morgan designed the estate's largest building in a mixture of Gothic, Italian, and Spanish architectural styles. Work began on the building in 1922 and took nearly twenty years to complete. The structure has tall twin towers with a brilliant white stone exterior. Underneath the stone facade is Morgan's favorite building material—reinforced concrete. Hearst named the magnificent structure "Casa Grande," which is Spanish for "grand house." Inside the building are a private film theater and a dining room that seats thirty people. Hearst filled Casa Grande's rooms with rare artworks. The largest room in the building, for example, contains a sixteenth century tapestry once owned by European kings. The library holds priceless Greek pottery from the third and eighth centuries B.C.E. Hearst's bedroom contains rare Italian paintings, including the "Madonna and Child" by Segna da Bonaventura. The wondrous artworks displayed in Casa Grande are too numerous to describe. Awed by Casa Grande's spacious grandeur, early guests referred to it as the "Hearst Castle," the name by which it is still internationally known.

By 1935, the San Simeon estate contained a total of 129 rooms: fifty-eight bedrooms, forty-nine baths, eighteen sitting rooms, two kitchens, and two libraries.

Morgan also designed two wondrous pools. The outdoor pool is called the Neptune pool, and the indoor pool is known as the Roman pool. The Neptune pool is a splendid example of engineering expertise and classic beauty. It is made of green and white Vermont marble that shines brilliantly in the California sun. It holds an amazing 345,000 gallons of water. On one side of the pool stands a Roman temple that Hearst had imported from Rome. The Neptune pool is situated on the side of a steep hill, and one corner of the pool juts out beyond the supporting ground. This part of the pool is held up by reinforced concrete beams and has withstood the damaging effects of earthquakes. The Neptune pool was one of Morgan's greatest engineering triumphs. The Roman pool is made of shiny blue tiles outlined in real gold. Surrounding the indoor pool are alabaster lamps that cast a soft glow on the water. Adjacent to the pool is a small wading pool designed to imitate a classic Roman bath. The Roman pool is located beneath the estate's tennis courts. Building the Roman pool in this location was quite an engineering challenge for her, but the pool's design was a complete success.

By 1936, Hearst had spent nearly $8 million on San Simeon, but it still was not complete. By 1945, he ran out of money and was unable to continue construction at San Simeon. Both wings of Casa Grande remained unfinished, as did the patio walls and much of the landscaping. Not long after the work stopped at San Simeon, Julia Morgan became ill, suffering a series of small strokes in the early 1950's. She died in 1957 at the age of eighty-five. Designing and building the Hearst Castle represented the peak of Morgan's architectural career. The state of California ultimately took over the ownership of San Simeon and declared it a historical monument. Every day, thousands of visitors tour Casa Grande and marvel at her splendid work.

Summary

Julia Morgan was a bold woman who achieved great success in an era dominated by men. She was the first woman to receive a degree in engineering from the University of California at Berkeley. Following that triumph, Julia was awarded a degree in architecture from the prestigious École des Beaux-Arts in France. It took Morgan three years just to be admitted to this previously all-male school. Once she had established her own office, she became the first woman to train other women in her field. She also provided her most talented trainees with college tuition. Morgan was ambitious and worked hard in her profession. She accepted more than a hundred building commissions in the years immediately after the San Francisco earthquake. Among her San Francisco commissions, she is most noted for her fine renovation of the Fairmont Hotel. This project gained for her the universal respect of her colleagues. Indeed, Morgan had a busy career during a time when most women stayed at home and reared their children.

Julia Morgan once said, "[My] buildings will be my legacy." An innovative architect, she was among the first to use reinforced concrete successfully. She introduced her American colleagues to this superior new building material through her use of it in the Mills College Bell Tower. This construction material has been especially important because it is more resistant to earthquakes.

In addition, Morgan had innovative design ideas for her buildings. The Asilomar YWCA, for example, is built with natural pine and redwood to blend with its natural environment. The rooms of Asilomar's Merrill Hall are decorated with a seascape motif that brings a touch of the nearby ocean to the building's interior. Besides Asilomar, Morgan designed ten other YWCAs. In these structures, she was concerned with providing ample light for the tenants. She accomplished this by including skylights, courtyards, and balconies in her designs.

San Simeon stands as Julia Morgan's most prestigious accomplishment. Stunning and grand, it is one of the world's most visited architectural sites. She spent twenty-six years designing and building San Simeon, and this magnificent estate preserves her memory and assures her place in history.

Bibliography

Boutelle, Sara Holmes. *Julia Morgan, Architect*. New York: Abbeville Press, 1988. A well-researched volume on Morgan's life and career. Contains many fine photographs of Morgan's buildings and a list of all structures known to have been built by her.

James, Cary. *Julia Morgan*. New York: Chelsea House, 1990. Examines Julia's life and career from a feminist point of view. Includes some poignant childhood photographs of Julia.

Longstreth, Richard. *Julia Morgan, Architect*. Berkeley, Calif.: Berkeley Architectural Heritage Association, 1977. This small book summarizes Morgan's early career and presents an illuminating discussion of her talents.

Wadsworth, Ginger. *Julia Morgan: Architect of Dreams*. Minneapolis, Minn.: Lerner, 1990. Written for young readers, this book presents a fine account of Julia's life, especially her early years. Contains many photographs of Julia and her work.

Winslow, Carleton, et al. *The Enchanted Hill: The Story of Hearst Castle at San Simeon*. Millbrae, Calif.: Celestial Arts, 1980. This book traces the development of the San Simeon estate. Includes many color photographs of Morgan's buildings and Hearst's artworks.

Pamela Kett-O'Connor

TONI MORRISON

Born: February 18, 1931; Lorain, Ohio

Area of Achievement: Literature

Contribution: Morrison was the first African American woman to win the Nobel Prize in Literature. Her work includes some of the most engaging contributions to American literature in the last hundred years.

Early Life

Toni Morrison was born Chloe Anthony Wofford in Lorain, Ohio, on February 18, 1931. She was the second of four children born to George Wofford and Ramah Willis Wofford. Her father's occupations included car washing, steel mill welding, road construction, and shipyard work, which typified the eclectic labor lifestyle of African American men living during the Great Depression of the late 1920's and 1930's. Her mother worked at home and sang in church. Both parents had strong Southern roots. Morrison's father was from Georgia and had vivid memories of racial violence in his childhood, while her mother's parents were part of the migration of African Americans from Alabama, via Kentucky, who sought to find a better life in the North.

Morrison's parents taught her much about understanding racism and growing up in predominantly white America. Her father was not very optimistic about the capacity of whites to transcend their bigotry toward blacks and remained acutely untrusting of all white people. Her mother's judgment about whites was less pessimistic, although she adhered to the thinking that strength and hope in the black community had to be secured from within that community and not from without. These community values—values of the village—have become the cornerstone of Morrison's literary and political thinking. Her focus is consistently directed within the black community, a focus that reflects her confidence in the tangible culture of black America and its crucial role in shaping strong and talented people.

In her childhood, Morrison's eclectic literary tastes introduced her to such literary works as Gustave Flaubert's *Madame Bovary* and the works of Leo Tolstoy, Fyodor Dostoevski, and Jane Austen. Morrison was quite aware of the disparity that existed between the largely white worlds of these works and her own black female experience. Her reading enabled her to understand the value of cultural specificity in literature and the universality of the particular. It also demonstrated that her own culture, values, dreams, and feelings were not being represented in the literature she was reading. In many ways, her movement toward writing fiction was spurred by a need to redress what she felt was a woeful silence about black experience in the literature she read.

After completing high school in Lorain, Morrison went on to receive her B.A. from Howard University. She became involved with theater and had the opportunity to travel through the South performing before black audiences. Those trips gave her a better understanding of the geographical reality of the black American experience, a grounding that would be reproduced in her fiction. In 1953, she went on to Cornell University, where she completed her master's degree, studying suicide in the work of William Faulkner and Virginia Woolf. These writers were fitting figures against which she could react as a writer. Faulkner, because of his white vision of the Southern experience, and Woolf, because of her white treatment of the female experience in a male-dominated world, provided Morrison with models upon which she would later improvise.

Morrison taught at Texas Southern University for two years and then taught at Howard. There she honed her political views on black America, arguing against the current desegregation rhetoric by suggesting that blacks needed greater economic independence and needed to be wary of distorting their own culture and values through assimilation.

At Howard she married Harold Morrison, a Jamaican architect with whom she had two sons. The marriage was not a positive experience for Morrison; it left her feeling powerless and unsatisfied. She left Howard in 1964, divorced her husband, and assumed a post at Random House in New York City as an editor. Morrison continued her teaching career despite her intense work with Random House as a senior editor for so many years. She has taught at Yale University, Bard College, the State University of New York campuses at Purchase and Albany, and Princeton University.

Life's Work

In 1993, Toni Morrison was awarded the Nobel Prize in Literature in recognition of her achievements as a novelist of outstanding talent. The award represented the culmination of a series of accolades that have followed Morrison after the publication of each of her six novels. These novels have become classics in American literature and have been the subject of extensive critical study. Morrison has also published remarkably intelligent discussions of her works in numerous interviews and essays. She forces literary critics to reevaluate their innate suspicion of writers who write and speak about their own works. The combination of the novels and Morrison's engaging commentaries produces an insight into the deeply committed psyche and spirit of this woman. Her reviews and critical articles published in *The New York Times* and its *Review of Books* (to which she has been a regular contributor for years) constitute a significant body of critical approaches to literature and culture. Her commitment is to her African American experience, and her goal has been to evolve a literary aesthetic that is intrinsically African and American.

Morrison wrote her first novel, *The Bluest Eye*, during her painful marriage. The instinct to write was shaped by a need to read something with which she could identify. In this regard, Morrison identifies with the discourse of the postcolonial writer who seeks to evolve a voice that will articulate her experience in a way that allows it to overwhelm the domination of the culture of the colonizer. In *The Bluest Eye*, Morrison deftly treats the issues of identity and race with language and poetics that echo the writing of Frantz Fanon. At the core of the novel is the psychological trauma of Pecola, a black girl's experience of her racial identity in a predominantly white society. Her desire to have blue eyes represents the painful refutation of her own sense of self-worth as a black child. The novel is posited as a parable—a tale that painfully explores issues of incest, maturation, friendship, racism, and sexual violence through poetic language that is at once simple and startlingly complex. Morrison's achievement with this first novel was to contribute a series of vivid images and literary insights (complete with their paradoxes and complexities) to the raging debate around the Black Power movement of the late 1960's. Morrison provided a grounding for these ideas.

Her commitment to the black experience continued in her second novel *Sula* (1973), in which she makes the community that she describes a living character. In this community, the individuals are distinctive and complex. They range from the schizophrenic war veteran Shadrack to the doggedly independent and mysteriously explosive Eva, a virtual matriarch who commits an act of violence in the work. The central, character, Sula, is posited as a dangerous figure. She does not fit easy stereotypes but is, ultimately, associated with evil. Many black critics appear to share the view that *Sula* is one of Morrison's best works because of its deconstruction and reconstruction of myths surrounding motherhood, race, gender, and class in American society.

Morrison's third novel, *Song of Solomon* (1977), has a male protagonist, Macon, or "Milkman," who embarks on a journey South to discover a lost family treasure. His mammon-centered quest becomes a quest for self-discovery and a discovery of his ancestry. Morrison structures this narrative around a series of folktales. The work climaxes in the dramatic and magical flight of Macon—a flight associated with the African slave's narrative of escape from the drudgery of slavery, which has been passed down through African American culture. *Song of Solomon* established Morrison's reputation as a writer. The work was awarded the National Book Critics' Circle Award and the National Book Award for best novel. Critics and reviewers commended the work for its narrative force and its complex examination of the history of the African American community.

In *Tar Baby* (1981), her fourth novel, Morrison expands her geographical boundaries, setting part of the novel in a fictional Caribbean island. The novel is a complex treatment of theories of sexuality and race that is couched in the African folktale of the "tar-baby." Morrison also includes in this text some examination of the traditions of black rebellions, as demonstrated in the Maroon lifestyle of Caribbean blacks during slavery.

In 1987, Morrison published *Beloved*, a frightening narrative about a slave woman who murders her child to prevent the child from becoming a slave. This horrifying act becomes a challenge for Morrison, who tries to articulate the realities that could make such an act possible. *Beloved* is layered with images and ideas that demonstrate Morrison's commitment to using actual historical "texts" as the basis for her consistently mythic approach to fiction writing. *Beloved* was awarded the Pulitzer Prize in 1988. In this work, as in all her novels, Morrison demonstrates a desire to speak to her own community or from that community. Morrison bluntly states that she writes for a black audience because she is writing for the village.

She demonstrates this trend most vividly in her novel *Jazz* (1992), in which she uses the most fascinating elements of this African American music form to shape her work. In *Jazz*, which is set in the 1920's during the heyday of jazz music and black innovation in the arts, Morrison applies the discipline and classical grounding of the music, its capacity to evoke the blues-like lament of black experience and history, and its improvisational nature to create a novel that is not explicitly about jazz music but is in fact jazz. The Nobel Prize in Literature was awarded to Morrison largely on the strength of this, her sixth novel.

Summary

Toni Morrison has done in her fiction writing what August Wilson has achieved in drama since the 1970's. These writers share the distinction of providing American literature with an insight into the dignity and richness of African American culture in a manner that both chronicles the history of this culture and celebrates its uniquely brilliant ethos through the use of language, folk forms, and narrative traditions. As a commentator on her own work, Morrison has brilliantly analyzed her lyrical sensibility and has managed to contextualize the experience of the African American artist in American literature. Her work represents possibility and legitimizes the inclination of African American artists to delve into the African American experience without fear of being deemed irrelevant, inaccessible, or parochial. She has also demonstrated this commitment in her editorial work. Her crucial role in the publication of Middleton Harris' *The Black Book* (1974) demonstrates her concern for preserving images of African culture in America's collective consciousness.

Apart from her talent as an artist, Morrison brings an intensely political engagement to her art. She constantly speaks of the irrelevance of work that is not political. Politics, for her, embraces the elements of relevance, accountability, and truth. She is a leading voice among African American women writers who are not afraid to emphasize their political discourse. Others who share this ethos and who speak of Morrison's leadership in this regard include Toni Cade Bambara, Ntozake Shange, Alice Walker, and Maya Angelou.

Morrison has worked as a teacher and an editor for most of her adult life, and she continues to bring these skills to bear on her own work. She is a committed defender of the rights of women and speaks up against injustices against women. More important, she has supplied intelligent and cogent criticism of the white feminist movement from the perspective of an African American woman.

Bibliography

Bell, Roseann P., Betty J. Parker, and Beverly Guy-Sheftall, eds. *Sturdy Black Bridges: Visions of Black Women in Literature*. Garden City, N.Y.: Anchor Press, 1979. An eclectic compilation of critical essays, prose pieces, and creative work from Africa and the African diaspora which places Morrison squarely and comfortably in the evolving milieu of writers whose roots are in Africa.

Christian, Barbara. *Black Feminist Criticism: Perspectives on Black Women Writers*. New York: Pergamon Press: 1985. A wide-ranging examination of black women's writing which contains an intelligent examination of the politics of Toni Morrison's early works.

Evans, Mari, ed. *Black Women Writers, 1950-1980: A Critical Evaluation*. Garden City, N.Y.: Anchor Press/Doubleday, 1984. Contains Morrison's seminal essay "Rootedness: The Ancestor as Foundation," as well as several insightful critical discussions of Morrison's writing.

Ruas, Charles. *Conversations with American Writers*. New York: Alfred A. Knopf, 1984. Contains an enlightening interview with Morrison in which she defines her place in American letters.

Tate, Claudia, ed. *Black Women Writers at Work*. New York: Continuum, 1983. This book is made up of interviews with Morrison and other black women writers. The Morrison interview contains some of her most cogent and forthright expressions of her commitment to politics in writing and a black or Afrocentric aesthetic.

Wilentz, Gay. *Binding Cultures: Black Women Writers in Africa and the Diaspora*. Bloomington: Indiana University Press, 1992. Wilentz writes informatively about Morrison's use of African folklore and folk patterns in the generation of her literary work.

Kwame Dawes

GRANDMA MOSES

Born: September 7, 1860; Washington County, near Greenwich, New York
Died: December 13, 1961; Hoosick Falls, New York
Area of Achievement: Art
Contribution: A self-taught artist, Grandma Moses developed a distinctive style of painting, a form of Primitivism also referred to as naïve art or folk art.

Early Life

Anna Mary Robertson, of Scotch-Irish descent, was born on September 7, 1860, on a farm in Washington County, in eastern New York. Her parents were Russell King Robertson, a flax grower, and Margaret Shannahan. Anna Mary was the third of ten children. Her parents called her Sissy, her siblings, Molly, and her husband, Mary, but to the world she was known as Grandma Moses.

In her autobiography, she described the pleasures of her childhood and the work on the farm. Her memories of these happy days, as she called them, were the resources upon which she drew for her art. She learned early to express herself in a creative way. She remembered how her father liked to see his children occupy themselves with drawing. He would buy large sheets of white blank newspaper that cost only a penny. Paper was cheaper than candy and lasted longer.

Her school days were limited. At the age of twelve, Anna Mary left home to earn her living as a hired girl, working neighborhood farms for the next fifteen years. In November of 1887, she married Thomas Salmon Moses, a hired man who worked on the same farm. On their wedding day, they left New York to settle on a dairy farm in Staunton, Virginia. They had ten children, only five of whom survived.

In December, 1905, the family returned to eastern New York and bought a farm at Eagle Bridge. For the next twenty-two years, Anna Mary's main occupation was to work on the farm, care for the family, and keep up their house. On one occasion, she was wallpapering the parlor when she ran out of paper. Her solution became her first known painting. She applied some white paper to the empty space and painted a landscape, the *Fireboard* (1918). It is housed in the Bennington Museum.

When her husband died in 1927, her youngest son, Hugh, and daughter-in-law Dorothy took over the farm. She now had fewer responsibilities. She enjoyed embroidery, creating worsted yarn landscape pictures that she composed herself. When her rheumatism made embroidering difficult, she turned to painting. These were mainly done for amusement and given as gifts to friends. Sometimes she sold a few with her homemade preserves and jams in the Women's Exchange in the W. D. Thomas Pharmacy in Hoosick Falls.

Life's Work

The turning point in Grandma Moses' artistic career came in 1938. Louis J. Caldor, an art collector and engineer, is credited with discovering her talent. He had stopped in Hoosick Falls while on vacation. As he walked by the Thomas Pharmacy, he noticed the Moses paintings in the window. He bought three and inquired where he could buy more. The prices were reasonable, usually between $3 and $5. Moses priced her paintings according to size. When Caldor left for New York the next day, he had an additional ten pictures, some painted and some embroidered in yarn.

The subjects of Moses' paintings were memories of scenes and events she knew well. Landscape paintings of the four seasons dominate: white for winter paintings, light green for spring, deep green for summer, and brown and yellow for fall. Her early paintings were strongly influenced by illustrations, such as Currier and Ives lithographs, which she found in magazines. Sometimes she cut out figures that she moved around to find a composition that pleased her. Her usual practice was to work from memory, without a preliminary sketch.

Caldor tried for a year to interest someone in the Moses pictures. When he heard about the exhibition "Contemporary Unknown American Painters" at the Museum of Modern Art, New York City, from October 18 to November 18, 1939, Caldor entered three paintings: *Home*, *In the Maple Sugar Days*, and *The First Automobile*.

In 1940, these paintings were included in the artist's first solo exhibition. Caldor had finally located an art dealer, Otto Kallir, who was interested in folk art and who agreed to arrange an exhibition. Kallir selected thirty-three paintings and one worsted picture. The exhibition "What a Farm Wife Painted" was held at Kallir's gallery, St. Etienne, in New York, from October 9 to October 31, 1940. The artist, who had just turned eighty, did not come to the opening; as she said, she knew all the paintings.

An art critic in the *New York Herald Tribune*, on October 8, 1940, noted that in Washington County the artist was known as Grandma Moses. This was the first time the name appeared in print.

The reaction to her work was overwhelmingly positive. Requests came from everywhere for her paintings, in the beginning mainly for copies. This explains why so many paintings have the same or similar names, such as *Sugaring Off* or *Turkey Hunt*.

Before the exhibition closed, plans were under way for the next exhibition. The Gimbels Department Store in New York City invited Grandma Moses to show her work from November 14 to November 25, 1940. She was also asked to attend the opening. She accepted and appeared with complete self-confidence before an audience of more than four hundred people.

Now began a long series of exhibitions in the United States, including the New York State Art Show, where *The Old Oaken Bucket* (1941) received the State Prize. Her works were also shown abroad, first in 1949 in Canada and then in traveling exhibitions to Europe. In Grandma Moses' lifetime, her paintings were shown in about eighty exhibitions.

Grandma Moses' reputation continued to grow as she received other honors. On May 14, 1949, she accepted the Achievement Award of the Women's National Press Club in Washington, D.C., and received a standing ovation from seven hundred dinner guests when she entered the hall. President Harry S Truman presented the award to her and five other women, including Eleanor Roosevelt. The president, who was much impressed by Grandma Moses and her lively conversation, arranged to meet her the next day at Blair House. Later, Grandma Moses' mentor and friend Otto Kallir offered the White House her painting *July Fourth* (1951).

More recognition came to Grandma Moses. She was the recipient of two honorary doctorate degrees: in 1949, from Russell Sage College, Troy, New York, and, in 1951, from the Moore Institute of Art, Philadelphia. A documentary film about her, completed in 1950, received a Certificate of Nomination for Award from the Academy of Motion Picture Arts and Sciences. Edward R. Murrow, a well-known broadcast commentator, interviewed her for the CBS *See It Now* television series. The interview aired on June 29, 1955.

In the film, Grandma Moses explained and demonstrated her work method. Neither a heat wave nor the hot camera lights bothered the almost ninety-five-year-old artist. The CBS film crew followed the creation of a painting from the beginning to the end. The subject that Grandma Moses chose was one of her favorites: a sugaring-off scene.

She selected a Masonite board. With a broad house painter's brush, she applied flat white paint for the ground. When the surface was dry, she penciled in the horizon to see how high it would be. Then she indicated trees, bushes, and houses. Her painting began with the sky. A winter sky, she explained to the camera crew. She worked steadily, occasionally closing her eyes as if to conjure up the scene in her mind. Sometimes she put a dab of bright red or blue on the board. This would soon turn into a recognizable figure. When she finished painting the white snow, she sprinkled glitter over it, ignoring those who said that glitter was inappropriate for a painting. She argued that anyone who had seen snow in sunlight knew it glittered.

One exception from her practice to paint only from memory was the painting of the *Eisenhower Farm* (1956). To honor President Eisenhower on the anniversary of his inauguration, the president's cabinet wanted to give him a Grandma Moses painting. Working from numerous photographs of the farm, she accomplished her task to the president's satisfaction. She was paid $1,000, the largest amount she ever received for a painting.

Grandma Moses completed almost 1,600 paintings, of which some twenty-five were done after her one-hundredth birthday. After she entered a nursing home in July of 1961, she was not allowed to paint. This was a great disappointment to her. Her death, on December 13, 1961, was announced on all radio networks and reported on the front pages of newspapers nationwide.

The Bennington Museum in Bennington, Vermont, holds the largest public collection of Grandma Moses' work. The old schoolhouse from Eagle Bridge, now moved to the museum grounds, exhibits memorabilia from her life.

Summary

Grandma Moses, a talented untrained artist, created a unique style of painting. Unlike those of most nonacademic artists, especially in the nineteenth century, her artistic career was successful. She received international fame during her lifetime and furthered the cause of nonacademic art in both the United States and Europe. She helped to increase critical appreciation and popular acceptance of primitive, or naïve, art, the genre to which her works are usually thought to belong. In her art, she celebrated the virtues of American rural life, and through her example she taught thousands of people the value of a simple and uncomplicated manner of living. At an age in life when most people are retired, she started to work professionally and thereby became an inspiration to senior citizens. She demonstrated that age need not be a hindrance to a fulfilled life. In connection with Senior Citizens Month, in May of 1969, honoring all older Americans, the U.S. government issued a stamp to commemorate Grandma Moses, a distinction given to few artists. The commemorative stamp depicts a detail of *July Fourth*, 1951, the painting that hangs in the White House, Washington, D.C. Interest in Grandma Moses has not declined. In 1989, Cloris Leachman played Grandma Moses in a play, *American Primitive*, covering the years from 1905, when Grandma Moses moved back to New York, until 1960. The play, which was on tour from April 26 to July 9, 1989, went to fourteen major cities across the country.

Bibliography

Biracree, Tom. *Grandma Moses: Painter*. American Women of Achievement Series. New York: Chelsea House, 1989. With an introduction by Matina S. Horner, president of Radcliffe College, the book gives a clear account of the artist's life and career. It has a good selection of black-and-white photographs and eight pages of color reproductions, and it should be useful to high school students as well as to general readers.

Kallir, Jane. *Grandma Moses, The Artist Behind the Myth*. New York: C. N. Potter, 1982. The writer, granddaughter of Otto Kallir, see below, discusses several other nonacademic artists contemporary with Grandma Moses, such as John Kane and Joseph Pickett. Describes Grandma Moses' personal growth and artistic development and notes that the artist did not adopt any established style but invented her own.

Kallir, Otto. *Grandma Moses*. New York: Harry R. Abrams, 1973. This is the major work on Grandma Moses. It contains valuable biographical information and a catalog of all of her nearly 1,600 paintings, her worsted pictures, and her tiles. The book includes 253 large illustrations, of which 135 are in color, plus 1,203 documentary illustrations.

____________, ed. *Grandma Moses: American Primitive*. Introduction by Louis Bromfield. New York: Doubleday, 1947. Grandma Moses' autobiographical comments, reproduced in her own handwriting, accompany the forty reproductions (two in color) of her paintings. Gives a clear description of how an untrained person came to take up painting.

Moses, Anna Mary (Robertson). *Grandma Moses: My Life's History*. Edited by Otto Kallir. New York: Harper & Row, 1952. Encouraged by Kallir, Grandma Moses wrote several autobiographical sketches focusing on her early childhood and her married years. Includes photographs and reproductions of sixteen paintings in color.

Oneal, Zibby. *Grandma Moses: Painter of Rural America.* Women of Our Time Series. New York: Viking, 1986. A brief (58 pages), illustrated, very readable text written to interest children seven to eleven years of age. Focuses on Grandma Moses' country childhood and hard work as a farm wife. She is presented as an independent woman who found the time to be creative.

Elvy Setterqvist O'Brien

BELLE MOSKOWITZ

Born: October 5, 1877; New York, New York
Died: January 2, 1933; New York, New York
Areas of Achievement: Social reform and government and politics
Contribution: A social reformer in the early 1900's, Moskowitz became the most politically influential woman in the United States when she served New York governor and 1928 presidential candidate Al Smith as a close adviser.

Early Life

Belle Lindner was born in New York City on October 5, 1877, the daughter of Isador Lindner, a watchmaker, and Esther Freyer Lindner, both immigrants from the northeastern corner of Germany known as East Prussia. Belle was the sixth of seven children, but three of her older siblings had died in infancy. Her parents, who owned their own home at Third Avenue and 127th Street in Harlem, then a suburban neighborhood, removed Belle from the city's overcrowded schools at age fourteen so she could attend Horace Mann, a laboratory school run by faculty from Teachers College at Columbia University. In 1894, Belle entered Teachers College herself, but left after a year to take private drama lessons. With a strong voice and expressive ability, she excelled in dramatic readings and gave private lessons in elocution and drama. Although the most familiar pictures of Belle show her as a stout, middle-aged woman, in her twenties she was slender and unusually attractive. Her drama instructor encouraged her to seek a career on the stage, but her parents objected that the theatrical world was not suitable for a virtuous young woman.

As a young woman, Belle had participated in welfare activities provided by Temple Israel, where the Lindners worshiped. In 1900, she took up social work at the Educational Alliance, a settlement directed by prosperous American Jews of German ancestry for the benefit of the impoverished Jewish immigrants from Eastern Europe then crowding into New York and other cities in the United States. Belle lived at the Alliance for three years, during which time she directed the settlement's program of exhibits and entertainment and devoted particular attention to children's drama.

Life's Work

In 1903, Belle Lindner left the Alliance to marry Charles Israels, an architect who had done volunteer work there. Although she is best known as Belle Moskowitz (the family name of her second husband, Henry Moskowitz), Belle made her initial professional reputation as Belle Israels. To supplement her new husband's uncertain income, she began to work writing pamphlets and other publications for the United Hebrew Charities. She used the extra money to hire a nurse for her first-born child and to pursue her interests in social reform. Charles Israels was supportive of his wife's activities.

In 1903, Belle Israels joined the New York Section of the Council of Jewish Women, an organization committed both to the study of Judaism and to social service.

Israels gave special attention to the needs of delinquent girls. Although she held traditional moral views and opposed premarital sex, Israels did not condemn pregnant teenagers and young unmarried women out of hand. Rather, she helped raise the money to operate the Lakeview Home for Girls, where an unwed mother could stay and learn a skill that would allow her to keep and support a child.

Israels also found rewards from her association with the New York State Conference of Charities and Corrections. Drawing on her experience at the Educational Alliance, she organized exhibits for the conference that focused on such concerns as the prevention of tuberculosis, the need for legislation to protect children in the work force, the funding of parks and playgrounds, and the improvement of housing codes.

Between 1908 and 1913, Israels put much effort into the growing movement to reform dance halls through legislation. Music and dancing have often been at the center of social controversy, from the rap of the 1990's back to the rock and roll of the 1950's and before that to jazz. Prior to World War I, new dances such as the bunny hug, the grizzly bear, and the tango were attracting concerned comment, since they featured close embraces between the partners and movements that were considered unseemly. The tango, an import from Argentina, raised many eyebrows with its dips and sways.

Israels' work with teenage mothers had made her familiar with data on the use of alcohol and the prevalence of other improper behavior at the dance halls that were then popular among working-class girls. Israels was sympathetic to their need for recreation, but she also wished to establish certain controls over individual behavior. Working initially through the Committee on Amusements that she had organized among members of the Council of Jewish Women, Israels conducted an investigation of dance halls, publicized the results of the study, and then attempted to mobilize public opinion to secure the enactment of regulatory legislation. Her methods and concerns were common among Progressive reformers.

Israels and her fellow reformers hoped to secure the enactment of a licensing law that would curtail the sale of liquor at dance halls. She also attempted to raise funds to operate model dance halls where weapons would be checked at the door and respectable dances such as the polka, the jig, and the new Austrian glide popularized. Youngsters might then forget their enthusiasm for the more outrageous dances such as the tango and the turkey trot. Although several laws of the sort Israels favored were enacted, enforcement was often lax, parents seemed unconcerned, and teens resented controls. The ban on the sale of liquor was, however, widely accepted.

Although she was an active reformer, Israels' first commitment was to her family. Between 1904 and 1911, she gave birth four times (the last child died at birth). Widowed in 1911, Israels had three children to rear and only a modest legacy with which to support her family. She therefore turned to full-time work, writing "how-to" articles for various women's magazines and in 1912 taking the position of commercial recreation secretary for the Playground and Recreation Association of America.

For several years, Israels also worked in the labor department of the Dress and Waist Manufacturers' Association (DWMA), an organization of some three dozen manufacturers of clothing that constituted a major employer of women in the New York area. Her task was to help manage and refine a grievance procedure to curtail the strife that had bedeviled labor-management relations in the dress and shirtwaist business. These difficulties had been punctuated by the disastrous Triangle Shirtwaist Factory Fire of 1911, in which nearly 150 employees had died. The fire had followed a long period of ill will between management and labor. In 1913, Israels was dismissed for supposedly being excessively sympathetic to the side of labor. Relations between the two sides quickly deteriorated, however, and the DWMA asked Israels to take charge of the association's labor policy. Feuding factions of manufacturers and increasingly aggressive labor demands marred her efforts, and, in 1916, her contract was terminated.

By this time Belle Israels had remarried. In 1914, she was married to a longtime acquaintance, Henry Moskowitz, who was equally well known among social workers and Progressive reformers. The Moskowitzes had grown to believe many of the nation's ills could best be solved by political leaders committed to reform. Both Henry and Belle Moskowitz agreed that many sought-after reforms—such as the institution of safety standards in the aftermath of the Triangle Shirtwaist Factory Fire—needed to be codified in law and enforced by state inspectors.

This concern had led Belle to support Theodore Roosevelt's Progressive Party in the 1912 presidential election. She and numerous other reformers believed that Roosevelt had the strongest commitment to social justice of any of the three major presidential candidates. Roosevelt was defeated, but Belle's interest in woman suffrage and other political issues grew.

In 1918, Belle Moskowitz gave her support to Al Smith in the New York gubernatorial contest. In his successful effort to win the governorship, Smith, who had been reared in the lower East Side slums of New York City, had to overcome the liability of a long association with Tammany Hall, New York City's powerful political machine that had frequently been tarred with charges of corruption. Most New York women of the era regarded Smith as just another machine politician. Others, such as Frances Perkins, were impressed by Smith's work in the New York state legislature, where he had done much to secure the enactment of laws governing factory safety. Belle Moskowitz asked Perkins to recommend her for a place in Al Smith's campaign organization.

Moskowitz was placed in charge of the newly established Women's Division of the Smith campaign organization. The division focused on the social concerns of women—health, working conditions in industries where women were employed in large numbers, fire prevention, and woman suffrage. (Women had just gained the franchise in New York, but were still struggling to secure woman suffrage throughout the United States.) Moskowitz was also helpful in broadening Smith's contacts among those professionals who were dubious about his background.

Once elected, Smith increasingly came to rely on Belle Moskowitz and named her executive secretary of the Reconstruction Commission, an agency charged with recommending changes to streamline the state's inefficient administrative structure.

The commission was also expected to deal with employment opportunities, a popular idea at a time when millions of World War I veterans were soon to be discharged from service. Moskowitz's special skills were in publicity, and she showed much imagination in using motion pictures to highlight the commission's efforts.

Although the two were about the same age, Moskowitz seemed to regard Smith as a mother might, hovering near him to guard his image and further the causes for which he fought. Between 1918 and his 1928 campaign for the presidency, Smith won four two-year terms as governor of New York. Smith would have been pleased to appoint Moskowitz to state office, but she preferred to remain an adviser. She aided Smith in writing and revising innumerable articles, speeches, and state messages and represented him in many meetings with influential groups of New Yorkers. With men she was self-effacing and disguised her assertiveness; almost invariably they came away from meetings thinking the decisions reached were theirs even though Moskowitz had done much to shape these decisions. With women she was much blunter and also made clear her opposition to the divisive new issue of equal rights. While assisting Smith, Moskowitz also collaborated with her husband in managing a public relations firm, one of the first in that newly established field. Among its clients were private businesses, the Smith campaign organization, and occasionally a public agency such as the Port and Harbor Development Commission.

In 1924, Smith made his first bid for the White House, but was unable to gain his party's nomination. Four years later Smith won the Democratic nomination. In the race for president, however, there were liabilities he could not overcome—his lingering reputation as a machine politician, the fact that he was the first Catholic to seek the presidency, and his well-known dislike for Prohibition, then the law of the land. For perhaps the first time in her association with Smith, Moskowitz herself floundered, unable to discern how best to reach Americans in the South, Midwest, and the West. She was also at a loss to understand how Smith might respond to a vicious whispering campaign that spread stories that he was a drunkard and that he favored legalized prostitution. Even had his campaign been more adroit, many experts believe in hindsight that Smith could not have won the presidency in 1928. With the much admired Herbert Hoover as their standard bearer, the Republicans had too many advantages for Smith or any other Democrat to overcome.

Despite Smith's defeat, Moskowitz hoped to continue her involvement in public service. Through Smith and others, she approached New York's governor-elect, Franklin D. Roosevelt, about securing a place in his administration, perhaps as his personal secretary. According to Frances Perkins, who joined Roosevelt's staff in New York and became the first woman to secure a cabinet position when Roosevelt was inaugurated as president in 1933, Eleanor Roosevelt did much to eliminate any chance Moskowitz had to secure a place in FDR's inner circle. Eleanor Roosevelt had worked cordially with Moskowitz on several occasions and appreciated her abilities, but she reportedly counseled FDR that to appoint Moskowitz as his secretary would mean turning the governorship over to her. Whether the story Perkins related has validity is uncertain. Nevertheless, Roosevelt clearly had pressing reasons of his own to distance himself from the defeated Smith and from Smith's closest advisers.

Rebuffed by Roosevelt, Moskowitz continued to serve Smith. When he opened offices in the new Empire State Building in 1931, the Moskowitzes transferred their own offices there. She worked with her husband on several public relations accounts and assisted Smith, who remained a public figure, with his speeches and in writing his memoirs. Her hopes that Smith might again secure the Democratic presidential nomination in 1932 were thwarted when the party turned to a candidate untainted by defeat, Franklin Roosevelt. Moskowitz died in New York City in 1933.

Summary

Belle Moskowitz had one of the most distinguished careers of any American woman in the first decades of the twentieth century. During her years at the Educational Alliance, she was introduced to many of the era's social concerns and subsequently participated in studies of the crucial issue of factory safety. Her efforts to bring stability to the traditionally bitter management-labor relations in New York's garment industry are also noteworthy. Moskowitz then became increasingly involved in politics.

For a decade she aided Smith who, as governor of New York State, brought about significant improvements in administration, the development of one of the nation's earliest public park systems, and advances in social welfare. Her association with Smith also brought her great personal benefit: By the time he ran for president, she was recognized as the most powerful woman in politics. She did not exercise power on her own, and perhaps it would have been impossible for a woman to do so at that time. She might even have denied that she wanted power; to her, access to Smith meant a chance to bring about reform. Smith turned to the Right after Roosevelt's presidential victory in 1932, but Moskowitz's biographer believes that had Moskowitz lived she would not have accompanied Smith on that political journey. In any event, her career was a remarkable one, studded with accomplishments in social reform, business, and politics.

Bibliography

Caro, Robert A. *The Power Broker: Robert Moses and the Fall of New York*. New York: Alfred A. Knopf, 1974. A decade younger than Moskowitz, Moses was also a member of Smith's inner circle and was subordinate to Moskowitz on the Reconstruction Commission and on other occasions. This massive study shows that Moses often chafed at her leadership.

Cohen, Julius Henry. *They Builded Better Than They Knew*. New York: Julian Messner, 1946. Like other men who knew and worked with Moskowitz, Cohen attributes much of her success in what had been and was still a man's world to "womanly intuition."

Eldot, Paula. *Governor Alfred E. Smith: The Politician as Reformer*. New York: Garland, 1983. The most thorough assessment of Smith's governorship, this study makes clear Moskowitz's contributions to his success.

Hacker, Louis, and Mark D. Hirsch. *Proskauer: His Life and Times*. University: University of Alabama Press, 1978. This biography of Proskauer, an influential New York attorney and jurist, is especially valuable in describing the resentment Tammany leaders, in the early 1900's still mainly Irish in background, felt toward Smith's reliance on Moskowitz, Proskauer, and Robert Moses, all Jewish.

Handlin, Oscar. *Al Smith and His America*. Boston: Little, Brown, 1958. This brief biography of Smith evaluates the New Yorker's place in history as the first Catholic and the first candidate reared in the slums of a major city to run for the presidency.

Josephson, Matthew, and Hannah Josephson. *Al Smith: Hero of the Cities*. Boston: Houghton Mifflin, 1969. Has much to say about Moskowitz. The authors acknowledge that her first great love was Charles Israels, her late husband. They speculate that for Smith she displayed both ambition and "sublimated love."

Perry, Elisabeth Israels. *Belle Moskowitz: Feminine Politics and the Exercise of Power in the Age of Alfred E. Smith*. New York: Oxford University Press, 1987. This fine example of an academic biography was written by Moskowitz's granddaughter. Provides much documentation on Moskowitz's life and career.

Lloyd J. Graybar

LUCRETIA MOTT

Born: January 3, 1793; Nantucket, Massachusetts
Died: November 11, 1880; near Philadelphia, Pennsylvania
Areas of Achievement: Social reform and women's rights
Contribution: An eloquent advocate of the abolition of slavery and of equality for women, Mott devoted her life to working toward these goals.

Early Life

Lucretia Coffin was the daughter of the master of a whaling vessel. Her parents, Thomas and Anna Folger Coffin, were hard-working Quakers. Although public education was not available, Lucretia learned to read and write as a young child, probably attending Quaker schools. In 1804, Thomas Coffin, who had lost his ship, moved the family to Boston, where he became a successful merchant. Here the children could be educated, and when Lucretia showed particular talent, she was sent to Nine Partners Boarding School, a Quaker academy in Southeast New York. She became an academic success, met James Mott—her future husband—and got a lesson in discrimination when she discovered that James was paid five times as much as a woman with the same title at the school.

In 1809, the Coffin family moved to Philadelphia, and James Mott followed, taking a job in the family business. In 1811, James and Lucretia were married. They experienced several years of hard times because of the depression that followed the War of 1812, but eventually they settled in Philadelphia, where James established a successful business. Lucretia, despite having two small children, took a job teaching. Four more children followed, but Mott's son Thomas died in 1817. As the children began to spend time at school and her husband prospered, Mott had time to read many books, including Mary Wollstonecraft's *Vindication of the Rights of Women* (1792), which had a strong influence on her. Mott began to speak in Quaker meetings and in the early 1820's was approved as a Quaker minister.

Life's Work

For Lucretia Mott, faith was always important, and it led her to desire justice for all, including slaves and women. Although she always wanted to avoid controversy, when issues she cared about arose, she was often very outspoken. In the early 1830's, she befriended William Lloyd Garrison, a leading abolitionist who founded the New England Anti-Slavery Society. When women's groups were called for, Mott helped found the Philadelphia Female Anti-Slavery Society and held some office for virtually every year of its existence. Mott was soon a leader in the Anti-Slavery Convention of American Women, and when its 1838 meeting was met by riots and arson in its meeting hall, it was the Mott home at which convention leaders reconvened.

Mott soon found equality an issue within the abolitionist movement. In 1838, the Massachusetts branch of the Anti-Slavery Society gave women the right to vote. A decision on the issue was blocked at a regional meeting, and a debate began at the

1839 national convention. After the five sessions adjourned without a decision, Garrison managed to get agreement that the organization's roll would include all persons, but a number of leading abolitionists were opposed, maintaining that the organization was being diverted from the issue of slavery. In 1840, the British and Foreign Anti-Slavery Society issued invitations for a world convention, and Mott was elected as one of the American delegates. The British group had indicated that women were not wanted, and Mott arrived to find that the credentials of female delegates were not being honored. Despite an angry debate, the decision stood, and Mott had to sit in the visitors' gallery, where she was joined by Garrison and the other American delegates. Mott did not speak at the convention, preferring to defer to proper authority even when it was mistaken.

After the convention Mott traveled in Britain—it was her one trip abroad—and visited such luminaries as Harriet Martineau. In Scotland, it was suggested that she address the Glasgow Emancipation Society, but the directors demurred. The city's Unitarian church, however, welcomed her, and she gave her address there. During this trip, she also began a friendship with Elizabeth Cady Stanton, with whom she would fight discrimination against women. The two were close until Mott's death in 1880.

Mott's attitude about slavery was quite clear: It was unmitigated evil and should be ended forthwith. She rejected any idea of compensation for slave owners as adding to the immorality, and urged abolitionist groups to stop debating the ethical and philosophical implications of the institution—for her, these were settled anyway—and stick to the practical question of ending it. She argued for "free produce"—that is, refusing to conduct any trade in goods produced by slaves—but Northern economic interests in Southern goods and commerce were too large for such a boycott to win many friends even among abolitionists. In theory, she rejected colonization and even flight as solutions to slavery because the numbers who escaped did not even equal the natural increase of the enslaved population. In practice, however, she supported the Underground Railroad, freely opening her home to fugitives. She was an active supporter of many escapees, including Henry "Box" Brown, who had himself nailed into a packing box and shipped to her friend Miller McKim.

In the early years of the 1840's, Mott was often ill. Her husband, however, had become prosperous enough to give up his business so that the family could pursue other interests. The Mott home was known for its hospitality to its many guests, including Garrison, Theodore Parker, Frederick Douglass, and Sojourner Truth. As her health allowed, Mott continued her preaching, mostly at Quaker and Unitarian meetings. Having rejected orthodox Quaker theology in 1827, she faced charges of heresy as well as denunciations for daring, as a woman, to speak in church. Never ruffled, she spoke to hostile audiences—including slave owners—forthrightly and firmly.

Although she never gave up her work toward abolition, in the later 1840's Mott became more and more involved in the crusade for women's rights. In 1845, she made her first public call for woman suffrage in a speech to the Yearly Meeting of Ohio Quakers. Three years later, in an address to the American Anti-Slavery Society entitled "The Law of Progress," she lamented the lack of improvement in the condition of women. It was after this speech that Mott fell in with a suggestion by Elizabeth Cady Stanton that there should be a women's rights convention.

The future stars of the women's movement, Stanton and Susan B. Anthony, were virtually unknown, so the much better known Mott emerged as the person in the public eye at the first Women's Rights Convention, which met at Seneca Falls, New York, July 19 to 20, 1848. Mott and others drew up a Declaration of Sentiments modeled on the Declaration of Independence, but the women were so unsure of themselves that they asked James Mott to preside at their meeting. The convention then debated the Declaration paragraph by paragraph, ultimately passing them all unanimously. Mott had been somewhat reluctant to press the issue of suffrage, but, urged on by Stanton and Frederick Douglass, she agreed to it. In the end, she was the most frequent speaker at Seneca Falls. At a follow-up meeting two weeks later in Rochester, New York, she responded to critics who asserted that the women were ignoring St. Paul's injunction that they be subservient to their husbands by noting that most of the complainers had ignored the saint's advice not to marry. The 1853 convention met in Philadelphia only to be so disrupted by hostile demonstrations that Mott, the presiding officer, was forced to adjourn it. An invitation to move to Cleveland was accepted, and despite some tension, the meeting was completed without interruption.

Although she was beginning to experience some physical decline in the 1850's, Mott made many efforts on behalf of the abolitionist and women's rights crusades. In 1849, she agreed to make a speech to counter the traditional misogynist position taken by Richard Henry Dana during a lecture series in Philadelphia. Her "Discourse on Women," tracing the history of women's achievements and reiterating her position that female inferiority was a function of systematic repression and denial of opportunity, was printed. A second edition appeared in 1869 in response to requests from feminists in England. In the early 1850's, she confronted Horace Mann and the new National Education Association on the issue of equal pay for women teachers, though without much immediate success. She also continued to speak for the abolitionist cause, traveling as far south as Maysville, Kentucky, where, despite some significant hostility, she presented her case for freedom. Although she took no public position on John Brown's raid on Harpers Ferry—Quaker principles of pacifism overrode even the urgency of freeing slaves—she did shelter Mrs. Brown while she was trying to visit her husband in the weeks before his execution.

In 1857, the Mott family moved to Roadside, a comfortable estate between New York and Philadelphia. The move was intended in part to get Lucretia away from the stress of her numerous commitments. Although her health was somewhat restored by rest, she was sixty-four years old and beginning increasingly to feel her age. A pacifist, she was torn by the Civil War, but after the conflict she tried to preserve the antislavery society to support the freedmen. She was also active in the Free Religious Association, which had been formed in 1867 to encourage an end to sectarian strife. She also continued her activities with the Equal Rights Convention.

When that organization began to split in the 1870's, Mott tried vainly to heal the breach. The feminists divided into the National Woman Suffrage Association, led by

Elizabeth Cady Stanton and Susan B. Anthony, and the American Woman Suffrage Association, headed by Lucy Stone and Julia Ward Howe. Mott remained with her longtime friends Stanton and Anthony but deeply regretted the split. Mott's activities decreased steadily throughout the late 1860's and 1870's. She died on November 11, 1880, at Roadside.

Summary

Lucretia Mott was an unusual woman. In an age when most people objected to women ministers, she was an eloquent advocate for her faith. Not only did she speak effectively within Quaker meetings, but she also had the confidence to challenge the leadership on points of theology. Her preaching and erudition won the respect of many, although no woman in the first half of the nineteenth century could have achieved full acceptance in the pulpit. Believing that she was in the right, she was unruffled by criticism and continued to speak as she deemed appropriate.

Mott was less unusual in the ranks of the abolitionists, which included many women, white and black. Nevertheless, her dignified mien and public speaking ability gave her a leadership role. The strength of her conviction led her to take risks, speaking out in the 1830's when the antislavery position was far from popular and going into hostile areas—even the South. She fought diligently for her view that the antislavery forces should insist on total abolition immediately and should use the economic weapon of refusing to trade in products produced by slave labor. Although she was unsuccessful in winning support for the latter position, she provided the abolitionist movement with one of its best examples of idealism and principle.

Faced with serious sexual discrimination within the ranks of the abolitionists, Mott emerged as a champion of women's rights. At a time when most of the eventual champions of the feminist movement were young and unknown, Mott was a respected and respectable leader. If Elizabeth Cady Stanton and Susan B. Anthony, in 1848, could be dismissed as part of a radical fringe, Lucretia Mott could not. As a minister whose knowledge and conviction were well established and as a mainstay of the abolitionist movement, she gave the fledgling women's movement a credibility that would have taken much time and effort to gain without her leadership. She did not live to see the triumph of equal rights for women, but she did much to give the movement the impetus necessary to obtain them.

Bibliography

Burnett, Constance. *Five for Freedom: Lucretia Mott, Elizabeth Cady Stanton, Lucy Stone, Susan B. Anthony, Carrie Chapman Catt*. Reprint. New York: Greenwood Press, 1968. Originally published in 1953, this is an effective and well-written biography that gives a thorough account of Mott's life and career.

Cromwell, Otelia. *Lucretia Mott*. Cambridge, Mass.: Harvard University Press, 1958. A scholarly, well-researched biography that sets Mott's life and activities in the context of nineteenth century America, this work is somewhat lacking in critical analysis of the subject.

Hallowell, Anna. *James and Lucretia Mott: Life and Letters*. 5th ed. Boston: Houghton Mifflin, 1896. An early biography made particularly valuable by the inclusion of correspondence. Oversupportive of the Motts.

Mott, Lucretia. *Lucretia Mott: Her Complete Speeches and Sermons*. Edited by Dana Greene. New York: Edwin Mellen Press, 1980. A convenient source of much of Mott's writing that provides an excellent means of gaining an understanding of her philosophy and ideas.

Stewart, James B. *Holy Warriors: The Abolitionists and American Slavery*. New York: Hill & Wang, 1976. A useful survey of abolitionism that is extremely valuable in setting Mott's work and views in the context of the movement as a whole.

Fred R. van Hartesveldt

SHIRLEY MULDOWNEY

Born: June 19, 1940; Schenectady, New York

Area of Achievement: Sports

Contribution: The first female driver in the male-dominated sport of drag-racing, Shirley "Cha Cha" Muldowney went on to win seventeen National Hot Rod Association titles. Her achievement of three Top Fuel world championships has not been matched by any other driver.

Early Life

Shirley Roque was born in 1940, the daughter of Belgium Benedict "Tex Rock" Roque and his wife, Mae, in a working-class neighborhood in Schenectady, New York. Tex Rock was a boxer, taxi driver, and violinist who taught his young daughter to drive at the age of twelve. These early driving lessons appealed to her more than school, and by the age of fourteen she was drag racing late at night in Schenectady. Drag racing, a high-speed race down a straight track or street against another vehicle, was the sole domain of male drivers and mechanics at that time. Most teenage girls either rode along for support or cheered their boyfriends on from the sidelines. Shirley's involvement as a driver attracted local attention and numerous racing challenges. At the age of fifteen, she met her boyfriend and future husband, Jack Muldowney, a driver and mechanic who soon built her first race car. By the age of sixteen she had dropped out of high school, gotten married to Jack, and begun her racing career. With Jack on her team, she began to acquire a reputation that drew boys and their cars from all over New York to try to beat her time. Shirley acknowledged that the first time she took her own life in her hands, she became aware of the extent of her capabilities. It was this knowledge that propelled her to turn professional in 1959 at the age of nineteen.

Life's Work

Shirley Muldowney was a small woman who, at five feet, four inches and 108 pounds, hardly fit the image most fans had of a tough, fast driving drag racer. In the mostly blue-collar and conservative world of drag racing, Shirley, in her pink racing helmet and halter tops, infuriated and threatened both the male drivers and their fans. Though petite in stature, she was fully capable of controlling a fiberglass "funny car," a race car built to duplicate a street car yet designed to protect the driver within a sturdy steel cage. The funny cars only look like a standard car—they contain a full racing engine in a dragster steel frame. When her sheer daring and courage at high speeds were combined with her husband's superb mechanical skills, they created an ideal racing enterprise. Although she was booed roundly and routinely by spectators and treated as a freak attraction to build audience numbers, Shirley nevertheless became the first and only woman licensed by the National Hot Rod Association (NHRA) to drive a dragster in 1965. By the early 1970's she had won several regional titles, but her divorce from Jack Muldowney in 1972 demanded that she reduce her racing activities in favor of rearing their teenage son. Later that year, however, Shirley Muldowney was approached by drag racer Conrad "Connie" Kalitta, who offered to sell her his backup funny car. Kalitta coined her nickname, "Cha Cha," and booked her successfully at drag racing venues across the country.

In 1973, the thirty-three-year-old Muldowney was in her fourth crash, one that required her to undergo plastic surgery around her eyes. The crash was serious enough to force her to consider quitting funny car racing and move to Top Fuel dragsters. Her decision to change cars established another professional milestone when she became the first woman licensed to drive this high-speed machine. Her Top Fuel car was a twenty-five-foot arrow-shaped car capable of traveling down a quarter-mile track in less than six seconds. The car's 2,500 horsepower engine could attain a speed of 250 miles an hour or more, and required a parachute to slow it down after the finish. The engine ran on a powerful fuel of nitromethane and methanol that completely destroyed the engine, making it necessary to rebuild it after each race.

Acknowledged to be an expert starter by even her most strenuous opponents, Muldowney was considered to be the fastest driver off the starting line. Muldowney considered her small size and killer instinct to be an exceptional advantage in her sport. She was convinced that a light touch helped her swift starts, and she found that her mind cleared when she was pushed and goaded by the crowd or her opponents. She was often quoted as saying she got better when she was mad, not flustered and scattered. When asked why her race cars and helmets were a trademark hot pink, Muldowney replied that she used her gender as a weapon and a nudge to motivate the male drivers. Primping dramatically before a race in front of the male drivers built up a tension she used to inspire fear in her opponents.

Muldowney eventually compiled an impressive racing record, winning seventeen NHRA titles—more than any other driver except Don "Big Daddy" Garlits—and was the only driver ever to win three Top Fuel championships for running the quarter-mile track in less than six seconds. Despite these achievements, she continued to struggle financially in her career. In her best year, 1980, she only cleared $5,000 after expenses. Generally, most race car drivers avoid paying all touring, fuel, transport, and car maintenance expenses by attracting a corporate sponsor. For advertising privileges on the vehicle and crew or driver uniforms, the sponsor will subsidize expenses and provide supplies allowing the driver to pay staff salaries and reap some profits. Muldowney always blamed her difficulty in maintaining a lucrative sponsorship on sexism, but her opponents attributed it to her often fiery personality.

After Twentieth Century-Fox approached her for permission to make a film version of her life from childhood to champion. Muldowney served as creative consultant on the picture, entitled *Heart Like a Wheel.* The film was released in 1983 and starred Bonnie Bedelia as Muldowney and Beau Bridges as her former lover and crew chief, Connie Kalitta. After a miserable initial release, *Heart Like a Wheel* was rereleased as an art film. It was screened at the New York Film Festival, was fairly successful with audiences, and received positive critical reviews. In addition to presenting the pressures and difficulties of the sport authentically, the film also chronicled the story of a woman's search for independence. While the film attracted mass public attention, it did not bring Muldowney the endorsements or broadcasting contracts she had hoped would materialize. Deferring any plans for an early retirement, Muldowney actively continued her racing career.

On June 29, 1984, an inner tube in one of Muldowney's front tires snapped and wrapped around the front wheel spindle of her racer, locking the wheels and causing the car to crash in a destructive 600-foot-rollover on a track in Montreal, Canada. Muldowney suffered a severed right thumb, a partially severed foot, a fractured pelvis, three fractures to her right ankle and leg, torn cartilage in her left knee, an injured neck, and two broken fingers. She spent more than four months in the hospital and accumulated hospital bills in excess of $100,000. Donations, even from her old nemesis, Don Garlits, helped to defray these expenses. She was advised never to race again. Still, she persevered and, after a year of recovery and physical therapy, returned to the track in 1986.

In the wake of her accident, Muldowney and Garlits have shelved the fierce rivalry that raged between them during the 1970's and 1980's. While most of their hostility was publicity hype to sell tickets to "Battle of the Sexes" races, it was rumored that Garlits had a dartboard with Muldowney's picture on it. Muldowney's near-fatal crash in 1984 went a long way to reconcile the opponents. They eventually combined talents to focus on Muldowney's career with Garlits hired as a "special adviser" on her Top Fuel car. In the contemporary drag market, drivers soon needed more than one million dollars to keep a Top Fuel car competitive. Garlits became responsible for running a computer diagnosis center in the pit to help fine tune Muldowney's car.

During her comeback season in 1986, Muldowney established her career-best time of 5.42 seconds, and she continued to rank among the top ten racers in the national standings for her division through 1990. In that year, she was inducted into the Motorsports Hall of Fame of America, and she continued to compete as a Top Fuel drag racer into the early 1990's.

Summary

Shirley Muldowney not only broke speed barriers on the track but also broke barriers that prevented women from participating fully in a male-dominated sport. As the first woman licensed to drive professionally for the National Hot Rod Association, she endured and even seemed to relish the taunts of spectators, who were unused to seeing a woman anywhere outside of the stands. Instead of hiding or ignoring her gender, Muldowney called attention to it with her trademark hot pink equipment and cars and made a point of filing her nails before entering the race. Instead of trying to join in with the men in their own atmosphere, she playfully flaunted a stereotypical feminine image in order to goad her competitors. This playful selling of her femininity stopped, however, when it came to demonstrating her driving ability.

Shirley Muldowney served as an inspiring example to women, particularly those from lower-middle-class or working-class backgrounds, by proving that a woman who was a high-school dropout at sixteen can achieve respect as a professional race car driver and complete a General Equivalency Diploma by age twenty-four. She exemplified the struggles of working single mothers while rearing a child on the road as she worked in a field that had been traditionally dominated by men.

In the area of driver safety, the devastating 1984 accident that nearly ended Muldowney's career resulted in the improvement of the front wheels and tires of later dragsters. A tire-retaining groove became required equipment on the front wheels of any vehicles in NHRA races, and Goodyear even came out with special tubeless tires for use on these cars.

Generally acknowledged to be one of the best drivers of either gender, Muldowney compiled one of the finest records in the sport and achieved a reputation for being unbeatable as a Top Fuel driver off the starting line. She was the first racer of either sex to win the NHRA Top Fuel world championship three times. Muldowney opened the way for other female drivers, but few have been able to achieve either her record or her longevity.

Bibliography

Baechtel, John. "It's What I Do." *Hot Rod*, May, 1986, 60-63. An interview with Muldowney discussing her career, accidents, and the major risks inherent in drag racing.

Duden, Jane. *Shirley Muldowney*. Mankato, Minn.: Crestwood House, 1988. This biography, written for junior high students, focuses on Muldowney's career challenges in a predominantly male field in a simplified style. While the book does not go into much personal detail, it does present highlights of Muldowney's career. Of particular value are the list of Muldowney's awards, records, and racing statistics.

Moses, Sam. "The Best Man for the Job Is a Woman." *Sports Illustrated*, June 22, 1981, 16-25. A lengthy article written early in Muldowney's career highlighting the difficulties she had in succeeding in the male-dominated field.

Vader, J. E. "Two Foes Bury the Hatchet, but Not the Competition." *Sports Illustrated* 71 (September 4, 1989): 22-27. A magazine article discussing the collaboration of Muldowney with retired driver and old rival, Don Garlits. Muldowney has hired Garlits as a special adviser to consult on the modification of her Top Fuel race car. Their long-standing rivalry is documented and the reasons for its demise are listed.

Laurie Dawson

CARRY NATION

Born: November 11, 1846; Garrard County, Kentucky
Died: June 9, 1911; Leavenworth, Kansas
Area of Achievement: Social reform
Contribution: An activist in the temperance and women's rights movements, Nation gained international notoriety by smashing saloons. She demonstrated the strength and place of women in temperance reform.

Early Life

Born to George Moore and Mary Campbell Moore, Carry (written in her illiterate father's hand in the family Bible using this spelling) Amelia Moore grew up in the slave culture of Kentucky. Her father was a prosperous planter and stock trader; her mother suffered from a delusionary mental illness and assumed she was Queen Victoria, demanding the appropriate degree of respect from those around her.

At age ten, Carry was converted at a Campbellite revival, an event that had a profound effect on her spiritual development. Her early secular education was limited because her family moved at least a dozen times between Kentucky, Missouri, and Texas before she was sixteen. She did manage, however, to attend a teacher's college in Missouri, where she earned a teaching certificate.

Her father lost his slaves and land as a result of the Civil War, and took his family back to Missouri, settling in Belton. Carry met and fell in love there with a young army physician, Charles Gloyd. They were married on November 21, 1867; however, because of Gloyd's alcoholism and fierce devotion to the Masonic Lodge, the marriage deteriorated soon after the nuptials. Despite her love for Charles, she never persuaded him to stop drinking, which he did in the company of his fellow Masons, and within two years of their marriage he was dead, leaving Carry with an infant daughter, Charlien, who may have grown up insane, an elderly mother-in-law, and an intense dislike for both alcohol and secret societies. For several years, Carry supported herself, her daughter, and her mother-in-law by teaching in a primary school in Holden, Missouri. In 1877, she married David Nation, an attorney, minister, and editor who was nineteen years her senior. They had little in common, and for Carry it proved to be an unhappy match. They lived for several years in Texas, where Carry supported the family by running a hotel. In 1890, they moved to Medicine Lodge, Kansas, where David became a minister and then left the pulpit to practice law. His practice grew large enough to free Carry from the necessity of supporting the family, and as a result, she became active in the temperance movement as well as in religious and civic reform. Because of her interest in charitable activities, the residents of Medicine Lodge called her Mother Nation. Her second marriage also deteriorated, however, and in 1901 Carry's husband divorced her.

Life's Work

Before David and Carry Nation moved to Kansas, a constitutional amendment adopted in 1880 had made it a dry state. This occurred nearly half a century before the passage of the Eighteenth Amendment and fifty years after the beginning of the temperance movement in the United States. In Kansas, a legal technicality allowed liquor in its original container to be served. Carry, believing that she had a divine mission to stop the drinking of alcoholic beverages, organized a chapter of the Women's Christian Temperance Union (WCTU) with the intention of driving out the "wets" (those who drank). Her first major confrontation took place in 1899, when, in the company of several other WCTU members, she managed through nonviolent means to shut down seven liquor distributors. During the following year, she changed her tactics when she traveled twenty miles by buggy to smash three "joints," or saloons, using rocks and brickbats, in Kiowa, Kansas. Carry rationalized that because those establishments were illegal, they had no protection under the law; therefore, she had the right to destroy them. From Kiowa she went to Wichita, where she used a hatchet to destroy the bar in the Hotel Carey. This venture resulted in several thousand dollars of property damage for the saloon owner and seven weeks in jail for Nation. From there it was on to Enterprise and then the state capital, Topeka, for several days of bar chopping. Each incident earned for her more time in the local jail, usually for disturbing the peace.

Prior to her appearance in Topeka, Nation's activities had been of the hit-and-run variety. She would typically break up a few saloons and then either leave town or go to jail. Realizing that she could not single-handedly close down all the offending liquor establishments in Kansas, she intended to use Topeka as a focal point for an organization that, she hoped, would achieve her goal.

After holding an unsuccessful meeting with the governor of Kansas, Carry Nation set about to organize her mostly feminine supporters into an army of Home Defenders. Led by General Nation, who was ably supported by assistant generals, the force numbered several hundred. Nation accepted numerous speaking engagements to spread her message that the only way to close the joints was to increase the agitation against them. In keeping with her message, she took her Home Defenders on the offensive, smashing the ritzy Senate Saloon. In the melee, Nation, who was often in physical danger, received a nasty cut on the head. Despite the destruction, the bar reopened within hours, selling beer, whiskey, and souvenirs from the wreckage.

Carry Nation's actions exacerbated the split in the temperance movement: on the one hand, between the sexes, and on the other hand, between those who supported such violence as necessary and those who took a more passive and traditional approach to the liquor control issue. Nation helped to focus the issue of prohibition in Kansas. Generally, the Prohibitionists, who represented the more radical fringe, supported her tactics, while the Women's Christian Temperance Union leadership, made up mostly of Republicans or Populists, opposed them. Those who opposed Nation disliked her taking the law into her own hands, and they rejected her argument that the joint owners, being lawbreakers themselves, deserved to be put out of business violently.

Nation supported herself and paid her fines by means of lecturing, stage appearances, and the sale of souvenir miniature silver hatchets. For a time, she earned as much as $300 a week. To help with her finances, she employed a management firm, and she later hired her own manager, Harry C. Turner. Unfortunately, Nation had little business sense, giving away most of her money to the poor and to temperance groups, not all of which were legitimate.

Nation also took on a few publishing ventures to spread the word. At varying times, *The Smasher's Mail*, *The Hatchet*, and *The Home Defender* appeared. While in Topeka, she wrote her autobiography, *The Use and Need of the Life of Carry A. Nation* (1905).

Although she spent the majority of her time in the temperance crusade in Kansas, she did venture to the East Coast, where she visited both Yale and Harvard. Unfortunately, on both occasions she allowed herself to be portrayed as a buffoon, thus adding to the negative image surrounding her. She later toured England, where again her welcome was less than expansive.

Physically, Carry Nation was a large woman. Nearly six feet tall, she weighed approximately 175 pounds and was extremely strong. When she and her minions broke up the Senate Saloon, she lifted the heavy cash register, raised it above her head, and smashed it to the ground.

After less than a decade in the public spotlight, however, her health failed, and she retired to a farm in the Ozark Mountains of Arkansas. She spent the last several months of her life in a Leavenworth, Kansas, hospital and died there on June 9, 1911. After her death, friends erected a monument at her gravesite with the inscription "She hath done what she could."

Summary

Carry Nation's impact is both real and symbolic. She did show the nation that direct action can help to focus attention on a moral issue. When, in 1901, Nation went to speak to the Kansas legislature, she told them that since she was denied the vote, she would have to use a stone, and use the stone (or hatchet, to be more specific) she did. The joints she smashed were not significant in terms of her impact on temperance and prohibition. In fact, at least a few of them reopened within hours or days of her visit. Her impact had to do with her ability to rally support to her cause. She focused attention on the issue of alcohol consumption. Representing the views of a majority of Kansans, she showed them that one individual could make a difference.

Nation also had a significant impact on women's rights. She certainly broke with the traditional roles of woman as wife and mother, although she did fulfill both roles. At a time when few women engaged in public protest, Nation was at the cutting edge of that activity. She opened a home in Kansas City for women who had suffered at the hands of male alcoholics. She determined that her activity had been made necessary by a male-dominated world—as a woman, she did not have access to political power. As time went on, however, Nation appeared to be moving toward nonviolent direct action and away from saloon smashing. The masthead of her newspaper *The Hatchet* (1905) encouraged women to seek the vote instead of resorting to the hatchet.

Carry Nation has been badly treated by most of her biographers. In part, she was responsible for her own bad reputation. In her autobiography, she perhaps revealed too much of her personal and religious life, thus exposing herself to criticism. She played into the hands of her critics when she made outrageous statements or visited college campuses where she should have expected to be placed in a bad light. Her methods appeared unfeminine in a decade when feminine virtue was extolled. She also became the victim of the eastern press, which delighted in poking fun at the crude ways of westerners by mocking Nation as a social misfit and a religious freak.

Carry Nation died almost a decade before the passage of the Eighteenth Amendment, which outlawed the manufacture, distribution, sale, and consumption of alcoholic beverages. Whether people remembered her in 1919 is not of great importance; the amendment passed in part at least because she focused the attention of many Americans on the issue of prohibition. Whether one was for or against temperance, it would have been difficult in the first decade of the twentieth century to ignore the issue, especially when Carry Nation went storming into bars with hatchet in hand.

She also died a decade before the passage of the Nineteenth Amendment, which granted women the right to vote. Her statements to the Kansas legislature, as well as her newspaper's masthead, indicate that Carry Nation well knew the power of the ballot and the importance of working for the right of women to vote.

Bibliography

Asbury, Herbert. *Carry Nation*. New York: Alfred A. Knopf, 1929. This older biography paints Nation as a social misfit.

Bader, Robert Smith. *Prohibition in Kansas*. Lawrence: University Press of Kansas, 1986. This general history of prohibition in Kansas contains a very positive chapter on Carry Nation and her contribution to the temperance movement.

Flexner, Eleanor. *Century of Struggle: The Woman's Rights Movement in the United States*. Rev. ed. Cambridge, Mass.: The Belknap Press of Harvard University Press, 1975. Provides an excellent starting point for anyone interested in the women's rights movement.

Gusfield, Joseph. *Symbolic Crusade: Status Politics and the American Temperance Movement*. Urbana: University of Illinois Press, 1963. An interesting and useful history of the temperance movement from its nineteenth century roots to the passage of the Eighteenth Amendment.

Lewis, Robert Taylor. *Vessel of Wrath: The Life and Times of Carry Nation*. New York: New American Library, 1966. A relatively recent biography written in negative terms.

Nation, Carry. *The Use and Need of the Life of Carry A. Nation, Written by Herself*. Topeka, Kans.: F. M. Steves & Sons, 1905. Nation's autobiography sets the negative tone for her biographers.

Duncan R. Jamieson

MARTINA NAVRATILOVA

Born: October 18, 1956; Prague, Czechoslovakia

Area of Achievement: Sports

Contribution: As a leading figure in women's tennis since the mid-1970's, Martina Navratilova was one of the first women athletes to demonstrate that women's sports could be as exciting as men's and that professional women athletes deserved comparable financial rewards.

Early Life

Martina Navratilova was born Martina Subertova in Prague, Czechoslovakia, on October 18, 1956. Her parents were divorced a short time after her birth, and her mother married her second husband, Mirek Navratil. Martina lived a robust outdoor life in the Krknoše Mountains until the age of five, when her family moved to Revnice near the capital city of Prague. She started skiing before she was three years old and became an excellent skier by the time she was five. She preferred to play rough games such as soccer with the boys rather than playing with girls. From earliest childhood she exhibited exceptional strength and athletic ability. Her mother and stepfather were concerned about her "unfeminine" behavior, but were impressed by her physical gifts; they believed she would become a champion if she could find the right sport on which to focus her energies.

In the densely populated urban environment near Prague, Martina found that opportunities for vigorous physical activity were limited. Nevertheless, the city offered ample facilities for playing tennis. Her whole family played the game. Her maternal grandmother, Agnes Semanska, had been a national champion before World War II. Both of Martina's parents competed in amateur tournaments and served as tennis administrators for the Czech government. They were on the courts practically every day and brought Martina with them. Her stepfather cut down an old racket for Martina to use, and he became her first tennis instructor. She immediately became enthusiastic about the game and was competing in junior tournaments by the age of eight. Soon she was beating players five and six years older than herself.

By age sixteen, Martina had won three national women's championships with her aggressive play. She was ecstatic when selected by the Czechoslovakian Tennis Association to tour the United States in 1973 with a team of the best men and women players. She was enchanted by the freedom she found in the United States, which was so much different from the repressed spirit of her Communist-dominated homeland. Fascinated by American music, American fashions, and American food, she was twenty pounds heavier when she returned home. Her first trip to the United States made an impression that changed her life. She realized that many of the bad things she had heard about the United States were merely Communist propaganda.

Martina became pregnant when she was seventeen and had an abortion. She later said that she regretted the whole affair because she had not truly been in love. She eventually acknowledged that she felt a strong sexual attraction to women. After being granted American citizenship, she would become candid about her homosexuality, something that would have been impossible to acknowledge in ultraconservative Czechoslovakia.

While still a teenager, Martina asked the American government for political asylum and applied for citizenship. For years she lived in fear of being kidnapped by her government's secret police because her act created bad publicity for the whole Communist system. In defecting, Martina knew she was cutting herself off from home and family, because she would not be allowed to visit her homeland after becoming an American citizen. She bravely faced the future in a strange new land with only a limited knowledge of the English language.

Life's Work

Martina Navratilova is universally referred to as "Martina." In her autobiography, *Martina*, she explains that her last name should be pronounced *Nav-RAH-tee-low-VAH*, with emphasis on the second and last syllables. She prefers to be called by her first name because Americans, including sports announcers, have so much trouble pronouncing her surname.

Once Martina discovered tennis, she devoted her life to it with the intensity that is her outstanding characteristic. Women's tennis had been a game of finesse until Martina burst upon the scene. She turned it into a game of speed and power—one that was less "ladylike" than it had been in the past, but far more interesting to spectators. Martina brought to professional tennis a cannonball serve that was clocked at a higher speed than the serves of some of the better professional male players. She was left-handed, which is considered an asset in tennis, and was noted for her powerful forehand as well as her aggressive charges to the net.

Her rivalry with Chris Evert became legendary. For years, the two women battled for first place at the world's most important tournaments: the Australian Open, the U.S. Open, the French Open, and Wimbledon in England. Martina won so many titles on the grass courts of the historic All English Lawn Tennis and Croquet Club that people said she owned Wimbledon. Despite their rivalry, Chris and Martina became good friends and often played as partners in doubles matches. Martina's record at doubles became almost as impressive as her singles record.

Martina was not a popular player when she entered professional tennis. Because she possessed a steely determination and demeanor unmatched since Helen Wills Moody was champion, spectators thought of Martina as an iceberg. Her limited knowledge of English made it difficult for her to communicate with the press, and she had a subtle sense of humor that did not translate easily into English. Because of her size and strength, she gave the impression that she beat other women players simply by overpowering them. This was not true, although she could hardly be blamed for making the most of her physical assets.

Martina quickly became wealthy from prize money and endorsements. She brought her parents to the United States and gave them a beautiful house near her own home in Texas. She continued to pursue an active professional schedule into the 1990's, one which included travel, public appearances, and all sorts of athletic activities. Martina also began exploring other interests, and signed a contract with a New York publisher to write mystery novels.

Martina has established an example for women who are not considered "feminine" in the conventional sense; she has proved that there are as many different types of women as there are different types of men, and that each woman has the option to develop to her fullest potential. She has always loved America because it is the one country that offers opportunity to everyone and has led the world in promoting women's rights.

In the twilight of her professional tennis career, Martina Navratilova had become one of the most popular personalities in the game. It was a tearful crowd that saw her play her tennis matches at Wimbledon in 1993. She made it to the semifinals, but had to bow to talented younger players, such as Monica Seles and Steffi Graf, who were only half her age and had learned to play her aggressive style of tennis. Success had made Martina feel more relaxed and amiable, while at the same time the public had come to understand that her impassive exterior concealed a sensitive temperament. Like Jimmy Connors and John McEnroe, two of the greatest men tennis players of all time, she was disliked at the beginning of her career, but came to be adored for courage and dedication to excellence.

As an international superstar, Martina's personal life has been a subject of great media interest. She soon realized that it was impossible to conceal her homosexuality or her intimate relationships with various women. One of the biggest news stories had to do with her so-called "palimony" legal battle with Judy Nelson, who sued Martina for half of the money she had earned during the years they had lived together. The suit was finally settled out of court, with Nelson receiving an expensive house in Aspen, Colorado, and an undisclosed amount of cash.

In 1994, shortly before Martina announced her retirement from professional tennis, she had won her 167th singles title by defeating Julie Halard of France in the $400,000 Paris Women's Open. This set an all-time record for career singles championships for both women and men. Martina had also earned more money in prizes than any other male or female tennis player in history. In addition to the nearly $20,000,000 in prize money she had won during her professional career, she had received a huge amount of additional money for sponsoring various products. This was a fantastic achievement, considering that when she entered professional tennis the lion's share of the big prizes as well as the lucrative advertising fees went to men.

Summary

Martina Navratilova contributed greatly to women's tennis and to women's sports in general by demonstrating that women could compete just as fiercely as men and could play with as high a degree of technical excellence. Many sportswriters suggested that she was sufficiently strong and aggressive to compete with the best male players. Shrugging off such speculations, she helped to popularize women's tennis as a spectator sport, thereby attracting larger attendances as well as much broader television coverage.

Martina also had a tremendous impact in the area of gay rights because she was one of the few public figures who lived openly as a homosexual and was outspoken in her views on the subject of homosexuality. Particularly offended by a growing trend in the United States to pass discriminatory legislation targeting the homosexual community, Martina called for greater public understanding and tolerance.

The publicity generated by Martina Navratilova on and off the tennis courts naturally increased the value of professional women athletes as endorsers of products such as tennis racquets and tennis shoes, further motivating more and more women to compete in sports. Martina's stardom helped to strengthen the case for professional women athletes being compensated at the same level as men. Her fame and fortune set an example for young girls to follow, helping to encourage more young women to enter professional sports and women in general to lead vigorous, healthy lives.

Bibliography

Faulkner, Sandra, with Judy Nelson. *Love Match: Nelson vs. Navratilova*. New York: Carol Publishing Group, 1993. A full-length book about the notorious "palimony" suit brought against Martina by her live-in lover, Judy Nelson. Brings out much information about Martina's character outside the public view.

Henry, William A., III. "The Lioness in Winter." *Time* 140 (November 30, 1992): 62-63. A brief retrospective article on Martina's career and her feelings about professional sports, gay rights, and life in general as she was approaching the end of her illustrious tennis career.

Jacobs, Linda. *Martina Navratilova: Tennis Fury*. St. Paul, Minn.: EMC Corporation, 1976. A short book covering Martina's childhood and tennis career up until the day in 1975 when she defeated the world's number-one women's tennis player, Chris Evert. Contains many interesting photographic illustrations.

Kort, Michele. "Ms. Conversation." *Ms.* 16 (February, 1988): 58-62. An interesting interview with both Martina Navratilova and another great tennis player, Billie Jean King, who discuss their views on women's tennis, their personal lives, and other subjects.

Navratilova, Martina, with George Vecsey. *Martina*. New York: Alfred A. Knopf, 1985. A frank and revealing autobiography in which Martina describes her unhappy childhood and conflicts over homosexuality. Portrays her as a very sympathetic and human personality, in dramatic contrast to the ice-cold, aggressive image she projected on the tennis courts.

Vecsey, George. "Martina's Last Bow? (1993 Wimbledon)." *Tennis* 29 (July, 1993): 90-97. Discusses Martina's forthcoming appearance in the 1993 Wimbledon tennis tournament and the unsurpassed record she established at this prestigious event, beginning in 1974. Paints a word picture of historic All England Lawn Tennis and Croquet Club. Illustrated with photographs.

Bill Delaney

ALICE NEEL

Born: January 28, 1900; Merion Square, Pennsylvania
Died: October 13, 1984; New York, New York
Area of Achievement: Art
Contribution: Described by some as a "collector of souls," Alice Neel spent six decades producing expressionistic, intense portraits, cityscapes, and still lifes that document the human condition. Often compared to works by Edvard Munch, Vincent van Gogh, Frida Kahlo, and other great artists, Neel's portraits reflect her belief in the importance of the human image to communicate values and beliefs.

Early Life

Alice Hartley Neel was born on January 28, 1900, in Merion Square, Pennsylvania. Her parents were George Neel, a descendant of several generations of Irish opera singers in Philadelphia, and Alice Concross Hartley, whose lineage included a signer of the Declaration of Independence. Alice adored her gentle, passive father, whose position as head clerk in the accounting department of the Pennsylvania Railroad provided a modest middle-class income. The Neel family was actually ruled by the elder Alice, a forceful and dominating matriarch.

The younger Alice loved the beauty of the countryside that surrounded her home in the small town of Colwyn, Pennsylvania, but she hated the isolation and boredom. A fearful, anxiety-ridden child, she loved painting and used it as therapy. Under constant pressure to be a dutiful daughter and often reminded by her mother that girls should be satisfied with practical expectations in life, Alice gave up art courses in high school to take typing and stenography. Intelligent but insecure, she was popular for her beauty and wit. In her teens, Alice Neel found that dating boys provided the approval she could not find in other parts of her life, and she used the attention as a distraction from unhappiness.

The extremes of repression of her own needs and the hysteria of her social life pushed Alice into a minor nervous breakdown at age seventeen. When she recovered the following year, she supplemented the family income for three years with her paycheck as a clerk at the Army Air Corps. After taking evening classes at the School of Industrial Art, Alice convinced her mother to allow her to study illustration at the Philadelphia School of Design for Women. Without telling her mother, Alice later changed her major to fine arts and received a full three-year scholarship. It was there that Alice learned to assert herself on canvas; by her second year, she was disagreeing with the conservative painting rules of many of her teachers. During this time, Alice enrolled in the Chester Summer School of the Pennsylvania Academy of Fine Arts, where she fell in love with Carlos Enriquez, a handsome upper-class Cuban. Carlos was recalled to Cuba by his angry parents, and Alice returned to finish her final year at the Philadelphia School.

Enriquez returned shortly after graduation, and he and Alice were married. They moved to Cuba, where they painted and sketched the poverty and colorful nightlife of the Afro-Cubans. They were dependent, however, on Enriquez's wealthy family. In 1927, several months after the birth of her first child, Santillana, Neel had an exhibition of her work in Havana. Ambivalent about motherhood and fearful of the traditional role that her husband's family wanted her to accept, Neel returned to her parents' house with her daughter several months later. After Enriquez rejoined her later that fall, they moved to an apartment in New York City to pursue careers in art.

Life's Work

Alice Neel was excited by New York City, and she and her husband roamed the neighborhoods, recording life on the streets. Unable to afford oils, they painted in watercolors, and Alice began shaping a style that would translate powerfully to her later oil canvases. Neel was devastated when Santillana died unexpectedly of diphtheria in 1927. By her own admission, her ambivalence about motherhood manifested itself in an intense guilt that left her unable to paint. Less than a year later, Alice gave birth to another daughter, Isabetta, welcoming her with the watercolor "Well Baby Clinic," an anguished portrait of impoverished motherhood in a neighborhood clinic. In 1930, Enriquez fled their troubled marriage, taking Isabetta with him to Cuba.

Neel threw herself into her art. After only a month of productivity, the impact of Neel's abandonment by her husband and the loss of her second child caused Neel to have a nervous breakdown. She was hospitalized for some time and attempted suicide on several occasions. Eventually, she began to draw again, recording the patients and the wards where she lived. A summer in a private sanatorium restored Neel, and she reconnected with the art world, painting intense, often nude portraits of her friends and their visitors. In 1932, she moved to Greenwich Village in New York City to live with Kenneth Doolittle, an offbeat politico.

This move marked an important period in Neel's painting and the emergence of a small but loyal group of admirers of her work. Even in the bohemian, left-wing ambience of Greenwich Village in 1932, Neel's use of symbols, faces, and exaggerated features was shocking, particularly in a period when pastoral landscapes reflected the current aesthetic. Although Neel socialized with writers, artists, and politicos, she remained independent, refusing to be associated with a particular group or school. In the summer of 1932, she entered the Greenwich Village Art Festival, which led to an exhibit at a small bookstore and gallery in the Village.

Later that year, Neel was included in an international show at the Boyer Gallery in Philadelphia. These exhibits established Neel's credentials as a professional artist. She was selected to receive a grant from the Public Works of Art Project (PWAP), a government-sponsored Depression relief effort for artists. The public recognition and the security of having an income gave Neel the courage to break away from a sometimes violent relationship with Doolittle.

Although her grant from the PWAP ended abruptly after six months, the Works Progress Administration, another federal program designed to support artists, selected Neel to participate in the professional category of the elite easel division. Neel's subjects reflected the wretched and elegant extremes of New York City's neighborhoods. These portraits, with Neel's trademark moroseness, were often rejected by city administrators charged with the duty of selecting paintings to adorn public buildings. This, combined with Neel's independence, frequently threatened her decade-long tenure with the WPA.

A number of artists, however, strongly believed in her extraordinary talents and worked hard to help Neel become recognized. Finally, after Neel had experienced a number of major disappointments, the Contemporary Arts Gallery in 1938 gave her a solo show. Immediately following that show, she exhibited with the New York Group at the A.C.A. Gallery, which featured social and political art by undiscovered painters. Marginalized by her style and gender, Neel and her work were largely ignored by the critics.

Neel distanced herself from the intellectual/artistic milieu of Greenwich Village. She believed that it had become too middle-class, and she moved to Spanish Harlem, a lively but impoverished Puerto Rican ghetto where she would live for nearly thirty more years. Within two years, she gave birth to two sons, the first fathered by José Santiago, a nightclub performer who abandoned Neel, and the second by Sam Brody, a complex intellectual who alienated many of Neel's friends. Although they never married, Neel's tumultuous relationship with Brody lasted for seventeen years. Neel continued to paint in isolation from the artistic community, recording the suffering and poverty of her neighborhood on canvases too disturbing for most buyers.

In 1944, Neel had a solo show at the Pinocotheca, a small but prestigious uptown gallery whose owner, Rose Fried, was noted for promoting unconventional work. The critics acknowledged Neel's talent but were repelled by her disturbing images, and no paintings were sold. At the same time, the galleries were infatuated with abstract expressionism as a postwar social statement. Neel's work, once considered risky, was now out-of-date. Her commitment to social realism was rooted in her long affiliation with the political Left. Unlike many others, who abandoned the Communist Party with the advent of McCarthyism, Neel remained loyal to the ideals of social activism.

She continued to paint social realist themes but remained fiercely attached to her own style, refusing to conform to art world trends. Neel would not compromise and would often lose clients because they did not like the searing truths of their portraits. During much of this period, she was barely surviving from her art commissions and was only able to make ends meet with financial assistance from John Rothschild, a longtime admirer. In 1950, she showed again at the A.C.A. gallery to mixed reviews and no buyers. Ironically, Neel's connections with left-wing circles provided her with her most appreciative audience: She exhibited and lectured in political venues. Unfortunately, few in that group could afford to buy art.

Neel became increasingly despondent about her lack of recognition, and in her late fifties she underwent two years of psychoanalysis. As a result of her successful treatment, she took control of her life, broke off her relationship with Sam Brody, and sought out subjects for her portraits who would help her career. Her two portraits of poet Frank O'Hara and her contacts with key art critics led to several major gallery shows.

By 1962, the Museum of Modern Art's show "The Return of the Figure," coupled with a feature article devoted to Alice Neel in *ARTnews* magazine, established her as a leading figure in the art world. Still, Neel remained true to her own vision and would not modify her work. She continued to paint the souls of the disenfranchised, was vociferous in denouncing the Vietnam War, and was a spokesperson for the growing women's liberation movement. Pressure from Neel, the support of numerous political groups, and the art world's recognition of her major contribution culminated in Neel's greatest triumph: a one-woman retrospective at the Whitney Museum in 1974.

Until her death in 1984, Neel continued to paint and remained an active and prominent figure both in the art world and popular culture. She appeared on television, was featured on popular magazine covers, and received an award from President Jimmy Carter.

Summary

Alice Neel's work defies categorization. From her earliest work in the 1920's to her contributions in the 1980's, in her capturing of the spirit of an era, or what she called the "Zeitgeist," Neel maintained a commitment to a style transcending the trends of those decades. She believed that the personal is political and that the human image is the essential medium. Even her nonportraits have a remarkable sense of human presence. Her cityscapes have been described as anthropomorphic. For feminists, Neel is a symbol of the historical repression of the woman artist. She was restricted by confining social models of behavior that forced female artists to choose between motherhood and the pursuit of an artistic career. As an artist, she was marginalized and diminished in the male-dominated art world. The women's liberation movement of the 1960's and 1970's provided an appreciative audience for Neel's recounting of years of "underground" feminism and her struggle with the forces that inhibited her recognition until she was in her sixties. Her eloquent portraits, still lifes, cityscapes, and landscapes not only are historically significant as a documentation of her artistic career but also speak in powerful images of the universal pain, injustice, and vulnerability of the human condition. Alice Neel's works serve as a testament to her indomitable character as well as her significance in the history of American art.

Bibliography

Belcher, Gerald L., and Margaret L. Belcher. *Collecting Souls, Gathering Dust: The Struggle of Two American Artists, Alice Neel and Rhoda Medary*. New York: Paragon House, 1991. A compelling and readable biography that contrasts Neel's life with that of her talented friend and classmate Rhoda Medary, who gave up art for marriage.

Higgins, Judith. "Alice Neel." *ARTnews* 83 (October, 1984): 70-79. A comprehensive discussion of Neel's life and work based on the author's interview with Neel at her son's home in Vermont.

Hills, Patricia. *Alice Neel*. New York: Harry N. Abrams, 1983. Beautiful black-and-white and color reproductions of Neel's works are accompanied by autobiographical and critical commentary by Hill. Includes interviews with, as well as extensive autobiographical commentary from, Neel.

Neel, Alice. *Alice Neel: Exterior/Interior*. Medford, Mass.: The Gallery, 1991. Focuses on Neel's still lifes and landscapes rather than on her portrait work. The catalog's thirty-five pages of analysis discuss this important but often ignored component of Neel's work and analyze it in terms of possible artistic influences. Includes many color plates.

Nemser, Cindy. *Alice Neel, the Woman and Her Work*. Athens: Georgia Museum of Art, 1975. The book is part of an exhibit of Neel's work at the Georgia Museum of Art. The museum's director, William D. Paul, provides an excellent preface analyzing her work. Contains photographs of Alice Neel, biographical sketches, discussions of Neel's work by several portrait subjects, and a revealing autobiographical statement by Neel taken from her doctoral address at Moore College of Art. Accompanied by an extensive chronology, a bibliography, and several black-and-white photographs.

Saltz, Jerry. "Notes on a Painting." *Arts Magazine* 66 (November, 1991): 25-26. Analyzes the art tradition to which Neel belongs, describing her work as a brilliant combination of European portraiture and modern photography. Saltz particularly focuses on Neel's 1932 painting *Symbols* and provides an in-depth discussion of the powerful associations it evokes.

Susan Chainey

LOUISE NEVELSON

Born: Early Autumn of 1899 (possibly September 23 or October 16); Kiev, Russia
Died: April 17, 1988; New York, New York
Area of Achievement: Art
Contribution: Louise Nevelson's original and unusual view of sculpture as environmental and transforming, as well as her innovative use of materials, made her a leading sculptor of the twentieth century and a major role model for twentieth century women artists.

Early Life

Louise Nevelson was born Leah Berliawsky in 1899 in Kiev, Russia. She was the second child of four born to Isaac and Zeisel Berliawsky. Isaac Berliawsky immigrated to America in 1902, and his family joined him in 1905; they settled in the small coastal town of Rockland, Maine. Isaac had been involved in the family lumber business in Russia. After settling in the United States, he supported his own family by selling "junk," building houses, and buying and selling properties.

As a working-class Jewish immigrant family, the Berliawskys were viewed as outsiders by the predominantly Protestant population of Rockland. From the beginning, Leah, now called Louise, felt a sense of isolation and alienation. Forced to change her name and to abandon her mother tongue in favor of English, she found her refuge in the arts. Both of Louise's parents enjoyed the arts, especially music. Louise's mother was interested in fashion and made her own unusual and extravagant clothes. Louise also enjoyed wearing her own "creations," and by the age of seven she was expressing a desire to become an artist. As a young girl, Louise took private voice lessons and piano lessons, drew, and painted in oil and watercolor.

After her graduation from high school in June of 1918, Louise became engaged to a wealthy shipowner from New York named Charles Nevelson, who was descended from Lithuanian Jews. In 1920, they married in Boston, settled in New York, and Louise began to live the lifestyle of an upper-class, socially elite lady. Louise's only child, Myron Irving Nevelson, was born in 1922.

At the same time Louise was functioning as a New York socialite, wife, and mother, she was unable to forget her interest in the arts. She continued to wear flamboyant fashions of her own creation, and by 1924 she was studying voice with Metropolitan Opera coach Estelle Liebling, attending Saturday afternoon drawing classes at the Art Students League, and taking private drawing lessons with the well-known artist William Meyerowitz. In 1926, she began studying acting at the International Theater Arts Institute in Brooklyn under the Italian actress, Princess Norina Matchabelli.

Throughout her life, Louise Nevelson was to retain a deep interest in theater and music, as well as dance; but the visual arts were to become her lifetime passion. She began her first serious, full-time study of art in 1929 at the Art Students League in New York, where she studied painting and drawing with the distinguished artist and teacher Kenneth Hayes Miller.

Almost from its inception there was strife in Louise's marriage to Charles Nevelson. Charles was a conservative businessman who desired his wife to play a more traditional role in family and social life. After the family business suffered losses during the mid-1920's, Charles moved the family to modest housing and expected his wife to help economize. She chose instead to develop her creative interests. Although she cared deeply for her son, Louise ultimately decided to dedicate her life exclusively to art. In 1931, she separated from her husband and left their son in his custody. She later divorced Charles in 1941.

Louise Nevelson went to Munich in 1931 to study with Hans Hofmann, who was one of the most influential avant-garde artists and teachers of the period. In Munich, she expanded her understanding of cubism, but because of general disappointment with Hofmann's program, she left after about three months. She traveled to Berlin and Vienna, where she played small roles in several films. After spending a few weeks in Italy and Paris, she returned to New York.

In 1932, Nevelson became an assistant on a series of frescos executed by the famous Mexican artist Diego Rivera at the New Worker's School in New York. She returned to the Art Students League to study drawing and painting with Hans Hofmann, who had moved to New York. She also began her long study of modern dance at this time, and took up the study of sculpture under the sculptor Chaim Gross.

Life's Work

It was in 1934 that Louise Nevelson began to make the transition from art student to professional artist. She rented an artist's studio in New York and exhibited paintings in her first gallery showing at Alfred Stieglitz's Secession Gallery. From 1935 to 1939, she taught art for the government-subsidized Works Progress Administration.

Although Nevelson continued to paint and draw throughout her life, by 1934, she was directing most of her artistic energy into sculpture, the art form for which she would become famous. Her early sculptures were primarily human, animal, or abstract forms made out of plaster or clay. She exhibited a sculpture for the first time at the Brooklyn Museum show entitled "Sculpture: A Group Exhibition by Young Sculptors" (1935).

In the 1930's and 1940's, two of the most influential avant-garde art styles were cubism and surrealism. Nevelson was inspired by both. In the 1940's, her work became increasingly more geometric, abstract, and complexly layered and was to reveal subtle metaphysical and surrealist tendencies in her creation of sculpture which included movable parts, viewer participation, and later, the erection of total, theatrical environments. By the 1940's, she was also constructing or assembling sculpture, in the manner that was becoming a major sculptural method of the twentieth century, rather than carving or modeling. Sculptural assemblage would become Nevelson's primary means of artistic expression.

During the 1940's, Louise Nevelson experienced severe financial difficulties. Although she exhibited widely at the Karl Nierendorf Gallery and elsewhere, her work received mixed reviews and rarely sold. It was not until Nevelson was in her fifties that her mature sculptural style developed and she began creating the enormous abstract environmental sculptures for which she became well known.

By 1955, Nevelson's work was being represented by the important but nonprofit Grand Central Moderns Gallery in New York. "The Royal Voyage" (1955), Nevelson's second solo exhibition at the Grand Central Moderns Gallery, was the first in a series of Nevelson's theme exhibitions that consisted of assembled wood painted entirely black. "The Royal Voyage" was an environmental installation created from dozens of large, rough wood pieces arranged to symbolize a king and queen (represented by huge beams) embarking on a mysterious, mystical sea journey.

After "The Royal Voyage" show, Nevelson presented other theme exhibitions in black wood at the Grand Central Moderns. "Moon Garden + One" (1958) was a huge black theatrical environment which featured her first wall, *Sky Cathedral*, a structure more than eleven feet high and ten feet long that was constructed out of boxes filled with a variety of wooden forms and objects arranged in a complex and abstract manner. The exhibition was lit dramatically in blue and emanated a mood of otherworldliness.

"Moon Garden + One" was highly applauded by critics and the national media. The show marked the beginning of Nevelson's critical success and her recognition as a major twentieth century sculptor. By this time, Nevelson had collected huge warehouses and storerooms full of "junk" and "odds and ends," mostly wood, that she assembled in large walls constructed of boxes or into immense environmental installations, most of which were painted uniformly in one color, usually black, white, or gold.

In 1960, Nevelson created her first totally white environment at the Museum of Modern Art in New York, in a show entitled "Sixteen Americans." Nevelson was given the biggest gallery for the installation of her "Dawn's Wedding Feast," which consisted of walls constructed of filled boxes, intricately constructed columns, hanging sun and moon assemblages, a nuptial pillow, a wedding chest, and a wedding cake made from Victorian finials and chair legs. The marriage theme was to be a recurrent one in Nevelson's work and can be seen as symbolizing traditional marriage ceremonies, marriage to life, or marriage to one's work.

By 1961, Nevelson was being represented by the prestigious Martha Jackson Gallery in New York and was receiving a guaranteed income. Fascinated by the allure of gold, she made a golden environment out of her walls of assemblage boxes called "The Royal Tides" (1961). Toilet seats, furniture parts, tools, and junk in abstract arrangements glowed in shimmering gold and were meant to evoke the mood of royalty, another of Nevelson's recurrent themes.

By the early 1960's, Nevelson had become an extremely famous and highly respected sculptor. In 1962, she was selected as one of the three artists to represent the United States at the important international exhibition, the XXXI Biennale, Internazionale d'Arte in Venice, Italy. She was awarded the grand prize in the First Sculpture International at the Torcuato di Tella Institute's Center of Visual Arts, Buenos Aires, in the same year. In 1963, she was given a Ford Foundation grant to work on printmaking at the Tamarind Lithography Workshop in Los Angeles, California. In 1964, Nevelson began her official affiliation with the important Pace Gallery in New York, which sold her work regularly and gave her a guaranteed income. The Whitney Museum of American Art gave Nevelson a retrospective exhibition in 1967, and she was elected to the National Institute of Arts and Letters in 1968.

Nevelson began to make large metal sculptures for public spaces in the late 1960's. She worked primarily with cor-ten steel, out of which she created immense abstract forms generally meant for permanent outdoor display. Princeton University commissioned the first of these, *Atmosphere and Environment X* (1969). In 1972, *Night Presence IV* (22½ feet high) was installed on Park Avenue in New York and *Atmosphere and Environment XIII: Windows to the West* (15 feet high) was erected in Scottsdale, Arizona.

In the late 1960's, Nevelson also began to work with plastics, plexiglas, and Lucite. She assembled these materials into abstract forms in the manner of the wood constructions, but these were smaller and more delicate in appearance. Sculptures such as *Ice Palace I* (1967) and *Canada Series I* (1968) featured overlapping transparencies and reflection of light.

The interior of the Chapel of the Good Shepherd in Saint Peter's Church, New York, was entirely designed by Louise Nevelson in 1977. Again taking on a large-scale project, Nevelson designed benches, vestments, and constructed wall sculptures in white, and created another of her total environments. In the same year, *Mrs. N's Palace* was being shown at the Pace Gallery, an installation of massive wooden forms which symbolized Nevelson's dream home or environment.

By the time of Louise Nevelson's death, she had become a major media celebrity and was recognized as a leader in twentieth century sculpture. Her vision of sculpture as environmental and transforming, and her incorporation of old, found objects and "junk" into works of art was highly innovative and daring. Nevelson received many honors and awards in the later part of her life. In 1978, Legion Memorial Square in Manhattan was renamed Louise Nevelson Plaza. In 1979, she was elected to the American Academy of Arts and Letters and was awarded their gold medal for sculpture in 1983. She was presented with a National Medal of the Arts by President Ronald Reagan in 1985.

Louise Nevelson continued to work as an artist almost to the end of her life. In 1988, after undergoing radiation treatment, she died of a brain tumor at her home in New York. A memorial service was held for her in the Medieval Sculpture Hall of the Metropolitan Museum of Art in New York.

Summary

Louise Nevelson was a truly independent woman whose life was entirely dedicated to her art. While her mode of dress was feminine and extravagant, she proved, through her art, that there was no limit to what a woman could accomplish or create if she was seriously dedicated. The materials, methods, and size of Nevelson's art were highly nontraditional for women. Early in her career, Nevelson was criticized for her choices, but she commanded her art so well that she eventually even overwhelmed and impressed most of her critics. Ultimately, she came to be acknowledged internationally for her originality and contribution to the history of sculpture, primarily because of her constructed environments and innovative use of materials.

Throughout her life, Nevelson identified herself as a feminist many times. She refused to be controlled by any strictures put upon her merely because she was a woman. During the 1940's, she came to associate more and more with other women artists in an effort to gain strength against the sexist attitudes which were predominant in the art world of the time. She participated in women artist exhibitions and was elected to the National Association of Women Artists in 1952. In 1979, Nevelson was chosen to be the New York Feminist Art Institute's guest of honor at the benefit given at the World Trade Center.

By the end of the 1970's, Louise Nevelson, because of her highly public presence, had become a major role model for women, and for women artists in particular. She was an example of a powerful woman who was able to claim her life for her own, mold it, control it, and devote it to the thing she cared about most deeply. She was flamboyant, outspoken, energetic, and resilient, and her art was daring, innovative, and supremely her own. She stopped at almost nothing to express her innermost self through her art and she always believed that what she had to express was important and valid. Since the time of Louise Nevelson, women artists have begun working widely in large-scale forums and nontraditional materials such as metals, plastics, and wood. Nevelson provided women artists with a truly inspiring example of female strength, creativity, and courage.

Bibliography

Glimcher, Arnold B. *Louise Nevelson*. New York: Praeger, 1972. Written by the director of the Pace Gallery, New York, who was Nevelson's friend and dealer. This book serves as an excellent introduction to her life and work up to 1972. Includes a list of major exhibitions and collections, as well as more than one hundred black-and-white and color photographs of her work. No bibliography.

Lipman, Jean. *Nevelson's World*. New York: Hudson Hills Press, 1983. With an introduction by the art critic, Hilton Kramer and an afterword by Louise Nevelson. This book focuses on the art of Nevelson with thorough discussions of her early work, wood sculpture, transparent and metal sculpture, as well as works on paper. Includes a bibliography and more than one hundred color and black-and-white reproductions.

Lisle, Laurie. *Louise Nevelson: A Passionate Life*. New York: Summit Books, 1990. An important, thorough examination of Nevelson's life, career, and work. This is an interesting, well-researched biography which analyzes Nevelson's development, from birth to death. Includes an excellent bibliography and black-and-white photographs.

Nevelson, Louise. *Dawns and Dusks*. New York: Charles Scribner's Sons, 1976. Based on taped conversations between Nevelson and her assistant, Diana Mac-

Kown, with whom Nevelson discusses her life and art. The focus of the book is on her career and her sculpture. Includes black-and-white photographs of Nevelson, family, and friends, as well as reproductions of art. Introduction by art historian John Canaday

———. *Louise Nevelson: Atmospheres and Environments*. New York: Clarkson N. Potter, 1980. A beautiful catalog published in conjunction with a 1980 exhibition of Nevelson's sculpture at the Whitney. Includes an introduction by Edward Albee and excellent color photographs of some of Nevelson's most important environmental exhibits, including "Moon Garden + One," "Dawn's Wedding Feast," and "The Royal Tides." With bibliography.

Wilson, Laurie. *Louise Nevelson, Iconography and Sources*. New York: Garland, 1981. Based on a Ph.D. dissertation finished in 1978, this book is an important contribution to the study of the meanings and background behind Nevelson's imagery. Wilson seeks the sources of Nevelson's symbolism, particularly of marriage, royalty, and death, in her life, studies, travel, and philosophy. Includes a bibliography and 191 black-and-white illustrations.

Nannette Fabré Kelly

JEAN NIDETCH

Born: October 12, 1923; Brooklyn, New York

Area of Achievement: Business and industry

Contribution: As the founder of Weight Watchers International, the world's most successful diet plan corporation, Jean Nidetch has helped millions of people lose weight and keep it off.

Early Life

Jean Slutsky was born on October 12, 1923, in Brooklyn, New York, the daughter of David Slutsky, a cab driver, and his wife, Mae Fried Slutsky, a manicurist. At birth, she weighed a moderate seven pounds three ounces. Her mother was overweight and, as Jean noted in her memoirs, *The Story of Weight Watchers* (1970), used food to reward her children for good behavior and to comfort them in unpleasant situations. The only one in the family who took little interest in food was their father. Both Jean and her younger sister Helen grew into chubby children.

At school, she was an outgoing girl who soon had a circle of friends who also suffered from weight problems. She appeared not to be bothered by her condition, but painful memories of those days remain with her, such as embarrassing moments in physical education classes or during fire drills when other children ridiculed her for being the last one out of the building.

Despite her weight problem, she was determined to make something of her life. After being graduated from Girls High School in Brooklyn in 1941, she enrolled at City College of New York. She planned on majoring in business administration. The next February, however, her father died, and she had to drop out of college. For a short time, she worked for the Mullin Furniture Company in Queens and then for a company called Man O'War that put out tip sheets for horse racing. In late 1942, she got a job with the Internal Revenue Service. During these years, she became a "professional dieter," trying every new diet pill and appetite suppressant on the market that promised instant weight loss. Often she would lose weight but gain it, and more, back.

In 1945, she met Martin Nidetch, a man from her Brooklyn neighborhood who had recently returned from U.S. Army service and who also shared her interest in food. After a courtship revolving around restaurants and eating, the two were married on April 20, 1947. Very soon afterward, she quit her job at the IRS when the couple moved to Tulsa, Oklahoma, where her husband began a job as credit manager for a chain of Federal stores.

In Tulsa, Jean Nidetch worked as a salesperson for Street's Department Store. The job lasted less than a year because Martin got a manager's job with another Federal store, and the couple moved to Warren, Pennsylvania, in January of 1948. In Warren, Jean Nidetch also worked for a while at Federal's, but then she got a job with Sylvania Electric. During this time, the couple's best friends were another couple who ran a restaurant, and Nidetch continued to overeat.

In 1949, Nidetch and her husband had their first child, a boy who died soon after birth. Two years later, their son David was born. In 1952, they returned to New York, where Martin worked as a driver for Carey, a limousine service. They bought an apartment in Little Neck and settled into life in the New York City suburbs. By 1956, Nidetch had another son. In addition to caring for two young children, she found time to join many organizations. Frequently, as she did in the North Hills League for Retarded Children, she became a leader because of her fund-raising skills.

Even with all of her activities, Nidetch continued to overeat and diet, each time returning to old habits. Her husband also became heavier and heavier, and the couple developed a routine of jokes and humor about themselves that made them popular socially and provided a defense against their weight problems.

Life's Work

By 1961, Jean Nidetch, at five feet, seven inches tall, weighed 214 pounds. She had tried every diet and diet doctor on the market. One day in the supermarket, a woman asked her when her baby was due. This embarrassing incident finally prompted her to go to the New York City Department of Health Obesity Clinic, and she began their recommended regimen. The clinic prescribed a diet with no substitutions. Following it, Nidetch would lose two pounds a week. Each week, she was to come to the clinic to be weighed.

She followed this for ten weeks. Each evening, however, she secretly gorged on cookies. Unable to confide this weakness to her family or anyone at the clinic, she decided to call up five overweight friends and invite them over to talk about their weight problems. She did, and Weight Watchers began.

This group discussion provided the format for freely confessing food excesses, and soon the women found that they could follow Nidetch's diet and actually lose weight. Each began to invite other overweight friends to the group. In two months, forty women were dieting and gathering weekly at Nidetch's home. Because these sessions enabled her to accomplish her goals, she quit the obesity clinic and, on October 30, 1962, reached her goal weight of 142 pounds.

Having successfully shed the pounds and kept them off, Nidetch went on to help her overweight family do the same thing. Meanwhile, the group meetings had outgrown the couple's apartment, and Nidetch moved them to the basement of their apartment house. She also began receiving calls from many overweight people and started to travel around the New York metropolitan area visiting individuals and helping to organize groups.

Finally, one couple who successfully achieved and maintained their weight through Nidetch's group meetings persuaded her to go into business. In May of 1963, Albert and Felice Lippert of Baldwin, Long Island, and Jean and Martin Nidetch formed the Weight Watchers Corporation. The business began in a loft above a film theater in Great Neck, Long Island.

Within four years, so many Weight Watchers groups had formed in the New York City area that the company began spreading across the country. The concept caught on almost everywhere a group was started, and by 1968, when it became a publicly held corporation, Weight Watchers had eighty-one franchises in forty-three states and ten franchises abroad.

On June 11, 1973, Weight Watchers celebrated its tenth anniversary by inviting members to a reunion at Madison Square Garden in New York City. The 16,000 members who attended were entertained by comedian Bob Hope, singer Pearl Bailey, and other well-known show people. In her interview with the press, Nidetch told *Newsday* food writer Barbara Rader that, of all the diets around, Weight Watchers was the only one that enabled a person to lose pounds and actually keep them off. That is the secret to the company's phenomenal success.

The Weight Watchers diet, essentially the one Nidetch was given by the New York Department of Health, prescribes a sensible regimen of meats, fish, dairy products, grains, fruits, and vegetables. It allows dieters to eat certain snacks between meals, so that by the end of the day, people find that they have eaten a remarkable amount of food. Once they reach their goal weight, they receive a maintenance diet composed of similar food groups but with more latitude in choices.

To join Weight Watchers, people should have at least ten pounds to lose and should have had a doctor's examination. Each week, members come to a meeting where they pay their weekly dues, are weighed in, and then attend the group meeting. Meetings vary in format, but most consist of a short lecture by the leader followed by group discussion of problems. People may, for their weekly dues, attend as many meetings as they wish. After they achieve their goal weight, meetings become monthly.

This format, begun by Nidetch in her home, continued to be the foundation of the corporation. Under the business direction of Albert Lippert, president and chairman of the board, the organization continued to grow during the 1970's. In addition to overseeing the franchises, he managed the company's other enterprises, including the monthly *Weight Watchers Magazine,* a television program, a number of summer camps for overweight children, and several food and beverage lines.

In 1978, the business became too large for Nidetch and the Lipperts to manage, and they sold the company to the food conglomerate H. J. Heinz. Although she is technically out of the business, Nidetch still continues as a consultant and spokesperson for the corporation. During the 1980's and early 1990's, she traveled to places as far away as Fiji, where she was welcomed with the same enthusiasm as she had been in New York City. She also appears at local shopping malls and supermarket openings, ever the evangelist for the company's nutritious, easy-to-prepare products and the food plan that is the foundation of the Weight Watchers program.

The program itself retains the fundamental features of Nidetch's original plan but keeps pace with changes in lifestyles. At least one major change is introduced each year, often at the suggestion of members. The company maintains a staff of dietitians, psychologists, and exercise physiologists, and frequently the corporate executives sit in on meetings to fine tune the new ideas. The diet is now called the food plan and includes three other elements: the support group, the exercise plan, and self-discovery aspects that deal with attitude and lifestyle changes. The company also has introduced a new program called the Inner Circle, which uses the same food plan but limits the number of participants in one group to eight or ten, who then form a stable group with no new members.

By 1988, Weight Watchers had more than 700,000 members in twenty-four countries. As a division of Heinz, the company employed some 7,000 people, many of whom were successful graduates of the program. It is still growing. Other weight-loss businesses, such as Jenny Craig, Physician's Weight Loss, Diet Center, and Nutri-System, offer stiff competition, but by using the ideas gleaned from Nidetch's first meetings in her apartment in New York, Weight Watchers has remained the foremost company in the industry.

Summary

Even though the company she founded is a division of H. J. Heinz, Jean Nidetch herself is chief public relations person. Blessed with a vivacious, sincere personality and a knack for performance, she continues to share her experiences with audiences all over the world. She is able to represent a giant business yet maintain a personal touch, speaking candidly of her own weight problems and the associated emotional anguish. As one of the first in the business to advocate lifestyle changes, she focuses on the personal and social features of the Weight Watchers plan that enable people to maintain desirable eating habits.

Throughout her career in helping people make these changes, Nidetch has been honored by many business and professional organizations. Many cities and states have named days and events after her. Her awards include Woman of Achievement, Professional Women's Club, and many others. She has also received awards for the many books and articles she has written, beginning in 1966 with the original *Weight Watchers Cook Book* and continuing through the years with other books such as *Ask Jean: Questions to Jean Nidetch, Founder of Weight Watchers* (1975) and *The Weight Watchers Quick Start Program Cookbook* (1984). For the many other cookbooks bearing the Weight Watchers name, she has written introductions.

In everything she does, Jean Nidetch continues to project the positive attitude that underlies the plan that has helped millions of people throughout the world to lose weight successfully and that has built Weight Watchers into a multimillion-dollar company.

Bibliography

Miller, Holly. "Hips, Hips Away!" *The Saturday Evening Post* 260 (November, 1988): 48-52. Focusing on the experiences of a thirty-three-year-old teacher who successfully used the Weight Watchers plan, the author marks the twenty-fifth anniversary of Weight Watchers. Includes a sidebar with comments by Nidetch that reflect her continuing enthusiasm for life and for the company. Includes photographs.

Nidetch, Jean. *Weight Watchers Cook Book*. New York: Hearthside Press, 1966. This original program cookbook is the basis for all the books that followed. It includes details explaining the plan, daily and weekly menus, and the Weight Watchers philosophy. Most of the book contains recipes arranged according to the program's food groupings.

____________. *Weight Watchers Quick Start Program Cookbook.* New York: New American Library, 1984. One of the updated versions of the basic Weight Watchers program.

Nidetch, Jean, with Joan Rattner Heilman. *The Story of Weight Watchers.* New York: New American Library, 1970. Full of before-and-after photographs of Nidetch and others, as well as family photographs, this book details the success story of Nidetch and the Weight Watchers concept that became a worldwide success. Written in an informal style, the book is full of personal details and anecdotes that reveal Nidetch's personality and enthusiasm.

Louise M. Stone

JESSYE NORMAN

Born: September 15, 1945; Augusta, Georgia

Area of Achievement: Music

Contribution: Gifted with an extraordinary voice, Norman has established herself as one of the leading figures on the opera stage and as a recording artist with an unusually broad repertoire.

Early Life

Jessye Norman was born on September 15, 1945, one of the five children of Silas and Janie Norman. The Normans were a prosperous, middle-class black family from Augusta, Georgia, whose children were expected to attend college. Norman grew up hoping to become a doctor or a nurse. Although she admired the singing of Leontyne Price, whom she recalls hearing when she was very young, and Marian Anderson, whom she saw on television when she was about eleven, she did not think that a person could simply decide to become a singer. Her family was quite musical—her father sang in church, her mother played piano, and she and all of her siblings took piano lessons from an early age. Norman spent her childhood singing at church and in school; although people often commented on her ability, she thought nothing of it.

When Norman was thirteen it was suggested to her parents that she start voice lessons, but they refused. Norman later commended her parents for what she saw as their good judgment in this area. She was convinced that too much training too early would have resulted in damage to such a heavy voice as her own. Norman sang as often as she could, performing for the Girl Scouts, in Sunday school, and at PTA meetings. She began learning arias with the help of her high-school music teacher and listened to Metropolitan Opera radio broadcasts on Saturday afternoons.

When Norman was sixteen, she entered the Marian Anderson Foundation scholarship auditions in Philadelphia, at the encouragement of her music teacher. She did not win anything, but on the way back from the auditions she was introduced to Carolyn Grant, a voice teacher at Howard University. Grant was so impressed with Norman's voice that she asked the university to offer Norman a full four-year scholarship to Howard. The offer was made immediately, even though Norman was not be able to take advantage of it until her graduation from high school, a year and a half later. Norman began matriculating at Howard in the fall of 1963.

Life's Work

Although Jessye Norman had not had formal voice lessons prior to her years at Howard University, her voice had been well exercised and developed during high school. Her teachers in later years encouraged her to specialize in a single voice classification, but she soon expanded her repertoire. Mezzo-soprano, spinto, dramatic soprano, and lyric soprano—most of these labels were applied to her vocal range at different times. At the beginning of her career she was most commonly identified as a mezzo, but her upper range was developed enough to allow her to sing roles few mezzos would even attempt. In Berlin, from 1969 to 1975, Norman was expected to be able to perform in roles that ranged from high coloratura to dramatic parts. By the early 1990's, she was generally recognized as a dramatic soprano, although she continued to perform other roles.

Howard University provided Norman with a community that allowed her to grow musically and personally. Besides her formal vocal training under Carolyn Grant, Norman became a paid soloist at two churches in the Washington, D.C., area; she also served as president of her sorority and as a member of various student government and music organizations. Upon her graduation in 1967, Norman went to study with Alice Duschak at the Peabody Conservatory in Baltimore. She was not happy there, however, and transferred after only one semester to the University of Michigan, where she studied with Pierre Bernac and Elizabeth Mannion. Her work with Bernac, especially, let to her development of a large repertoire of art songs, focusing particularly on the French chanson.

During both her undergraduate and graduate years, Norman participated in several vocal competitions. In 1965, she won first place in the National Society of Arts and Letters competition. She helped to fund her graduate study by auditioning for William Mathews Sullivan Music Foundation. In 1968, she entered and won the International Music Competition in Munich. This honor resulted in several professional offers to work in Germany, and Norman moved to West Berlin in 1969. She signed a three-year contract with the Deutsche Oper Berlin and made her operatic debut that same year as Elizabeth in Richard Wagner's *Tannhäuser*. The Berlin opera, like most European operas, expected its singers to fill in as needed on various parts. During her time in Berlin, Norman expanded her repertoire to include the unusually large number of operas Berlin considered standard. Upon the completion of her first contract, Norman re-signed for another three years, but she did not complete this contract. Unhappy with her lack of freedom to choose her own roles, she resigned from the Deutsche Oper Berlin in 1975.

While working with the Berlin opera, Norman had made debuts all over the world. In 1970 she appeared in Florence, Italy, singing George Friedrich Handel's *Deborah*, and in 1972 she sang as Aïda at La Scala in Milan. Also in 1972, Norman made her American opera debut in the same role, at the Hollywood Bowl under the direction of James Levine. A few months later, she debuted at the Royal Opera House at Covent Garden in London, singing a role which later won her even greater acclaim, that of Cassandra in *Les Troyens* by Hector Berlioz.

Despite the glowing reviews of her performances in these years, Norman was not satisfied. Although she is known for the wide variety of works she performs, in both style and vocal range, Norman has been exceedingly careful in avoiding roles she believes are unsuitable for her. The expectation that she act as a useful fill-in soprano at the Berlin opera went against the grain, and upon her resignation, Norman left opera altogether until 1980. From 1975 to 1980, she performed recitals of lieder and chanson, orchestral concerts, and opera excerpts throughout Europe and North and South America.

Norman has consistently recorded much of her repertoire, and it continues to be her recordings that earn for her the most critical acclaim. Not willing to limit herself to the tried and true, Norman has recorded opera, spirituals, the songs of Francis Poulenc, Erik Satie, and Jean-Philippe Rameau, lieder by composers from Gustav Mahler to Gabriel Fauré to Igor Stravinsky, and the work of contemporary composers often ignored by other musicians. In 1971, Norman signed an exclusive recording contract with Philips Classics, which expanded to include London and Deutsche Grammophon when the companies joined under one label.

Eventually Norman decided to return to opera. In 1983, she finally made her Metropolitan Opera debut in New York, once again as Cassandra in *Les Troyens*. She alternated this role with that of Dido in the same opera, switching off with Tatiana Troyanos throughout the season. On one memorable night during the first season, Norman ended up singing both roles in a single performance when the singer scheduled as Dido had to cancel. After her Met debut, Norman continued her concert tours and expanded her roles each year. She sang the French national anthem, *La Marseillaise*, before a television audience of millions for the French bicentennial. She is widely respected for her acting ability and her capacity to communicate on many levels through her music. Each summer she appears at prestigious music festivals such as Tanglewood and Salzburg. She has been awarded honorary doctorates from such universities as Howard, Michigan, Harvard, Sewanee, and Brandeis, as well as the Boston Conservatory. She is said to have been the inspiration for the French film *Diva* (1980) by Jean-Jacques Beineix, based on the obsession of a French fan, and released in the United States in 1982. This fan spent his entire income to attend Norman's concerts throughout Europe and to send her armloads of flowers. The Museum of Natural History in Paris has even named an orchid in Norman's honor.

Norman continues to maintain her family ties, returning to visit her mother (her father is deceased) in Georgia when she can. She has homes in London and in Westchester County, New York. Although Norman is careful to keep her private life private, she devotes much time to charitable work, raising money for black colleges, the Save the Children campaign, and the Girl Scouts. She performs regularly for the Metropolitan Opera in New York City and made history at that venue with her performance of Schoenberg's *Erwartung*, the company's first one-character production, in 1989.

Summary

Jessye Norman's career has continued to rise, but it is clear that she has already made a lasting impression on the music world. She has the rare quality of refusing to conform to the images others have of her. Her 1989 recording of Bizet's *Carmen*, for example, is not the standard interpretation of the part that most performers try to duplicate. Although she says she did not deliberately try to be different, her aim was to interpret the role so as to make it a comfortable role for herself. Her independence, both in interpretations and in her choice of music to perform and record, has helped to broaden the offerings to the musical public.

Norman is reticent about her life outside of music, but she has stated that she needs to feel connected to the world around her. She is concerned about political and social issues, remembering experiences from her childhood in the South before the Civil Rights movement. She has said that being an African American artist has not made any difference to her during her career. Although her identity as an African American clearly has shaped Norman's musical interests and opportunities to some degree, it is interesting to note that her statement, made less than two decades after Marian Anderson's debut as the first African American to sing at the Metropolitan Opera, clearly rejects the notion that racial identity has imposed any significant limitations on Norman's career.

Norman enjoys her reputation as an iconoclast. She dislikes being referred to as a diva—although, in the true sense of the word, no one would deny her the title—because of the connotations of temperament and pettiness that have come to be associated with that term. Although she takes great pride in her accomplishments, Norman also has a reputation for always arriving on time for rehearsals and for being fully prepared, unpretentious, and friendly—the epitome of professionalism.

Jessye Norman's persistent individuality and consummate musicianship are impressive. As she continues to shine on the opera stage, her example and her financial support have encouraged others to strive to achieve their dreams and to do their best at the work they love.

Bibliography

Garland, Phyl. "Jessye Norman: Diva." *Ebony* 43 (March, 1988): 52. Focusing on Norman's life outside music, this short article provides more information on her childhood than any other source. Of limited value otherwise, it has a few interesting quotes about growing up black in the South that reveal aspects of Norman's character not seen elsewhere.

Livingstone, William. "Jessye Norman." *Stereo Review* 54 (October, 1989): 102. This well-written article is composed from interviews with Norman and includes Norman's assessment of various roles and how she interprets them.

Mayer, Martin, "Double Header." *Opera News* 48 (February 18, 1984): 8-11. Although it includes little biographical material, this excellent article provides interesting critical commentary (bordering on the snide at times) on Norman's stage and recording careers.

Mordden, Ethan. *Demented: The World of the Opera Diva*. New York: Franklin Watts, 1984. Although this work mentions Norman specifically only a few times, it gives a picture of the world of opera unequaled elsewhere. Mordden's explanation of the types of voices and the operatic roles written for these voices is especially helpful for anyone trying to assess Norman's career. Knowledge of the opera repertoire is assumed. Bibliography and index included.

Story, Rosalyn M. *And So I Sing: African-American Divas of Opera and Concert*.

New York: Amistad Press, 1993. A history of African American women singers in the world of classical music, this work considers Norman in the perspective of other black artists. Index and bibliography included.

Margaret Hawthorne

MARSHA NORMAN

Born: September 21, 1947; Louisville, Kentucky

Area of Achievement: Literature
Contribution: The contention Marsha Norman's success has sparked among critics—either she is exploiting the status quo or candidly articulating the dilemma of women—suggests that expectations for female dramatists has remained a matter of debate well into the twentieth century's closing decades.

Early Life

Admittedly a lonely child, Marsha Williams Norman later recalled spending much of her young life reading. Her mother, Bertha Mae Conley Williams, a fundamentalist Methodist, forbid television and radio in the home, and declared films off-limits. The dramatist reflected that her mother "inadvertently" put her "in touch with the most dangerous things of all," those that exercised the imagination.

Because Mrs. Williams considered the neighborhood children not good enough to play with her daughter, Marsha created an imaginary friend, Bettering. The family lived in Audubon Park, a middle-class section of Louisville, Kentucky, where Marsha had been born September 21, 1947. Children's theater flourished in Louisville, and when performances were a school event, her mother permitted her to attend. Marsha later credited her eventual work in theater to this early exposure to the stage, as well as the isolated conditions of her childhood. During her high school years, Marsha found a creative outlet in writing. Validating her interest in writing, particularly about difficult subjects, Marsha's high school essay "Why Do Good Men Suffer?" won first place in a local literary contest. It was later published in the *Kentucky Bulletin*.

A scholarship student majoring in philosophy, Marsha received her B.A. in 1969 from Agnes Scott College, a small liberal arts school for women in Decatur, Georgia. Returning to Louisville, she married her former English teacher, Michael Norman.

In 1971, Marsha Norman earned an M.A.T. from the University of Louisville. Determined, in her words, to "put in some time saving the world," she accepted a job teaching emotionally disturbed youths at the Kentucky Central State Hospital. In 1973, she transferred to a school for gifted children and taught filmmaking. In 1974, she obtained a divorce from Michael Norman, but retained his last name. From 1974 to 1979, Norman served as book reviewer and editor of the *Louisville Times*, creating for the paper a weekend supplement for children, "The Jelly Bean Journal."

Life's Work

While writing for the *Louisville Times*, Marsha Norman began an association with Jon Jory, the artistic director of the Actor's Theatre of Louisville (ATL). She first approached Jory for advice on involving local young people in the performing arts. Eventually, Jory offered to commission from Norman a play about school busing, a controversial issue at the time. Norman had ambitions to be a playwright but admitted to Jory her lack of interest in dramatizing that subject. Jory counseled that, to focus herself dramatically, she write about an occasion in which she felt herself to be in physical danger.

Norman found her inspiration in the terror she felt at being confronted with a violent and abusive teen inmate during her teaching job at the State Hospital. The question that focused the writing of her first play was "What would happen to somebody like that when she was put in a place where she could not run away, not get out, what then?"

Norman herself later admitted that she was prone to "react violently to being trapped, either economically, emotionally, or physically." She referred again to her identification with her protagonist in an interview with *The New York Times*: "My whole life I felt locked up. I felt in isolation." For Norman, the writing of *Getting Out* became her own "opening of the door."

To ground the details of the play in first-hand experience, Norman interviewed fifteen female prisoners. The result was an examination of the psychological dynamics of a woman released from prison after an eight-year sentence for murder. Alternating scenes contrast the duality of the protagonist's life and personality as two actors share the stage, portraying the "rehabilitated" Arlene and her younger, unregenerate self, Arlie.

Originally produced in 1977 by ATL, *Getting Out* was also performed at the Mark Taper Forum in Los Angeles in 1978. In October of that year, the play opened Off-Broadway. Voted the best new play produced in a regional theater by the American Theater Critics Association, *Getting Out* appeared in *The Best Plays of 1977-1978* (1980), the first non-New York production to be so recognized.

As the recipient of a National Education Association's playwright-in-residence grant, Norman spent much of 1978 through 1979 with ATL. At about this time, Norman married her second husband, Dann C. Byck, Jr. In 1978, her two one-act plays, *The Laundromat* and *The Pool Hall* were presented together in a single production titled *Third and Oak*. The mundane settings of both plays offset the profound loneliness which brings their two characters together. Norman's association with ATL also produced *Circus Valentine* (1979), about a traveling circus on the small-town circuit, and a workshop mounting of *The Hold-up* (1980), based on her grandfather's tall tales about his days in New Mexico. In 1983, a revised version of this comedy-Western was performed by San Francisco's American Conservatory Theater.

As Norman's profile rose nationally, her writing appeared on television. In 1978, her teleplay *It's the Willingness* was shown as part of Public Broadcasting System's *Visions* series, while *Trouble at Fifteen* aired as a segment of NBC's *Skag*. *The Laundromat* was also produced on Home Box Office as a made-for-cable film directed by Robert Altman.

In March of 1983, Norman's Pulitzer Prize-winning play, *'night, Mother*, opened on Broadway, with her husband at the time, Dann Byck, Jr., as producer. Although acknowledging the difficulty of having the play "living in the house with the two of us," it was such a personal project that Norman did not "want it out of the family." Three months earlier, the play had been staged by Robert Brustein's American Repertory Theater, one of the nation's most prestigious regional houses.

The crisis dramatized by this two-character play is precipitated when Jessie announces to her mother, Thelma, that she intends to kill herself that evening. The issue of suicide, however, is subservient to that of options available to women for exerting control over their lives. Also central to the play is the complex relationship between mother and daughter, with its mix of bitterness, guilt, and longing.

'night, Mother received four Tony nominations for the 1982 to 1983 season, including one as best play. These nominations, along with the Pulitzer, boosted ticket sales, enabling the play to close on Broadway after a respectable ten-month run. The play's success drew the attention of Hollywood, and a film version, scripted by Norman, was released in 1986, starring Oscar winners Sissy Spacek and Anne Bancroft.

In *The Fortune Teller*, published in 1987, Norman again explored the fraying of a mother-daughter relationship. Beginning it as a play, the proliferation of characters and Norman's desire to "include things like fire engines and sex" caused her to flesh the story out into a novel.

Norman returned to Broadway in 1991, branching out into musical theater. *The Secret Garden* won her a Tony Award for best book for a musical and a Drama Desk Award. She also wrote the show's lyrics to music composed by pop star Carly Simon. Reviews noted a twentieth century overlay of psychoanalytic devices—memory, dream, desire—in Norman's adaptation of Frances Hodgson Burnett's celebrated children's book, first published in 1911.

Themes of loneliness, isolation, and parent-child tensions echo through this as well as much of Norman's other work. Her play following *'night, Mother*, *Traveler in the Dark* (1984), dramatized conflicts among fathers and sons as it explored the mysteries of faith.

Norman's next work for the stage, *The Red Shoes*, which opened on Broadway in December, 1993, was again a musical adaptation. This time the original was the 1948 film of the same name, and her collaborator the veteran Broadway composer Jule Styne. Despite these impressive credentials, the show quickly closed. Reviews targeted its failure to make the heroine's fatal breakdown when forced to choose between love and career credible in light of contemporary feminism.

Summary

Marsha Norman is among a group of American women playwrights to have emerged in the latter half of the twentieth century in equal numbers to the entire history of females writing for the stage. Feminist scholars have noted that women's authorship of plays has lagged behind other forms of writing, perhaps because drama is a public form of expression that seems far removed from the domestic sphere.

In an ironic twist, the critical and financial success of *'night, Mother* proved problematic for feminists. Because current feminist criticism in large part aimed to deconstruct the prevailing, male-dominated tradition, the acceptance of *'night, Mother* by the theatrical establishment rendered Norman suspect. Some critics attacked her adherence to drama's time-honored Aristotelian unities, expecting an undermining of such conventions by a woman playwright. Others condemned the play's focus on the individual rather than on societal and institutional forces, thereby weakening its power as a political document. Still others savaged what they saw as reinforcement of a stereotype of women as self-destructive. While much critical discussion of *'night, Mother* revolved around Jessie's suicide, some distinguished the play for exploring the struggle of older women such as Thelma to relinquish their hold on adult children. "We all lose our children," Norman, herself a mother of two, has commented. "You think for a lifetime they belong to you, but they are only on loan."

The dramatic tension Norman derives from family relationships is a quality noted not only in much women's literature but also in the classic American plays of Eugene O'Neill, Arthur Miller, and Tennessee Williams. Norman most closely identifies with fellow Southerner Williams. Referring to their shared view of the inescapability of family, she has remarked: "Our writing is absolutely linked to the problem of how do you change when the perception of the people around you doesn't change." Another feature Norman's work shares with a large part of American literature is its impulse to articulate the longings of "common" people. She identifies the people one passes "right by" on the street as the inspiration of her writing.

However the merits of Norman's influence may be judged, her place among the vanguard of women playwrights to emerge in the 1980's remains undisputed. For Norman herself, no longer having plays put in "a little box labeled 'women's theater' " promises "a time of great exploration of secret worlds, of worlds that have been kept very quiet."

Bibliography

Bigsby, C. W. E. *Beyond Broadway*. Vol. 3 in *A Critical Introduction to Twentieth-Century American Drama*. New York: Cambridge University Press, 1985. A primary reference for other works on the subject, this text seriously considers the sociopolitical context of plays and productions. Extensive notes and a bibliography, as well as an index, are provided.

Dolan, Jill. "Bending Gender to Fit the Canon: The Politics of Production." In *Making a Spectacle: Feminist Essays on Contemporary Woman's Theatre*, edited by Lynda Hart. Ann Arbor: University of Michigan Press, 1989. Dolan persuasively presents *'night, Mother* as a case study in how a woman playwright's intentions can be altered through the process of production and the impact of critical reaction.

Herman, William. *Understanding Contemporary American Drama*. Columbia: University of South Carolina Press, 1987. This introductory volume on American dramatists of the latter half of the twentieth century focuses on plays as literary texts. A brief section on Norman, one of only two women featured in the book, is relegated to a concluding chapter subtitled, "Other Voices." Notes, bibliography, and an index are included.

Murray, Timothy. "Patriarchal Panopticism, Or, the Seduction of a Bad Joke: *Getting Out* in Theory." *Theatre Journal* 35 (October, 1983): 376-388. This essay argues that the play offers audiences a theatrical diversion from social injustices, particularly those perpetrated by gender differences. Highly academic language threatens at times to blunt the sharpness of the critique.

Savran, David. *In Their Own Words: Contemporary American Playwrights*. New York: Theatre Communications Group, 1988. Norman is among four women selected for this collection of twenty interviews, each introduced by a short critical essay. As guided by the author, Norman discusses her early introduction to theater, her experiences with production, and her approach to writing, as well as her views regarding American theater.

Spencer, Jenny S. "Marsha Norman's She-Tragedies." In *Making a Spectacle: Feminist Essays on Contemporary Women's Theatre*, edited by Lynda Hart. Ann Arbor: University of Michigan Press, 1989. Spencer reconsiders an eighteenth century dramatic form to illuminate issues of passivity, domesticity, and sexuality in Norman's plays.

Amy Adelstein

MABEL NORMAND

Born: November 9, 1892; Staten Island, New York
Died: February 23, 1930; Monrovia, California
Area of Achievement: Film
Contribution: As a film actor and director during the heyday of the silent film era, Mabel Normand made lasting contributions to film comedy.

Early Life

Mabel Ethelreid Normand was fond of telling her friends that she was two years younger than her rival, Mary Pickford, but Normand was actually the same age as Pickford. Her parents were Claude G. Normand and Mary Drury, who had met in Providence, Rhode Island, and married against their parents' wishes. After their first three children had died of tuberculosis, the couple moved to Staten Island, where Claude took up carpentry and where three more children were born: Gladys, Claude, Jr., and Mabel.

As a child, Mabel Normand was very active, winning several awards for her prowess in swimming. Her beauty blossomed early, and she was encouraged to seek employment as a model. At sixteen, she began to pose for magazine illustrators, including James Montgomery Flagg, noted for his "I Want You" recruiting posters, and Charles Dana Gibson, immortalized by his famous Gibson Girl. Normand's image graced the pages and covers of such popular magazines as *The Delineator*, *Life*, and *The Saturday Evening Post*. According to one story, Normand was scheduled to sit for Gibson, but Gibson had to cancel their session to attend a funeral, and Normand decided to apply for a job as an extra in a motion picture. She soon found herself working for D. W. Griffith, the pioneer film producer and director, best remembered for his epic film *The Birth of a Nation* (1915).

When Griffith and his Biograph company moved temporarily to California in December of 1909, Normand was left behind, but actor Mack Sennett, already smitten by the wide-eyed Gibson Girl, promised to hire her as soon as he returned and was able to start his own film company. Meanwhile, Normand went to work for Vitagraph, another East Coast film company, and performed opposite John Bunny and Flora Finch, the quintessential fat-and-skinny comedy team. In only a short time, Normand became known as "Vitagraph Betty," the pretty voluptuary in such films as *Troublesome Secretaries* (1911) and especially *The Subduing of Mrs. Nag* (1911). Normand later returned to Biograph, again shooting on the East Coast, to make such films as *The Diving Girl* (1911) and *The Squaw's Love* (1911), which allowed her to hone her natural athleticism by diving off cliffs and swimming in icy water. Under Griffith's direction, she performed opposite Mary Pickford in *The Mender of Nets* (1911).

Life's Work

In 1911, Mabel Normand accompanied Mack Sennett to California, where they made more than twenty comedy shorts for Biograph, including *A Dash Through the*

Clouds (1912), in which Normand flies in a primitive airplane. When Sennett left Biograph to start the Keystone Film Company in late 1912, Normand went with him, partly because she desired greater artistic freedom. Sennett had a well-developed sense of humor and valued his star's talent, unlike Griffith, who was disdainful of comedy and favored melodrama.

Between 1912 and 1915, Normand starred in more than 100 Keystone comedies. These films are noteworthy because of their experimentation and raw energy and because they assembled in front of the same camera the variegated talents of such legendary silent film actors as Charlie Chaplin, Roscoe "Fatty" Arbuckle, Minta Durfee, Fred Mace, and Mabel Normand. In her years as a Keystone player, Normand was most frequently coupled with Arbuckle (more than forty films together), but she also worked with Mace and Chaplin. *Tillie's Punctured Romance* (1914), starring Normand and Chaplin, is regarded as Hollywood's first feature-length comedy.

Normand made her directorial debut in *Won in a Closet* (1914) and went on to direct Chaplin in four films, including *Caught in a Cabaret* (1914). Chaplin in turn directed her in at least five films, including *His Trysting Place* (1914), and the two comedians teamed up to codirect and star in *Mabel's Married Life* (1914). In *My Autobiography* (1964), Chaplin made disparaging comments about Normand as a director, perhaps because he resented being directed by a woman.

July 4, 1915, was the date set for Sennett and Normand's wedding, but something happened that ended their engagement and eventually separated them professionally. The night before their wedding, Normand found Sennett at the apartment of a young Keystone player named Mae Busch. In a heated argument, Busch allegedly smashed a vase over Normand's head and slammed the door. Dazed and bloody, Normand managed to take a taxi to Fatty Arbuckle and Minta Durfee's house. The driver carried the unconscious Normand to the doorstep, Arbuckle immediately summoned a doctor, and Normand was rushed to the hospital, where she lay in a coma for several weeks. This amazing story is told by Normand's biographer Betty Fussell in her work *Mabel* (1982). In *The Honeycomb* (1969), Adela Rogers St. Johns gives a different version of the story, based on her knowledge as a Hollywood reporter and friend of Normand. She confirms Sennett's infidelity on the eve of his wedding, but attributes Normand's concussion to a failed suicide attempt.

After her recovery, Normand returned to Keystone (which by then had become Triangle-Keystone) to make several more comedies with Arbuckle, mainly on the East Coast, away from Sennett. Fearing that Normand might go to work for producer Thomas Ince, Sennett offered her a new studio and her own Mabel Normand Feature Film Company, which she accepted graciously. Normand spent the next year making *Mickey* (1918), a feature-length romantic comedy that was delayed in its release because of production and distribution problems; it is often considered her best work.

Dissatisfied with Triangle's handling of *Mickey*, Normand signed a five-year contract with Samuel Goldwyn and called Sennett to break the news. Sennett was livid. He wanted to control Normand economically and sexually and was jealous of Goldwyn's encroachment on his "property." In any event, Normand's life during the ensuing years away from Sennett was turbulent and far from happy. It is likely that in late 1918, Normand gave birth to a stillborn child, alleged to be Goldwyn's son. The attendant nurse, Julia Benson, became Normand's lifelong friend and confidant, remaining with the comedian until her death. It is also possible that during this period Normand became addicted to the opium in her tuberculosis medicine, and this addiction may have led to cocaine abuse.

Between 1918 and 1920, Normand made sixteen films for Goldwyn, including *The Venus Model* (1918), *Sis Hopkins* (1919), and *What Happened to Rosa* (1920). Normand was Goldwyn's most profitable and loyal star. Transformed by the "Mabelescent" prose of Goldwyn publicist Norbert Lusk, she became one of the Goldwyn Glamour Girls, yet she continued to act in threadbare vehicles that did little to challenge her talent or change her image. In his autobiography *Behind the Screen* (1923), Goldwyn fondly remembers the day that Normand walked into his office with $50,000 in liberty bonds and suggested that he use the bonds to save his faltering company. Goldwyn declined, his company collapsed, and Normand was released from her contract in order to return to Sennett to make *Molly O'* (1921), *Suzanna* (1923), and *The Extra Girl* (1923).

Three scandals in rapid succession almost ended Normand's career and eventually crippled it permanently. The first scandal involved Fatty Arbuckle, who was charged with the 1921 rape and murder of actor Virginia Rappe. Though Arbuckle was acquitted of the charges, the scandal eventually drove him out of the filmmaking business. Normand suffered by association, incurring public scrutiny of her own lifestyle. As a result, the release of *Molly O'* had to be delayed by two months.

The second scandal involved William Desmond Taylor, a prominent film director and Normand's close friend, who had been tutoring her in literature and philosophy. On February 7, 1922, Normand visited Taylor at his bungalow to borrow a book. After she left, he was mysteriously murdered. Although Normand was never a serious suspect in the case, her reputation was seriously damaged by the lurid stories about her involvement that were published by the press. Sennett had to delay the release of *Suzanna* for a year because of the negative publicity surrounding Normand.

The third scandal involved Normand's chauffeur, who shot oil millionaire Courtland S. Dines on January 1, 1924, allegedly because Dines had insulted Normand at a party. Although Dines survived the shooting and refused to press charges, the public blamed Normand. There were calls to ban her films and investigate her personal life. *The Extra Girl*, released before the incident, was her last film for three years and the last successful film of her career. During the ensuing hiatus, Normand starred briefly in a Broadway play, but her voice was not suited for the stage.

On September 15, 1926, Normand married fellow actor Lew Cody as a party prank. Although she later regretted her action, she never divorced Cody, fearing another scandal. During the next two years, she made five films for producer Hal Roach. Normand was directed by Stan Laurel (of Laurel and Hardy fame) in *Raggedy Rose* (1926), and she performed with actors Boris Karloff and Oliver Hardy in *The Nickel Hopper* (1926). Her last film was *Should Men Walk Home?* (1927), directed by Leo

McCarey. On February 23, 1930, Normand died of pulmonary tuberculosis in a sanatorium in Monrovia, California, less than a month after her father's death from pneumonia. Pallbearers at her funeral included Griffith, Goldwyn, Chaplin, and Sennett.

Summary

Mabel Normand is sometimes referred to as the "Female Chaplin," but this epithet slights her unique contributions to film comedy. First, it must be remembered that she preceded Chaplin on the screen. In the Little Tramp's gestures and expressions, the careful observer can detect the extent of Normand's influence. Normand was a talented woman in a medium controlled by men. She is reputed to have said, "I made millionaires of more men I never saw than anybody ever in pictures." This caustic remark suggests the extent to which she was exploited by directors, producers, and businessmen, but it also bespeaks her popularity among filmgoers in the post-World War I years and early 1920's. While Mary Pickford was "America's Sweetheart," Normand was the undisputed "Queen of Comedy." Reporters collected and reprinted her witticisms, calling them "Mabelisms." Fans idolized her because she said and did whatever she pleased, seldom with regard to propriety or decorum. She was also one of the first female directors, with at least eight films to her credit. As an actor, Normand pioneered several classic slapstick comedy routines, including the pie-in-the-face gag. Unlike other female comedians of her time, she performed her own stunts, often risking life and limb for a laugh. Normand's physical brand of comedy inspired a long line of female comedians, including Lucille Ball, Carol Burnett, and Goldie Hawn. In addition, Normand's life with Mack Sennett served as the inspiration for the 1974 Broadway musical *Mack and Mabel*, starring Robert Preston and Bernadette Peters.

Bibliography

Fussell, Betty Harper. *Mabel.* New Haven, Conn.: Ticknor & Fields, 1982. This biography contains interesting chapters on Normand's Keystone years, her relationship with Goldwyn, and the Taylor murder. Fussell is the first writer to suggest that Normand had a miscarriage in 1918. She also discusses the star's decade-long struggle with tuberculosis and her cocaine addiction.

Giroux, Robert. *A Deed of Death: The Story Behind the Unsolved Murder of Hollywood Director William Desmond Taylor*. New York: Alfred A. Knopf, 1990. This book reexamines evidence in the Taylor murder. In an appendix, Giroux provides a transcript of the coroner's inquest, including Normand's testimony. He also supplies a lengthy bibliography of books and articles about the case. Another book on the Taylor murder is Sidney D. Kirkpatrick's *A Cast of Killers* (1986).

Normand, Stephen. "Mabel Normand: Her Grand-Nephew's Memoir." *Films in Review* 25 (August-September, 1974): 385-397. Stephen Normand defends his great-aunt against allegations of drug abuse. He also analyzes her work and provides interesting biographical information.

St. Johns, Adela Rogers. *The Honeycomb*. Garden City, N.Y.: Doubleday, 1969. St. Johns, a Hollywood reporter, discusses her personal and professional relationship with Normand in chapter 7. She offers valuable insights into Normand's character.

Sennett, Mack, and Cameron Shipp. *King of Comedy*. Garden City, N.Y.: Doubleday, 1954. Sennett discusses his relationship with Normand, including their early work together for Griffith and their frustrated wedding plans. He includes a brief (though somewhat inaccurate) biographical sketch of "the girl from Staten Island." He credits Normand with screen history's first pie-in-the-face gag in 1913.

Sherman, William T. "Love and Courage: A Look at the Films and Career of Mabel Normand." Parts 1-4. *Classic Images* (November, 1990-February, 1991). This seminal article offers an astute assessment of Normand's career. The first three installments provide biographical information and analysis. Part 4 is a detailed filmography of Normand's work.

Edward A. Malone

ANNIE OAKLEY

Born: August 13, 1860; Darke County, Ohio
Died: November 3, 1926; Greenville, Ohio
Area of Achievement: Sports
Contribution: An expert markswoman and consummate performer, Annie Oakley traveled throughout the United States and Europe demonstrating her expert shooting in an era when shooting was almost exclusively a man's sport.

Early Life

Phoebe Anne Moses, nicknamed Annie, was the fourth daughter born to the Quakers Jacob and Susan Moses of rural Darke County, Ohio. When Annie was still a young child, Jacob taught her to hunt and to trap. After Jacob's death from exposure in 1866, Susan and her eight children were left destitute. Young Annie was sent to the county poor farm, but she was soon chosen by a young farmer to be a companion for his wife and infant daughter. Although it was common for poor children to be farmed out, the ten-year-old Annie's fate was unusually cruel; she was overworked and physically abused by the farmer. For two years she was virtually a slave. In 1872, Annie fled, returning to the poorhouse, where she lived with the new superintendent and his wife as a member of their family. Under their care she attended school.

When Annie was fifteen, she returned to her mother. The enterprising young woman capitalized on her adroitness with firearms, entering into a business arrangement with a local merchant in which she supplied him with small game that was shipped to Cincinnati hotels. From that time forward, Annie earned her living with her shooting, proudly paying her mother's mortgage and boasting throughout her life that she had never had money other than what she personally had earned. From her early years of depredation Annie learned frugality. Throughout her life, she shrewdly managed and invested her earnings, thereby enabling Annie and her husband to live their retirement years in comfort.

Life's Work

Annie Moses—in 1882 she adopted the stage name Oakley—was twenty-one when she met her future husband, sharpshooter Frank Butler. Exhibition shooting was at its peak in popularity when Butler, who was traveling in Ohio with a variety show, competed in a contest against Annie Moses. Although women sharpshooters were relatively common, Butler was surprised by the youthful, petite Annie Moses, who appeared to him to be a little girl. Moses outshot Butler that day, which marked the beginning of their courtship. The two married one year later.

During their early married years, Oakley and Butler toured variety theaters and skating rinks. It was at one such show that Oakley met the Sioux chief Sitting Bull, who became fond of her, naming her *Watanya Cicilla*, or "Little Sure Shot." The two would meet again when they both worked for Buffalo Bill Cody's Wild West Show. Butler soon realized he was outdistanced by Oakley's prowess and her showmanship;

he retired from exhibition shooting to become Oakley's manager.

In 1884, after a short stint with the Sells Brothers Circus, the still relatively unknown Oakley applied to Buffalo Bill Cody for a sharpshooting position in his Wild West Show. Although he initially refused her, after the sudden departure of his star marksman, Captain Adam Bogardus, Cody gave Oakley a three-day trial. He was delighted with "Missie"—as he called her—and with only a brief interruption, Oakley remained with Cody's outfit until 1902.

Bursting into the arena sporting her trademark loose, dark, curly hair and her meticulously handsewn costumes of short skirts and leggings, Oakley was in constant motion during her ten-minute act. She leaped over a table to grasp her gun after a clay target had already been released, shot upside down, backwards while looking in a hand mirror, and occasionally from horseback and from a bicycle. She clowned with audiences by feigning horror over missed shots, which she did intentionally so that she would not be accused of cheating. She shot cigarettes from her husband's mouth and potatoes from her dogs' heads, and she split a playing card turned sideways. Athletic and quick, Oakley was one of the finest shots, and clearly the most engaging exhibition shooter, of her era.

At the height of its popularity in the 1880's, Buffalo Bill and his Wild West Show presented a spectacle of heroic cowboys and villainous horse-riding Plains Indians. Its massive cast of Indians, including for a year the famous Sitting Bull, and fancy-riding cowboys re-created shootouts, stagecoach attacks, and mock battles, thrilling audiences and generating an idealized image of the West in the minds of Americans and Europeans alike. Cody's outfit was the first and best of the numerous Wild West shows that became the inspiration for film Westerns of a later era. The youthful athlete Oakley became an audience favorite, attaining international superstar fame. Her life, along with Cody's, was mythologized.

After drawing record crowds at Staten Island and Madison Square Garden in 1886, the Wild West show traveled in 1887 to London, where Oakley was universally praised by audiences and reporters. In England, the once-poor country girl charmed royalty and traveled in upper-class social circles. Remarkably, Oakley was accepted at elite British gun clubs, where, despite being a woman, she was admired for her expert shooting. In London, she began teaching women to shoot, a tradition she continued for the rest of her life. Women were as capable of shooting as men, she believed, and she advocated the carrying of personal arms as a means of self-defense.

Oakley left Cody's show in 1887 for reasons that are obscured because neither Cody nor Oakley discussed the matter. During that year, she engaged in numerous exhibitions and matches, in which she had also participated when touring with the Wild West show in order to earn prize money and gain publicity. In 1885, for example, she attempted to shoot, after loading the guns herself, 5,000 glass balls in one day, scoring 4,722 and breaking a record for the last 1,000, of which she missed only 16. She set several other records, including one for American doubles scoring—two traps released simultaneously. During 1888, Oakley also traveled on the variety circuit performing trick shooting on stage, spent a short time with Pawnee Bill's Wild West

Show, and starred in her first theatrical play, *Deadwood Dick: Or, The Sunbeam of the Sierras*. Although the critics despised the play, they wrote favorable reviews of Oakley. By early 1889, Oakley returned to Cody's show, where she remained as a star performer until she retired in 1902.

By 1892, Oakley's legend was firmly established; she had charmed London society, had become the darling of the newspapers, had achieved recognition at shooting clubs in England and the United States, and had even had clubs named for her. In 1889, she had extended her reputation to continental Europe when she traveled with Cody's Wild West Show to France, Italy, and Germany. In 1893, even the United States Army admitted her expertise by sending representatives to learn from her while she performed at the Chicago World's Fair.

Oakley's apparent youthfulness generated much of her stage appeal. Only five feet tall and weighing approximately 110 pounds, the petite Oakley astounded audiences with feats of endurance with heavy guns. In 1902, when her hair suddenly turned white, and she could no longer project the image of a young girl, Oakley and Butler retired from the Wild West show. She again tried acting, with a play called *The Western Girl*, written expressly for her and showcasing her marksmanship. This time, the play was successful with both critics and the public.

In 1903, Oakley's relationship with the press was abruptly shattered when newspapers throughout the country printed a story originating in Chicago with William Randolph Hearst's newsservice. Reportedly, Annie Oakley had been arrested stealing a man's pants to support her cocaine habit. She was represented as a destitute drug addict. A woman claiming to be Annie Oakley had indeed been arrested, but the newspapers had failed to confirm her identity, and she was, in fact, merely a burlesque impersonator of Oakley. In one of the largest libel suits ever initiated, Oakley sued and won settlements from newspapers throughout the country. Her battle to clear her reputation lasted for nearly five years and absorbed much of her energy. During that time, she performed some of her best trapshooting, establishing her reputation among the elite of the sport.

Oakley officially retired from show business in 1913, after having spent a brief time with the Young Buffalo Wild West Show. Butler and Oakley moved to an idyllic spot on the Eastern Shore of Maryland, but after a lifetime spent on the road, they could not easily reconcile themselves to a sedentary lifestyle. They soon resumed traveling. During World War I, Oakley toured army camps demonstrating her shooting. She also campaigned for the Red Cross. Amid plans to reenter show business in 1922, Oakley was partially paralyzed in a car accident, which ended her career. She died on November 3, 1926, and was followed eighteen days later by her husband, Frank Butler.

Summary

In an era when shooting was considered a men's sport, Annie Oakley advocated that all women be taught to shoot. She viewed guns as providing a form of independence for women, who, when armed and trained, would no longer be forced to rely on men for their protection. During her lifetime, Oakley estimated that she had trained more than fifteen thousand women and considered that women were as capable as men. She advocated providing shooting instructors and rifle ranges in schools for both boys and girls.

In other ways, Oakley was patently less iconoclastic. She jealously guarded her social reputation among upper-class Britons and Americans, bridling at challenges to her femininity, and when she was not performing, she functioned in what she deemed to be ladylike fashion: dressing conservatively, refraining from alcohol, and sharing a close monogamous relationship with her husband. During the suffragist movement, she condemned bloomers, which she considered unladylike, and "bloomer women." She did not advocate women's voting rights. She claimed that women should not "go in for sport so that they neglect their homes." After retiring to the Eastern Shore of Maryland, however, Oakley found herself to be a failure at homemaking. "I went all to pieces under the care of a home," she reported. Interestingly, in 1898, during the Spanish-American War, Oakley had written President William McKinley, requesting to be sent to the Cuban front. During World War I, she likewise wrote to the secretary of war, proposing the establishment of an armed women's regiment for home defense. Although her suggestions were never seriously entertained, her intent was genuine. Annie Oakley, according to her own definition of femininity, achieved fame and success in a predominantly male field that required strength, stamina, and great skill.

Bibliography

Blackstone, Sarah J. *Buckskins, Bullets, and Business: A History of Buffalo Bill's Wild West*. Westport, Conn.: Greenwood Press, 1986. A concise, detailed account of Cody's Wild West, describing the variety of acts and the logistics of moving the massive show from one engagement to another. Blackstone provides the best analysis of the impact of Cody's show on the development of the myth of the American West.

Flory, Claude R. "Annie Oakley in the South." *North Carolina Historical Review* 43 (1966): 333-343. Flory concentrates primarily on Oakley's years after her retirement from the Wild West Show during which she and Butler lived in Florida and North Carolina, giving shooting exhibitions and shooting lessons.

Havighurst, Walter. *Annie Oakley of the Wild West*. New York: Macmillan, 1954. Havighurst utilizes contrived dialogue and melodramatic scenes throughout his book. Illustrated and indexed. Havighurst's biography is clearly superseded by Kasper's book.

Kasper, Shirl. *Annie Oakley*. Norman: University of Oklahoma Press, 1992. Extensively utilizing newspapers and Annie Oakley's own scrapbooks, journalist Kasper has written an interesting and detailed biography of Oakley in which she has attempted to separate myths from documentable facts about Annie Oakley's life. Easily supplants earlier works as a definitive biography. Contains photographs, an index, and a bibliography.

Rosa, Joseph G., and Robin May. *Buffalo Bill and His Wild West: A Pictorial*

Biography. Lawrence: University Press of Kansas, 1989. As its title indicates, this book is liberally illustrated. It contains a section summarizing Annie Oakley's career with, and apart from, Cody's Wild West Show. Contains a bibliography and an index.

Russell, Don. *The Lives and Legends of Buffalo Bill*. Norman: University of Oklahoma Press, 1960. Russell's nearly five-hundred-page book on Buffalo Bill places Oakley's life in the context of Cody's Wild West Show. Russell provides the most detailed history available of Cody's outfit.

Mary E. Virginia

FLANNERY O'CONNOR

Born: March 25, 1925; Savannah, Georgia
Died: August 3, 1964; Milledgeville, Georgia
Area of Achievement: Literature
Contribution: In her short lifetime, Flannery O'Connor created a small but significant body of fiction and nonfiction unique in American literature, Southern literature, Catholic literature, and feminist literature.

Early Life

Mary Flannery O'Connor was born in Savannah, Georgia, on March 25, 1925, the only child of Edward Francis O'Connor, Jr., and Regina Cline O'Connor, both of whom came from prominent Southern Catholic families. Flannery was a happy, sensitive, and independent child. When she was twelve, her father became critically ill with disseminated lupus, a rare and incurable metabolic disease, and the family moved from Savannah into the Cline home in Milledgeville, which formerly had been the governor's mansion (when Milledgeville was the capital of Georgia). Three years later her father died.

O'Connor attended Catholic elementary schools, Peabody High School, and Georgia College (then Georgia State College for Women) in Milledgeville, receiving an A.B. degree in 1945. While in college, she served as art editor and cartoonist for the school newspaper, editor of the literary quarterly, and feature editor of her yearbook.

She received a scholarship to study for an M.F.A. degree at the University of Iowa's School for Writers, under the direction of Paul Engle. In 1946, while still a student, she published her first short story, "The Geranium," in *Accent* magazine. She began work on her first novel, *Wise Blood*, which won her the Rinehart-Iowa Fiction Award in 1947. In 1947 and 1948, four short stories from her master's thesis, "The Heart of the Park," "The Train," "The Peeler," and "The Turkey," were published in prestigious "little magazines."

Life's Work

Flannery O'Connor's accomplishments in college and graduate school won for her a place in the fall of 1948 as writer-in-residence at Yaddo, an artists' colony in Saratoga Springs, New York. There she met writers Robert Lowell, Edward Maisel, and Elizabeth Hardwick. That year she also engaged Elizabeth McKee as her literary agent. She was then twenty-three years old.

Early in 1949, political turmoil at Yaddo surrounding the well-known journalist Agnes Smedley led many of the artists, including O'Connor, to withdraw. She returned briefly to Milledgeville, spent the summer writing in a furnished room in New York, and then moved in September to the Ridgefield, Connecticut, home of Robert Fitzgerald, a well-known poet and translator, and Sally Fitzgerald, also a writer.

O'Connor worked on her novel *Wise Blood* while helping the Fitzgeralds with the care of their children. During the train ride home to Milledgeville during the Christmas holidays in 1950, she suffered her first severe, almost fatal, attack of what was later diagnosed as disseminated lupus. With the help of ACTH, a cortisone derivative, O'Connor slowly recovered, and in July, 1952, she and her mother moved to their family farm, Andalusia, outside Milledgeville.

O'Connor gradually adjusted to her circumstances and organized her life around her work. She drew on her daily experience for the materials of her stories, entertained a wide variety of visitors, wrote numerous letters, and delighted in raising ducks, geese, and peacocks. While she was able, she accepted invitations to lecture at colleges and libraries. By 1955, the weakness of her bones made it necessary for her to use crutches, and except for one trip to Europe, she rarely left Andalusia.

During the first year of her illness, O'Connor completed revisions of *Wise Blood*. After five years' work and some unpleasant controversy with Rinehart over publishing rights, the novel was published in 1952 by Harcourt, Brace. Puzzling, misunderstood by many, considered by turns repulsive, dull, and precocious, *Wise Blood* marks the beginning of O'Connor's mature work.

In the next three years, O'Connor published a number of short stories in magazines and literary journals. In 1955, Harcourt, Brace collected these into *A Good Man Is Hard to Find and Other Stories*. The collection was greeted with critical acclaim. O'Connor's stories were characterized as violent, grotesque, and outrageously funny. Although readers praised her keen ear for the rhythms of Southern speech and her sharp eye for telling detail, many failed to appreciate or understand the orthodox Christianity that formed the foundation of her work.

In 1960, Farrar, Straus, and Cudahy published O'Connor's third book and second novel, *The Violent Bear It Away*. Like *Blood Wise*, the novel is condensed, intense, and poetic. Clearly more mature in vision and artistry than her earlier novel, it brought mixed reviews from secular readers and greater appreciation from Christians.

While working on the stories that constituted her second collection, *Everything That Rises Must Converge*, O'Connor's health began to fail. Farrar, Straus, and Giroux published the book in 1965, the year after O'Connor's death from kidney failure. The book was highly praised.

Other writings published after her death reveal the many facets of her genius and enhance her literary reputation. In 1969, Sally Fitzgerald and Robert Fitzgerald gathered O'Connor's lectures and miscellaneous nonfiction into *Mystery and Manners: Occasional Prose*. These writings, which are models of nonfiction prose style, provide insight into O'Connor's views on art, religion, and education. Also included in the collection is the lengthy introduction O'Connor wrote to *A Memoir of Mary Ann*, the true story of a remarkable little girl who suffered facial disfigurement and terminal illness with dignity and grace.

Flannery O'Connor: The Complete Stories appeared in 1971. This collection of thirty-one pieces includes twelve previously uncollected stories. O'Connor's first published story, "Geranium," and her last, "Judgment Day," a reworking of "Geranium," provide a framework for the chronologically ordered collection. The book received the National Book Award in 1972.

The Habit of Being: Letters (1979), edited by Sally Fitzgerald, is an extensive collection of personal and professional letters spanning O'Connor's adult life, from 1948 to 1964. These letters reveal something of the depth and details of Flannery O'Connor's rich personality, her numerous personal and professional relationships, and her religious faith, as well as her wide-ranging reading, her linguistic playfulness, and her sense of humor. Her letters are essential reading for anyone who wants to understand Flannery O'Connor and her work.

In 1983, Leo J. Zuber compiled *The Presence of Grace and Other Book Reviews*, a collection of the numerous book reviews O'Connor wrote for local publications. *Collected Works*, published by Literary Classics of the United States, appeared in 1988, thus firmly establishing O'Connor's place in American literature.

Summary

Critics have variously labeled Flannery O'Connor a black humorist, a regionalist, a Southern lady, and a Roman Catholic novelist. If she had to be labeled, she chose that of Christian realist. Working within the prevailing currents of prose fiction, O'Connor recognized her debt to such writers as Henry James, Joseph Conrad, Nathanael West, and Nathaniel Hawthorne. She profoundly interiorized her sense of place, the American South in which she was born and bred and whose idioms, cadences, and concerns she expressed. Her ultimate commitment was to what she might do with "the things of God" within the tradition of an orthodox Catholic faith. These three strands of her reality—literature, the South, and Catholicism—converged in her to produce a body of work that remains unique in American literature, in Southern literature, in Catholic literature, and in feminist literature.

Although no one has yet emerged to attempt a similar synthesis, the thirty years since O'Connor's death have brought increasing appreciation, understanding, and valuing of her life and work. The future will surely recognize her significant contribution in at least three areas: the understanding of the human condition, the appreciation of the relationship between art and religion, and the valuing of women as writers. As human beings acknowledge, accept, and understand the reality of spirit permeating matter, Flannery O'Connor's clarity and depth of vision will continue to attract new generations of admirers. As artists continue to address in their work the problem of the relationship between art and belief, Flannery O'Connor's "habit of art" will continue to evoke new depths of creativity. As women continue to claim their "true country" and their true voices, Flannery O'Connor's commitment, integrity, and faith will continue to inspire in them a transformed "habit of being."

Bibliography

Asals, Frederick. *Flannery O'Connor: The Imagination of Extremity*. Athens: University of Georgia Press, 1982. Asals finds that the power of O'Connor's fiction springs from a passion for extremes, the tension of opposites. His work explores some of these tensions. As O'Connor's work changed and developed, the focus of her imagination on extremes remained constant.

Coles, Robert. *Flannery O'Connor's South*. Baton Rouge: Louisiana State University Press, 1980. Coles, a highly regarded social psychologist, draws on O'Connor's letters and extensive interviews with Southerners to discuss O'Connor's social, religious, and intellectual milieu.

Feeley, Kathleen. *Flannery O'Connor: Voice of the Peacock*. New Brunswick, N.J.: Rutgers University Press, 1972. Feeley, a Catholic nun, studies the marked passages in O'Connor's personal books to uncover the theological foundations of her writing. Doing so, she discerns six recurring themes in O'Connor's art and belief and concludes that O'Connor saw reality through the eyes of an Old Testament prophet.

Fickett, Harold, and Douglas R. Gilbert. *Flannery O'Connor: Images of Grace*. Grand Rapids, Mich.: Wm. B. Eerdmans, 1986. This critical-biographical essay traces O'Connor's artistic development and the treatment of sin and salvation in her writings. More than thirty photographs of O'Connor, including one self-portrait, and the people and places close to her illustrate the text.

Friedman, Melvin J., and Beverly L. Clark, eds. *Critical Essays on Flannery O'Connor*. Boston: G. K. Hall, 1985. This collection includes representative reviews of most of O'Connor's works, four of the most moving posthumous tributes, and a dozen outstanding critical essays, presented in the order of their first appearance. It concludes with a bibliography, annotated in depth, of diverse and innovative criticism intended for beginning as well as experienced readers of O'Connor.

Getz, Lorine M. *Flannery O'Connor: Her Life, Library, and Book Reviews*. New York: Mellen, 1980. This indispensable book for serous students of O'Connor includes perhaps the best chronological account of O'Connor's life and work, a descriptive list of her personal library, and a list of her published book reviews.

Golden, Robert E., and Mary C. Sullivan. *Flannery O'Connor and Caroline Gordon: A Reference Guide*. Boston: G. K. Hall, 1977. This annotated guide to reviews, articles, and books about O'Connor and her work, published between 1952 and 1976, is especially helpful in interpreting her work and tracing the development of her literary reputation in the early years.

Hendin, Josephine. *The World of Flannery O'Connor*. Bloomington: Indiana University Press, 1970. Hendin provides a provocative reading that takes issue with much earlier criticism, downplaying O'Connor's Catholicism and contending that she wrote out of rage at the disease that was consuming her.

Hyman, Stanley E. *Flannery O'Connor*. Minneapolis: University of Minnesota Press, 1966. This is a brief, often controversial overview of O'Connor's imagery, symbols, and themes. It includes a biographical sketch and places O'Connor in a modern literary context.

McFarland, Dorothy T. *Flannery O'Connor*. Modern Literature Monographs. New York: Frederick Ungar, 1976. McFarland provides an excellent overview for undergraduate students, including a biographical sketch, contextual background, and brief but comprehensive discussions of O'Connor's style, techniques, imagery, and major concepts.

Orvell, Miles. *Invisible Parade: The Fiction of Flannery O'Connor*. Philadelphia: Temple University Press, 1972. Orvell establishes several contexts for O'Connor's works—the South, Christianity, and literature—and then examines individual works within those contexts. This book may provide a good orientation to O'Connor, especially for those who are uncomfortable with her religious beliefs.

Christian Koontz

SANDRA DAY O'CONNOR

Born: March 26, 1930; El Paso, Texas

Areas of Achievement: Government and politics and law
Contribution: O'Connor was the first woman appointed to serve on the Supreme Court of the United States.

Early Life

Born on March 26, 1930, in El Paso, Texas, Sandra Day was brought up on a rustic cattle ranch in southeastern Arizona. The oldest of three children, she proved to be a hardworking and self-reliant young woman. By age ten, Sandra was riding horses, repairing fences, and driving tractors. She also developed studious habits as a youngster, reading the many magazines and books provided by her parents. Encouraged to value education by her college-educated mother, Ada Mae Wilkey Day, Sandra was sent to live with her maternal grandmother in order to attend a private girls' school in El Paso. Between the ages of six and fifteen, Sandra alternated between spending summers with her parents on the ranch and school months away. She was graduated from high school in Austin, Texas, at the relatively young age of sixteen.

A very mature young student, Sandra Day entered prestigious Stanford University in California at age sixteen. She completed both her undergraduate and law degrees by the time she was twenty-two. Her progress through school was both rapid and marked by high achievement. She attained magna cum laude status for her B.A. degree in economics, and she ranked third in her law school's graduating class. She was chosen to be a member of the Society of the Coif, an exclusive honorary society for superior law students, and she served on the staff of the highly regarded *Stanford Law Review*. There she met, and shortly thereafter married, John O'Connor, who later was to become a senior partner in an Arizona law firm.

Life's Work

Despite her considerable academic achievements, Sandra Day O'Connor was unable to obtain a position in one of the traditionally all-male private law firms in California, except as a legal secretary. Denied this opportunity, O'Connor began what would turn out to be an extraordinary career in public service. She served briefly as deputy attorney for San Mateo County in 1952-1953 before moving to West Germany because of her husband's Army assignment. Upon returning to the United States, she proceeded to have and rear three sons, while maintaining a busy schedule of volunteer activities in Phoenix, Arizona. Still unable to secure a law firm position, she devoted herself to public service, becoming one of Arizona's assistant attorney generals in 1965 and then a state senator in 1969. She later became the first woman to hold the majority leader position in a state senate.

Although she enjoyed the respect of her senate colleagues and the support of her constituents, O'Connor preferred the intellectual challenge of the judiciary to the social demands of the legislature. She successfully sought election in 1974 as a state trial judge, and four years later she was appointed by Governor Bruce Babbitt to the Arizona Court of Appeals. As both a state legislator and a judge, she developed a reputation as an extremely diligent, intelligent, and fair-minded public servant. Influenced as a youth by her father, Harry Day, who had an intense dislike for Franklin Delano Roosevelt and the policies of the Democratic Party, O'Connor became a loyal Republican Party activist, serving on the Arizona committee to reelect President Richard M. Nixon in 1972 and working for Ronald Reagan's presidential nomination in 1976. Her judicial temperament, fidelity to the Republican Party, impressive academic credentials, and impeccable moral character made her a prime candidate for a federal court appointment.

Since its opening session in 1789, and for almost two hundred years thereafter, no woman had served on the Supreme Court of the United States. In fulfillment of a campaign pledge to appoint a qualified woman to the U.S. Supreme Court, President Ronald Reagan nominated Sandra Day O'Connor on July 7, 1981, to become the 106th justice in the Court's history. This historic decision by President Reagan followed a three-month-long search headed by Attorney General William French Smith, who, ironically, had been a partner in one of the California law firms that had refused to hire O'Connor years before. Despite some questions that were raised about her relatively brief experience as an appellate court judge, her nomination was enthusiastically supported by both conservatives and liberals. O'Connor impressed members of the Senate Judiciary Committee with her careful and prudent approach to such controversial legal issues as abortion and the death penalty, and she made clear her strong conservative belief that judges ought to restrain themselves from injecting personal values into their judicial decisions. Her merit being obvious to all, she was confirmed by the U.S. Senate by a vote of 99 to 0 in September of 1981. O'Connor's womanhood, for so long an obstacle to career advancement, now provided the occasion for her rise to the pinnacle of the legal profession.

Sandra Day O'Connor is a distinguished and highly respected associate justice of the Supreme Court. She immediately impressed colleagues with her disciplined work habits and dignified yet congenial manner. Shortly after arriving, she initiated an aerobics class in the Supreme Court gymnasium for all women employees, which she attends faithfully. Although slowed by a bout with breast cancer in 1988, O'Connor maintains one of the most grueling work schedules of any justice. Journalists often note that she is exceedingly well prepared for each case, citing the incisive questions she poses to counsel when the Court conducts oral arguments.

On the Supreme Court, O'Connor has had a significant influence on some of the most controversial issues in constitutional law. Her moderately conservative judicial opinions have been particularly important in the areas of abortion, religion, affirmative action, federalism, and women's rights. On the nine-member Court, she has often cast the deciding vote, repeatedly discovering some reasonable middle-ground position between her more ideological liberal and conservative brethren.

O'Connor has defined the standard by which states must abide as they devise ways to regulate abortion. Rejecting both the arguments of conservatives that the Constitution does not prevent states from prohibiting abortions and the arguments of liberal feminists that states could place no constitutional restrictions on a woman's right to choose an abortion, she argued persuasively in *Planned Parenthood of Southeastern Pennsylvania v. Casey* (1992) that states could regulate abortion up to the point that these restrictions become an undue burden on the woman seeking the abortion.

In the controversial area of religion, O'Connor has again been a voice of moderation. Against liberals who advocate a virtually total separation of religion from state activities and against conservatives who argue that the Constitution allows active government support and encouragement of religion so long as the government does not establish one preferred religion, O'Connor has articulated the position that a government policy violates the Constitution if it intends, or appears, to endorse religion. She has said, however, that government ought not to impede private citizens who wish to engage in religious activity, even within public institutions.

O'Connor has actively participated in moving the Court to a more conservative stance on affirmative action even while defending such programs against more conservative justices who would abolish them in all circumstances. In a case that displayed her sensitivity to discrimination against women as well as her support for some types of affirmative action programs, she argued in *Johnson v. Transportation Agency of Santa Clara County* (1987) against the complaint of a white male who was passed over for a skilled job in favor of a woman who, though well qualified, scored slightly lower on an interview score. At the time, none of the 237 skilled positions in the agency was held by a woman. For O'Connor, this was sufficient evidence that the county had discriminated against women. In subsequent cases, she has tried to limit government affirmative action programs only to those circumstances in which they function as a remedy for evident, actual race or gender discrimination. Justice O'Connor has taken increasingly conservative positions in other areas of civil rights, such as voting rights. In 1993, for example, she ruled in *Shaw v. Reno* against the reorganization of legislative districts to maximize the voting power of African Americans.

O'Connor is the only one of her colleagues on the Court to have been an elected state legislator. This fact, combined with her fundamentally conservative values, has made O'Connor a strong advocate of limits on the power of the federal government over the states. This stance is reflected in her ardent defense of state court jurisdiction over criminal justice matters such as capital punishment. Her conservative views on federalism have emerged in such important decisions as *Gregory v. Ashcroft* (1991), in which, writing for the majority of the Court, O'Connor ruled that Missouri's constitutional requirement of mandatory retirement for judges did not violate the federal Age Discrimination in Employment Act. Similarly, in *New York v. U.S.* (1992), O'Connor's majority opinion declared that the federal government could not order state governments to assume ownership of nuclear waste if they failed to create adequate disposal sites as required by federal law. Justice O'Connor has become the leading judicial proponent of state sovereignty.

As for women's rights, O'Connor has stood forcefully for certain principles—that the Constitution mandates gender equality and that civil rights laws protect women against discrimination in education and employment. As a state senator, she supported the Equal Rights Amendment. In 1993, Justice O'Connor wrote an opinion for a unanimous court in *Harris v. Forklift Systems* which made sexual harassment in the workplace easier to prove. Although she is not a liberal feminist, O'Connor's efforts to preserve a woman's constitutional right to choose abortion, her votes on the Court to end discrimination against pregnant workers, and her opposition to the exclusion of women from men's private clubs demonstrate her commitment to gender equality.

Summary

Sandra Day O'Connor's pathbreaking rise to the Supreme Court was a significant moment in the greater transformation of women's lives in American society during the last half of the twentieth century. Her celebrated nomination to the Court, applauded by people of all political views, reflected the growing consensus that women were deserving of high political office and that they had been unjustly excluded from these positions for far too long. Her appointment to the Court also coincided with the increase in popularity of conservative political ideas in the 1980's, to which trend she contributed.

O'Connor's accomplishments go beyond the circumstances of her appointment. On the Court, she has influenced many important areas of American law, often casting pivotal votes in highly controversial cases. Scholars have proposed that O'Connor brings a uniquely feminine perspective to cases heard by the Court, marked in part by her consistent ability to see both sides of complex issues and her tendency to forge a reasonable compromise that is consistent with her basic conservative values. Other scholars have documented the fact that several of the justices became noticeably more receptive to arguments in favor of gender equality after O'Connor's arrival on the Court. O'Connor was joined by the second woman justice after President Bill Clinton nominated Ruth Bader Ginsburg to fill a vacancy on the Supreme Court in 1993.

Although women continue to be underrepresented in political office, O'Connor retains a unique public profile as one of the most popular and readily recognized Supreme Court Justices ever. Her determination to succeed in the predominantly male world of law and politics, and her ability to combine motherhood and family with a career dedicated to public service, make her a positive role model for many young women.

Bibliography

Abraham, Henry J. *Justices and Presidents*. 2d ed. New York: Oxford University Press, 1985. Contains a detailed and perceptive analysis of the political circumstances surrounding O'Connor's appointment to the Supreme Court, written by one of the best Supreme Court scholars.

Behuniak-Long, Susan. "Justice Sandra Day O'Connor and the Power of Maternal Legal Thinking." *The Review of Politics* 54 (Summer, 1992): 417-444. One of the more accessible scholarly analyses of O'Connor's jurisprudence. The author argues that O'Connor has a particularly feminine, though not feminist, perspective that influences her adjudication of legal controversies.

O'Connor, Sandra Day. "Portia's Progress." *New York University Law Review* 66 (December, 1991): 1546-1558. An illuminating lecture given by the justice in 1991 on the subject of women in the legal profession. O'Connor reviews her personal experience with societal discrimination and the history of Supreme Court cases dealing with women. She also explains how her views differ from those of many feminists.

Savage, David G. "Sandra Day O'Connor." In *Eight Men and a Lady: Profiles of the Justices of the Supreme Court*. Edited by the staff of the National Press. Bethesda, Md.: National Press Books, 1990. The best short biography of O'Connor, with a fine account of her appointment to the Court and an analysis of her decisions through her first four years on the Court.

———. *Turning Right: The Making of the Rehnquist Supreme Court*. New York: John Wiley & Sons, 1992. Biographical information on O'Connor and analyses of her votes in key cases are presented in the context of a comprehensive and penetrating journalistic account of the Supreme Court in action from 1986 to 1992.

Philip Zampini

GEORGIA O'KEEFFE

Born: November 15, 1887; Sun Prairie, Wisconsin
Died: March 6, 1986; Santa Fe, New Mexico
Area of Achievement: Art
Contribution: Breaking with European traditionalism, Georgia O'Keeffe pointed to new ways to perceive the world about her, creating precise, sometimes stark depictions of nature and of urban scenes.

Early Life

For her first twenty-eight years, Georgia Totto O'Keeffe was an artistic revolution waiting to erupt. Georgia, the second of seven children born to Francis and Ida Totto O'Keeffe in rural Wisconsin, was fascinated by art. By age ten, she wanted to be a painter, although she did not know what that entailed. When people pressed her to tell them what kind of painter she wanted to be, she invariably replied, "A portrait painter."

O'Keeffe's early training in art began with a local art teacher and continued in a parochial school. When the nun who taught art told the impressionable child that she was painting things too small, Georgia obliged by painting her subjects large, sometimes so large that her pictures overflowed their boundaries, as many of her later floral paintings would.

In 1905-1906, O'Keeffe attended the Art Institute in Chicago, where she was embarrassed to paint nude men and where she was schooled in an ultraconservative, highly traditional European style of painting. She spent the following year at the Art Students League in New York City, where, as had been the case in Chicago, her painting received favorable comment and won prizes.

O'Keeffe, however, was not receiving the kind of instruction she needed. Unwilling to go through life painting dead rabbits and pastoral scenes, she gave up painting in 1908, becoming a commercial artist in Chicago. She designed the rosy-cheeked girl who still graces cans of Dutch Cleanser. O'Keeffe hated commercial art but, needing to earn a living, she stayed with it until she fell ill, suffering a temporary impairment to her vision. She returned to her family, who had relocated in Virginia in 1903.

During this interval, O'Keeffe took a summer course at the University of Virginia, which did not admit women but allowed them to study in summer school. The instructor, Alon Bement, was a disciple of Arthur Dow of Columbia University, an artist who, influenced by Oriental art, had broken away from European artistic conventions. O'Keeffe eventually studied with Dow, who changed forever the way she saw things and re-created them.

From 1912 to 1914, O'Keeffe taught art in Amarillo, Texas, where she was intrigued by the big sky and the broad, seemingly endless plains. In 1915, she spent an abortive semester teaching at Columbia College in South Carolina, but the following fall she became an art instructor at West Texas State Normal School in Canyon.

It was during this teaching stint that O'Keeffe sent some of her charcoal drawings to her New York friend Anita Pollitzer, who showed them to photographer Alfred Stieglitz. He exhibited them in 1916—without O'Keeffe's knowledge or consent—at his 291 Gallery. This showing marked the beginning of Georgia O'Keeffe's future as an artist.

Life's Work

When Georgia O'Keeffe, recently arrived from Texas to continue her studies with Arthur Dow, learned that Alfred Stieglitz had shown her work without authorization, she stormed into his studio to confront him. When the two met, however, Stieglitz's enthusiastic assessment of her work mollified her.

Stieglitz, whose reputation in the art world was solid, held another exhibition of O'Keeffe's work in 1917. She was in Texas when this exhibition was held, but Stieglitz won O'Keeffe's heart by rehanging the entire exhibition for her alone when she arrived in New York shortly after the closing.

During her years in west Texas, O'Keeffe imbibed its stark landscape and intense colors, regularly painting the nearby Palo Duro Canyon, a favorite subject. Her artwork, always precise, began to show a new depth and originality in both its use of light and its angularity.

O'Keeffe was developing one of her most significant skills, an ability to paint something as static as a tree or flower yet imbue the painting with incredible motion and dynamism. Nothing in an O'Keeffe still life is at rest; everything moves. The charcoal sketches that first attracted Stieglitz's attention reflect this motion, but as O'Keeffe experimented with color and light, the motion in her still lifes became explosive.

By 1918, O'Keeffe was ready to leave west Texas. When Stieglitz arranged for her to receive a subvention in support of her painting, she willingly moved to New York and soon was living with Stieglitz. Her years in west Texas did much to shape O'Keeffe's later work. She had discovered the unique quality of light in the southwestern desert. Also, in search of objects for her students to paint, she stumbled upon the notion of using sun-bleached animal bones, which were plentiful in the surrounding desert.

Although she did not herself begin to paint animal skulls and pelvises until more than a decade later, she had gained an appreciation for the kind of patina that sun-drenched bones acquire and for their translucence. For the next decade, however, O'Keeffe, who had first visited Santa Fe, New Mexico, just before her return to New York, remained in the East. In 1924, she was married to Stieglitz, now divorced from the wife he had left in 1918.

The life O'Keeffe and Stieglitz had established in 1918—summers at the Stieglitz family home at Lake George in New York's Adirondack Mountains, winters in New York City—continued throughout the 1920's. O'Keeffe, Stieglitz's favorite model, spent much of her time and creative energy posing for his photographs, which he exhibited widely.

O'Keeffe was finding subjects for her own painting both at Lake George and in

New York City. In 1925, the couple moved into an apartment on the thirtieth floor of Lexington Avenue's Shelton Hotel from which O'Keeffe commanded a view that extended to the East River. Here she painted her famed New York cityscapes.

Her paintings of industrial scenes along the East River and of various buildings in New York City marked a new direction in O'Keeffe's career as an artist and reflected the influence of John Marin, whose paintings of industrial scenes impressed her when she first saw them in 1915.

In the 1920's, O'Keeffe also painted many still lifes—particularly flowers—and scenes from the Lake George summers. Perhaps the most interesting of her urban paintings is *The Shelton with Sunspots* (1926). The towering building in which O'Keeffe and Stieglitz lived springs from the bottom of the canvas like the prow of a ship, many of its details obscured by blinding sunspots that bounce off the hotel's windows. O'Keeffe imbues this painting of a bland, commonplace skyscraper with conflict. It has been suggested that O'Keeffe, who suffered from migraine headaches, replicated in this picture the play of light that sometimes accompanies that malady.

In 1929, Mabel Dodge Luhan invited Georgia O'Keeffe, who by now was well known, to visit her ranch in Taos, New Mexico. Because Stieglitz refused to venture west of the Hudson River, O'Keeffe went to New Mexico alone, remaining at the Luhan ranch from April until August. This trip heralded a new direction in O'Keeffe's life and work.

From that point on, she would spend most of her summers in New Mexico, doing so until 1946, when Stieglitz died. O'Keeffe moved permanently to Abiquiu, north of Santa Fe, in 1949. She had bought a house at Ghost Ranch, fifteen miles north of Abiquiu, in 1940 and occupied both houses until encroaching feebleness necessitated her final move to Santa Fe in 1984.

In Taos, O'Keeffe learned to drive and bought a car. Every day during her New Mexican summers, she packed her equipment into her car, which rode high off the ground, and drove into the desert to paint. When the desert heat oppressed O'Keeffe, she stretched out beneath the car's chassis.

The desert paintings represent a large portion of O'Keeffe's most celebrated work. Her paintings of animal bones—*Cow's Skull: Red, White, and Blue* (1931), *Ram's Head with Hollyhock* (1937), and *Pelvis with Moon* (1943)—representing an extended period in her artistic career, are among her most puckish works.

O'Keeffe enjoyed painting the soft, flowing lines and angles of adobe buildings, as seen in such paintings as her *Ranchos Church* (1930) or *Black Patio Door* (1955), to which such Lake George paintings as her *Stables* (1932) and *Barn with Snow* (1933) contrast sharply.

After Stieglitz's death, O'Keeffe became a world traveler. Many thought she had now entered her abstract period. Actually, many of the paintings she produced between 1946 and 1980 were photographically realistic representations of scenes she observed from more than 30,000 feet up as she jetted across the sky. Among her most famous paintings of this period is an enormous canvas, *Sky Above Clouds II* (1963).

Living to be nearly a hundred, Georgia O'Keeffe painted until failing eyesight forced her into a brief retirement with her companion, Juan Hamilton, and his family in Santa Fe. There she died quietly on March 6, 1986.

Summary

Georgia O'Keeffe always insisted that she was an artist, not a woman artist. She denied that gender had much to do with accomplishment and, from her earliest exhibitions, demonstrated that she could hold her own with her masculine competitors. Indeed, as an artist, she was superior to most of them.

During nearly a century of life, Georgia O'Keeffe continually grew professionally. She constantly tried new things. She considered no subject lacking in artistic potential, as her preoccupation with bones, paper flowers from New Mexican graveyards, conventional urban buildings, and scenes of smokestack industries clearly demonstrates.

O'Keeffe saw things as no one else saw them. Many subsequent artists have tried to imitate her floral paintings, for example, producing huge flowers crammed into canvases too small to accommodate them. Somehow, O'Keeffe could do that and, in the process, communicate something about the essence of a flower that no one had captured before. Her imitators end up with crowded canvases that look cramped. Perhaps an artist's imitators suggest more accurately than words can the true greatness of the artist they seek to copy.

In O'Keeffe's work, one finds the zeal for life that so well characterized her as a person. O'Keeffe left a legacy of hope to artists in all fields who dare to deviate drastically from artistic convention. O'Keeffe neither disparaged her predecessors nor imitated them. She was truly and completely her own person.

Bibliography

Ciboire, Clive, ed. *Lovingly, Georgia: The Complete Correspondence of Georgia O'Keeffe and Anita Pollitzer*. New York: Simon & Schuster, 1990. Georgia O'Keeffe maintained a correspondence with Anita Pollitzer, a classmate at Columbia University, for more than forty years. Much of it is reproduced here.

Didion, Joan. *The White Album*. New York: Simon & Schuster, 1979. Didion's "Georgia O'Keeffe" discusses O'Keeffe's reaction to "the men," the power structure that determined the artistic and aesthetic principles of the art world of her day.

Eisler, Benita. *O'Keeffe and Stieglitz: An American Romance*. New York: Doubleday, 1991. Eisler provides crucial insights into the sometimes stormy but always symbiotic relationship that existed between O'Keeffe and Stieglitz for the forty years they knew each other. Contains many of Stieglitz's photographs of O'Keeffe.

Lisle, Laurie. *Portrait of an Artist: A Biography of Georgia O'Keeffe*. Albuquerque: University of New Mexico Press, 1986. A sensitive and accurate biography of O'Keeffe. The author understands the artist's artistic orientation and how she uses her environment artistically.

Messinger, Lisa Mintz. *Georgia O'Keeffe*. New York: Metropolitan Museum of Art, 1988. This book, aside from O'Keeffe's autobiography, contains the best reproductions of O'Keeffe's work. It offers reproductions of the twenty-nine works in the collection of the Metropolitan Museum of Art. Well written and insightful.

O'Keeffe, Georgia. *Georgia O'Keeffe*. New York: Viking Press, 1976. If one could read only one book relating to O'Keeffe, this autobiography would be the sensible choice. An indispensable book for anyone seriously interested in O'Keeffe.

Peters, Sarah Whitaker. *Becoming O'Keeffe: The Early Years*. New York: Abbeville Press, 1991. Peters offers a sensitive and spirited look into the making of an artist. Excellent illustrations.

Robinson, Roxana. *Georgia O'Keeffe: A Life*. New York: Harper & Row, 1989. The most comprehensive biography of Georgia O'Keeffe to date. Well written and amply illustrated. The illustrations, however, do not include reproductions of O'Keeffe's work, which are readily available in the autobiography.

Shuman, R. Baird. *Georgia O'Keeffe*. Vero Beach, Fla.: Rourke, 1993. Intended for the nonspecialist, this book contains excellent illustrations, a chronology, and an annotated bibliography. It provides accurate coverage of O'Keeffe's life and work.

R. Baird Shuman

JACQUELINE KENNEDY ONASSIS

Born: July 28, 1929; Southampton, New York
Died: May 19, 1994; New York, New York
Area of Achievement: Government and politics
Contribution: Jacqueline Kennedy was one of the most famous First Ladies of the twentieth century. The American people associate her with the glamour and excitement of her husband's brief presidency, his tragic death, and the troubled history of her celebrated family.

Early Life

Jacqueline Lee Bouvier was born on July 28, 1929, to John Vernou Bouvier III and Janet Lee Bouvier in Southampton, Long Island, New York. Her father was a stockbroker and a member of a wealthy Roman Catholic family of French heritage. Her mother came from a prominent family in New York whose wealth was based on banking. During her early years, Jacqueline and her younger sister, Lee, grew up in comfortable circumstances. A local reporter covered her second birthday party, and the press noted her appearances in horse shows with her mother.

The Bouvier marriage encountered problems during the mid-1930's. After several separations, the couple divorced in 1940. Jacqueline and Lee lived with their mother but saw their father on weekends. His lessons about social behavior and the way that young women interacted with men made a great impression on Jacqueline. Her mother later married Hugh D. Auchincloss, also a prosperous stockbroker. Jacqueline attended Miss Chapin's School in New York City and entered Miss Porter's School in Connecticut when she was fifteen. She was presented to society in 1947. One columnist named her his "Debutante of the Year."

Jacqueline entered Vassar College in 1947. She spent her junior year in France, attending the University of Grenoble and the Sorbonne in Paris. She finished her college education at George Washington University, from which she was graduated in 1951. She won *Vogue* magazine's Prix de Paris contest but declined the award. After a summer trip to Europe in 1951, she worked at the *Washington Times-Herald* as the Inquiring Photographer, asking questions and taking pictures for a daily feature column. John F. Kennedy was one of the people she interviewed. She was briefly engaged to John G. W. Husted, Jr., but they ended the engagement by mutual agreement.

In 1951, friends introduced Jacqueline to Congressman John F. Kennedy of Massachusetts. They met again the following year, when Kennedy was a candidate for the United States Senate. After his victory in November of 1952, they saw each other more frequently. Their engagement was announced on June 24, 1953. They were married on September 12, 1953, with 750 wedding guests, 3,000 spectators, and extensive news coverage.

Life's Work

The early years of her marriage to John F. Kennedy were not easy ones for

Jacqueline Kennedy. She did not like politics or the routine of campaigning, at which her husband excelled. The senator's health was also poor, and she helped him recover from surgery in 1954 and 1955. Jacqueline provided particular assistance in the writing of his Pulitzer Prize-winning book *Profiles in Courage* (1956). She also had two miscarriages before her first child, Caroline, was born on November 27, 1957.

As John F. Kennedy made his run for the White House in 1960, his wife participated grudgingly in the early days of primary campaigning. Despite her reluctance to do so, she proved to be very popular with the people who saw her. The announcement of her pregnancy during the summer of 1960 enabled her to limit her campaign activities. A "Campaign Wife" newsletter, written for her by Kennedy aides, radio broadcasts, and several news conferences were her direct contribution to John Kennedy's narrow victory over Richard M. Nixon. Following the election, her son, John F. Kennedy, Jr., was born on November 25, 1960.

Jacqueline Kennedy had mixed feelings about her ceremonial role as the president's wife. She disliked the term "First Lady" and asked the White House staff not to use it. She was also unwilling to meet on any regular basis the various social and charitable delegations that came to the White House or sought her patronage. In her place, she sent the wife of the vice president, Lady Bird Johnson. Jacqueline Kennedy's relations with the press were often strained. She would have preferred that reporters not attend White House parties, and she sometimes referred to female journalists as "harpies."

Other aspects of her new position engaged Jacqueline Kennedy's enthusiastic interest. She regarded the White House itself as a potential national showplace for art and culture that previous administrations had ignored. She told her staff that she intended to make the mansion a grand place for the American people. Over the next three years, Jacqueline embarked on an ambitious program to obtain antiques and historical artifacts that would transform the White House into a replica of what existed during the era of Thomas Jefferson.

Jacqueline called upon wealthy friends to assist her in locating antiques suitable for the White House. The mechanism for receiving these funds and carrying on her work was the White House Historical Association. She obtained legislation from Congress that declared White House furnishings to be government property. To finance her campaign, the First Lady arranged for the sale of guidebooks to the White House. Jacqueline displayed what she had done when she conducted a televised tour of the White House on February 14, 1962. The program received critical praise for her taste and skill. Popular interest in the White House grew dramatically during the early 1960's because of Jacqueline Kennedy's efforts.

A related part of her agenda as First Lady was to promote cultural events. She and the president hosted more informal evenings than their predecessors had, and noted artists and performers entertained the dignitaries. Among those who appeared were noted cellist Pablo Casals, violinist Isaac Stern, and actor Frederic March. The social side of John Kennedy's "New Frontier" was a glittering success, and invitations to the Kennedy evenings at the White House became highly sought after.

Jacqueline Kennedy traveled with the president on some of his foreign tours and made several trips abroad on her own as well. When President Kennedy went to Paris in 1961, Jacqueline was such a success that her husband wryly remarked: "I am the man who accompanied Jacqueline Kennedy to Paris—and I have enjoyed it." The First Lady's trip to India in 1962 was another popular triumph for her.

Recent research has revealed that Jacqueline Kennedy was more of an adviser to the president than had been known previously. She attended some meetings of the National Security Council as an observer, and John Kennedy trusted her judgment on numerous issues. Though their marriage had experienced strain because of the president's infidelities, the couple drew closer together during their years in the White House. The death of their son Patrick in August of 1963, shortly after his birth, was a source of sadness.

Jacqueline Kennedy was riding with her husband in Dallas on November 22, 1963, when he was killed by an assassin. She supervised the details of the funeral in a way that made the ceremonies a moment of intense national mourning. Her stoic bearing and graceful dignity during the aftermath of the tragedy and through the funeral that followed impressed the world. In a conversation with a journalist shortly thereafter, she described her husband's presidency as an American "Camelot" and asked that his memory be preserved.

The five years after her husband's murder saw Jacqueline Kennedy endeavor to build a new life for herself and her children amid unrelenting newspaper publicity about her every move. She left Washington and lived in New York City. A difficult controversy with author William Manchester about the accuracy of his book on President Kennedy's death underscored her unique position with the public. Seeking to escape the constant scrutiny that followed her everywhere, she was married to Aristotle Onassis, a wealthy Greek ship owner, on October 20, 1968. The news shocked a nation that had regarded her as a perpetual presidential widow and thus recoiled from what appeared to be a marriage of convenience.

Her marriage to Onassis lasted for seven years, until he died in 1975. Publicity and photographers still surrounded her, and every aspect of Jacqueline Onassis' life was discussed in the media. In the years after the death of her second husband, she worked as an editor for several publishers in New York City and produced some best sellers for these firms. Her two children grew up, and she became a grandmother. In her mid-sixties, she was still a favorite subject for magazine covers and media attention. She refused to give interviews, wrote no memoirs, and made no comments on the many books written about her life and her years as Mrs. John F. Kennedy.

In January of 1994, Jacqueline Kennedy Onassis began to receive treatments for non-Hodgkin's lymphoma, a form of cancer. Her lymphoma was highly aggressive, and she died at home in New York City on May 19, 1994. She was buried in Arlington National Cemetery in Washington, D.C., next to her first husband, John F. Kennedy.

Summary

Jacqueline Kennedy Onassis was one of the most popular and famous of all First

Ladies. She is forever associated in the public mind with the brief years of the Kennedy presidency and its tragic conclusion. During the early 1960's, her restoration work at the White House, the glittering parties that she and her husband gave, and the image of worldly sophistication that she presented took the role of the First Lady to levels of international prominence that it had never previously attained. Her gallant bearing in the aftermath of her husband's murder gained for her a unique place in American social consciousness.

During the three decades between November of 1963 and her death in 1994, Jacqueline Kennedy Onassis saw her public image shift from the negative reaction when she married Aristotle Onassis in 1968 to a more positive assessment since the mid-1970's. Her success as a mother, editor, and cultural figure kept her in the news. Biographies and articles about her continued to attract a large readership. Jacqueline Kennedy Onassis's life offers striking evidence of the extent to which fame and celebrity have shaped the way in which Americans evaluate First Ladies as historical figures.

Bibliography

Anthony, Carl Sferrazza. *First Ladies: The Saga of the Presidents' Wives and Their Power*. 2 vols. New York: William Morrow, 1990-1991. Contains a sympathetic evaluation of Jacqueline Kennedy as First Lady.

Birmingham, Stephen. *Jacqueline Bouvier Kennedy Onassis*. New York: Grosset & Dunlap, 1978. A thoughtful and well-written biography that relies heavily on the work of other authors for its factual information.

Caroli, Betty. *First Ladies*. New York: Oxford University Press, 1987. An overview of the institution of First Ladies with some interesting insights about the performance of Jacqueline Kennedy in the White House.

Davis, John H. *The Bouviers: Portrait of an American Family*. New York: Farrar, Straus & Giroux, 1969. Davis is a member of the Bouvier family, and his access to important source materials and insights make this a very valuable volume about the Bouviers.

Gutin, Myra G. *The President's Partner: The First Lady in the Twentieth Century*. New York: Greenwood Press, 1989. Focusing on First Ladies as communicators and political surrogates for the president, this book appraises the impact of Jacqueline Kennedy's White House years.

Heymann, C. David. *A Woman Named Jackie*. Secaucus, N.J.: Carol Communications, 1989. A full biography that mixes original research in Jacqueline Kennedy's White House Social Files at the Kennedy Library with an equal amount of gossip.

Kelley, Kitty. *Jackie Oh!* Secaucus, N.J.: Lyle Stuart, 1978. A sensationalized biography that includes every lurid tale about its subject that the author could find. Some anecdotes may be true, but the book should be used cautiously.

Smith, Nancy, and Mary C. Ryan, eds. *Modern First Ladies: Their Documentary Legacy*. Washington, D.C.: National Archives and Records Administrations, 1989. This book of essays has an illuminating chapter on Jacqueline Kennedy's records at the John F. Kennedy Library and further information that helps to place her role as First Lady in historical context.

Thayer, Mary Van Rensselaer. *Jacqueline Kennedy: The White House Years*. Boston: Little, Brown, 1967. This volume draws extensively on Jacqueline Kennedy's Social Office Files at the John F. Kennedy Library. It is a valuable source, since so many of those files are still unavailable for research.

Lewis L. Gould

KATHERINE DAVALOS ORTEGA

Born: July 16, 1934; Tularosa, New Mexico

Area of Achievement: Government and politics
Contribution: As one of the first Latinas to hold a high government position, Ortega provided a role model and example for all women with political aspirations.

Early Life

Donaciano Ortega and Catarina Davalos, the parents of Katherine Davalos Ortega, were from pioneer families that in the 1800's settled in what later became the state of New Mexico. The couple married and had nine children, with Katherine the youngest. Donaciano held many different jobs, including that of deputy U.S. marshal, which he began at the age of sixteen. He also worked at a copper mine, had a blacksmith shop, and did carpentry work. The family moved to Tularosa, a town with fewer than three thousand inhabitants, so that the children could attend high school. The family owned and operated a restaurant and dance hall in Tularosa, then a restaurant and a furniture store in nearby Alamogordo, New Mexico. Katherine's oldest sister, Ellen, founded the Otero Savings and Loan Association there in 1974. The businesses were moderately successful, but the family had a modest income.

Working in the family restaurant provided Katherine with early training in business skills. Even at the age of ten, she showed such facility with numbers that she was allowed to work the cash register. All the Ortega children participated in the family business, and each had a say in its operation.

Donaciano Ortega encouraged his children to learn English, though Spanish was their first language, and Katherine attended schools where Spanish was used rarely or never. While a senior in high school, she worked at the Otero County State Bank in Alamogordo. After high school, she worked in a bank for two years to save money to pay her college tuition.

Katherine Ortega was graduated with honors from Eastern New Mexico University in 1957 with a bachelor's degree in business and economics. She also studied secondary education, giving some thought to teaching high school business courses, but she was told not to bother applying for jobs in the eastern part of the state because her Hispanic background would disqualify her. She decided to abandon teaching, disgusted with the discrimination that kept her from pursuing her preferred career to the level of her ability and in a location of her choice.

Life's Work

Soon after her graduation, Katherine Ortega started an accounting firm in Alamogordo with her sister, Ellen. She held several accounting positions in New Mexico and later in California, after she moved to Los Angeles in 1967. From 1969 to 1972, she worked as a tax superviser with Peat, Marwick, Mitchell and Company, one of the largest accounting firms in the United States. In 1972, Ortega was recruited by Pan

American National Bank of Los Angeles to serve as its vice president and cashier. Her accounting skills and bilingualism aided in her work with the local Hispanic community. In December, 1975, she was selected as president and director of the Hispanic-owned Santa Ana State Bank, becoming the first woman to be president of a commercial bank in California. In 1978, respecting the wishes of her mother, who was in ill health, Ortega returned to New Mexico. She became a consultant to the family-owned Otero Savings and Loan Association, which grew to have assets of $20 million while she was associated with it. She became a certified public accountant (CPA) in 1979.

Ortega had been active in the Republican Party since college and had joined the Young Republicans soon after graduation. Following her return to New Mexico, Ortega's involvement in politics intensified. She worked as a precinct chair for the party in Alamogordo and assisted in the campaign of Senator Pete Domenici. The Republican Party called on her to serve as a liaison with Hispanic and women's organizations.

Ortega was rewarded for service to the Republican Party in April, 1982, with her first presidential appointment, when Ronald Reagan named her to the ten-member Advisory Committee on Small and Minority Business Ownership. In December of that year, she was appointed to the five-person Copyright Royalty Tribunal, which was created in the late 1970's to set royalty fees that cable television systems had to pay to copyright holders of broadcast programs. Among other duties, the tribunal also set the fees that jukebox operators paid to copyright holders of music.

While Ortega was serving on the Copyright Royalty Tribunal, Reagan recognized her professional abilities. On September 12, 1983, on the recommendation of Senator Domenici, who was then chair of the Senate Budget Committee, Reagan nominated Ortega as treasurer of the United States. Ortega would replace Angela M. Buchanan, who left office after the birth of her first child. The nomination came at a ceremony marking the beginning of Hispanic Heritage Week. Reagan's nominating speech pointed out the positive influence of the strength and decency of the Hispanic family. At the ceremony announcing her nomination, Ortega stressed the opportunities increasingly becoming available to women but noted the importance of self-reliance.

Ortega was sworn in on October 3, 1983, becoming the thirty-eighth holder of the position of treasurer of the United States. After being sworn in by Treasury Secretary Donald T. Regan, she signed special forms that were later used to add her signature to printing plates from which U.S. currency would be produced. Ortega was the tenth woman, and the second Latina, to be U.S. treasurer, following Romana Acosta Bañuelos, who served in the position from 1971 to 1974. Beginning in the mid-twentieth century, the position traditionally was given to a woman as a reward for service to her party and to the president. Ortega's new appointment made her the highest-ranking Hispanic in the Reagan Administration.

As U.S. treasurer, Ortega supervised the Bureau of Engraving and Printing, the U.S. Mint, and the U.S. Savings Bond Division. At the time of her appointment, Ortega oversaw five thousand employees and a budget of $220 million; her salary was

$63,800 per year. The treasurer is a senior member of the staff of the secretary of the treasury, who is a member of the president's cabinet. The Bureau of Engraving and Printing produces U.S. currency as well as other documents and postage stamps. Ortega's signature soon began to appear in the lower left-hand corner on the front of each unit of U.S. paper currency. In 1985, Ortega was given the responsibility of promoting the sale of U.S. Liberty Coins, special gold and silver commemorative coins designed to raise $40 million to pay some of the costs of restoring the Statue of Liberty.

During 1984, Ortega traveled around the country speaking to various Hispanic and Republican groups. Although hers was not a policy-making position, she was important in articulating the Republican Party position on policy issues. Ortega's most important speaking engagement came at the end of the year, when she was chosen to give the keynote address at the Republican National Convention in Dallas, Texas. This honor recognized her accomplishments as a government official. She noted at the time that she was firmly committed to Reaganomics and the Republican Party, saying that she was "born a Republican." Political analysts widely expected a woman to be chosen to deliver the keynote address, but Senator Nancy Kassebaum and cabinet members Elizabeth Dole and Margaret Heckler, all with much more tenure at high levels of the federal government, were considered more likely to be chosen for the honor. In her speech, Ortega referred several times to her Hispanic heritage, and she included several phrases in Spanish. She noted how many people of Hispanic descent were leaving the Democratic Party and welcomed them to the Republican fold.

Ortega's high profile at the convention served to dispel complaints that the Reagan Administration was not committed to appointing women to high positions. Ortega made a point in her many speeches of emphasizing the many subcabinet positions that Reagan had filled with women.

Ortega served as treasurer of the United States from 1983 to 1989. She was married to Lloyd J. Derrickson on February 17, 1989. After leaving government service, she was primarily self-employed. She also served as an alternative representative to the United Nations and was on the boards of directors of several major corporations, including Ralston Purina Company and the Kroger Company.

Summary

Katherine Davalos Ortega serves as an example of how determination and hard work can lead to success in a chosen field. Although she came from a modest background and suffered discrimination that made her abandon teaching, her first career choice, she earned professional credentials and through her dedicated work won the recognition of the Republican Party. She was well qualified when President Reagan looked for a candidate, preferably a Hispanic woman, to fill the position of U.S. treasurer.

In that position, Ortega was one of the highest ranking Hispanic members of the Reagan Administration. She provided a positive role model, and her service likely played some part in the increasing numbers of appointments of people of Hispanic descent to high government positions. The administration of President Bill Clinton, for example, included two Latinos, Henry G. Cisneros and Federico F. Peña, in cabinet-level positions as secretary of Housing and Urban Development (HUD) and secretary of transportation, respectively.

Ortega's life achievements and government service have been recognized and honored by many groups. She was given the 1977 Outstanding Alumni Award from Eastern New Mexico State University and also earned the California Business-woman's Achievement Award and the Damas de Comercio Outstanding Woman of the Year Award. She was willing to serve as an example to other Hispanics, noting that everyone encounters obstacles of some sort. When faced with discrimination, she chose a career path on which her abilities would speak for themselves.

Bibliography

Brownstein, Ronald, and Nina Easton. *Reagan's Ruling Class: Portraits of the President's Top One Hundred Officials*. Washington, D.C.: Presidential Accounting Group, 1982. Provides details about the people with whom Ortega worked in Washington, D.C., but does not discuss her. Useful for providing context on Reagan's other appointees.

Clines, Francis X. "Reagan Names Hispanic Woman as Treasurer of the United States." *The New York Times*, September 13, 1983, p. B14. Brief article announcing Reagan's nomination of Ortega. Notes that the announcement, made at a White House ceremony for Hispanic Heritage Week, came at a time that the Republican Party was trying to attract Hispanic voters.

Edmunds, Lavinia. "Women to Watch at the Republican National Convention." *Ms.* 13 (August, 1984): 22. Places Ortega in the context of women at the convention, at which the Republican Party had vowed to have about half of its delegates be women. Notes that Ortega was firmly committed to Reaganomics and that cabinet members Elizabeth Dole and Margaret Heckler, along with Senator Nancy Kassebaum, had been considered more likely to be chosen as keynote speaker.

Gonsior, Marian C. "Katherine D. Ortega." In *Notable Hispanic American Women*, edited by Diane Telgen and Jim Kamp. Detroit: Gale Research, 1993. A three-page biography of Ortega. Useful for details about her early life, with many of Ortega's thoughts included as quotations. The volume as a whole provides an overdue look at the contributions of Hispanic American women.

McFadden, Robert. "Choice for Treasurer: Katherine Davalos Ortega." *The New York Times*, September 13, 1983, p. B14. A brief biography with some quotations from Ortega regarding her background.

Morey, Janet, and Wendy Dunn. "Katherine Davalos Ortega." In *Famous Mexican Americans*. New York: E. P. Dutton, 1989. An eight-page biography, containing details of the duties of the U.S. treasurer. Appropriate for middle-school readers. Contains a photograph of Ortega as treasurer of the United States.

Salkowski, Charlotte. "GOP Keynoter Radiates Self-Help Ideals." *The Christian*

Science Monitor, August 17, 1984, pp. 1, 32. An article about Ortega written near the time of her keynote address at the Republican National Convention. Notes her modest background and opinions concerning the character-building nature of hard work and self-sufficiency.

A. J. Sobczak

GERALDINE PAGE

Born: November 22, 1924; Kirksville, Missouri
Died: June 13, 1987; New York, New York
Areas of Achievement: Theater and drama and film
Contribution: A dedicated stage and screen actress of consummate skill, Geraldine Page first earned great critical acclaim for her interpretation of sensual, neurotic women in plays by Tennessee Williams. She was a brilliant method actress who, for thirty years, had few serious rivals in the mastery of that technique.

Early Life

Geraldine Page, born on November 22, 1924, in Kirksville, Missouri, was the first of two children reared by Leon Elwin and Edna Pearl Page. When she was five, her father, an osteopathic physician, moved the family to Chicago, where she grew up with her younger brother, Donald. She attended Englewood High School, developing an interest in music and art. After graduation, she briefly attended the University of Chicago.

Geraldine took up theater only after considering other career possibilities. She had first wanted to be a concert pianist, but because the family could not afford the cost of her training, she decided to try art, choosing acting only after her attempts at painting proved frustrating. She realized acting's great appeal when, at seventeen, she played in an amateur, Sunday-school production of *Excuse My Dust* and found she could evoke a strong emotional response in her audience. She also credited her father with nudging her in the right direction, though he wanted most for her to try her hand at writing.

Another amateur staging, of Louisa May Alcott's *Little Women*, in which she played Jo, compelled her father to honor his promise to send her to the Goodman Theatre Dramatic School, from which she was graduated in 1945. With the advice of her dean, she helped form an acting company that performed in summer stock productions at Lake Zurich, outside Chicago, but she also took leading parts in productions at Woodstock, Illinois. During winter seasons, Page went to New York, taking all kinds of odd jobs to pay her room and board while looking for role assignments. For each of four frugal years she faced disappointment, but she persisted, despite niggling doubts about chances of success. At night, when not studying Shakespeare, she ushered or checked hats in theaters, and during the day sold books or wound thread cones at the International Thread Company, her only stable job.

In 1949, Page enrolled in New York's famous Actor's Workshop, studying the method acting techniques taught by Lee Strasberg and Elia Kazan. Although she made important contacts, for three years she could secure only an occasional part in Off-Broadway productions. Fortunately, one role she played, that of the Pagan Crone in a 1951 production of Federico García Lorca's *Yerma* (1934) staged by the Loft Players at the Circle-in-the-Square in Greenwich Village, convinced the show's director, Jose Quintero, to give her the lead part in the 1952 Circle-in-the-Square production of Tennessee Williams' *Summer and Smoke* (1948). Page's brilliant portrayal of Alma Winemiller, a complex character with an intense but repressed sexuality, astounded all the play's reviewers, and their raves soon compelled skeptical Broadway producers and directors to trek downtown to see her perform. Most went back as ardent believers, and it was obvious long before the play's ten-month run ended that Page, suddenly a hot property, was about to take a giant career step forward.

Life's Work

Summer and Smoke brought Geraldine Page offers from Hollywood agents, who promised screen tests and big dollar contracts, exciting opportunities for an actress who had still been working as a dress-shop clerk and lingerie model when she first got the role of Alma. She reluctantly declined initial offers because she wanted first to land a major part in a Broadway production, but she finally agreed to a seven-year film contract with Charles Feldman, an independent producer who agreed to let her continue her stage work.

Before the end of 1952, she accomplished her immediate goal of securing a Broadway role, getting the part of Lily in Vina Delmar's *Midsummer*, which opened at the Vanderbilt Theatre in January of 1953 and ran for more than a hundred performances. Her portrayal of the uneducated wife of a schoolteacher won great critical acclaim, confirming her right to headline billings, but the play itself was at best damned with faint praise.

Page, as she confided in a 1953 interview, quickly discovered that success exacted a heavy toll, often leaving her exhausted. But it was also exhilarating, and she continued to work with enduring dedication. She sought to master the method style of acting, continuing study under Uta Hagen, from whom she learned how to keep a role fresh and challenging.

Although she had played a bit part in an earlier film made in New York, her first major film role was in *Hondo* (1953), a Warner Bros. western featuring John Wayne. Page played a spirited and resourceful woman striving to survive on the frontier during an Apache uprising. She did well enough to get her first Oscar nomination and the promise of additional screen assignments, but it would actually be seven years before she got another role. Perhaps, as she later confided, she was unofficially blacklisted, stigmatized in the McCarthy era anticommunist hysteria because she had once appeared with Paul Robeson in *Othello*. Still, in 1953 her prospects seemed very good. Her salary climbed from $40 to more than $300 per week, ensuring her survival in a tough, unforgiving business.

Although Page would continue to work in film throughout her career, her greatest early triumphs were on the stage, first as Alma Winemiller, then, in 1959, as the jaded and fading film queen, Alexandra del Lago, in another Tennessee Williams play, *Sweet Bird of Youth*, for which she won the Drama Critics Award for Actress of the Year. She reprised the parts of both Alma and Alexandra in film versions of the two works, playing opposite Laurence Harvey in *Summer and Smoke* (1961), and Paul Newman in *Sweet Bird of Youth* (1962), both highly regarded screen adaptations. The actress, however, always preferred the stage versions, bristling at Hollywood's insistence on glamorizing both parts and defusing much of the playwright's raw power.

For a time, Page seemed to run the risk of being permanently identified with her roles in Williams' two plays. Her soft, husky voice, shy but slightly tawdry looks and mannerisms, including an imposing array of nervous tics and facial twitches, seemed to suit the playwright's decadent and emotionally tormented heroines to perfection and threatened to leave an indelible impression on critical minds. Within a decade, however, Page turned in other fine stage performances, establishing both her range and versatility, although throughout her career a few critics would carp at what they considered her excessive histrionics.

She worked both in New York and in regional theaters, convinced that good theater should be available to general audiences everywhere. Her reputation, strong from the beginning, was further enhanced by her performances in, among other new plays and revivals, N. Richard Nash's *The Rainmaker* (1954), an adaptation of André Gide's *The Immoralist* (1954), Eugene O'Neill's *Strange Interlude* (1964), Anton Chekhov's *The Three Sisters* (1964), Lillian Hellman's *The Little Foxes* (1974), Alan Ayckbourn's *Absurd Person Singular* (1974), John Pielmeier's *Agnes of God* (1982), Sam Shepard's *Lie of the Mind* (1985), and Noel Coward's *Blithe Spirit* (1987), in which she was still performing at the time of her death. In fact, her love for and fascination with live theater never diminished, and she remained a lifelong student of her craft. She also promoted theater, and with her husband, actor Rip Torn, whom she married in 1961, she founded the Sanctuary Theatre, a repertory company. Her work in touring shows was almost always done from love and dedication rather than necessity.

Yet, while theater remained her first passion, her film roles gave her a wider, more popular and bigger audience, and, financially, even greater success. For a long time, however, she had the dubious distinction of being nominated for more Academy Awards without winning an Oscar than any other actor except Peter O'Toole. Seven films secured her nomination for either Best Actress or Best Supporting Actress: *Hondo*, *Summer and Smoke*, *Sweet Bird of Youth*, *You're a Big Boy Now* (1967), *Pete 'n' Tillie* (1972), *Interiors* (1978), and *The Pope of Greenwich Village* (1984). Finally, after being nominated for the eighth time, she won an Academy Award for Best Actress for her brilliant depiction of Carrie Watts, an aging, nostalgic, beleaguered, but spunky woman, in the last major film of her career, *The Trip to Bountiful* (1985). Her performance was considered by many to be her cinematic masterpiece. With her characteristic theatrical flair, Page declined to attend the award ceremony and made her acceptance remarks from New York in the presence of her repertory company.

A heart attack claimed Geraldine Page's life in 1987, only a year after her Oscar win for *The Trip to Bountiful*. She was only sixty-two at the time of her death, and had just seemed to have taken a new turn in her superb career, showing that age alone could not foil her great, enduring genius.

Summary

Geraldine Page's last significant film and stage work, in *The Trip to Bountiful* and

Blithe Spirit, which earned for her a Tony nomination, demonstrated her great resourcefulness as an actress. Hers was an extraordinary talent, but her dramatic range was in some measure obscured by her tremendous success in specific roles. Perhaps that is the ironic risk of the method style of acting, which encourages actors to become the character they play.

It was in her less celebrated parts that Page revealed her adaptability to atypical roles, as, for example, that of the comic mother, Margery Chanticleer, in the film *You're a Big Boy Now* (1966), her two Emmy-winning roles in televised adaptations of two Truman Capote stories, "A Christmas Memory" (1967) and "The Thanksgiving Visitor" (1969), or as the marvelous voice of Madame Medusa in the Disney animated feature, *The Rescuers* (1977). If she was often cast for her ability to depict eccentric women, she nevertheless demonstrated that eccentricity did not necessarily mean a stereotypical performance. It was, after all, her ranging artistic genius that garnered her a host of national and international awards.

Above all, Page was a devoted student and practitioner of her craft, with a great ability to sway the passions of her audiences. Although she had unrelenting professional dedication and great confidence in her talent, she also valued her privacy and independence offstage. She was kind, easygoing, and personable, an actor who was particularly respected and loved by those who worked with her in theater, a world in which egos have all too often have gotten in the way of talents far inferior to hers.

Bibliography

Hochman, Sandra. "Geraldine Page: A Self-Portrait in Words." *The New York Times*, June 21, 1987, p. H5. This is a brief, posthumous selection of the last recorded reflections of the actress on her career, gleaned from an interview conducted by Sandra Hochman. It is full of engaging charm and humor, and includes a photograph taken just before her death.

Hutchins, David. "After Seven Oscar Snubs, Geraldine Page May Trip off to Bountiful at Last." *People Weekly* 25 (March 24, 1986): 72-76. An illustrated essay covering Page's career, this piece focuses on her admirable professional commitment. It also recounts some intimate details, including insights into Page's marriage with Rip Torn. It is helpful as one of the last profiles of the actress published before her death.

Kalter, Joanmarie. *Actors on Acting: Performing in Theatre and Film Today*. New York: Sterling, 1979. A collection of in-depth interviews with ten men and women actors from a range of performing backgrounds. Geraldine Page's interview touches on her motivation in becoming an actor, her training with various practitioners of method acting, and her struggles to perfect her craft on stage and screen. Rich with anecdotes from her career up through the filming of Woody Allen's *Interiors* (1978).

Yacowar, Maurice. *Tennessee Williams and Film*. New York: Frederick Unger, 1977. This study critiques all film adaptations of Williams' plays through the period of his great successes. It fits Page's film performances in *Summer and Smoke* and

Sweet Bird of Youth into a critical framework focusing on each film's strengths and weaknesses and its director's artistic vision.

Young, William C. *Famous Actors and Actresses on the American Stage*. 2 vols. New York: R. R. Bowker, 1975. This collection of critical excerpts includes an interview segment, an early profile of Page, and reflections by Walter Kerr from *The Theatre in Spite of Itself* (1963). Combined, they give important, intimate insights into Page and her early career.

John W. Fiero

ALICE FREEMAN PALMER

Born: February 21, 1855; Colesville, New York
Died: December 6, 1902; Paris, France
Area of Achievement: Education
Contribution: The second president of Wellesley College, Palmer championed the cause of educational reform for women, greatly influencing attitudes of educators and society at large concerning the need for quality education for women at every level.

Early Life

Alice Elvira Freeman was the oldest of four children born to James Warren Freeman and Elizabeth Josephine Higley Freeman on a farm in Colesville, New York. When Alice was nine years old, her father decided to pursue his interest in medicine in hope of improving the family economic situation. Elizabeth Freeman assumed full support of the children for two years and her husband received his degree from the Albany Medical College in 1864. Alice's early education came mostly from her parents. Her mother and grandmother had experience as schoolteachers, and her father was adventurous and inquisitive. The family was deeply religious and active in promoting moral and social causes. Alice was given household responsibilities that often included the care of younger siblings. She gained much practical knowledge and developed a deep love of nature which she carried into adulthood. At three years of age, Alice had taught herself to read; by the next year, she began to attend the village school. In the one-room school, however, educational stimulation was limited.

In 1865, Dr. Freeman moved his family to the nearby village of Windsor, New York, to begin his medical practice. Alice was enrolled at Windsor Academy, a coeducational preparatory school where she came into contact with formal, rigorous education for the first time. The academy's teachers came from prestigious institutions such as Harvard and Andover, and Alice excelled in her work. At age fourteen, she became engaged to a theology professor. She soon realized, however, that her own goals in life depended on her receiving adequate education. She viewed marriage as an equal partnership that would be impossible without an education equal to that of her mate. Six months after the young professor left for seminary at Yale, Alice broke the engagement.

The Freeman family lived in relative poverty to which the members responded with a certain resourcefulness and creativity. Although the parents valued education, for financial reasons it was decided that the funds available must go to Alice's brother, who would one day likely be in a position of supporting a family of his own. Alice had been preparing diligently at Windsor to enter college and was willing to sacrifice whatever was necessary to attend. She bargained with her parents that if they would even partially finance her higher education, she would take on no family responsibilities of her own until each of her three siblings had received the education they desired, and her father gave his consent.

Alice had thought of entering newly founded Vassar College, but was not satisfied that the college would offer women as rigorous an education as men received at the finest schools. Instead, she chose to travel far from home and take entrance examinations at the University of Michigan, one of the few universities in the country offering a coeducational program. Unfortunately, she failed the examinations. During her interview, however, she attracted the attention of the university president, who interceded on Alice's behalf. She was allowed six months to prove her suitability as a student. This she did admirably and, after years of financial hardship and sometimes ill health, graduated in 1876, with a bachelor of arts degree. Family finances had deemed it necessary for Alice to interrupt her studies in 1875 and take a temporary position as preceptress at a struggling high school in Ottawa, Illinois. From the outset, her skill as an administrator was evident. She negotiated smoothly with faculty and students and designed quality courses of study. Nevertheless, finishing her own education was her priority, and she returned as soon as possible to the university despite pleas from the community to remain.

Life's Work

After graduation from the University of Michigan, Alice Freeman embarked on a succession of difficult years as she fulfilled her resolution to help her family and educate her siblings. Jobs were low paying and not always of her choice; however, her record of achievements was no less than excellent in each situation. She taught in a girls' seminary in Lake Geneva from 1876 to 1877 and from 1877 to 1879 at the high school of Saginaw, Michigan. In 1877, she received her first invitation to teach at Wellesley College as an instructor of mathematics, but refused for personal reasons. In 1878, Henry Fowle Durant, the founder of Wellesley, contacted her again with the offer of a position in the Greek department. Her sister Stella, to whom she was devoted, was ill and needed her care. Again, she declined. Stella died in 1879, and, although it was a time of deep sorrow for Alice, she was freed to go about her work with a more independent spirit. When Durant called for the third time, she accepted the chairmanship of the History department in 1879, and went to Wellesley.

The college had been founded by Durant and his wife in an effort to promote the same kind of education for women that was offered to men in the United States. The ideals were in close kinship with those that Freeman upheld, and she worked tirelessly with the young women whom she taught. The college was experimental and liberal in its program of studies, and Durant was insistent that research and laboratory work were more important than simply learning from a textbook. This placed a large demand on the faculty not only to lecture but also to prepare detailed reading lists from which the students worked. Shortly after Durant's death in 1881, Ada L. Howard, the president of Wellesley, resigned. Alice Freeman, whose work had shown dedication and consummate skill, was chosen at age twenty-six to be vice president of the college and acting president. In 1882, she became the second president of Wellesley, where her talent as an administrator and organizer of human resources found an ideal outlet.

During her six years as president, much of Freeman's time was spent stabilizing the academic and administrative structure while implementing goals Durant had set for the college. She organized the Academic Council composed of heads of the academic departments to which she turned often for advice and consultation in academic matters. Standing faculty committees were formed and a building program was begun which included a gymnasium and dormitories. Networks were created with feeder high schools in the country and the preparatory school was discontinued. Freeman's full energy then went into improving the collegiate program by raising academic standards and simplifying and standardizing the courses of study that were offered. Although tuition was increased, Freeman also endeavored to make more scholarships available to students. Her contacts in the field and keen sense of people's abilities also culminated in successful efforts to build the faculty.

Alice Freeman's professional life was not restricted to the Wellesley campus, but extended to matters of general education. She was instrumental in establishing the Association of Collegiate Alumnae in 1882 (forerunner of the American Association of University Women), which brought together educated women nationwide who were interested in raising standards of education for women. She served two terms as president in 1885-1886 and 1889-1890. In 1884, she was one of three American delegates elected to attend the International Conference on Education in London.

In 1887, Alice Freeman's life took a new turn. A friendship with Harvard philosopher George Herbert Palmer developed into a romance, and the two were married on December 23. Having decided that her work at Wellesley was finished and the college was ready for a time of quiet growth and the watchful care of someone new, she resigned her position shortly before her marriage, much to the despair of the college and of her public, especially those who felt she had compromised her profession for marriage. Instead, she envisioned her future as an opportunity to continue to pursue her goals within the comfort of a lifestyle that for the first time included leisure. She was constantly available for public addresses and gave unselfishly of her time to any organization that supported the ideals of excellence in education, particularly that of women. She remained on the executive committee of the Board of Trustees at Wellesley until her death and was active as well in the founding of Radcliffe College as separate from, but affiliated with, Harvard. Her work was separate from that of her husband, but each received ample support and respect from the other. The couple spent several sabbaticals in Europe, where they traveled many miles on bicycle enjoying the countryside. Alice and her husband also spent many summers at the Palmer family farm in Boxford, Massachusetts, twenty-five miles north of Boston, where they enjoyed tranquility not possible in the city.

In 1891, Alice Palmer was one of five delegates from Massachusetts chosen to attend the World Columbian Exhibition in Chicago, an event that highlighted the work of international women in many professions, including education. In 1892, she received a Ph.D. degree from the University of Michigan. In the same year, she was invited by the new University of Chicago to serve as their dean of women. Although Alice and her husband were both offered positions, they decided not to leave Boston. The university's president, William Rainey Harper, was determined to entice the most capable woman he knew in the field and persisted in modifying the conditions until she agreed to serve. She was required to spend only twelve weeks' residence in Chicago, allowed to elect her own sub-dean, and released from any teaching responsibilities. She stayed until 1895, having established policies on which others could build.

Her professional activity continued and included work with the Woman's Home Missionary Society of the Presbyterian Church and the Women's Educational Association, an organization founded in Boston in 1891 and of which she was president for nine years. The Massachusetts Board of Education appointed her to its membership in 1889, and she helped to raise levels of high school education in the state and ensure free high school education for every citizen. In 1902, while on sabbatical with her husband, Alice Palmer died in Paris of a heart attack at the age of forty-seven.

Summary

Alice Freeman Palmer was a true pioneer in the field of education for women. Her life was spent in preparation for her work and in professional endeavors that helped to drastically change the quality of academic opportunity offered to women in the United States. Her accomplishments were numerous, and, fortunately for society, came early in her brief life. She had a gift for working among people that called for the best from them and herself. Recognition included honorary degrees from Columbia University in 1887 and Union University in 1896. In 1920, she became the second youngest person to be named to the Hall of Fame at New York University, which recognizes professionals from a variety of fields. She left no writing for posterity other than a few articles and a book of romantic poems called *A Marriage Cycle* (1915). Her lasting mark was made, however, through her interaction with students and faculty and her willingness to involve herself fully with important causes in cooperation with others, thus bringing many worthwhile ideas to fruition. Her efforts made a difference for all women who have followed her as she opened the doors to educational and professional challenges never before possible.

Bibliography

Bordin, Ruth B. *Alice Freeman Palmer: The Evolution of a New Woman.* Ann Arbor: University of Michigan Press, 1993. The most recent biography of Palmer, Bordin's work gives an excellent account of Palmer's achievements, impact, and interaction with other prominent figures in the struggle for equal education for women.

Palmer, George Herbert. *The Life of Alice Freeman Palmer.* Boston: Houghton Mifflin, 1924. Written by her husband, this biography offers an intimate look at Alice Palmer's life and work. Some correspondence and poetry are included.

Palmieri, Patricia A. "Here Was Fellowship: A Social Portrait of Academic Women at Wellesley College, 1895-1920." *History of Education Quarterly* 23 (Summer, 1983): 195-214. A scholarly article that discusses the lives of various figures encountered by Palmer during her tenure as professor and then as president of the college.

Storr, Richard J. *Harper's University: The Beginnings*. Chicago: University of Chicago Press, 1966. This history of the University of Chicago gives insight into Palmer's tenure as the first dean of women.

Weimann, Jeanne Madeline. *The Fair Women*. Chicago: Academy Chicago, 1981. This account of the Women's Building at the World Columbian Exposition discusses Palmer's involvement with the education exhibition.

Wein, Roberta. "Women's Colleges and Domesticity: 1875-1918." *History of Education Quarterly* 14 (Spring, 1974): 31-47. The article explores activity at Wellesley and Bryn Mawr at a time when decisions made had a major effect on whether female education would continue to perpetuate feminine passivity or foster independence.

Sandra C. McClain

DOROTHY PARKER

Born: August 22, 1893; West End, New Jersey
Died: June 7, 1967; New York, New York
Area of Achievement: Literature
Contribution: Parker's ironic wit, astute observations, and acute verse, along with her place at the Algonquin Round Table, made her one of the twentieth century's most popular writers.

Early Life

Dorothy Rothschild was born on a rainy August night in 1893, at her family's summer home on the shore of West End, New Jersey. Her father, Jacob Henry Rothschild, was the son of German-Jewish immigrants who came to the United States in the wake of the revolutions that spread across Europe in 1848. J. Henry, as he preferred to be known, joined his father in the men's furnishings business. In 1868, he fell in love with his neighbor, Eliza Annie Marston, the daughter of Christian English gun merchants. The disapproval of her family kept the two apart for ten years, during which time Eliza took a job teaching public school; they finally married in 1878.

Dorothy, who was born when Eliza was forty-two years old, was the last of four children. The family lived the comfortable lives of the upper middle class, hiring Irish maids and residing on the fashionable Upper West Side. Disaster, however, does not acknowledge wealth: On July 20, 1898, when Dorothy was four years old, Eliza died of a combination of acute colic and heart disease.

Within less than two years, Henry married another well-educated gentile, Eleanor Francis Lewis. Dorothy cordially despised both her and the Blessed Sacrament Academy where Eleanor convinced Henry to enroll her as a day student. Eleanor's determination to see Dorothy accept Christian dogma kept the two at constant loggerheads. Their struggles ended in April, 1903, when Eleanor died suddenly of a cerebral hemorrhage.

After Eleanor's death, Dorothy attended the academically rigorous Miss Dana's School in Morristown, New Jersey, where she learned Latin and French and was required to recite poetry. She graduated in 1911. From that moment until her father's death in 1913, Dorothy's social life revolved around tedious parties, piano playing, and composing silly rhymes to send to her father while she sat on the wide verandas of various seaside hotels.

Henry's death on December 28, 1913, marked the end of Dorothy's comfortable, middle-class life for a time. After the siblings divided up the household goods, Dorothy was forced to support herself by playing the piano at various Manhattan dance schools. She amused herself in the off-hours by writing light verse. Although she professed not to think of verse as a serious vocation, she thought enough of her efforts to send pieces to various publishers, including Franklin Pierce Adams, writer of the newspaper column "The Conning Tower," and to Frank Crowninshield at *Vanity Fair*.

Acceptance finally came in 1914, when Crowninshield sent a letter accepting Dorothy's poem "Any Porch" and a payment of twelve dollars. Thrilled, Dorothy immediately proposed that he might offer her a job as well. When he declined, she continued banging out tunes for would-be flappers. A few months went by, followed by another letter from Crowninshield, this time offering Dorothy a job at *Vanity Fair*'s sister publication *Vogue*. Her career was about to begin.

Life's Work

At *Vogue*, Dorothy's wit showed itself in the advertising copy and picture captions she was assigned to write. "Brevity," she quipped in one of her most-quoted captions, "is the soul of lingerie." During this period, she met her first husband, a handsome young stockbroker named Edwin Pond Parker II. The two married over the protests of his well-connected Protestant family but lived together only briefly; Parker enlisted as an ambulance driver and shipped out to the battlefields of Europe almost immediately.

By 1918, Parker's clever way with words had finally earned her a position on the editorial staff of *Vanity Fair*. Only twenty-four years old, Parker became New York's only woman drama critic, replacing P. G. Wodehouse during his leave of absence. The reviews she wrote, penned in her highly individual style, attracted her first broad audience and put her name on the lips of sophisticated New Yorkers.

At *Vanity Fair*, Parker met two lifetime friends, Robert Benchley and Robert Sherwood, witty, relatively unknown writers who, like Parker, were poised on the brink of success. The three went everywhere together, including the first luncheon of the group that was to become the renowned Algonquin Round Table. Alexander Woolcott, Edna Ferber, Harpo Marx, George Kaufman, Irving Berlin, and many other celebrated authors, critics, artists, and songwriters gathered around this table for daily, lunchtime exchanges of ideas, observations, and witty repartee. Parker was reputedly the wittiest of the bunch, waiting calmly in the midst of the daily babble until she saw an opening for her deadly, often profane barbs, which the petite brunette delivered in a soft, cultivated voice.

Parker was fired by Crowninshield in 1920 for writing unfavorable reviews of three plays produced by prominent advertisers. Her marriage was also in trouble. Her husband, always a heavy drinker, had not stayed sober in Europe; in fact, his troubles with alcohol accelerated and became further complicated by his introduction to opiates. By the time he returned home in 1919, he and Dorothy had become strangers. By 1920, he was one of her most useful humorous topics at the Round Table; they separated in 1922 and divorced in 1928.

The friendships she developed at the Round Table and the ability of her friends to keep her name in the public eye helped Parker begin her long and successful freelance career. Harold Ross begged her to join the founding board of *The New Yorker*, where, under the pseudonym "The Constant Reader," she wrote book reviews. Her short stories and verse appeared in a large number of publications, including *The American Mercury*, *The Bookman*, "The Conning Tower," and others. In 1929, her short story

"The Big Blonde" won the O. Henry Prize. All told, between 1926 and 1933 she published three collections of verse—*Enough Rope* (1926), *Sunset Gun* (1928), and *Death and Taxes* (1931)—which, along with two collections of short stories, *Laments for the Living* (1930) and *After Such Pleasures* (1933), captured the spirit of the times and enjoyed outstanding sales.

Parker's life always contained heartaches as well as triumphs. She learned from her former husband the art of drinking to avoid pain; during the 1920's, she and her Algonquin compatriots made cocktail hour a day-long experience. Her love life was flamboyant; she boasted of her many lovers, preferred men younger than herself, and knew no moderation in her feelings. When her relationship with playwright Charles MacArthur ended in abortion and abandonment, she attempted suicide, an act that she repeated four times between 1923 and 1932. The first time, she slashed her wrists with a razor; later, she tried Veronal, barbiturates, and even a bottle of shoe polish. The pain and confusion in her life provided the material for her short stories. Her technique seduced her readers into laughter at human foibles that transformed, at the story's resolution, into an anguished cry of despair. Parker turned even suicide into laughter: "Resume," one of her best-known verses, lists methods of self-annihilation and their drawbacks, finally concluding, with regret, "You might as well live."

Writing was never an easy process for Parker; even during the productive 1920's, she struggled over every word. As her life progressed, her output declined. She often missed deadlines, and she produced, over the course of her lifetime, a surprisingly small volume of work. What she did write, however, spoke volumes about the rage in her life, which, as she aged, turned from gender issues to social injustice. In 1927, she marched through the streets of Boston, protesting the pending execution of Sacco and Vanzetti. She was arrested on charges of "public sauntering" and reported from inside the prison on the course of the execution.

The decade of the 1930's, which for most Americans held the hardships of the Great Depression, were years of wealth and happiness for Parker. In 1933, at the age of forty, she married Alan Campbell, a handsome actor eleven years her junior. They moved from New York to Hollywood, where they were paid exorbitantly as a screenwriting couple, at one point making a combined salary of $5,200 a week. They were hired because of Parker's fame, but many people attribute their success to Campbell's powers of organization and careful tending to Dorothy's every need. Together they worked on dozens of screenplays, the most famous of which was made into the 1937 hit, *A Star is Born.*

In 1937, during the height of the Spanish Civil War, Parker and Campbell went to Spain. Parker's experiences there, immortalized in her short story "Soldiers of the Republic," further radicalized her. She returned to the United States determined to raise money to feed the starving children she had encountered. This involvement blossomed over the years into work opposing Nazi Germany. She conducted her political work largely by serving as a figurehead and public speaker for organizations she found worthy. In the 1950's, this involvement resulted in threats from the House Committee on Un-American Activities, which considered her a communist. Although this charge was never proved, Parker was blacklisted in Hollywood.

By the 1940's, Parker's career and her marriage to Campbell had disintegrated. The couple divorced in 1947. Parker wrote a play based on the life of Charles Lamb, *The Coast of Illyria*, with beau Ross Evans in 1949, but it never made it to Broadway. She and Campbell remarried in 1950. They separated less than a year later, then reunited briefly in 1960, near the end of Campbell's life. Writing became more difficult with the passing years; Parker wrote book reviews for *Esquire* but accomplished little creative work on her own. The years of high earnings in Hollywood had been accompanied by years of lavish spending. After Campbell's death, Parker lived alone in two rooms at the Volney Hotel in New York City, strapped for money and starved for company. Typically, she immortalized this life in a play written with Arnaud d'Usseau, *Ladies of the Corridor*. Parker died of a heart attack on June 7, 1967.

Upon her death, Parker left her estate of $20,000 to the Reverend Martin Luther King, Jr., naming the National Association for the Advancement of Colored People (NAACP) as the residual beneficiary. Lillian Hellman, her fellow writer and long-time friend, was named Parker's literary executor.

Summary

Dorothy Parker flourished as a professional writer at a time when women's lives and interests were still largely confined to their homes. She provided readers with brilliant, witty descriptions of her world and the people who inhabited it, painting their foibles and her own in a clear, unsentimental light. She has been praised for the economical language of her stories, for her evocative and funny verse, and for the sparkle of her conversation. She drew a compelling portrait of women in a rapidly changing world.

Despite her continual drinking, ruinous love affairs, and a tendency to waste her talents in endless hours of self-hatred, she created a body of work that has lasted well beyond her lifetime. The works collected into *The Portable Dorothy Parker* have proved to be enduring favorites, keeping Parker's work in print for more than fifty years. Readers looking for insight into the literary world of the early twentieth century would do well to study Dorothy Parker, whose trenchant observations bring that world alive in a way unmatched by the work of her peers.

Bibliography

Acocella, Joan. "After the Laughs." *The New Yorker* 69 (August 16, 1993): 76-81. A critical and biographical article in which the author argues that Parker let her personal insecurities cloud her artistic potential.

Keats, John. *You Might as Well Live: The Life and Times of Dorothy Parker*. New York: Simon & Schuster, 1970. This work, the first popular biography of Parker, is both thorough and readable. Contains an index and a bibliography.

Kinney, Arthur F. *Dorothy Parker*. Boston: Twayne, 1978. Kinney combines a brief biography with detailed literary criticism of Parker's work.

Meade, Marion. *Dorothy Parker*. New York: Villard Books, 1988. A thorough biography that places Parker squarely in the middle of New York's literary society. The author stresses the personal side of Parker's life, referring to Parker's literary work only to illustrate biographical material.

Parker, Dorothy. *The Portable Dorothy Parker*. Rev. ed. New York: Viking Press, 1973. Parker's own selections of her work to be included in the Viking edition of 1944 are joined here with new material and introductions by Brendan Gill and W. Somerset Maugham.

Susan E. Keegan

ROSA PARKS

Born: February 4, 1913; Tuskegee, Alabama

Area of Achievement: Civil rights
Contribution: Rosa Parks, who is well known for her refusal to relinquish her bus seat to a white passenger in Montgomery, Alabama, on December 1, 1955, was a civil rights advocate before she committed her historic and heroic act.

Early Life

The oldest of two children, Rosa Lee McCauley was born on February 4, 1913, to Leona Edwards McCauley and James McCauley. Her mother was an educator; her father, a carpenter. The influences in young Rosa's life included her mother and her grandparents. According to Parks, half of her life was spent in a segregated South that "allowed white people to treat black people without any respect." Rosa's parents were separated a great deal of the time. His occupation in carpentry and construction took James away from home often. Her mother resented being left alone. By the time her brother was born, her parents had separated. She did not see her father again until she was five. Rosa, her mother, and her brother moved in with her maternal grandparents. They lived in Pine Level, Alabama, where Rosa was to spend her formative years. Her brother, who was two years and seven months younger, doted on Rosa's every word and action. She became his protector and primary caretaker while her mother worked.

Rosa was small for her age. Her health was poor and her growth appeared to be stunted. She also suffered from chronic tonsillitis. These problems kept her out of school for a year.

Rosa observed the many differences between the white and black schools. Blacks had to build and heat their own schools, whereas white schools were funded by the town, county, or state. There were no buses to transport blacks, and black children attended school for five months, while white students went for nine. Such a discrepancy existed because the majority of black parents were sharecroppers, and their children were needed in the spring and fall to plow, plant, and harvest.

Rosa's great-grandfather (her grandmother's father) was a Scots-Irishman who migrated to the United States in the nineteenth century. He was an indentured servant who married an African slave. He and Mary Jane Nobles married and had two daughters and one son before slavery was abolished in 1865. After emancipation, six other children were born to the couple. Rosa grew up in a home where family history was important. She listened to stories about slavery, segregation, and the Ku Klux Klan.

As a young girl, Rosa worked as a field hand, tended to household chores, and cared for her ill grandparents. Her mother spent much of her time teaching. Soon, her mother decided that Rosa should go to a nine-month school. This could only be done if Rosa moved away from Pine Level. Consequently, Rosa was shipped to Montgomery, Alabama, to live with her maternal aunt. She attended a private girls' school. While enrolled in the Montgomery Industrial School for Girls, Rosa was responsible for doing household chores and domestic work outside the home.

By the time she was eleven, Rosa's childhood seemed far behind. She cleaned two classrooms at her school in exchange for free tuition. After graduation, she enrolled in Booker T. Washington High School. After her mother became ill, she dropped out of school to care for her. Rosa's outlook on discrimination and segregation was influenced by family stories, her tenure at the Montgomery Industrial School for Girls, and her experiences as a child. She detested the plight of blacks and the advantages that whites possessed, often at the expense of African Americans.

As a teen, she sewed, read, and attended the local African Methodist Episcopal (A.M.E.) church. Her love for singing and praying continued throughout her life. Active in the Allen Christian Endeavor League, Rosa kept busy as a member of the A.M.E. church.

In her nineteenth year, Rosa met Raymond Parks through a mutual friend. Both had been previously unlucky in love, and they did not pursue a romantic relationship immediately. Raymond Parks was a barber and an active participant in the Civil Rights movement. Rosa resisted his advances, but his persistence wore her down. Their common interest in civil rights tended to bond them. During their many conversations, she discovered that their interests and backgrounds were often the same. Both were born in February in the segregated South, were committed to the advancement of the black race, and were of mixed racial heritage. Like herself, Raymond cared for an ill mother and grandmother. They both shared a love of God, and like Rosa, Raymond was an active participant in his church.

In December of 1932, Rosa and Raymond were married in her mother's house. In 1933, she obtained her high-school diploma at the age of twenty. The couple settled in Montgomery, Alabama. Rosa engaged in a variety of occupations in an effort to augment her spouse's income. She became a seamstress, a domestic, and an office clerk. She became the secretary of the Montgomery chapter of the National Association for the Advancement of Colored People (NAACP) in 1943. She was also an adviser to youth organizations. She became a member of the Montgomery Voters League and began to encourage blacks to become politically empowered. Her thirst for education continued. She attended seminars and workshops whose topics dealt with the civil rights struggle. Rosa waged her own personal battle against segregation. Instead of riding on segregated buses, she often opted to walk home. She went out of her way to avoid drinking from segregated water fountains. At the age of forty, Rosa was a well-known civil rights activist in her community.

Life's Work

"The only tired I was, was tired of giving in." These were the words spoken on Thursday, December 1, 1955, by Rosa Parks. Parks was returning home from her job as a seamstress. She boarded the segregated bus in the manner usual to Montgomery. Blacks would enter the front, pay, get off, and reenter to take their seats through the back door. The front of the bus was reserved for whites, while African Americans occupied the rear. On this particular day, however, the front of the bus quickly filled up. The area where blacks were designated to sit would have to be vacated. A white male passenger required a seat and there was none available in the white section. Consequently, the blacks in the front of the black section were asked to move. They were told by the driver to relinquish their seats. All complied except for Rosa. She was dealing with the same driver who had evicted her more than a decade earlier from his bus. Rosa remained adamant on this occasion. This particular request was not to be taken lightly.

The majority of the riders were black. The black patrons believed that they were within their rights in requesting better treatment in exchange for their consistent patronage. Other blacks in the community had defied the driver's requests to move. Rumblings of boycotts and demonstrations ensued, but there was no mass organized effort. Parks was arrested on the evening of December 1, 1955, for refusing to relinquish her seat to a white patron, thereby violating the segregation laws of Montgomery, Alabama. A white lawyer, Clifford Durr, was hired to take her case. She was released on a one-hundred-dollar bond.

The African American community quickly mobilized. An organization called the Women's Political Council passed out thousands of pamphlets, asking for a one-day bus boycott. A community meeting was held on December 5 in the Holt Street Baptist Church. The Montgomery Improvement Association was created, and a young, charismatic minister, the Reverend Martin Luther King, Jr., was elected its president. Rosa agreed to allow her case to serve as the focus of the civil rights struggle. The one-day bus boycott was considered a success. By the time Rosa was tried and found guilty, the boycott was in its second month. The cooperation of the black ridership was 100 percent. Rosa was fined ten dollars and told to pay an additional four dollars in court fees. She refused to pay and appealed.

Because seventy-five percent of Montgomery's ridership was black, the bus company was quickly sliding into bankruptcy. Rosa and her husband lost their jobs. They were harassed with phone calls, letters, verbal threats, and intimidation. As a result of 381 days of boycotting, segregation was banned on municipal buses. On December 21, 1956, Rosa sat in the front of the newly integrated city buses in Montgomery, Alabama. As a result of her part in the boycott, Rosa and her husband were unemployable.

Because she was unable to find work, and with Raymond suffering from ill health, Rosa, her mother, and Raymond moved North. They settled in Detroit, where her brother Sylvester resided. After spending a year there, Rosa opted to take a job at the Hampton Institute in Virginia as a hostess in the Holly Tree Inn. The inn was a residence and guest house on the historically black college campus. Thinking that her husband and mother would find positions in Virginia, Rosa took the position, but the job market in Virginia was not as favorable as she had hoped. Raymond and Leona remained in Detroit for the year Rosa was in Virginia. She returned to Detroit in 1959 and took a position as a seamstress. She continued her work in the African American community, joining another civil rights group, the Southern Christian Leadership Conference.

On March 1, 1965, Rosa was hired as a staff assistant to U.S. Representative John Conyers. She worked for him for twenty-three years. During her tenure in Conyers' employ, Rosa lost her brother, spouse, and mother. Raymond's demise came in 1977 after a five-year struggle with cancer. Three months later, her brother Sylvester met the same fate. In 1979, her mother, Leona, also died of cancer. Having had no children, Rosa was left alone, except for distant relatives. Despite personal tragedy and failing health, Rosa continued to work tirelessly for the rights of all people. In August of 1994, Parks was briefly hospitalized for injuries she sustained after a thief broke into her Detroit home, robbed her of fifty dollars, and hit her. Community outrage over her assault led to the quick arrest of her assailant.

Summary

Hailed as the Mother of the Civil Rights movement, Rosa Parks has garnered a place in human history. The recipient of innumerable awards, Rosa maintains that she is unaccustomed to being a public person. By her own admission, she possesses more honorary degrees, awards, and plaques than she is able to count. Yet she continues to accept all invitations to speak, lecture, or simply be honored. She humbly accepts her status as a national treasure and symbol. Her many awards include the Spingarn Medal (1979), the Martin Luther King, Jr., Nonviolent Peace Prize (1980), and the Eleanor Roosevelt Women of Courage Award (1984). She possesses more than ten honorary degrees. On February 28, 1991, the Smithsonian Institution unveiled a bust of her. She has established the Rosa and Raymond Parks Institute for Self-Development. She continues to raise funds for the NAACP and is an active member of her church and of the Southern Christian Leadership Conference. It is the latter organization that has sponsored the Rosa Parks Freedom Award, which is awarded annually. Streets in Detroit and in Montgomery, Alabama, have been renamed Rosa Parks Boulevard. The African-American Museum in Detroit unveiled her portrait in January of 1988, in time for her seventy-fifth birthday. She was honored in 1990 at the Kennedy Center in Washington, D.C. Her eightieth birthday was spent in California, where she was on a national tour to promote her autobiography.

Parks remains a dignified individual who continues to influence society. She symbolizes many things to many people. For those in the 1950's and 1960's, she ignited a movement that was dormant for far too long. For individuals in the 1990's, she is important because of her tireless efforts to alter society for the better. Future generations will still feel her influence. Her courage has inspired others to take chances, work for the betterment and advancement of all people, and continue to challenge and change society's foibles and discriminatory actions.

Bibliography

Metcalf, George R. *Black Profiles*. New York: McGraw-Hill, 1971. This book documents the life and contributions of black individuals. Parks is one of the featured individuals.

Miller, Judi. *Women Who Changed America*. New York: Manor Books, 1976. This anthology discusses women in America, including Parks, who have contributed to American life. It demonstrates how these women altered life in the United States in a positive manner.

Parks, Rosa. *The Autobiography of Rosa Parks*. New York: Dial Books, 1990. This autobiography is an insightful look into the life, times, and experiences of Rosa Parks. Through her own works, Parks reminisces about her childhood, family influences, marriage, and civil rights activities.

Robinson, Jo Ann. *The Montgomery Bus Boycott and the Women Who Started It*. Edited by David J. Garrow. Knoxville: University of Tennessee Press, 1987. This text focuses on the historic 381-day boycott. Parks is discussed in this book in great detail.

Smith, Jessie Carney, ed. *Notable Black American Women*. Detroit: Gale Research, 1992. The lives and contributions of African American women in all fields are highlighted. Parks is one of hundreds discussed.

Annette Marks-Ellis

ELSIE CLEWS PARSONS

Born: November 27, 1875; New York, New York
Died: December 19, 1941; New York, New York
Area of Achievement: Anthropology
Contribution: As a wealthy patron and an influential writer, Parsons contributed to feminism, sociology, and anthropology. In her own life and in her writings, she challenged traditional conventions of behavior for women.

Early Life

Elsie Worthington Clews was born in New York City on November 27, 1875, the first child of Henry Clews and Lucy Madison Worthington Clews. Her father, an immigrant from Britain, had made a fortune as a stockbroker on Wall Street. In 1874, Henry Clews married Lucy Worthington, whose aristocratic Kentucky family boasted James Madison as an ancestor. Elsie grew up in the family home in New York and in a resort mansion in Newport, Rhode Island. Lucy Clews hoped to instill in Elsie the manners and behavior thought proper for ladies of wealthy Manhattan society, but Elsie rebelled as a young girl and adult. Elsie disagreed with her mother on the necessity of fancy clothes, proper decorum with young men, and education for women.

Elsie was taught by private tutors and attended Miss Ruehl's School for Girls in New York. In 1892, she chose to attend Barnard College against the wishes of her mother, who thought that the rigors of study would ruin Elsie's health and leave her ill-prepared for social life. Elsie was determined to pursue serious subjects, and in 1896 she was graduated Phi Beta Kappa from Barnard. She continued the next year at Columbia University, where she took her M.A. in 1897 and her Ph.D. in 1899. Both graduate degrees came in sociology. Her doctoral dissertation, completed under Franklin H. Giddings, was an analysis of education in colonial America. Elsie taught sociology at Columbia from 1899 to 1906. Her first book, *The Family* (1906), developed as a textbook from her class lectures.

In 1900, Elsie married Herbert Parsons, a lawyer and, later, a Republican congressman from New York. The couple had six children, four of whom lived to adulthood: Elsie ("Lissa"), born in 1901, John Edward (1903), Herbert (1909), and McIlvaine (1911). Elsie Clews Parsons' wealth allowed her to hire governesses for her children when they were young and to send them to private schools. Her unconventional but companionable marriage allowed her great freedom for travel, intellectual work, and separate friendships.

Life's Work

During her early career, Elsie Clews Parsons distinguished herself as a feminist sociologist. Just as she had rebelled against the conventions of her social class, so she challenged the accepted beliefs about the family in society. Her first book, *The Family*, raised a furor for advocating trial marriage and suggesting that women occupied a subordinate role that was reinforced by marriage conventions. Her most prolific time of feminist writing came in the period 1912 to 1919, when she was associated with several radical intellectual groups in New York. She attended the salons of Greenwich Village radical Mabel Dodge, where she befriended other like-minded iconoclasts such as Floyd Dell and Max Eastman, editors of *The Masses*, and Walter Lippman, founder of *The New Republic*. She became a frequent contributor to these and other radical and liberal journals.

Parsons wrote several sociological studies focusing on the theme of social restraint across cultural lines. Her books *The Old Fashioned Woman* (1913), *Religious Chastity* (1913), *Fear and Conventionality* (1914), and *Social Freedom* (1915) all discuss the role of women in various cultures and argue that woman's experience is universal. These works reveal her belief that women are excluded from male affairs and are restrained by rituals, taboos, and conventions, whether they belong to primitive tribes or so-called civilized societies.

During World War I, Parsons joined many other radical thinkers in opposing the war. Her pacifism strained her marriage when her husband volunteered to serve with the Army in Europe. Like many others of her generation, she was disillusioned by the war and seemed to lose hope in social reform and progress. After 1919, her intellectual life took a different path, although she had been gradually turning toward anthropology and folklore for several years. She had been acquainted with the Columbia anthropologist Franz Boas and his graduate students Alfred Kroeber, Robert Lowie, and Pliny Goddard since her teaching days at Columbia, and gradually they became her close intellectual associates.

Parsons' interest in anthropology coincided with her introduction to the American Southwest. In 1910, she first traveled to New Mexico, where she dabbled in archaeology and fell in love with the landscape and native peoples. Over the next thirty years, Parsons returned frequently to the Southwest, where she lived among the Zuni, Laguna, Acoma, Jemez, Isleta, and Hopi Indians. She gathered a huge amount of ethnographic data about these and other peoples of the Southwest. Although she published numerous studies on the Southwest, including *Notes on Ceremonialism at Laguna* (1920), *The Social Organization of the Tewa of New Mexico* (1929), and *Hopi and Zuni Ceremonialism* (1933), her two-volume work *Pueblo Indian Religion* (1939) stands as her most significant contribution to anthropology. This was the first synthesis of material on Pueblo religious traditions, and it contained much information never before known outside of Pueblo societies. The book also caused much controversy, particularly among the Pueblos whom she had studied and who resented her prying into their secret affairs. Her data had been based upon observation when possible, but when observation was not possible, she relied upon paid informants who clandestinely gave her information that was not supposed to be passed on to outsiders. Although this practice did make available much material that was of value to anthropologists, it also caused dissension within Pueblo communities and hardship for her informants, who were thereafter ostracized.

Her theories about Southwestern Indians contributed to an understanding of the diffusion of culture. Parsons argued that while the social organization of each Pueblo tribe varied, the distribution of cultural traits could be traced by means of comparative studies of each group. Her comparative approach also led her to research the relationship between Indian and Hispanic cultures to determine what cultural borrowing occurred in their common history. This work eventually took her to Mexico and Ecuador to conduct ethnographic research into Indian groups that still preserved their pre-Hispanic heritage. She wrote *Mitla, Town of the Souls and Other Zapoteco-Speaking Pueblos of Oaxaca, Mexico* (1930), and *Peguche, Canton of Otavalo, Province of Imbabura, Ecuador: A Study of Andean Indians*, which was published posthumously in 1945.

Though Elsie Parsons was not a student of Franz Boas, he was nevertheless a mentor to her as well as a friend. In 1919, she and Boas conducted fieldwork together at the Laguna Pueblo in New Mexico, and they often collaborated thereafter. Parsons conducted ethnographic work in the Boasian tradition of amassing an abundance of detailed data, from which conclusions could be drawn about cultural diffusion and history. She believed that it was possible to trace the origins of cultural practices using comparative ethnographic data and documentary sources. She believed that different American Indian tribes could be identified as belonging to a cultural area in which all the tribes shared certain traits as a result of diffusion. Thus, their cultural history could be reconstructed. This work led to a greater understanding of American Indian prehistory as well as insight into cultural interaction.

Parsons also shared Franz Boas's interest in folklore. She believed that folktales were a vital conduit for the transmission of social values and cultural traits. Between 1916 and 1927, she zealously pursued Caribbean and African American folktales, conducting fieldwork in Virginia, North and South Carolina, Florida, the Bahamas, Barbados, Jamaica, Grenada, Puerto Rico, Haiti, and Nova Scotia. This research resulted in many articles and books, including *Folk-Tales of Andros, Bahamas* (1918) and *Folk-Lore of the Sea Islands, South Carolina* (1923). After working among Portuguese blacks who had immigrated to Massachusetts from the Cape Verde Islands, she published her results in *Folk-Lore from the Cape Verde Islands* (1923).

Although she did not focus particular attention on women in her anthropological writings, Elsie Parsons was an influential supporter and benefactor of women anthropologists of the 1920's and 1930's. Her personal wealth allowed her to pursue her own travels and fieldwork, and to give financial assistance to others, including Gladys Reichard, Ruth Bunzel, and Ruth Benedict.

Elsie Clews Parsons died on December 19, 1941, from complications following an appendectomy. She had just returned from fieldwork in Ecuador and had been scheduled to attend the annual convention of the American Anthropological Association, of which she was president.

Summary

By the examples of her life and her intellectual work, Elsie Clews Parsons defied traditional roles for women. She attended a woman's college and graduate school despite the objections of her parents to higher education for women. She demonstrated that women of her era and class could resist social pressure to spend their time in idle consumerism and frivolous entertainment. In her intellectual work, she contributed new ideas to feminist thought, sociology, folklore, and anthropology. She ridiculed rigid gender roles, sexual customs, taboos, and rituals that were used to restrict women to a narrow sphere of activity. In all of her work, she championed the principle of free expression, examining the various ways in which societies denied self expression of individuals, especially women. As a woman of wealth, she had the freedom and means to do what she wanted, and she chose to pursue serious study and fieldwork. She also gave financial support to other women working in anthropology, thereby encouraging their participation in a scientific field that was not then supportive of women.

Parsons made her greatest mark in the fields of anthropology and folklore. She advanced the Boasian method of anthropology by amassing a huge amount of data on Pueblo societies. She made previously unknown material available to scholars and laid the foundation for further anthropological work on the Pueblo peoples. In her studies, she demonstrated that many cultural traits had been diffused among the Pueblos, with cultural borrowing from neighboring Indian tribes and Hispanics. She also gathered folklore from American and Caribbean communities to show the diffusion of cultural traits from African roots. Her significance was acknowledged by her profession, as evidenced by her election to the presidencies of the American Folklore Society (1918-1920), the American Ethnological Association (1923-1925), and the American Anthropological Association (1940-1941).

Bibliography

Gacs, Ute, Aisha Khan, Jerrie McIntyre, and Ruth Weinberg, eds. *Women Anthropologists: Selected Biographies*. Urbana: University of Illinois Press, 1989. This compilation offers concise biographies and selected bibliographies of Parsons and many of her contemporaries. An excellent reference source for readable, straightforward information on Parson's generation of women anthropologists.

Hare, Peter H. *A Woman's Quest for Science: Portrait of Anthropologist Elsie Clews Parsons*. Buffalo, N.Y.: Prometheus, 1985. A personal biography written by Parsons' great-nephew, using many private papers not available elsewhere. The book makes use of extensive quotes by Parsons but does not interpret Parsons' work in context of anthropological trends.

Herskovits, Melville J. "Some Next Steps in the Study of Negro Folklore." *Journal of American Folklore* 56 (January-March, 1943): 1-7. This article assesses the work of Parsons in collecting African American folklore, giving her credit for first applying the modern field method to this study.

Lamphere, Louise. "Feminist Anthropology: The Legacy of Elsie Clews Parsons." *American Ethnologist* 16 (1989): 518-533. This article discusses Parsons' early feminism and her anthropological work. It suggests that Parsons' feminism did not influence her anthropological thought as much as did Boasian thinking. It compares her to modern feminist anthropologists.

Reichard, Gladys E. "Elsie Clews Parsons." *Journal of American Folklore* 56 (January-March, 1943): 45-56. Offers a biographical sketch of Parsons at the time of her death, with personal impressions of her by a longtime colleague. Contains a complete bibliography of Parsons' writings.

Spier, Leslie. "Elsie Clews Parsons." *American Anthropologist* 4 (1943): 244-251. This article, written at the time of Parsons' death, assesses the impact of her anthropological work. It credits Parsons with being the first to study Pueblo Indians seriously and with laying the foundation for future work with the Southwestern Indians.

Zumwalt, Rosemary Levy. *Wealth and Rebellion: Elsie Clews Parsons, Anthropologist and Folklorist*. Urbana: University of Illinois Press, 1992. This is the most thorough biography of Parsons' intellectual work and personal life. Also explains the intellectual milieu of Boasian anthropologists.

Lynne M. Getz

DOLLY PARTON

Born: January 19, 1946; rural Locust Ridge, Sevier County, Tennessee

Area of Achievement: Music
Contribution: A major force in bringing women to the forefront of country music, Parton also fashioned successful pop music as well as films and television.

Early Life

A true child of Appalachia, Dolly Rebecca Parton was born in Eastern Tennessee, in the foothills of the Smoky Mountains, the fourth of twelve children. In her family's one-room cabin, there was no electricity, running water, or indoor plumbing.

Her father was a farmer and construction worker, and although the Parton family was quite poor, this did not seem to doom young Dolly to an unhappy life. Her mother was a singer of ballads and old-time songs, and as a very young child, Dolly Parton made up songs for her mother. In time, Dolly Parton took up playing the guitar and banjo on the local radio and, later, on television in nearby Knoxville. She was the first member of her family to graduate from high school.

She had appeared on the Grand Ole Opry as a child and thereafter knew what she wanted to do with the rest of her life. Dolly Parton was nothing if not determined, so in June of 1964, immediately after she was graduated from high school, she took a bus to Nashville to make her name in the country music business.

Life's Work

With her move to Nashville, Dolly Parton struggled to make herself a star. The way for women to succeed in country music had been demonstrated by Kitty Wells, Patsy Cline, and Loretta Lynn. At first, Dolly Parton lived with her uncle, Bill Owens, with whom she wrote songs. In 1966, when Bill Phillips made a minor hit of Dolly Parton's composition *Put It off Until Tomorrow*, her career as a songwriter formally commenced.

Parton's husband Carl Dean (they were married in 1966) always played a supportive role in helping her professional career. Her performing career took off in 1967, when she had hits with two novelty songs: *Dumb Blonde* and *Something Fishy*. That same year, she joined the Porter Wagoner television show as a female soloist and frequent duet partner with Wagoner.

During this part of her career, Dolly Parton sang as a high soprano; there was a sharp contrast between the lyrics she sang, which were about hardship and pain, and her delicate singing voice. In a short time, "Porter and Dolly," as they were known to their legions of fans, became country music's top duo, winning national awards in 1968, 1970, and 1971.

Wagoner helped Dolly Parton secure a contract with RCA, and she began to fashion her career as a recording artist. By the mid-1970's, singing songs she claimed she had made up while trying to survive growing up in grinding poverty, Parton, with her sensitive lyrics and fragile vocal stylings, became a star. At this point in her career, she was trying to find her own style, exploring a wide variety of themes and sounds. Among her early recordings were conventional hymns, moral tales, and the usual country music stories of love lost. She seemed to be trying everything and anything that had worked for women in country music since the days of Kitty Wells, whom Dolly Parton had admired.

Dolly Parton was not satisfied with being atop the country music charts. She set out to map territory that only Patsy Cline before her had tread—stardom in pop music. She left Wagoner in 1974 and a few years later made her move with a series of Los Angeles-influenced albums. In 1977, when Dolly Parton recorded *Here You Come Again*, written by veteran New York City pop music writers Barry Mann and Cynthia Weill, the song rose to number three on the mainstream pop charts and set in motion a whole new career for Dolly Parton.

Dolly Parton wanted to put behind her the traditional country associations she had worked so successfully to build up in the years with Porter Wagoner. No one mistakes her later duets—with Kenny Rogers and the BeeGees—for hard-core hillbilly music. The new Dolly Parton was aimed directly at mainstream musical tastes.

Dolly Parton's new goal was to become a film star. In the late 1970's, she hired an agent, and soon she was appearing regularly on *The Tonight Show with Johnny Carson*. She formally began working in films in 1980, when she gave an engaging performance as a Southern secretary opposite Lily Tomlin and Jane Fonda in *Nine to Five*. Dolly Parton also wrote and sang the film's title song, which earned for her an Oscar nomination, a Grammy award, and a hit album—on both country and pop charts.

The song "Nine to Five" has a big-band introduction and two basic melodies as it liltingly expresses working-class frustration. A full studio backup band (no country music combo here) beats at a disco-like pace. This song, the ultimate crossover hit, contains elements of most forms of pop music of the late 1970's and early 1980's, from disco to country-pop. Thereafter, Dolly Parton continued to work regularly in Hollywood, starring (and frequently singing as well) in *The Best Little Whorehouse in Texas* (1982), *Rhinestone* (1984), and *Steel Magnolias* (1989).

As her career prospered, Dolly Parton took full control of her business, creating, with her manager Sandy Gilmore, Sandollar Production Company and, in 1986, opening her own theme park, Dollywood, located in the Smoky Mountains, not far from where she was born. Dolly Parton has regularly graced the covers of *Redbook*, *Vanity Fair*, and *People* magazines. She has been as famous as any Hollywood personality during the closing years of the twentieth century.

Dolly Parton even had her own television series from late September of 1987 through May of 1988 on the ABC television network. The network brass were looking for someone to revive the variety show genre, which had been moribund since the demise of *The Carol Burnett Show*. ABC made a two-season, $44 million commitment to *Dolly*, believing that Parton could cross over the generation gap and make a hit. Dolly Parton sang from her rustic living room, complete with a roaring fire, and *Dolly* seemed to be the perfect show for the nostalgic Reagan era of the 1980's. Unfortunately for both ABC and Dolly Parton, the glitzy, big-budget hour finished forty-seventh in the ratings for its first and only season. If anything, Dolly Parton's considerable talents and appeal were overused; she appeared in every segment, singing duets with guest stars and performing in comedy skits. Indeed, except for a four-man vocal harmony group called the A Cappellas, Dolly Parton was the lone show regular.

In 1991, Parton starred in a critically acclaimed made-for-television film about battered women: *Wild Texas Wind*. In 1992, she starred in and helped to produce the film *Straight Talk*. Parton continued to release new albums and singles, including duets with young country singers such as Randy Travis, Ricky Van Shelton, and Billy Ray Cyrus; some of her songs were produced as videos that were aired on television video programs such as VH-1 and The Nashville Network. In the fall of 1994, HarperCollins published Parton's autobiography, *Dolly*.

Summary

The life of Dolly Parton is a wonderful version of the all-American success story. As the "Cinderella of the South," Dolly Parton started with almost nothing, save her talent and iron will to succeed. Before she turned thirty, she had become a national star. By the time she was forty, she was a millionaire.

She became a tough businesswoman, a very talented songwriter and singer, and a television and film star. In the long term, Dolly Parton should be remembered as a songwriter whose lyrics expressed the feelings of children and women in contemporary rural and urban American society.

A major force in bringing women to the forefront of country music, Dolly Parton followed the stylings of Kitty Wells and Patsy Cline. Fashioning a smooth sound to traditional country music instrumentation, she created a popular commercial product intended to appeal to a national pop music audience. In turn, she inspired a score of country-pop female singers, including Emmy Lou Harris and Linda Ronstadt, with whom she recorded the highly successful album *Trio* in 1987.

As a recording artist, Dolly Parton moved ever further into the heart of the pop music tradition, abandoning her earlier pure country style, much to the sorrow of many critics. These traditional critics argue that to appreciate Dolly Parton's genius fully one has to go back to two pathbreaking albums from the early 1970's: *Coat of Many Colors* and *My Tennessee Mountain Home*. The song "Coat of Many Colors" carefully tells the tragic story of a rag coat that Dolly Parton's own mother made for her poor young child one winter. The album also includes a dark song dealing with madness, "If I Lose My Mind," and a pondering of religion, mountain style, in "The Mystery of the Mystery." *My Tennessee Mountain Home* presents a wonderfully engaging oral history lesson complete with a vision of Nashville ("Down on Music Row"), a pair of musical essays about hard times and grinding poverty ("Daddy's Working Boots" and "In the Good Old Days"), and a trio of lyrical oral histories ("Dr. Robert F. Thomas," "I Remember," and "My Tennessee Mountain Home").

Despite her widespread popularity, Dolly Parton is a real country artist. This petite (five feet, two inches) blonde woman, with her towering wigs and skin-tight fashions, seems to epitomize that curious mixture of hillbilly fashion and heartfelt singing that Nashville likes to project.

People who know little about country music frequently underestimate Dolly Parton. She embodies conservatism, the all-American virtues of family, and down-home music, but she was able to become a pop cultural icon. Country stars before her have become famous, but few have matched the range and level of success as a performer that Dolly Parton has achieved.

Bibliography

Brown, Charles T. *Music U.S.A.: America's Country and Western Tradition*. Englewood Cliffs, N.J.: Prentice-Hall, 1986. This valuable survey of the history of country music in the United States includes a major section on Dolly Parton. The best part of this well-illustrated book is its musical analysis of top country hits, including "Nine to Five."

Bufwack, Mary A., and Robert K. Oermann. *Finding Her Voice: The Saga of Women in Country Music*. New York: Crown, 1993. A well-documented history of the impact of women in the field of country music. The bibliography is extensive. Chapter 14 is the best piece yet written about the latter part of the career of Dolly Parton. Well illustrated.

Kingsbury, Paul, and Alan Axelrod, eds. *Country: The Music and the Musicians*. New York: Abbeville Press, 1988. Do not be fooled by the appearance of this lavish, beautifully illustrated, oversized picture book. Its sixteen essays cover all the basics of the history of country music. Chapter 16 examines Dolly Parton.

Malone, Bill C. *Country Music U.S.A.* Rev. ed. Austin: University of Texas Press, 1985. This is the standard one-volume scholarly history of country music. Its detailed bibliography and guide to recordings ought to be required reading for anyone seriously interested in this genre of popular music. The career of Dolly Parton is treated in considerable detail.

Nash, Alanna. *Dolly*. Los Angeles, Calif.: Reed Books, 1978. A popular biography with a number of color photographs, a score of black-and-white photographs, and a short discography—only reference material is lacking. This is the best full biography of Dolly Parton, although it does not cover her career beyond 1978.

Parton, Dolly. *Dolly*. New York: HarperCollins, 1994. Parton's autobiography is a frank account of the singer's life—one that, if not entirely revealing, at least provides a glimpse of the hardship and challenges that Parton overcame in her quest to succeed in the world of country music and beyond.

Scobey, Lola. *Dolly: Daughter of the South*. New York: Zebra Books, 1977. This popular biography is inferior to Alanna Nash's *Dolly*. There are few details, and only a handful of black-and-white photographs are included. No footnotes, bibliography, or discography.

Douglas Gomery

ALICE PAUL

Born: January 11, 1885; Moorestown, New Jersey
Died: July 9, 1977; Moorestown, New Jersey
Area of Achievement: Women's rights
Contribution: The leader of the radical wing of the woman suffrage movement that helped pass the Nineteenth Amendment, Paul also introduced the Equal Rights Amendment.

Early Life

Born on January 11, 1885, in a farmhouse near Moorestown, New Jersey, to a wealthy Quaker (Society of Friends) family, Alice Paul entered the women's movement at a very early age. Her father, William Paul, served as president of the Burlington County Trust Company, and her mother, Tacie Parry Paul, was clerk of the Moorestown Friends' Meeting. Both strongly encouraged young Alice's interest in equal rights.

Alice's early life focused almost entirely upon her Quaker heritage. The Friends created a humane, optimistic religion during the seventeenth century, and they were one of the few sects that preached equality between the sexes. The fact that the Quakers allowed women to become missionaries and ministers created a unique religious environment. Although not much is known about Alice Paul's childhood, many scholars agree that it was the egalitarian, flexible, and tolerant nature of Quaker society that allowed her to develop as perhaps America's greatest radical feminist.

Although both of Alice's parents encouraged her independent attitudes, her mother served as her chief mentor. Alice's father died before she reached adulthood. Tacie Paul was one of many Quaker women (such as Lucretia Mott) who were involved in the nineteenth century American woman suffrage movement.

Alice followed in her mother's footsteps, enrolling in the Moorestown Quaker school and later graduating from another Friends' institution, Swarthmore College. During these formative years, Alice also used Lucretia Mott as her role model. Mott, one of the founding mothers of the American woman suffrage movement, helped organize the first women's rights convention in 1848 at Seneca Falls, New York, where she and Elizabeth Cady Stanton wrote the Declaration of Sentiments. Alice began her great crusade for equal rights as a graduate student at England's Woodbridge Quaker College and the London School of Economics, where she joined Emmeline, Christabel, and Sylvia Pankhurst, the radical British feminists who taught her the aggressive tactics that later produced American congressional support for the Nineteenth Amendment.

During Paul's years in Britain, she formed a close, lifelong friendship with another American suffragist, Lucy Burns, who also belonged to the Pankhursts' Women's Social and Political Union. Nearing the end of this political apprenticeship, Paul resolved to bring confrontational feminism to the United States.

Life's Work

When Alice Paul returned to the United States in 1910, she found Susan B. Anthony's bill granting women the right to vote still stalled in a congressional committee. Even though Anthony had submitted her bill in 1896, American women still lacked "The Franchise." Paul concluded that the situation in America called for drastic measures.

Paul persuaded the National-American Woman Suffrage Association (NAWSA) to allow her to coordinate its lobbying effects in Congress and promptly organized a huge march on the White House backed by a suffrage army estimated at a half-million people. Her dramatic entrance into Washington politics duly impressed the new president, Woodrow Wilson, whose inauguration occurred the next day. Immediately after the opening of the new Congress, Paul employed her aggressive tactics on the returning politicians in order to secure the Anthony Bill's release from committee to the floor of the House of Representatives. It would have been an overwhelming task for any lobbyist. Given Paul's extreme shyness, introverted Quaker personality, and lack of rhetorical skills, the bill that Congress passed, the president signed, and the states ratified became a signal triumph for her organizational genius.

During World War I, Paul quickly became the radical leader of the feminist movement. First, she changed NAWSA's lobbying focus from the states to the national legislature. She became a public relations expert at a time in history when such experts were rare. Paul's training in British circles enabled her to overcome opposition from the Washington, D.C., police, who wanted her marchers to parade on Sixteenth Street in front of the foreign embassies (instead of picketing the White House). She stood her ground, insisting that the ladies must be seen by President and Mrs. Wilson. She won the debate—the first of many such victories resulting in the ratification of the Nineteenth Amendment to the Constitution.

In 1917, when the United States declared war on Germany and President Wilson declared that the "world must be made safe for democracy," Paul decided that the time was right for another parade and picketing of the White House. "Why should American women support the war to make the world safe for democracy," her pickets emphatically asked, "when they have no democracy since they cannot vote?" When the White House called the police, Paul and her loyal "soldiers," facing arrest and imprisonment, followed tactics learned in England and refused to eat. Force-fed by law enforcement officials afraid of the possible public outcry produced by the hospitalization or death of a suffragist, Paul turned that tactic as well to the advantage of her cause.

Not everyone in the suffrage movement approved of Paul's tactics. More radical than the mainstream NAWSA's moderate leadership, she organized the National Woman's Party in 1913. The Quaker activist incorporated the party on September 20, 1918, but kept it largely inactive until the passage of the Nineteenth Amendment became a certainty.

After the Congress and the states approved woman suffrage, Paul reactivated the National Woman's Party in 1921. Although most women perhaps believed that equal rights would result automatically from the ratification of the Nineteenth Amendment, Paul and her colleagues remained unconvinced.

The principal philosophical ideas Paul wrote into the National Woman's Party platform reflected her skepticism that voting rights would lead to equal rights. Women, she argued, would no longer constitute the "governed half" of the American people. In the future, they would participate equally in all aspects of life.

The National Woman's Party organized most of the serious agitation—such as jail-ins, marches, fasts, and picketing—that occurred before the ratification of the Nineteenth Amendment. When ratification occurred, the more moderate NAWSA transformed itself into the League of Women Voters. Paul, however, believed that the battle would not be over until equal rights had been achieved for all Americans, regardless of sex.

For Alice Paul, true freedom extended far beyond the simple attainment of suffrage. She single-mindedly pursued the goal of removing all legal obstacles for women throughout the United States. After careful consideration and examination of the tactics and strategies that won the battle for woman suffrage, she concluded that the only means to legal equality was the passage of a federal Equal Rights Amendment (ERA). This was an extremely radical idea when Paul introduced it in 1923 at Seneca Falls, New York, where the first women's rights convention had been held in 1848. The central point she expressed focused on the philosophy that women would never be subjugated again "in law or in custom, but shall in every way be on an equal plane in rights." In this way, her Woman's Party gave birth to the Equal Rights Amendment.

Paul's proposed amendment split the women's movement. Some women believed that voting rights naturally would produce equality, making a second amendment unnecessary. Since the ERA radically redefined power relationships between men and women, even stronger opposition than originally existed to the Nineteenth Amendment developed within the male establishment.

Critics dismissed Paul as either a harmless but misguided "bleeding heart liberal" or a dangerously deranged radical. Democrats and Republicans alike warned the public against being receptive to her ideas. As the nation turned more conservative during the 1920's, with the election of President Warren Harding and the widespread repudiation of progressivism, the popularity of Alice Paul and her party declined, and she did not resurface as a significant force until the reintroduction of the ERA in 1972.

Following Paul's creation of the National Woman's Party and the introduction of the Equal Rights Amendment, the popularity of women's rights declined in the United States during the Depression of the 1930's. As the fight for jobs excluded more and more American women, Alice took her campaign to Europe, where she founded the World's Woman's Party. Since Paul always expressed strong opposition to the League of Nations' failure to allow female political participation, she continued her lobbying efforts on behalf of women until the organization collapsed during World War II. When the League gave way to the United Nations, Paul played a key role in introducing an equal rights provision in the preamble to the U.N. charter.

Following Paul's European experiment, she returned to the United States, where she resumed her efforts to pass the new, revamped Equal Rights Amendment. During the late 1960's, Paul campaigned against the Vietnam War while working for the ERA. Still marching and fighting for equal rights at the age of eighty-five, she finally surrendered to old age and moved to a Quaker nursing home in her native Moorestown, New Jersey, where America's great radical feminist died on July 10, 1977, at the age of ninety-two. She never lived to see the passage of the amendment to which she had devoted her entire life.

Summary

Few leaders in the politics of women's liberation were more significant than Alice Paul. Her longevity and radical proclivities outdistanced others who garnered more press and historical notice. For sixty-five years, from 1912 until her death in 1977, Paul stood ready to give her best to the cause of equal rights.

Despite her reputation for radical measures, Paul was not an abrasive personality. Although some thought her insensitive, perhaps what they perceived was the absent-mindedness of an intellectual who received her Ph.D. in sociology in 1912, before she launched her suffrage career. She understood both the politics and the economics of equal rights. The real struggle, she once argued, would not be won in state or even national legislatures. Women would have to win economically before they could win politically. Political forms would crystallize, she hypothesized, only when women had gained economic power. More important, she emphasized that having money was not enough. Knowing how to use money to attain political ends was the key.

Paul was not as well known as other feminists of her day—Susan B. Anthony, Lucretia Mott, and Elizabeth Cady Stanton. Her strategies and tactics, however, have since been considered to have been paramount in obtaining the Nineteenth Amendment to the Constitution. Although she died without realizing victory in her struggle to institute the Equal Rights Amendment, many of the goals she sought came to pass nevertheless, partly because of the half-century of supreme effort she exerted in order to realize her great dream.

Bibliography

Barker-Benfield, G. J., and Catherine Clinton. *Portraits of American Women: From Settlement to the Present*. New York: St. Martin's Press, 1991. A collection of scholarly articles on significant American women from Pocahontas to Betty Friedan. The article on Alice Paul by Christine A. Lunardini presents a particularly effective analysis.

Becker, Susan D. *The Origins of the Equal Rights Amendment: American Feminism Between the Wars*. Westport, Conn.: Greenwood Press, 1981. An analysis of Paul's postsuffrage role in reorganizing the women's movement along the international lines of the World's Woman's Party.

Flexner, Eleanor. *Century of Struggle: The Woman's Rights Movement in the United States*. Rev. ed. Cambridge, Mass.: The Belknap Press of Harvard University Press, 1975. A classic history of the women's movement (highlighting Alice Paul's role) by one of the great feminist historians.

Gallagher, Robert S. "I Was Arrested, of Course . . ." *American Heritage* 25, no. 2 (February, 1974): 16-24, 92-94. A fascinating and penetrating interview conducted with Paul three years before her death.

Irwin, Inez Haynes. *The Story of Alice Paul and the National Woman's Party*. Fairfax, Va.: Denlinger's, 1977. This is the primary history of the National Woman's Party.

Morgan, David. *Suffragists and Democrats: The Politics of Woman Suffrage in America*. East Lansing: Michigan State University Press, 1972. This is a narrow British interpretation of the politics of the American woman suffrage movement.

Stevens, Doris. *Jailed for Freedom*. New York: Boni & Liveright, 1920. Reprint. Freeport, N.Y.: Books for Libraries Press, 1971. This primary source focuses on the militant feminists who campaigned for the vote between 1913 and 1919. The work includes a valuable chapter on "General Alice Paul."

J. Christopher Schnell

JANE PAULEY

Born: October 31, 1950; Indianapolis, Indiana

Area of Achievement: Broadcast journalism

Contribution: Starting off as one of the youngest women to ever coanchor a major network morning show, Pauley parlayed her girl-next-door charm and solid journalistic skills into huge ratings at the *Today* show and left at the height of her popularity to launch her two successful prime-time newsmagazines: *Real Life with Jane Pauley* and *Dateline NBC*.

Early Life

Margaret Jane Pauley was born on October 31, 1950, in Indianapolis, Indiana. Her father, Richard Pauley, was a salesman with a food products corporation; her mother, Mary Patterson Pauley, was a former office clerk. Along with her older sister Ann, Jane grew up in a typical middle-class neighborhood in Indianapolis. Together, the two sisters enjoyed producing plays in a makeshift theater in their garage, worked hard to earn good grades, and went to church with their parents on Sundays. Although her father was often away from home on sales trips, Jane was encouraged to emulate his dedication to hard work; she also found occasion to exhibit something of her mother's sturdy self-reliance. A shy young girl who endured being called "Margaret" throughout second grade because she hesitated telling the teacher that she preferred being called by her middle name, Jane eventually overcame her timidity to become an award-winning competitive debater on her high-school speech team. One of her toughest rivals in statewide debate competitions was Fort Wayne native Shelley Long, who later achieved fame for her acting role on the long-running television show *Cheers*.

After graduating from high school, Jane moved to Bloomington to attend Indiana University, where she majored in political science and joined the campus chapter of Kappa Kappa Gamma sorority. Jane's excellent study habits and enthusiasm for her chosen major allowed her to complete her course work in three and a half years and graduate with her bachelor of arts degree at the end of 1971. Although she had tentative plans to enter law school, Jane left the school after completing her undergraduate work in order to pursue her interest in politics. She volunteered to work as an aide for New York City Mayor John V. Lindsay, who had launched his campaign for the 1972 Democratic presidential nomination. Despite the objections of her parents, who were concerned about her career plans and were also longtime Republicans, Jane traveled to Arizona to work on the team to generate support for Lindsay in that state's primary election. After Lindsay withdrew from the race for the nomination, Jane returned to Indianapolis in the spring of 1972 in order to work for her home state's Democratic Central Committee. Unenthusiastic about the prospect of returning to college that fall to pursue a law school degree, Jane eagerly accepted a chance to interview for a job as an entry-level television reporter with the local CBS affiliate station, WISH-TV, in Indianapolis. Within weeks of her hiring, at a salary of $125 per week, she was given the chance to cover the election day results in November of 1972. Despite the disappointing outcome of her work on behalf of Democratic presidential candidate George McGovern, Jane Pauley had launched her career in television journalism.

Life's Work

At WISH-TV, Jane Pauley advanced from being a twenty-one-year-old news writer with no experience in print or broadcast journalism to serving as coanchor of the station's noontime broadcast and as anchor for the weekend evening news within her first fifteen months on the job. As the first woman reporter working in the station's newsroom, Pauley realized that her presence not only fulfilled the television station's affirmative action compliance for FCC licensing purposes but also would affect the hiring of other women who would follow. After being passed over for a coanchor position at the station, she was pleasantly surprised when an NBC network representative encouraged her to audition for a job with that network's Chicago affiliate, WMAQ-TV. The station was looking for a way to overcome its last place ranking in the local Chicago ratings and thought that gambling on a fresh new face would attract new viewers. Flattered by the network's attention, Pauley agreed to travel to Chicago for interviews and an on-camera audition. As a twenty-four-year-old woman, Pauley believed that she had no serious chance of being hired as a big city coanchor. Despite Pauley's personal misgivings, her fearlessness, poise, and relaxed demeanor during her audition evidently convinced the station's owners that she could handle the job.

Pauley was hired in September of 1975 to serve as coanchor of WMAQ's prime-time broadcasts at five and ten o'clock each evening. Because of her lack of experience, she was teamed with a veteran male broadcaster, and she became Chicago's first female coanchor. Despite murmured criticism among staffers and unfriendly accusations in the Chicago press that her all-American good looks had had more to do with her hiring than her experience or ability as a news reporter, Pauley managed to weather her first year on the job and began to contribute special reports and to attain greater maturity as a broadcaster.

As luck would have it, Pauley was fortunate to be selected as one of six finalists to replace longtime *Today* show cohost Barbara Walters when she left NBC in 1976 to serve as coanchor of ABC's evening newscasts. Selected from among more than 250 applicants, Pauley and the other five finalists were invited to participate in on-the-air tryouts during the summer of 1976. After the auditions were broadcast, NBC conducted a poll of viewers in its largest regional television markets and discovered that Pauley was the undisputed favorite among the majority of the show's viewers. After she was hired in October, Pauley joined the show's official host Tom Brokaw, a seasoned young journalist who had previously served as the network's White House correspondent before joining the *Today* show. Pauley and Brokaw developed an excellent rapport, and her arrival improved the show's ratings almost immediately.

As a result of their friendship, Brokaw and his wife, Meredith, introduced Pauley to her future husband, political cartoonist Garry Trudeau, in 1977. Pauley and Trudeau were married in June of 1980 and soon began planning for a family despite their high-profile careers. After two miscarriages, Pauley gave birth to healthy twins, Rachel and Ross, in 1983, and came back from her first maternity leave in 1984 to find that *Today* show viewers responded enthusiastically to her return. In 1986, she gave birth to another son, Thomas. Able to juggle the demands of work and family since her husband's career allowed him to work at home, Pauley became more focused on streamlining her work routine in order to spend time with her children.

Known for her affability and team spirit, Pauley was able to overcome her disappointment concerning the departure of her friend Tom Brokaw in 1982, and she soon established a comfortable camaraderie with the show's new host, former sportscaster Bryant Gumbel. Although she felt that her own seniority on the *Today* show should have earned her a chance to fill the top spot, Pauley realized the significance of Gumbel's hiring as the first African American to anchor a top news program and gracefully accepted his addition to the show.

After returning from her maternity leave in 1986, Pauley celebrated her tenth anniversary on the *Today* show and announced her satisfaction in signing a new five-year contract to remain on the program—a contract that would establish her as one of the most senior members on any network morning show. Although her longevity as a coanchor coincided with a series of network switches and promotions for many of her female broadcasting peers, including Diane Sawyer, Connie Chung, and Mary Alice Williams, Pauley seemed comfortable with her morning show berth. Unfortunately, NBC executives began to consider Pauley's lengthy tenure to be more of a liability than an asset, and *NBC News at Sunrise* anchor Deborah Norville was given a position as the permanent newscaster on the *Today* show in 1989 at a salary only a fraction below that of Pauley. Soon, Norville began sharing the broadcasting sofa with Gumbel and Pauley instead of reading the news behind the desk, as was customary for previous newscasters. As it became clear that Norville was being groomed to become her eventual successor, Pauley began to contemplate her options. Although she initially sought to terminate her contract with NBC, Pauley was aware that contract stipulations would prevent her from seeking a similar position at another network for two years. Ultimately, Pauley negotiated a new deal that would allow her to leave the *Today* show in late October of 1989, but remain with the network as a regular substitute for her old friend Tom Brokaw on the *NBC Nightly News* and as the host of a new prime-time newsmagazine entitled *Real Life with Jane Pauley*, which was launched in 1990.

As the network's most successful prime-time news vehicle ever, *Real Life with Jane Pauley* cemented its host's reputation as a ratings winner. Although she felt somewhat guilty that the backlash of public opinion in response to her replacement on the *Today* show brought about a measurable ratings drop, Pauley was embarrassingly pleased that her work on her new program was enjoying such popularity while providing her with a greater outlet of writing and coproducing stories about which she was personally interested in reporting. The show was less successful during its second season, however, and was canceled. Nevertheless, the network sought to capitalize on Pauley's draw with prime-time audiences and teamed her with a young male broadcaster, Stone Phillips, who was recruited from ABC. Together, the two hosted the show *Dateline NBC*, which debuted in the spring of 1992 and earned a regular broadcast slot during the 1993-1994 television season. Responding to the public popularity of reality-based, informational news programming—a form of episodic broadcasting that was far cheaper to produce than the situation comedies and dramatic shows that commonly dominated prime-time television—NBC found that Pauley's new show established a welcome niche and provided the network with a springboard for launching a similar vehicle teaming Tom Brokaw with *Today* show coanchor Katie Couric.

Summary

In pursuing her career as one of America's leading female broadcast journalists, Jane Pauley successfully negotiated her way past a rocky beginning to establish herself as a talented professional. She could be counted upon to cover stories ranging from interviews with Hollywood celebrities to in-depth pieces on current issues at the same time she was expected to earn ratings honors by conducting live broadcasts from exotic locales. Despite the behind-the-scenes manipulations of the male-dominated staff of NBC television executives, Pauley survived one of the greatest challenges of her career without flinching. Having attained a level of professional recognition and celebrity during her thirteen years on the *Today* show, Pauley demonstrated her ability, in 1989, to capitalize on her appeal in order to negotiate a new contract that provided her with far greater opportunities than she could have pursued as cohost of a morning news program. Adroitly sidestepping the trap of belittling her own accomplishments and the pitfalls of accepting the network's assessment of her importance to the *Today* show, she managed to convince NBC executives to take her concerns regarding her future with the network seriously rather than interpreting her stance as a calculated play for greater power on the *Today* show itself. Pauley was most gratified that she was able to make a graceful departure from the show and still maintain the respect of her colleagues. By refusing to compromise her own goals or belittle the aspirations of the broadcasters with whom she worked, Pauley has become an example of how women can succeed in the high-profile world of broadcast journalism without losing their sense of perspective or their credibility with viewers.

Bibliography

Alter, Jonathan. "Real Life with Garry Trudeau." *Newsweek* 116 (October 15, 1990): 60-66. Although this piece focuses on the life and career of Pauley's husband, cartoonist Garry Trudeau, it does provide unusually frank insights into Pauley's personal life and demonstrates the self-deflating and effusive sense of humor that helps Pauley and Trudeau keep their individual successes in perspective.

Hoban, Phoebe. "The Loved One." *New York* 23 (July 23, 1990): 24-31. A cover story on Pauley that appeared on the eve of the premiere of *Real Life with Jane Pauley*.

Although the article expresses an almost cloying adulation of Pauley, it does provide a thorough overview of her career from her debut as a novice broadcaster in 1972 through her role as the star of her own prime-time newsmagazine in 1990. Includes various comments by network colleagues and peers regarding Pauley's professional demeanor, particularly in the face of the changes on the *Today* show that precipitated her departure.

Holloway, Diane. "In the Wake of *Today*, Jane Pauley Learns America Loves Her." In *Television News Anchors: An Anthology of the Major Figures and Issues in United States Network Reporting*, edited by Thomas Fensch. Jefferson, N.C.: McFarland, 1993. As one chapter in an entire anthology devoted to the subject of television news reporters, Holloway's article discusses Pauley's reaction to the public uproar that resulted from her decision to leave her post on *Today*. Explores the strange reversal of attention that occurs when a high-profile reporter attains such a level of celebrity that his or her actions become the focus of news reporting.

McIntosh, Claire. "Here *Today*, Gone Tomorrow: When Jane Pauley *Should* Have Quit." *Working Woman* 15 (May, 1990): 82-83. In this interview, New York-based executive recruiter John Lucht charts the various turning points in Pauley's career and discusses the strategies she might have pursued in order to negotiate a better contract with NBC before the well-publicized arrival of Deborah Norville prompted Pauley to leave the *Today* show to seek other broadcasting opportunities at the network. Particularly useful for its handy time line, which places Pauley's salary and responsibilities within the context of those awarded to her male colleagues and her female competitors on other networks.

Zoglin, Richard. "Surviving Nicely, Thanks." *Time* 136 (August 20, 1990): 76-78. A brief profile of Pauley that touches on her successful jump from daytime to prime-time television news. In spite of her well-publicized desire to keep her family life private, Pauley does discuss her own early life, her broadcasting career, and her perspective on the fate of the *Today* show after her decision to leave.

Wendy Sacket

ELIZABETH PALMER PEABODY

Born: May 16, 1804; Billerica, Massachusetts
Died: January 3, 1894; Jamaica Plains, Massachusetts
Area of Achievement: Education
Contribution: Elizabeth Palmer Peabody, who was independent, intellectual, and devoted to education, helped to introduce the kindergarten into the United States.

Early Life

Elizabeth Palmer Peabody was born into a solid, well-established American family. Her parents, who married in November, 1802, were of old New England stock. Her mother, the former Elizabeth Palmer, was a bright, zealous woman. Nathaniel Peabody, a teacher, eventually yielded to his wife's urgings to become a physician, which he did by serving an apprenticeship with a practicing physician. Nathaniel, who was always manually dexterous, finally gravitated to dentistry. It became his chief occupation, although he was also qualified to practice medicine.

As the first child, Elizabeth early assumed responsibility for looking after her two younger sisters, Mary and Sophia, born in 1806 and 1809, respectively. At four, Elizabeth was already attending her mother's school in Salem.

After her brothers arrived—Nathaniel in 1811, George in 1813, and Wellington in 1815—Elizabeth's responsibilities increased. Her father's innovative dental practice attracted wealthy patients. When an economic downturn in 1819 diminished their income and his, however, the ensuing financial reverses forced the family to move from Salem to Lancaster, Massachusetts.

Elizabeth's mother immediately opened a school in Lancaster. She gave birth to a daughter, Catherine, in the same year. Catherine died after seven weeks, leaving the mother devastated. Grief-stricken, she transferred many of the responsibilities of her school and her household to Elizabeth, who was then fifteen.

For the next sixteen years, Elizabeth was essentially a school mistress, although at times she served as governess—once as far away as Maine—to children of the wealthy, whose extensive libraries she devoured in her spare moments. She had already mastered Latin when, in 1822, a neighborhood intellectual, Ralph Waldo Emerson, then nineteen, agreed to tutor her in Greek. She later learned Hebrew and also read widely in European literature.

From 1834 to 1836, Elizabeth taught at Bronson Alcott's Temple School in Boston. In 1839, Elizabeth opened a bookshop at 13 West Street in Boston. This establishment became a gathering place for New England's intellectuals. The concept of Brook Farm was hatched there.

Elizabeth published books by New England authors who were to become legendary but whose books, at that time, did not sell enough copies to cover expenses. During a term as editor of *The Dial*, Elizabeth learned about the financial hazards of being a publisher.

Elizabeth seemed inevitably destined for spinsterhood. Her romance with Horace

Mann led to her sister Mary's marriage to the renowned educator. Her romance with the novelist Nathaniel Hawthorne ended in her sister Sophia's marrying him. These disappointments engendered some temporary family difficulties, but the sisters were soon close again. Elizabeth had an excellent and enduring rapport with Horace Mann, although her relationship with Hawthorne was sometimes strained.

Life's Work

Elizabeth Peabody, who was dynamic and well-disciplined intellectually, is remembered for her work in many capacities: author, teacher, publisher, editor, trainer of teachers, and, most significant, founder of the first English-language kindergarten in the United States. Each successive step in Peabody's life contributed significantly to professional activities that lay in her future.

Her studying of Greek with Emerson led to a long friendship during which, with his encouragement, she became a bookshop owner, an editor, and a publisher. Although her romance with Hawthorne led not to her marriage but to her sister's, Elizabeth became one of Hawthorne's early publishers.

Elizabeth's continuing professional association with her brother-in-law Horace Mann helped her to develop a utopian view of education. She believed, like Mann, in the perfectibility of humankind. This deeply rooted, strongly held belief led her to do her most memorable and widely recognized work.

In 1849, before anyone in the United States advocated doing so, Peabody, writing in *Aesthetic Papers*, a journal she founded, called for the introduction of art, music, and dance into the public school curriculum. She also called upon a nation that was hemorrhaging money to fund the Mexican War to divert its resources to public education.

The bookshop, which was never profitable, continued to attract an impressive clientele who came more to talk than to buy. William Ellery Channing, for whom Peabody served as an unpaid secretary and with whom she had a complex relationship, was among its most ardent patrons before ill health grounded him.

Ever excited by new educational ideas, Elizabeth heard that a Polish general, Josef Bem, had developed a foolproof system for learning dates in history. After studying Bem's complicated method, Elizabeth set herself to making sets of Bem's historical charts, which were intricately color-coded by hand because Elizabeth lacked money to pay a printer.

She was convinced that the key to her future fortune lay in these charts, which she thought she could persuade the Boston school system to buy in quantity. Peabody traveled extensively to promote her charts among skeptical educators everywhere. Her efforts, which extended over a period of years, were futile. Through them, however, she made valuable contacts with educators and learned about educational policymaking.

It was not until 1860, when Peabody was fifty-six years old, that a major turning point occurred in her life. She discovered a kindred soul in education, Friedrich Froebel. Although this early advocate of kindergartens had recently died, Elizabeth felt a considerable affinity with his ideas, which ran counter to much she encountered in her work with Bronson Alcott, who was ever the educational autocrat.

Froebel shared Elizabeth's (and Horace Mann's) Rousseauvian notion that humans are innately good at the time of their birth. When they deviate from goodness, it is because society has transmitted its evil to them. Froebel deplored the corporal punishment that was a major controlling factor in most of the schools of his day. He believed in discipline but was convinced that, to be effective, discipline must come from within.

Froebel glorified rather than suppressed the senses. He encouraged children to be curious, to explore the world around them by touching, seeing, smelling, tasting, and listening to its wonders. Froebel considered it unnatural for children to sit quietly and passively while learning. Physical activity was a major component of his curriculum.

Peabody's *Universal History: Arranged to Illustrate Bem's Charts* (1859) drew the attention of some noteworthy educators. In 1861, inspired by what she had leaned about Friedrich Froebel's ideas, she opened a kindergarten based upon them. Her sister Mary, Horace Mann's widow, sold her house in Concord in 1866 and bought a house in Cambridge in which her sons, entering Harvard, could live during their college years. Elizabeth lived in Mary's house.

Elizabeth and Mary had recently collaborated on *Moral Culture of Infancy and Kindergarten Guide* (1866), which soon went into a second edition. Elizabeth was gaining visibility as a lecturer at teacher training institutions. Her kindergarten succeeded well enough that she hired Mary as her assistant.

A fundamental principle of Elizabeth's school was that its students should be happy. The old notion that infants trailed into the world vestiges of Original Sin that had to be beaten out of them was alien to Peabody's educational and religious philosophy. She, like Mann, firmly believed that if children were shown the right path, they would follow it.

By 1867, Peabody's kindergarten was sufficiently solvent that she was able to make her first trip to Germany to see Froebel's dream manifested in schools run by his followers. When she got to Berlin, Elizabeth visited the "Kindergarten Seminary," presided over by the Baroness von Marenholz Bülow, who had studied with Froebel. This visit was the fulfillment of Elizabeth's dream. Here, in what seems like a precursor of the Montessori Schools of the next century, she witnessed instruction that engaged all of the children's senses.

This trip convinced Elizabeth of the rectitude of her mission. She had met Carl Schurz and his wife when they were in Boston in 1852, before they continued to Wisconsin, where they set up the first kindergarten in the United States, but theirs was a German-language kindergarten. Peabody's was the first kindergarten to use English as the medium of instruction.

Elizabeth returned from Europe bristling with ideas. Her reputation spread so quickly that no normal school considered its program legitimate if it had not included a visit by this renowned educator whose career had begun at an age when most people retire. She spread the word of the kindergarten movement in the United States by founding *Kindergarten Messenger* and editing it from 1873 to 1877. In 1888, she published *Lectures in Training Schools for Kindergartners* (1888).

Peabody lived to be almost ninety. In her eighties, she lobbied in Washington on behalf of American Indians, particularly the Piutes. She was active almost to her last day. She looked with eager anticipation to the twentieth century, which was about to dawn, and reveled in such advances in her own century as electrical power, the telephone and telegraph, and the railway.

Summary

Elizabeth Palmer Peabody, perhaps because she was never a wife or mother, accomplished what someone living in her mother's era and situation could not. The first Elizabeth Peabody, a vibrant, intelligent woman, bore the responsibility of rearing six children and endured the sorrow of losing one. Her responsibilities and her deep sorrow served to limit her influence. Her daughter Elizabeth did what her mother could only yearn to do.

The progression of Peabody's contributions to education stem from her many failures. Elizabeth taught at Bronson Alcott's Temple School, whose methods of instruction made her question how children learn most effectively. She then ran a bookshop that attracted New England's intellectual elite, and from it ran a printing press that published the earliest works of Nathaniel Hawthorne but failed financially. Her next project was the Bem charts, which were designed to teach students significant dates in history. Although the charts never attracted the following that Peabody envisioned, they led her to write a book that brought her to the attention of American educators. Having gained the credibility that this book generated, Peabody opened the first kindergarten in the United States that used English as the medium of expression. This led to her becoming a trainer of teachers and to her having an impact on American education the likes of which only a handful of educators can lay claim.

Bibliography

Baylor, Ruth M. *Elizabeth Palmer Peabody: Kindergarten Pioneer*. Philadelphia: University of Pennsylvania Press, 1965. This thorough book is the most complete Peabody bibliography extant, although it is somewhat dated. The focus is on Peabody as an educator, but the book also provides interesting comments about Ralph Waldo Emerson, Nathaniel Hawthorne, William Ellery Channing, Horace Mann, and others.

Brooks, Gladys. *Three Wise Virgins*. New York: E. P. Dutton, 1957. Brooks is strong on reporting Peabody's early life and those of her sisters. She gives one a strong sense of the family solidarity that characterized Elizabeth's makeup.

Fenner, Mildred Sandison, and Eleanor Craven Fishburn. *Pioneer American Educators*. Washington, D.C.: National Education Association, 1944. The succinct chapter (pages 73-80) on Peabody is accurate. Of interest also are related chapters on Horace Mann (pages 17-24) and Bronson Alcott (pages 57-64), with both of whom Peabody was closely associated.

Peabody, Elizabeth Palmer. *The Piutes: Second Report of the Model School of Sarah Winnemucca*. Cambridge, Mass.: John Wilson, 1887. This fascinating work on Peabody's interest in American Indians is still available in many libraries. It demonstrates Peabody's activity in her eighties.

Ronda, Bruce A. *The Letters of Elizabeth Palmer Peabody: American Renaissance Woman*. Middletown, Conn.: Wesleyan University Press, 1984. Ronda's carefully collected, well-edited collection of Elizabeth Palmer Peabody's correspondence provides an excellent look at the intelligentsia of her day. A valuable resource.

Tharp, Louise Hall. *The Peabody Sisters of Salem*. Boston: Little, Brown, 1950. Despite its age, this book remains a preeminent study of the Peabody sisters and, particularly, of Elizabeth, the most dominant of them. Well researched and ably written.

R. Baird Shuman

FRANCES PERKINS

Born: April 10, 1880; Boston, Massachusetts
Died: May 14, 1965; New York, New York
Area of Achievement: Government and politics
Contribution: Perkins, as secretary of labor for twelve years under President Franklin Delano Roosevelt, was the first woman to serve in a president's cabinet. As secretary of labor, she was instrumental in developing legislation to improve labor conditions for workers. Her most notable achievement was to chair the committee responsible for developing the social security system.

Early Life

Frances Perkins was born on April 10, 1880, in Boston, Massachusetts. In 1882, her family moved to Worcester, Massachusetts, where her father prospered in the stationery business. Known as Fannie Coralie Perkins until her twenty-fifth year, she was raised in the fashion typical of middle-class girls of her generation. Her conservative, New England family upbringing influenced her early life. She was taught to behave like a lady, to be seen but not heard, and to accept her father's authority on all matters. Her childhood was comfortable and sheltered. She learned to read at a young age and was encouraged to do so by her father. Although she was extremely shy as a young girl, at school she discovered her ability to express herself through words.

School broadened her range of experiences, and she was very involved in a variety of activities. Her ability to debate enabled her to pass her courses with ease, and she was graduated from high school in 1898. Not sure what she wanted to do with her life, Perkins decided that she would pursue teaching because that was an acceptable occupation for a woman of her time. She convinced her father that attending college would help her find a good teaching position, so he agreed to let her attend Mount Holyoke College in western Massachusetts.

Perkins entered Mount Holyoke with no particular direction for her studies. After taking a required chemistry course, however, she discovered her skills and interest in the sciences. She pursued chemistry as her major, but in her last year at Mount Holyoke she took a course that changed her life. It was an economics course, but unlike other courses, it involved the direct observation of factories and industry. Perkins was deeply affected by the working conditions of women and children in the factories. This experience gave Perkins an awareness of social conditions that affected her the rest of her life.

After she was graduated in 1902, Perkins taught briefly at several girls' schools until finding a permanent job teaching chemistry at Ferry Hall School in Lake Forest, Illinois, outside of Chicago. Although it was far from her family, her father agreed to let her go, and in 1904 she left for Chicago.

Perkins taught for two years, spending her free time in Chicago working with many of the social reformers there. She was greatly inspired by the efforts of settlement workers, and in 1906, she left teaching to live at Hull House, the settlement house founded by Jane Addams. Although she was there for only six months, the time greatly influenced her, and Perkins was convinced that her calling was to strive to change working conditions for laborers, particularly women and children.

Life's Work

Frances Perkins' first paid employment in reforming labor conditions came in 1907, when she left Chicago to become the secretary of the Philadelphia Research and Protection Association. The organization helped immigrant girls from Europe and African American girls from southern states who came to Philadelphia looking for work. The young girls were often preyed upon by unscrupulous employers or forced into prostitution. As secretary, Perkins was responsible for gathering facts and using them to pressure city officials to legislate changes in employment practices. In this first job, Perkins developed skills she used throughout her professional life. She learned to gather data on working conditions and use it to influence policymakers to develop laws to protect workers. Perkins felt that the best way to help workers and the poor was through government action.

Perkins left in 1909 and went to study at the New York School of Philanthropy. In 1910, she graduated with a master's degree in political science from Columbia University. With her social work and political science training, she was well prepared to follow her chosen path of working for labor reform and rights. Perkins became the executive secretary of the New York City Consumers' League in 1910. In this position, she was responsible for investigating the conditions that existed in industries dominated by women workers. Living in Greenwich Village near many of the factories, Perkins witnessed the Triangle Shirtwaist Factory fire of 1911, the worst factory fire in New York history. The sight of young women jumping out of windows because there were no fire escapes reinforced Perkins' commitment to social and labor reform. After witnessing that event, she realized that organizing and union efforts, while important, were not enough. She became convinced that only through the power of legislation could there be real change.

The aftermath of the Triangle Shirtwaist Factory fire did bring legislative action. The New York State assembly founded the New York State Factory Commission in 1911. Perkins was director of investigation for the commission until 1913.

In 1912, while serving on the State Factory Commission, Perkins took the position of executive secretary of the New York Committee on Safety. Already experienced in lobbying from her work with the Consumers' League, she was active in influencing the passage of numerous regulations protecting workers and improving labor conditions. Included in her legislative efforts were reorganizing the state labor department and limiting the workweek for women to fifty-four hours. These were the first legislative efforts at labor reform by any state.

In 1913, Perkins married Paul Wilson, an economist and budget expert with the Bureau of Municipal Research. As intensely private people who were committed to their work, they kept their personal lives separate from their public lives. Perkins chose to keep her birth name, for she felt she had made much progress and saw no reason to take her husband's name. Over the next few years, she maintained her work with the Committee on Safety. In 1916, after experiencing two unsuccessful pregnancies, she gave birth to a daughter Susanne, her only child. Perkins limited her travels and lobbying, but stayed with the Committee on Safety until 1917.

Perkins' years with the Consumers' League and work on state commissions brought her close to a number of New York politicians. In 1918, she campaigned for Al Smith, a legislator who had supported her early labor reform efforts. Smith was elected governor of New York and after he took office in 1919, he appointed Perkins to her first public position, as a member of the New York State Industrial Commission. Perkins served in Smith's administrations until 1929. During those years, she mediated strikes between workers and management, improved factory inspections, regulated working conditions, and administered workers' compensation. When Smith, who ran unsuccessfully for president, was replaced as governor by Franklin D. Roosevelt, Perkins was appointed industrial commissioner of the State of New York. Perkins thus became the first woman to serve on a governor's cabinet.

With the full support of Roosevelt, Perkins was able to make significant reforms in working conditions in New York. She expanded employment services, increased factory investigations, and created data-gathering systems to provide information necessary to support legislative change. Among her legislative initiatives were reducing the work week for women to forty-eight hours, creating a minimum wage, and developing unemployment insurance. These efforts proved to be the blueprint for the work she did with Roosevelt years later in Washington.

Perkins served under Governor Roosevelt until his election as president of the United States. Without hesitation, President Roosevelt asked Perkins to serve as his secretary of labor. In 1933, Frances Perkins became the first woman ever to be appointed to a cabinet-level position. She accepted the position with the understanding that she was free to pursue the social reforms she had begun in New York and had advocated throughout her professional career.

Initially, labor and business leaders were critical of the idea of a female secretary of labor. Fully aware of that fact, Perkins developed a leadership style that brought together labor and management through cooperation and conciliation. As secretary of labor, Perkins also tried to bring together different factions of the labor movement. With the Great Depression looming, Perkins viewed reforming labor conditions as a way to improve economic conditions.

Over time, Perkins was successful in facilitating legislative reforms. Major relief legislation passed during Perkins' first years included the establishment of the Federal Emergency Relief Administration, the Civilian Conservation Corps, and the Public Works Administration. These programs represented the first major employment efforts by the federal government. Additional legislation was passed to regulate minimum wages, child labor, and work hours.

Perkins' major contributions as secretary of labor were the development of a data system to track statistics on employment and unemployment, standardization of state industrial legislation, and the development of the social security system. Perkins chaired the Committee on Economic Security, which crafted the Social Security Act of 1935. For both Perkins and Roosevelt, the Social Security Act represented a major accomplishment because it established minimum securities for workers through national insurance. In 1938, Perkins realized another major labor reform through the Fair Labor Standards Act, which set minimum wages, maximum work hours, and child labor prohibitions.

Perkins remained secretary of labor throughout Roosevelt's years as president. She resigned in 1945 and served on the U.S. Civil Service Commission until 1953. Her last years were spent writing and teaching at Cornell University. Frances Perkins died on May 14, 1965, in New York City.

Summary

Frances Perkins' work demonstrated a rare blend of social concern and political action. Her early years in settlement houses and investigating working conditions propelled her to work toward changing the American labor system and improving the lives of working women and men. Perkins was convinced that what the labor system needed was legislative reform, not a complete overhaul. She devoted her professional career to influencing legislation that supported the needs of workers, particularly women and their families.

Perkins' role as a member of the presidential cabinet paved the way for future women to be directly involved in government action. She held public office before women could even vote. As a lobbyist and public official, she was instrumental in establishing government as a developer and regulator of legislation to protect workers. Under her influence, programs such as workers' compensation, unemployment insurance, minimum wages, and social security were formed. Such social legislation changed the face of labor forever and formed the foundation of modern workers' rights.

Bibliography

Martin, George W. *Madam Secretary*. Boston: Houghton Mifflin, 1976. A comprehensive and extensive biography based on Perkins' oral history, this book provides a very personal view of Perkins' life.

Mohr, Lillian Holmen. *Frances Perkins: That Woman in FDR's Cabinet!* Croton-on-Hudson, N.Y.: North River Press, 1979. A biography of Perkins with some emphasis on the role of Perkins as a woman in government.

Severn, Bill. *Frances Perkins: A Member of the Cabinet*. New York: Hawthorn Books, 1976. Chronicles Perkins' life from her youth throughout her years in government.

Sternsher, Bernard, and Judith Sealander, eds. *Women of Valor: The Struggle Against the Great Depression as Told in Their Own Life Stories*. Chicago: Ivan R. Dee, 1990. This collection of essays by various women includes a piece by Perkins, excerpted from her book *The Roosevelt I Knew*. It gives insight into the kind of government official she was.

Wandersee, Winifred D. "I'd Rather Pass a Law than Organize a Union: Frances

Perkins and the Reformist Approach to Organized Labor." *Labor History* 34, no. 1 (Winter, 1993): 5-32. Describes Perkins' approach to working with organized labor during her cabinet years.

Elizabeth A. Segal

JANE CAHILL PFEIFFER

Born: September 29, 1932; Washington, D.C.

Area of Achievement: Business and industry
Contribution: Pfeiffer served as vice president of communications at International Business Machines in 1972 and chairman of the National Broadcasting Corporation in 1978, when she was the highest-paid female executive in the United States.

Early Life

Jane Pennington Cahill was born on September 29, 1932, in Washington, D.C., to John Joseph and Helen Reilly Cahill. When Jane was seven, her father died suddenly and left her mother with the responsibility of supporting Jane and her older brother Jack. Helen Cahill's career success provided an example for her only daughter. Eventually, Helen Cahill's hard work led her to become the highest-paid woman in the federal civil service as the chief nutritionist for the Veterans Administration.

Majoring in speech and drama and minoring in mathematics, Jane was graduated from the University of Maryland with a B.A. in 1954. The following year, she took graduate courses in philosophy at Georgetown and Catholic Universities. Following the completion of her formal education, she entered a Roman Catholic novitiate to begin training to become a nun. Jane left after only six months, when she decided that the religious life was not what God wanted her to do with her life.

Life's Work

In 1955, Jane Cahill went to work for International Business Machines (IBM) as a systems engineering trainee, responsible for instructing customers in computer programming. Getting into that organization when it was on the verge of explosive growth provided her with opportunities for experience and responsibility that were open to few women in American industry at that time. In addition, Cahill's intelligence, hard work ethic, and willingness to gain broad experience through changing assignments, were a perfect match for the IBM corporate culture. As a result, her performance was rewarded with many promotions in the rapidly expanding corporation.

Cahill's ability to get things done is illustrated by an incident that occurred in 1960 when she was serving as site manager for the Mercury space program's missile-tracking program in Bermuda. When the IBM payroll did not arrive on time, she simply took out a loan with a local bank, paid her employees, and requested reimbursement from corporate headquarters to repay the loan. Such ingenuity brought her performance to the attention of IBM's top executives.

In 1966, she was granted a one-year leave of absence from IBM to serve as the first female White House Fellow in a program designed to increase understanding between business and government. Her assignment in the Department of Housing and Urban Development provided her with experience and government contacts that would later prove to be valuable to her career.

After Cahill returned to IBM, her career was on the fast track. In 1967, she became the administrative assistant to IBM chairman Thomas J. Watson, Jr.; in 1970, the secretary of the management review committee; in 1971, director of communications; and in 1972, the vice president in charge of corporate communications and government relations—IBM's first female vice president since World War II. As vice president, Jane Cahill was instrumental in involving IBM in sponsoring quality television programs that would appeal to businessmen who would be making computer purchasing decisions. As a result, IBM profited by being identified with quality news programming such as *Face the Nation*, as well as televised productions of William Shakespeare's *Much Ado About Nothing* and Miguel de Cervantes' *Don Quixote*.

On June 3, 1975, Cahill married Ralph A. Pfeiffer, Jr., the senior vice president of IBM's World Trade Corporation. Marriage brought instant motherhood: She became stepmother to his ten children from a former marriage—six boys and four girls. Citing the difficulties of two vice presidents from the same organization being married to each other and the demanding time requirements of their positions, Jane Cahill Pfeiffer resigned from her job at IBM nine months after her marriage. The next two years were eventful. Pfeiffer began freelancing as a consultant, capitalizing on her excellent reputation as a manager and her high-level corporate and government contacts. Her clients included such well-known organizations as IBM, Bank of America, Yale University, Bethlehem Steel, and the Radio Corporation of America (RCA), a relationship that would later prove to be quite important. When she was offered a cabinet-level post as secretary of commerce in 1976 by President-elect Jimmy Carter, Pfeiffer refused the opportunity, citing her recent recovery from thyroid cancer and her decision to remain with her family while her husband still worked for IBM in Armonk, New York.

A call on Kenneth W. Bilby, RCA's executive vice president for corporate affairs, to solicit a donation for the University of Notre Dame would change her life. Bilby introduced Pfeiffer to Edgar H. Griffiths, president of RCA, who retained Pfeiffer as a consultant. Earning $125,000 a year for working two or three days per week, she was assigned projects such as negotiating agreements with officials from the People's Republic of China for the sale of RCA television sets and communications systems and then obtaining the necessary federal government approval for the sale of such technology to a communist nation.

Part of her work with RCA involved improving the management of one of its wholly owned but poorly performing subsidiaries, the National Broadcasting Corporation (NBC). At that time, NBC was gearing its programming toward younger viewers by broadcasting expensive miniseries, movies, and specials instead of developing popular series that would attract a loyal following week after week. As a result, rival networks ABC and CBS were winning the ratings wars and were therefore able to charge more for advertising time. Pfeiffer knew Fred Silverman, the successful head of ABC Entertainment, as a result of her involvement with television advertising at IBM. Consequently, she was asked by RCA management to contact Silverman about the possibility of becoming president of NBC.

After negotiating through Pfeiffer, Silverman accepted the NBC position as president and chief executive officer in June of 1978. At Silverman's request, Pfeiffer spent most of her RCA consulting time working with Silverman during his first four months on the job. On October 4, 1978, again at Silverman's request, Pfeiffer was elected to the RCA board of directors and became chairman of NBC. Her three-year contract stipulated an annual salary of $225,000 plus bonuses ranging from $66,000 to $200,000 per year—a compensation package that made her the highest-paid female executive in the United States. Although a corporate president traditionally reports to the chairman of an organization, Pfeiffer's relationship with Silverman at NBC clearly reversed this pattern.

During her tenure at NBC, Pfeiffer worked on improving the company's planning, decision making, and budgeting processes. In an attempt to gain a larger audience, she increased the news budget by 23 percent, revamped the news format, and hired a retired CBS news president. Although many of her decisions were good for the business, some of them also made enemies for her within the organization. She reduced the board of directors from eighteen to nine members by eliminating some NBC executives. She also managed the investigation of a million-dollar embezzlement scheme that resulted in criminal charges being brought against ten employees and the firing of many unit managers and a vice president.

In spite of all of the changes made by Silverman and Pfeiffer to institute higher-quality programming and improve the news broadcasting, NBC's ratings remained the lowest of the three major networks. On July 8, 1980, Fred Silverman surprised the broadcasting community by announcing that he was relieving Pfeiffer of her duties; on July 11, she formally resigned.

There are many theories about Pfeiffer's sudden departure from NBC. They range from inadequate performance on her part to the diligent but righteous way that she handled the embezzlement scandal. Some people believed that Pfeiffer's honest, straightforward, and outspoken manner was more suitable to a corporate environment such as IBM than to the less structured, more political television industry. After leaving the broadcast industry, Pfeiffer returned to the consulting business, maintaining an office in Greenwich, Connecticut.

In addition to her professional life, Jane Pfeiffer has had a long and extensive history of public, corporate, and community service. She has served as a member of the President's Commission on White House Fellows, the President's Commission on Military Compensation, the Council on Foreign Relations, and the Board of Governors of the American Red Cross. In addition, she has served as a director for the Bache Group, Chesebrough-Ponds, Incorporated, Ashland Oil Company, Mony Financial Services, the International Paper Company, and the J. C. Penney Company, and as a trustee of the Kettering Foundation, Carnegie Hall, Catholic University, the University of Notre Dame, and the Rockefeller Foundation.

Pfeiffer has received well-deserved recognition for her accomplishments. She has been awarded honorary degrees from Pace College (1978), the University of Maryland (1979), Manhattanville College (1979), Babson College (1981), and the University of Notre Dame (1991). In addition, she is the recipient of the Achievement award from Kappa Kappa Gamma, the Eleanor Roosevelt Humanitarian Award, Centennial Alumna Medallion for the University of Maryland, the Humanitarian Award for the New York League for the Hard of Hearing, and the Humanitarian Award for the National Organization for Women.

Summary

Jane Cahill Pfeiffer broke through the "glass ceilings" of two major American corporations at a time when few women were able to do so. She managed to combine femininity with toughness and marriage with a high-powered career. Her success in great part can be attributed to her dedication to hard work, a sense of commitment, and her ability to use her network of contacts within the corporate culture; her failure at NBC can be attributed to a lack of understanding of the political nature of the broadcasting industry. Because she has been at a level of corporate responsibility that few women experience, Pfeiffer's expertise is highly valued. As a result, she has been sought after and has served on many corporate and nonprofit boards of directors.

Bibliography

Adams, Jane. "Fallen Idols." *Working Woman* 6 (February, 1981): 63-65. A comparison of the factors involved in the firings of two high-profile corporate women: Jane Pfeiffer of NBC and Mary Cunningham of the Bendix Corporation. In this article, Pfeiffer emerges as an accomplished and experienced businesswoman who responded to her job loss with style and grace.

"Jane Pfeiffer Named NBC Chairman." *Broadcasting* 95 (September 18, 1978): 28-29. An inside explanation of the job shifts and turmoil that occurred as NBC struggled to regain audience share.

Moritz, Charles, ed. "Jane Cahill Pfeiffer." *Current Biography Yearbook*. New York: H. W. Wilson, 1980. An extremely complete and detailed biography of Pfeiffer's background and career. This article also provides a comprehensive description of Pfeiffer's life history.

"NBC's Jane Pfeiffer: Making Overachieving Seem Ever So Easy." *Broadcasting* 95 (October 23, 1978): 89. A comprehensive short biography that details Jane Pfeiffer's personal and career history.

Schuyten, Peter J. "A Sure-Footed Climb to the Top." *New York Times Biographical Service* 9 (December, 1978): 1239-1240. A report written during Pfeiffer's early days at NBC that contains some background information on her life and several quotations about her aspirations to turn around the situation at the network. It is particularly interesting to read her optimistic views about beginning her job in the light of her subsequent firing.

Carol P. Harvey

MARY PICKFORD
Gladys Louise Smith

Born: April 8, 1892; Toronto, Ontario, Canada
Died: May 29, 1979; Santa Monica, California
Area of Achievement: Film
Contribution: Early in the history of the film industry, Pickford established herself as the first name box-office draw, and hence the first star, of American cinema. While the attraction of her name and image shaped the economics of motion pictures for decades, Pickford also became an early role model for independent women who took charge of their own destinies.

Early Life

The actress known as Mary Pickford was born Gladys Louise Smith on April 8, 1892, in Toronto, Canada. Poverty and early widowhood led Gladys' mother, Charlotte Hennessey Smith, to place her children on the stage. In 1898, at the age of six, Gladys appeared in *The Silver King* at Toronto's Princess Theatre. Her early success on the stage, and her mother's example, soon made the little girl the principal source of income for her family, a burden, she wrote later, that she felt keenly at an early age. This sense of fiscal responsibility led to an early maturity in which the young performer fought aggressively for salary increments and contract rights.

Gladys' theater career began in earnest when she appeared with the Valentine Stock Company's production of *The Little Red Schoolhouse* in April of 1901; her performance earned for her a part in the touring version of that play, which went on the road in November of 1901. During the next four years, Gladys went on tour—usually accompanied by her mother Charlotte—with several plays. Touring companies in those days followed a hard schedule, frequently playing one night and then moving on, staying in cheap hotels. Gladys endured, however, even though she never had time for more than six months of formal education, because even as a child she was determined to keep her family out of poverty. She educated herself on the road and somehow learned to read.

Sometimes her success led to parts for her mother or her brother and sister, Jack and Lottie, but it was Gladys' ability and determination that enabled the family to stay together. Devoted to her career, Gladys worked hard, observing the work of established performers whenever possible. By the age of about twelve, she decided that she would try to become a "success" by the age of twenty.

Life's Work

In fact, Gladys did not need to wait that long. Although she was suffering from exhaustion in 1907, a successful audition with David Belasco, a famous Broadway producer, brought her a part in *The Warrens of Virginia*. Belasco also urged Gladys to find a more appealing stage name. In those days, a part with Belasco was a sign that an actress had "arrived," and this association was to be a launching pad for the Belasco actress now known as Mary Pickford.

In 1909, when Pickford found herself temporarily out of work, her mother urged her to talk to the director D. W. Griffith, who had begun making "flickers" for Biograph studios in New York. Although Pickford was reluctant—stage actors considered work in films to be a sign of failure—she was not only able to find work with Griffith at a salary higher than that she had earned with Belasco, but she was also able to dictate her own terms to Griffith, who was more than pleased to have a Belasco veteran in his company. Pickford's determination at age sixteen to have some control over her work was to be a hallmark of the rest of her career.

Griffith did not allow his players to be known by name, fearing that prominence would lead them to demand more money, but Mary Pickford, known to audiences as "Little Mary" (the name of one of her screen characters) or "The Girl with the Golden Curls," soon became popular anyway. Her fame during this period came partially from her appearances in child roles, which, because of her slight physical stature and youthful looks, she was able to play until well into her thirties.

In 1911, Pickford left Biograph for IMP pictures, but she returned in 1912; shortly thereafter, she left to join Adolph Zukor's Famous Players, where she established herself as the industry's first individual box-office draw, or "star." Pickford demanded and got from Zukor the unprecedented salary of five hundred dollars a week; moreover, her growing popularity led to a series of raises, and by 1916 she was earning ten thousand dollars a week plus bonuses. In 1917, Zukor created Artcraft Pictures Corporation, a division of Famous Players-Lasky, to produce Mary Pickford films exclusively. By now, Pickford was making feature-length films (as opposed to shorts) that were commercial as well as artistic successes; *Poor Little Rich Girl* (1917) was the first of these films.

Poor Little Rich Girl was one of many period melodramas that appealed to the values of middle and working classes, but it was also distinguished by the cinematographic art of director Maurice Tourneur, who was breaking new ground with lighting, camera angles, and dream sequences. The film's ultimate success, however, was equally the result of Pickford's comedic scenes (such as a mudfight), which relieved the film's otherwise somber tone and which Pickford inserted over director Tourneur's objections.

Pickford's control over this film is another hallmark of her career. When she began her next film for Zukor, *Rebecca of Sunnybrook Farm* (1917), she demanded—and got—Marshall Neiland as director and Frances Marion as writer. In 1918, Mary Pickford obtained the rights to scripts for *Pollyanna* and *Daddy Long-Legs* and demanded complete control, with Famous Players-Lasky functioning solely as distributor. When Zukor balked, Pickford signed with First National, which formed its own division, Mary Pickford Co., which had complete control over production.

Two years later, Pickford and her husband Douglas Fairbanks joined with Griffith and Charlie Chaplin to form United Artists Corporation, a company that served as a distributor for independent producers, frequently the stars themselves, who were able to keep the profits from each picture, select or reject any role, and control publicity.

By contrast, 1930's stars who worked for large studios such as Metro-Goldwyn-Mayer (MGM) or Twentieth Century-Fox worked under contracts that paid them a straight salary for a given number of pictures, with acting roles being chosen by the studio heads or their subordinates. During the early days of United Artists (UA), Pickford produced some of her most famous films: *Pollyanna* (1920), *Little Lord Fauntleroy* (1921), and *Rosita* (1923). A less-known but critically acclaimed UA production was *Sparrows* (1926), which was noted for its gothic texture and brooding cinematography. In all, Pickford acted in sixteen films for United Artists between 1920 and 1933; after her acting career ended, she produced several other films during the thirties and forties.

The late twenties and early thirties were a difficult time for Mary Pickford. Her marriage to Douglas Fairbanks was becoming shaky, and the advent of "talking pictures" threatened many actors whose careers were built in the silent era. Pickford's first talkie, *Coquette* (1929), was a commercial success that won her the first Academy Award for Best Actress, but it was a critical failure that even horrified Pickford herself, who did not like what the new sound technology did to her voice. The only film Pickford and Fairbanks did together, an adaptation of Shakespeare's *The Taming of the Shrew* (1929), was a failure with the critics and at the box office, as were Pickford's remaining talkies. Although the Depression was probably partly responsible for the commercial failure of these films, Pickford, always insecure even at the height of her success, halted production before her last film, *Secrets*, was completed. The film was never released, and Pickford, only forty-two in 1933, never acted again. She was disheartened by her commercial failures, as well as by the death of her mother—whose business sense had helped to build Pickford's wealth—and the impending collapse of her marriage to Fairbanks.

In 1936, she and Fairbanks were divorced, and Pickford married Buddy Rogers, her former leading man who had remained devoted to her. Rogers and Pickford adopted two children, and she was able finally to play in real life the mother role she had played in films such as *Sparrows*. Although she continued to produce films, with indifferent success, Pickford gradually retired from public life, secluding herself at Pickfair, the estate she and Fairbanks had once shared, as she grew older. In 1953, she and Chaplin, the surviving founders, relinquished control of United Artists. In 1977, a few years before her death, Mary Pickford was given a Life Achievement Academy Award, but even this did not draw her out of seclusion, and the award ceremony had to be filmed at Pickfair.

Summary

Mary Pickford's contributions to the film industry are manifold. Her curly-headed "Little Mary" character became the prototype for child stars of later years; Shirley Temple was only the first in a long line that includes recent roles on television situation comedies. In all of her roles, moreover, Pickford's acting style created an important bridge between the silent and sound period; critics have noticed that Pickford could convey emotions in the silent films with subtle gestures and facial expressions, unlike the exaggerated styles of many silent actors.

Pickford's greatest contribution to the film industry was her popular appeal. The rise of stars such as Pickford and Chaplin, with whom audiences could identify, led to the growth of the film industry from a curiosity featuring short films to a serious art form with feature-length productions. Her independence paved the way for United Artists, which she cofounded, and which provided opportunities for creative producers such as Alexander Korda, David O. Selznick, and Samuel Goldwyn.

For women, moreover, Pickford was a trailblazer. Although she probably never considered herself a feminist (she was very conservative politically and socially), her life and work nevertheless provided a valuable role model for women. On the screen, her interpretation often gave her heroines a kind of plucky independence despite the overlay of middle-class conventionality that her audiences demanded. In an era when Victorian mores still predominated, she emerged as one of the few financially independent women of her era, one who had earned her fortune through hard work and gritty determination. For the time in which she flourished, that was a considerable achievement.

Bibliography

Balio, Tino. *United Artists: The Company That Changed the Film Industry*. Madison: University of Wisconsin Press, 1987. Although the focus of this treatment is on the history of United Artists after Pickford and Chaplin sold their interest in 1951, it still offers a good, if brief, perspective on the early years.

Eyman, Scott. *Mary Pickford: America's Sweetheart*. New York: Donald I. Fine, 1990. A thorough treatment of Pickford's life, with a critical discussion of her major films and her artistic contributions. More than forty photographs illustrate Pickford's life from childhood to old age. Probably the best treatment of Pickford's life and work, this book has few competitors.

Gomery, Douglas. *The Hollywood Studio System*. New York: St. Martin's Press, 1986. Case histories of each of the five major studios (Twentieth Century-Fox, Paramount, MGM, RKO, Warner Bros.) are followed by an eight-page, concise history of United Artists (under "Specialized Studios"), with an account of the founders' roles in its successes and failures.

Herndon, Boonton. *Mary Pickford and Douglas Fairbanks*. New York: W. W. Norton, 1977. An examination of Pickford's and Fairbanks' careers, emphasizing their married years. A good supplement to Eyman's book.

Pickford, Mary. *Sunshine and Shadow*. Garden City, N.Y.: Doubleday, 1955. Pickford's autobiography, although subjective and not always entirely reliable, remains one of the principal sources of information on her life.

Schickel, Richard. *D. W. Griffith: An American Life*. New York: Simon & Schuster, 1984. A detailed biography of the director who brought Pickford to the screen as "Little Mary," did much to shape her career, and later joined her as cofounder of United Artists. This book is valuable for its bibliography alone.

Timothy C. Frazer

SUSAN LA FLESCHE PICOTTE

Born: June 17, 1865; Omaha Indian Reservation, Nebraska
Died: September 18, 1915; Walthill, Nebraska
Areas of Achievement: Medicine and social reform
Contribution: As the first female Native American physician, Picotte served her tribe as medical missionary and community leader for twenty-five years.

Early Life

Susan La Flesche was born June 17, 1865, on the Omaha Indian Reservation in northeast Nebraska. Her father, chief Joseph La Flesche (also known as Iron Eye), was the son of a French fur trader and his Indian wife. Adopted by Omaha chief Big Elk, Iron Eye succeeded him as one of the two principal chiefs of the tribe in 1853. Susan's mother, Mary Gale La Flesche (also known as One Woman), was the daughter of a white army surgeon and his Omaha wife. The La Flesches believed that some accommodation to the ever-advancing white world was essential if their tribe were to survive. As the youngest of Iron Eye's four remarkable daughters, Susan grew up in a family much influenced by assimilation-oriented missionaries. Her parents converted to Christianity, adopted the white man's lifestyle, and encouraged their children to seek formal education. Her oldest sister, Susette (Bright Eyes), ultimately gained fame as a speaker, journalist, and Indian rights advocate; Rosalie enjoyed a successful business career in the livestock industry; and Marguerite became a teacher among the Omahas.

Reared on the reservation, Susan attended agency day schools run by Quaker and Presbyterian missionaries. At the age of fourteen, she and seventeen-year-old Marguerite traveled to New Jersey to attend boarding school at the Elizabeth Institute for Young Ladies, returning home to Nebraska two and a half years later. From 1882 to 1884, Susan taught at the mission school before continuing her education at the Hampton Normal and Agricultural Institute in Virginia. Established in 1868 to educate freed slaves (and later, Indians as well), Hampton emphasized vocational training; however, Susan and Marguerite could read and write English fluently and were encouraged to pursue an academic program. Susan was graduated second in her class in 1886. Urged to study medicine by the school physician, Dr. Martha Waldron, she eagerly accepted a scholarship to Woman's Medical College of Pennsylvania. On March 14, 1889, Susan was graduated at the head of her class of thirty-six women, becoming the first female Native American to acquire a medical degree.

Life's Work

Following a four-month internship at Women's Hospital in Philadelphia, Susan La Flesche accepted the position of government physician to the Omaha agency school. Of all the Nebraska tribes, the Omahas were considered the most successful in trying to accommodate to white ideas of "progress." The Omaha Allotment Act of 1882 had divided much of the reservation into individual farms, and more and more Indian families were sending their children to the agency school. Despite this seeming progress, drought, grasshoppers, unscrupulous white neighbors, and inept government agents all combined to create desperate poverty among the Omahas. With this social upheaval and deprivation came malnutrition and disease. Influenza, dysentery, and tuberculosis were endemic on the reservation, as were periodic outbreaks of cholera, smallpox, diphtheria, and typhoid fever. Within weeks of her arrival, the twenty-four-year-old La Flesche also took on the arduous task of treating the entire adult population, giving her a patient load of more than twelve hundred.

The size of the reservation—thirty by forty-five miles—and the absence of paved roads forced La Flesche to travel huge distances by horse and buggy or on horseback, often in severe weather. In 1891, the Women's National Indian Association, which had financed her medical training, asked her to take on additional duties as their medical missionary to the tribe. That same year, she gained membership in the Nebraska State Medical Society. Soon La Flesche experienced the first of several bouts with osteomyelitis, a painful infection of her facial bones which later caused deafness and eventually led to her premature death. Exhausted and temporarily bedridden by the disease, she resigned as agency doctor in October of 1893.

Despite her frail health and enormous professional responsibilities, La Flesche became increasingly involved in tribal and family affairs during the 1890's. Ever the missionary, she taught Sunday school at the Presbyterian church, acted as interpreter for non-English speaking Omahas, and worked closely with Marguerite to upgrade sanitary conditions on the reservation. To everyone's surprise, on June 30, 1894, she married Henry Picotte, an uneducated French-Sioux from the Yankton Agency who was a brother of Marguerite's late husband, Charles. The Picottes settled for a time in Bancroft, on the southern edge of the reservation, where Henry farmed the La Flesche allotment and Susan bore two sons: Caryl, born in 1895, and Pierre, born in 1898. While rearing her children and caring for her ailing mother, she continued to practice medicine, treating both Indian and non-Indian patients. Before long she was also nursing Henry, whose excessive drinking undermined his health and ultimately caused his death in 1905.

For Susan Picotte, the scourge of alcoholism went beyond the boundaries of a personal family tragedy. Her father had waged a successful campaign against whiskey peddlers and liquor consumption on the Omaha reservation. After Iron Eye's death in 1888, however, the situation deteriorated. Picotte eventually came to regard "demon rum" as the principal health hazard threatening her people. In temperance lectures, newspaper articles, and letters to government officials, she argued that alcohol abuse not only increased violence and crime but also made her tribesmen easy prey for all sorts of deadly diseases, especially tuberculosis and pneumonia. Moreover, she charged, local politicians and bootleggers routinely used whiskey to cheat tribal members out of their allotments. She lobbied the Bureau of Indian Affairs (BIA) for stricter enforcement of the 1897 congressional ban on selling liquor to Indians. By 1906, she had convinced the secretary of the interior to ban all liquor sales in any new town carved out of the Omaha reservation.

Picotte and her sister Marguerite (who had remarried) bought property in the new town of Walthill, where, in 1906, they each built modern homes. Over the next nine years, Picotte actively participated in the civic and professional life of the community, despite her own failing health. The Presbyterian Board of Home Missions hired her as their missionary to the Omahas, the first nonwhite to hold such a post. She served several terms on the Walthill Board of Health, during which time she led campaigns to eradicate the communal drinking cup and the household fly as agents of disease. She organized the Thurston County Medical Association, served a three-year term as state chair of the Nebraska Federation of Women's Clubs' public health committee, and began an intensive study of tuberculosis.

In 1909, the Omaha tribe sought Picotte's help in solving serious problems arising out of the allotment system. By law, individual allotments were to be held in trust by the government for twenty-five years, until Native American owners were deemed sufficiently "assimilated" to handle their own financial affairs. Meanwhile, government red tape and dictatorial agency control deprived tribal members of desperately needed trust funds. Making matters worse, the BIA instituted new restrictions in 1909; consolidated the Omaha and Winnebago agencies; and announced plans to extend the trust period an additional ten years, despite the Omahas' high literacy rate and well-educated leadership. Picotte wrote a series of blistering newspaper articles protesting the BIA's conduct. In February of 1910, barely recovered from a near-fatal attack of neurasthenia, she headed up a tribal delegation sent to Washington, D.C., to fight the new policies. Unsuccessful in getting the old agency restored, Picotte did persuade the secretary of the interior to cancel the ten-year trust extension, thus granting most Omahas control over their own property.

Picotte's main dream was to erect a centrally located hospital where she could provide better medical care for her Indian patients. Through her efforts, the Presbyterian Church provided $8,000, and Quakers gave an additional $500. Marguerite and her husband donated the land, and various other friends agreed to purchase the equipment. After Walthill Hospital opened in January of 1913, Picotte was able to practice there for only two years. The bone disease in her face and neck spread, taking her life on September 18, 1915. Her funeral was conducted jointly by Presbyterian clergy and a tribal elder; the medical facility she built was renamed the Dr. Susan Picotte Memorial Hospital.

Summary

As practicing physician, missionary, social reformer, and political leader, Susan La Flesche Picotte had a profound effect on the lives of her people. By 1915, there was scarcely an Omaha alive who had not been treated by her; even those who did not embrace all of her reformist ideals trusted her. As the Omahas' unofficial but clearly recognized spokesperson, Picotte defended their interests in the white world, even as she devoted her energies to their physical well-being at home. Beyond modern medical care, public health improvements, and vigorous leadership, she provided her tribe—and the larger world—with a vibrant example of what late nineteenth century reformers hoped to accomplish with their assimilationist policies. Like her father, Picotte believed that education, Christian principles, and legal rights were the key to her tribe's advancement. That she and her non-Indian mentors underestimated the difficulties facing Native Americans and overestimated the virtues of forced acculturation does not detract from her achievement. Susan Picotte walked with grace in two worlds; assimilated into middle-class mainstream American culture, she never abandoned her tribal roots or her overriding concern for her people. Few women, Indian or white, have left such an indelible mark on their communities.

Bibliography

Clark, Jerry E., and Martha Ellen Webb. "Susette and Susan La Flesche: Reformer and Missionary." In *Being and Becoming Indian: Biographical Studies of North American Frontiers*, edited by James A. Clifton. Chicago: Dorsey Press, 1989. Contrasting the lives of the two best-known La Flesche sisters, the authors conclude that both women were thoroughly assimilated into white culture; Susan, however, participated more directly in tribal life and harbored less bitterness toward non-Indians.

Green, Norma Kidd. *Iron Eye's Family: The Children of Joseph La Flesche*. Lincoln, Neb.: Johnsen Publishing Company, 1969. The pioneering work on the La Flesche family, and still the best source of detailed information on Picotte's life. Green explores the achievements of three generations of this large and fascinating clan. Included are the children of Iron Eye's secondary wife, Ta-in-ne, as well as a glimpse of the adult lives led by Picotte's two sons, Caryl and Pierre.

Hauptman, Laurence M. "Medicine Woman: Susan La Flesche, 1865-1915." *New York State Medical Journal* 78 (September, 1978): 1783-1788. Focuses on Picotte's experiences in medical school, emphasizing her enthusiasm and scientific curiosity. Hauptman makes good use of her correspondence to convey the image of a supremely self-confident young woman who also possessed a wry sense of humor.

Mathes, Valerie Sherer. "Dr. Susan La Flesche Picotte: The Reformed and the Reformer." In *Indian Lives: Essays on Nineteenth- and Twentieth-Century Native American Leaders*, edited by L. G. Moses and Raymond Wilson. Albuquerque: University of New Mexico Press, 1985. Mathes portrays Picotte's life and work as a manifestation of the late nineteenth century female reform tradition. This article also gives the most up-to-date diagnosis of the physician's own perplexing health problems.

Milner, Clyde A. *With Good Intentions: Quaker Work Among the Pawnees, Otos, and Omahas in the 1870's*. Lincoln: University of Nebraska Press, 1982. Places the La Flesche family's advocacy of accommodation in the larger context of the Quaker-inspired "Peace Policy" adopted by the government in 1869. For the Omahas' role within this framework, Milner relies heavily on a landmark study of the tribe published in 1911 by Picotte's half brother, ethnologist Francis La Flesche.

Wilson, Dorothy Clarke. *Bright Eyes: The Story of Susette La Flesche, an Omaha Indian*. New York: McGraw-Hill, 1974. Romanticized biography of Picotte's older, more famous sister. There is little material here on Susan herself, but more on her mother, Mary Gale, than is available elsewhere.

Constance B. Rynder

MARGE PIERCY

Born: March 31, 1936; Detroit, Michigan

Area of Achievement: Literature
Contribution: A popular poet and novelist, Piercy writes about working- and middle-class men and women, chronicling their relationships to nature, to society, and with one another in the context of a radical historical and feminist critique of the political and economic system.

Early Life

Born to a middle-European Jewish mother, who was passionate and imaginative but had only a tenth-grade education, and a Welsh Presbyterian father, who worked for Westinghouse most of his life and was an avid union man, Marge Piercy lived in an inner-city, working-class neighborhood in Detroit where she and an African American girl were the only two Jews in her school. After winning a scholarship to attend the University of Michigan, she became pregnant at eighteen and almost died of a self-induced abortion. After being graduated in 1957 as an English major who won prizes for both poetry and fiction, Piercy married Michael Schiff, a particle physicist, and completed an M.A. in English at Northwestern University. For the next ten years, she wrote much poetry and at least six novels while working at various part-time jobs in Chicago, such as secretary, sales clerk, telephone operator, and college instructor. Divorced and remarried in 1962 to Robert Shapiro, a computer specialist, she wrote about the textures of daily communal living as related to her left-wing political concerns, including involvement with antinuclear/peace movements and Students for a Democratic Society (SDS). Becoming increasingly conscious of the regressive sexual politics of the radical Left, by 1969 she had switched the primary focus of her political activity to the nascent feminist movement. In 1970, she and Shapiro bought land on Cape Cod, in Massachusetts, and Marge Piercy permanently settled in at Wellfleet, where she continues to write, garden, and commune with her cats.

Life's Work

Since the publication of her first novel, it has been Marge Piercy's practice to assemble a new poetry collection upon finishing each new novel. Piercy's first four apprentice works already embody her major themes and structures: She establishes a strong symbolic dichotomy between the organic and the mechanical, in which a nature-oriented, communal, subsistence-based lifestyle is contrasted with the technological, militaristic values of the media-created consumer culture of capitalism. The poems in *Breaking Camp* (1968) and *Hard Loving* (1969) are immediate, direct dramatizations of moments of consciousness; the novels use multiple, contrasting viewpoints. The least feminist of all of her novels, the first she had tried to write with a male protagonist, *Going Down Fast* (1969) deals with the destruction of an inner-city Chicago neighborhood by a university-sponsored urban renewal project. Her insider's analysis of political groups continues in *Dance the Eagle to Sleep* (1970), a surrealistically exaggerated account of the New Left youth movement, bordering on science fiction.

The works of Piercy's middle period chronicle her engagement with the critique of the then-emerging feminist movement. *Small Changes* (1973), which Piercy describes as "an attempt to produce in fiction the equivalent of a full experience in a consciousness-raising group," and *To Be of Use* (1973), which contains some of her most anthologized poetry, constitute a virtual encyclopedia of feminist themes. The novel contrasts the crisscrossing lives of two women: Beth, who starts out a mousy victim of the feminine mystique and an early abusive marriage but wins through to a self-reliant definition of herself as an activist lesbian and mother, and Miriam, who begins as an academic in computer science with all the advantages of class and education but fades into the baffled confusion of a neglected wife.

The third work of Piercy's high feminist phase is *Woman on the Edge of Time* (1976). A kind of feminist take on Ken Kesey's *One Flew over the Cuckoo's Nest* (1962) in which a possibly schizophrenic Chicana patient begins making visits to the future, Piercy's work combines the conventions of psychoanalytic novels of the 1970's with the science fiction conventions of a feminist utopia.

The end of the seventies saw the publication of three volumes of poetry, *Living in the Open* (1976), *The Twelve-Spoked Wheel Flashing* (1978), and *The Moon Is Always Female* (1980), and three novels, *The High Cost of Living* (1978), *Vida* (1979), and *Braided Lives* (1982). These works form a parabola created by the dissolution of Piercy's second marriage. Beginning with a denial of the possibility of romantic, heterosexual love, she goes through a period of ideological celibacy during which she exorcises her anger at her husband while debating the limitations of lesbian separatism. Eventually, she comes to accept her own heterosexuality and finds herself again willing to risk loving.

The first two works published in this period, the poetry collection *Living in the Open* (1976) and the novel *The High Cost of Living* (1978), are concerned with the difficulty of trying to live outside society's limiting myths and structures—in particular, outside the boundaries of what Adrienne Rich calls "compulsory heterosexuality." The novel is about the relationships among three characters: one young woman who is trying to grow up and out of a working-class background; another, slightly older, lesbian woman attempting the same class transition through graduate school; and a gay man.

The poems in *Twelve-Spoked Wheel Flashing* (1978) only begin to break out of these limitations through a celebration of natural cycles. The next novel, *Vida* (1979), explores another form of exile from society, that of violent political activism. The story of a political fugitive from the 1960's who is still living in an underground network that increasingly limits her personal choices, *Vida* compares the experiences of the political activist and her sister, who has chosen a more domestic but also explicitly feminist life.

With *The Moon Is Always Female* (1980), Piercy moves into a new phase of intense creativity exemplified by her "Lunar Cycle," a sequence of highly wrought poems, which represents a rich amalgamation of years of interest in myth, mixing Celtic, Greek, Jewish, and many other influences to make strong feminist statements about women's place in history and the need to respect women's many different life choices.

Braided Lives, published two years later (1982), reworks many of the feminist themes articulated in *Small Changes* and subsequent poetry in a more autobiographical mode. It is told from a single perspective—that of Jill Stuart, a successful and happily married poet aged forty-three (her birthday is the same as Piercy's). In the end, her former roommate dies of a botched abortion, leaving the heroine able to halt an unwise marriage and move on to become an activist for women's reproductive rights.

The early 1980's were something of a watershed for Piercy. Her mother died in 1981, and in 1982 she married Ira Wood, a playwright. That same year also marked the publication of a selection of poems from the previous seven volumes, *Circles on the Water*, as well as a collection of Piercy's essays, lectures, and reviews, *Parti-Colored Blocks for a Quilt*.

During the remainder of the 1980's, Piercy produced three more volumes of poems and three more novels. At first still circling the old wounds of her second marriage, her work increasingly rejoices in the daily labors of life, founded in a new depth of historical resonance. For example, the title poem of *Stone, Paper, Knife* (1983) moves from the childhood game of dominance toward a hope for a future created in every day's hard work. *My Mother's Body* (1985), although centered in her memories of her mother, also celebrates Piercy's rebirth in marriage, commemorating her identification with her mother by a deepening of references to Jewish traditions. *Available Light* (1988) includes a series of poems about European locations which evoke references to the heritage of suffering left by World War II and poems commemorating the dead, including her father, again focusing visions of rebirth through the rituals of Judaism.

The three novels published in the early 1980's follow a similar arc. In *Fly Away Home* (1984), a woman breaks out of a traditional marriage to a man who turns out to be engaged in criminal real estate practices, establishing her own career and a new relationship with a younger man. *Gone to Soldiers* (1987) is a 770-page World War II novel, chronicling the war from ten different characters' perspectives. Since six of the characters are women and six are Jewish, the novel represents an intentional connecting of Piercy to her mother's generation and religion. *Summer People* (1989) is a return to more familiar, domestic ground. The story of a ménage-à-trois going bad, the novel is set on Cape Cod among a group of artists and locals.

The two major works that Piercy produced in the early 1990's continued to expand her historic and thematic concerns. Piercy's first return to science fiction in fourteen years, *He, She, and It* (1990) is a complex interweaving of two Frankenstein stories which raises classic questions about responsibility for what one creates by means of esoteric knowledge. In a future earth ravaged by pollution and ruled mostly by large corporations, a brilliant scientist creates a cyborg whose consciousness and actions he then wants to control; his story is juxtaposed against the story that a Jewish grandmother (herself an expert computer programmer and partial creator of the cyborg) tells about a rabbi's creation of a golem in fifteenth century Prague.

The poems in *Mars and Her Children* (1992) carry on this theme of scientific responsibility for nonhuman creatures. (Mars is the name of a humpbacked whale Piercy has adopted through her support for whale research.) Grouped according to the colors of the rainbow, these poems revolve around the theme that all actions have consequences that affect the lives of all the creatures on the ark of planet Earth.

Summary

As a spokesperson for those most often ignored by society—the working class and women—Marge Piercy has established herself not only as a prominent voice of feminism but also as one of the few genuinely radical, left-wing writers enjoying sustained popular success. In the last twenty-five years, Piercy has produced thirteen volumes of poetry, eleven novels, and a collection of essays; all of her prose and all of her poetry published since 1982 is still in print in paperback, maintaining steady sales.

It is in the context of feminism that Piercy's work has received the most notice. Her essay "Grand Coolie Damn" (1969), published in Robin Morgan's early anthology *Sisterhood Is Powerful*, was one of the first critiques of the sexism of the New Left. Two of her realistic novels, *Small Changes* and *Braided Lives*, continue to be cited as definitive articulations of the central concerns of the women's movement. *Woman on the Edge of Time*, which has evoked more interpretive commentary than has any of Piercy's other works, provides a systematic working out of the ideas of radical feminism which may only have been matched by Margaret Atwood's *A Handmaid's Tale*, to which the novel is often compared.

Piercy's acceptance of feminism is never, however, monolithic or uncritical; her own life experiences cause her to question some aspects of the movement's ideology, especially its emphasis on lesbian separatism and its failure adequately to address issues of class and ethnicity. It is this scrupulous honesty, coupled with the coherence of her economic and ecological critique of the consumer culture's dangerous refusal of humane responsibility, that most characterizes Piercy's contribution to women's history.

Bibliography

Kress, Susan. "In and out of Time: The Form of Marge Piercy's Novels." In *Future Females: A Critical Anthology*, edited by Marleen S. Barr. Bowling Green, Ohio: Bowling Green State University Popular Press, 1981. Explores how the formal strategies of Piercy's first five novels show the development of her critique of capitalism, emphasizing the shifting balances between realism's concern with character and romance's concern with ideas.

Nowik, Nan. "Mixing Art and Politics: The Writings of Adrienne Rich, Marge Piercy, and Alice Walker." *The Centennial Review* 30, no. 2 (Spring, 1986): 208-218. Discusses the three writers' common rejection of training as English majors, and shows how other factors—in Piercy's case, her family background, the influence of Allen Ginsberg, and her political activism in the 1960's—caused them to commit to a political agenda for art.

Pearson, Carol. "Coming Home: Four Feminist Utopias and Patriarchal Experience." In *Future Females: A Critical Anthology*, edited by Marleen S. Barr. Bowling Green, Ohio: Bowling Green State University Popular Press, 1981. A condensation and revision of "Women's Fantasies and Feminist Utopias." *Frontiers* 2, no. 3 (Fall, 1977): 50-61. The original article places Piercy's *Woman on the Edge of Time* in the tradition of feminist utopias such as those by Joanna Russ, Ursula Le Guin, James Tiptree, Mary Bradley Lane, Charlotte Perkins Gilman, Dorothy Bryant, and Mary Staton (only the last four are discussed in the revision), systematically discussing their similar treatments of women's work, violence against women, sex roles, and the need to revolutionize economic structures, the nuclear family, and societal attitudes toward nature.

Piercy, Marge. *Parti-Colored Blocks for a Quilt*. Ann Arbor: University of Michigan Press, 1982. A collection of Piercy's essays and reviews, including important autobiographical pieces such as "Through the Cracks: Growing Up in the Fifties" and "Mirror Images" as well as numerous descriptions of her creative and revisionary processes, and several detailed interpretations of her own poetry.

Roller, Judi M. *The Politics of the Feminist Novel*. New York: Greenwood Press, 1986. Discusses *Braided Lives*, *Small Changes*, and *Woman on the Edge of Time* in the context of novels by Margaret Atwood, Kate Chopin, Erica Jong, Doris Lessing, Mary McCarthy, Judith Rossner, Alice Walker, and Virginia Woolf, among others, outlining their common feminist themes—identification with a female hero, analysis of the political power structure of intimate relationships, a call for fundamental societal change—and developing an explanation of how feminist ideals affect style and structure.

Walker, Sue, and Eugenie Hamner, eds. *Ways of Knowing: Essays on Marge Piercy*. Mobile, Ala.: Negative Capability, 1991. The first collection of essays on Piercy's work. The overview essay by Sue Walker presents a useful chronology; the primary bibliography at the end is definitive. Essays on poetry include two by Eleanor Bender, who, Piercy has said, has done the best detailed criticism of her poetry. Essays on the novels include two on *Small Changes* (one by Nancy Topping Bazin on feminist views of androgyny in the novel), two on *Woman on the Edge of Time*, and one on *Fly Away Home*. Other essays explore political themes and Piercy's sense of place.

Elisa Key Sparks

LYDIA ESTES PINKHAM

Born: February 9, 1819; Lynn, Massachusetts
Died: May 17, 1883; Lynn, Massachusetts
Area of Achievement: Business and industry
Contribution: Lydia Estes Pinkham developed a thriving business based on her patent medicine, influencing advertising and women's struggle to gain economic power.

Early Life

Born in Lynn, Massachusetts, Lydia Estes was the tenth of twelve children born to William and Rebecca Estes, members of one of the founding families of Lynn. Originally a shoemaker, William Estes founded a successful saltworks in 1812, which provided sufficient income for him to invest in real estate and increase his wealth even further. At the time Lydia was born, he owned a substantial farm as well as numerous other holdings.

The Esteses were Quakers who firmly believed in the cause of abolition of slavery, a cause viewed as highly radical by most of their contemporaries. Like most Quakers, they encouraged the education of their children and saw to it that Lydia and her siblings were exposed to the writings and ideas of the day's best philosophers, reform leaders, writers, and theologians, such as Frederick Douglass, William Lloyd Garrison, John Greenleaf Whittier, and Parker Pillsbury. After grammar school, Lydia studied at Lynn Academy and was graduated with high honors. Rebecca Estes was a follower of Emmanuel Swedenborg, and her introduction of his thinking to the rest of the family paved the way for Lydia's lifelong interest in spiritualism.

Although Lydia abandoned the Quaker faith as a teenager, the cause of abolition remained important to her. When she turned sixteen, she joined the Lynn Female Anti-Slavery Society, where her mother was already a member, and where she encountered Lucretia Mott and Abby Kelley. Mott and Kelley introduced her to the cause of women's rights, and she combined an interest in both reform movements. Later, Lydia became the secretary of the Freeman's Institute, a debating society and antislavery organization led by Frederick Douglass, who was a friend of the Esteses.

In September, 1843, Lydia married Isaac Pinkham, a shoe manufacturer whom she had met at the Freeman's Institute. Pinkham was a highly speculative businessman who hoped to follow in Lydia's father's footsteps by striking it rich in real estate. Lydia continued to work with various reform groups, but her participation diminished after the birth of her first child, Charles Hacker Pinkham, in December of 1844.

Life's Work

As Lydia Estes Pinkham continued to have children, Isaac Pinkham maintained his speculative career, becoming a farmer, a grocer, a building contractor, and a kerosene manufacturer, among other things. Lydia's father William died in 1848, leaving Lydia and her siblings with a small legacy. Isaac Pinkham tried unsuccessfully to parlay his wife's inheritance into greater wealth. In 1862, he moved the family to Wyoma

Village, a small town just outside of Lynn, hoping to establish a profitable farm. Two years later, flush as a result of land speculation, he moved the family back to Lynn, where he built a large house with a fountain in the front yard to signify his newfound affluence.

Lydia's interest in spiritualism grew throughout these years. She was also interested in medicine and health reforms, supporting women's right to medical education. She kept careful records of the cures she tried on her family, many of which were derived from American Indian lore. One medicine for female weakness proved to be particularly successful, and neighbors began asking for bottles of the liquid, which Lydia brewed at home.

Lydia's children worked to support the family's wavering finances. Isaac Pinkham's real estate holdings became worthless during the industrial depression of 1873. The bank threatened to arrest him because he could not pay the arrears on his mortgaged property, but a Pinkham cousin managed to persuade the bank to drop the suit. In searching for a way to support the family, Lydia's son Daniel proposed marketing the medicine his mother had developed for female weakness. Patent medicines were a profitable business at the time, and in 1875, the family decided to try their hand at it, working as a team. They named the medicine "Lydia E. Pinkham's Vegetable Compound," and its label proclaimed it "A Sure Cure for PROLAPSIS UTERI or falling of the Womb, and all FEMALE WEAKNESSES, including Leucorrhea, Painful Menstruation, Inflammation, and Ulceration of the Womb, Irregularities, Floodings, etc."

They manufactured the medicine at home. Because they were worried that Isaac's debts might swallow all the profits from the medicine, the family made one of Lydia's sons, William Hacker Pinkham, the sole proprietor. The members of Lydia's family worked as bottlers, brewers, salesmen, advertising writers, and distributors. William and Daniel went from door to door with circulars extolling the properties of the vegetable compound.

The ingredients for Lydia's recipe, which she patented in 1876, included false unicorn root, true unicorn root, life root, black cohosh, pleurisy root, and fenugreek seed, as well as alcohol, which was needed to preserve the mixture. Despite the entire family's strong support of the temperance movement, they believed that the alcohol used for medical purposes was a legitimate ingredient. They did, however, make a version of the medicine in pill form that contained no alcohol, for conditions that alcohol might aggravate.

One of Lydia's interests was in reforming medicine. Like many others of her time, she felt that doctors often caused needless suffering to their women patients. She saw her vegetable compound as an effective alternative to medical treatment. She responded to women who wrote seeking medical advice, counseling an approach based on diet and exercise. She also believed in homeopathy, an alternative medicine developed by Samuel Hahnemann that was popular at the time, and Grahamism, a health movement led by Sylvester Graham, which prescribed a diet of fruits, vegetables, and whole grains, as well as fresh air, cold water baths, celibacy, and exercise.

The family experimented with advertising. Daniel came up with the idea of calling cards with the words "Try Lydia E. Pinkham's Vegetable Compound. I know it will cure you, it's the best thing for Uterine complaints there is. Love, your Cousin Mary," written by hand on the back, which he dropped in parks and theaters, hoping that people would pick them up and read them. In order to widen the pool of possible customers, the words on the front pages of the circulars were changed to make it clear that the compound would cure men as well as women by adding the words "Weak and Diseased Kidneys" to the list of ailments that the vegetable compound professed to alleviate.

Some pharmacists thought the circulars too explicit and said that women would be too embarrassed or too sensitive to read them. The family proceeded to advertise the compound in a Methodist newspaper to counteract the charges. Encouraged by the results, they risked their limited money by placing a front-page advertisement in the Boston *Herald*. They were rewarded by a flood of orders from wholesalers, and the family resolved to embark on a newspaper campaign, going so far as to hire T. C. Evans to oversee their advertisements and to mortgage their house to pay for the campaign. Many of the advertisements contained testimonials from satisfied customers, attributing their cure to daily doses of the vegetable compound.

In 1879, Daniel Pinkham decided to change the label on the vegetable compound. He searched for a picture of a healthy woman who could demonstrate the advantages of regular partaking of Lydia's medicine. At last the perfect model presented herself: his mother, now sixty, who seemed ideal. Dressed in black silk with a pin at her lace-clad throat, Lydia, gazing slightly to her right, seemed wise and sympathetic, and sales boomed. The advertisements included the invitation to write to Lydia, who promised to answer all letters and did. Newspapers who had doubted Lydia's existence, claiming that the name was only an advertising gimmick, began to use her picture whenever they needed a picture of a famous woman.

The campaign was so widespread that Lydia Pinkham's name began to appear in songs, jokes, and anecdotes, including parodies sung by college glee clubs. Six months after the campaign began, an investor offered the family $100,000 for the business, insisting that the new trademark must accompany it. The Pinkhams turned him down.

In 1880, Daniel and William both died of tuberculosis, despite the best efforts of their mother, who plied them with every cure she knew. Lydia's interest in spiritualism redoubled, and she held séances every Saturday in an attempt to contact her sons. In 1882, she suffered a stroke. After several months of paralysis, she died on May 17, 1883. As she had requested, her funeral was held in spiritualist fashion, celebrating the fact that she had joined dead loved ones rather than mourning the loss of the living. The company she had helped found continued its success in the hands of her descendants.

Summary

Lydia Estes Pinkham was not a reform leader, but the company she founded influenced women's roles in society in several different ways. She worked to temper the often barbaric medical treatments of her day and encouraged women in healthful practices such as dressing sensibly and having regular exercise, fresh air, and a healthy diet. Nineteenth century America was full of harmful, sometimes bizarre, medical practices and cures, and Pinkham's Vegetable Compound proved an alternative to many of them. Woman after woman wrote letters to Pinkham, asking for medical advice, and she answered every one. She stressed the idea that women could be healthy and that illness was not a woman's natural condition.

Through her letters and writings, Lydia dispensed sound information regarding general hygiene to the American public. Her book on women's health, distributed under several different titles by the Pinkham Company, was acknowledged as being one of the best treatises of its kind, speaking unflinchingly of such delicate matters as puberty, conception, and menopause.

At a time when few women ran their own businesses, Lydia Estes Pinkham provided the first example of a successful woman who still embodied the ideal of motherhood. Her face appeared in newspaper after newspaper and was instantly recognizable to the women of her day. She used her advertising to campaign for social reform, such as the education of women, improving labor practices, and distributing information on birth control. After her death, her female descendants continued to take a hand in the running of the Pinkham company, demonstrating that women could combine business and family without detracting from their femininity.

Bibliography

Burton, Jean. *Lydia Pinkham Is Her Name*. New York: Farrar, Straus, 1949. This book provides more information than any other about Pinkham's family and tries to put her achievements and efforts in context, allowing the reader to appreciate their extraordinary nature.

Stage, Sarah. *Female Complaints: Lydia Pinkham and the Business of Women's Medicine*. New York: W. W. Norton, 1979. This useful overview traces the history of the Pinkham Company up to the present day. More space is devoted to the company's saga after Pinkham's death than before, but the text does include a chapter on her life.

Verbrugge, Martha H. *Able-Bodied Womanhood: Personal Health and Social Change in Nineteenth-Century Boston*. New York: Oxford University Press, 1988. A useful volume that sheds light on concepts of women's health during the period in which Lydia Estes Pinkham was active.

Washburn, Robert Collyer. *The Life and Times of Lydia E. Pinkham*. New York: G. P. Putnam's Sons, 1931. The earliest published piece (besides literature distributed by the Pinkham Company) about Lydia Pinkham, this text provides an overview of the times and social issues surrounding Pinkham and her enterprise, as well as some biographical information.

Catherine Francis

SYLVIA PLATH

Born: October 27, 1932; Boston, Massachusetts
Died: February 11, 1963; London, England
Area of Achievement: Literature
Contribution: As both poet and novelist, Plath adopted a self-analytical style that helped to inspire the "confessional" school of literature in the decade following her death.

Early Life

When Sylvia Plath was eight years old, her father died after a long illness. This early loss of a loved one affected Plath's poetry in a way that would be unparalleled by any other event in her life. Otto Emil Plath had been fifteen years old when he came to the United States from Grabow, a town near the Polish-German border. When Sylvia was an infant, he taught biology at Boston University and came to be nationally recognized as an authority on bees. After her father's death in 1940, Sylvia moved with her mother, the former Aurelia Shrober, and her younger brother, Warren (born April 27, 1935), to the Boston suburb of Wellesley, Massachusetts. There Sylvia's mother found work as a teacher, her grandmother took care of their home, and her grandfather helped to support the family by working as a maître d'hôtel at the Brookline Country Club.

At about the time of her father's death, Plath began writing poetry and short fiction. Her works won several newspaper contests and, in August of 1950, she sold her first story ("And Summer Will Not Come Again") to *Seventeen* magazine. A year later, another short story ("Sunday at the Mintons") won a fiction contest sponsored by *Mademoiselle* magazine.

In September of 1950, Plath began attending Smith College on a fellowship endowed by Olive Higgins Prouty, the author of *Stella Dallas* (1922). In 1952, Plath was one of two fiction authors to win a contest sponsored by *Mademoiselle* magazine. She spent the next summer as the student editor of *Mademoiselle*'s annual college issue. *Harper's* magazine also began to display an interest in Plath's work, paying $100 for three of her poems.

Despite this appearance of initial success, however, Plath fell into a deep depression. Hiding herself in an isolated part of the cellar, Plath took an overdose of sleeping pills. She was rescued in time and began to receive psychiatric treatment, including electroshock therapy.

Plath's initial suicide attempt and the incidents surrounding it were to become the basis for her autobiographical novel *The Bell Jar* (1963). Some of Plath's medical expenses following her attempted suicide were paid by Olive Higgins Prouty. Prouty had taken an interest in Plath as one of the recipients of the scholarship that she had endowed at Smith College. The older novelist's generosity toward Plath was to be repaid uncharitably when Plath caricatured Prouty as the novelist Philomena Guinea in *The Bell Jar*.

Life's Work

Appearing to be cured, Sylvia Plath returned to Smith College and was graduated summa cum laude with a Bachelor of Arts degree in 1955. The following year, she received a Fulbright Fellowship enabling her to go to England, where she attended Newnham College of Cambridge University. There Plath met the poet Ted Hughes; after a brief romance, they married in London on June 16, 1956. To Plath, Hughes—who was self-assured, decisive, and authoritarian—seemed to possess the qualities that she had both admired and feared in her father. In her later poetry, she described her initial attraction to Hughes as an attempt to bring her dead father back into her life.

In 1957, Plath received her master's degree from Cambridge and, with Hughes, returned to the United States. Later that same year, she took a teaching position at Smith College, her alma mater. Soon, however, Plath began to find that teaching did not satisfy her creative desires, and she decided to devote her full attention to writing. She attempted to find a publisher for the book of poems that would eventually become *The Colossus and Other Poems* and was disappointed to have it rejected a number of times. She continued to revise these poems and, in December of 1959, returned to England with Hughes. The following April, their daughter, Frieda Rebecca, was born.

In 1960, *The Colossus and Other Poems* was finally published by William Heinemann. With one major work already accepted for publication and with ideas for several others, Plath, in May of 1961, applied for a Eugene F. Saxton Fellowship with the intention of writing a novel. On November 6, 1961, Plath received a grant of $2,080 that would enable her to work on *The Bell Jar*. The year 1962 was a period of incredible activity for Plath. On January 17, she gave birth to her son, Nicholas Farrar, and less than a month later reported to the Saxton committee that the first eight chapters of her novel were in their final form. Despite a number of illnesses, Plath continued to work on *The Bell Jar* steadily throughout the year. She also accepted several assignments for the British Broadcasting Corporation and, in June, began to write the poems that would be published after her death as *Ariel*.

On August 1, 1962, Plath reported to the Saxton committee that she had begun the final stages of *The Bell Jar*. Suddenly, however, after a vacation in Ireland, Plath's world of hard work and domestic harmony began to unravel. In autumn, after learning that Hughes had been having an affair with the Canadian poet Assia Wevill, Plath separated from her husband. She moved to London, submitted the final draft of *The Bell Jar* for publication, and found an apartment in a house that had once belonged to the Irish poet William Butler Yeats.

The final months of Plath's life were marked by a prodigious amount of literary activity. Working each morning from four o'clock until seven (when her children awoke), Plath began writing far more spontaneously than she had ever done before. Abandoning the ornate and polished style of *The Colossus*, Plath produced several poems a day, in a remarkable burst of creativity that she began to refer to as the "blood jet." The works of this final period of her life are marked by natural, unpolished rhythms and are often attempts to work out her deep-seated feelings of loss, frustration, and anger.

In January of 1963, *The Bell Jar* was published, not under Plath's own name but under the pseudonym of "Victoria Lucas." Plath considered *The Bell Jar* to be a mere "potboiler . . . not serious work" and wanted her real name to be associated only with her poetry. In addition, Plath hoped to spare the feelings of friends and members of her family who appear in the novel thinly disguised as fictional characters.

The narrator of *The Bell Jar*, Esther Greenwood, is based upon Plath herself, and many incidents in the novel were drawn from the poet's own life. Esther loses her father at an early age, wins a number of writing contests, and undergoes psychiatric treatment for suicidal tendencies. Initial reviews of *The Bell Jar* were generally positive, but Plath's attention seemed drawn only to the criticism that the book received. Although appearing to be under great pressure, Plath gave her friends no indication of the severity of her depression. On February 11, 1963, she entered the kitchen of her apartment, placed towels around the doors to protect her children, and then committed suicide by turning on the gas.

Ever since her first suicide attempt at the age of twenty, death had been a frequent theme in Plath's writings. She occasionally referred to suicide as an act of purification and viewed death as merely another form of birth. In the late poem "Daddy" (written 1963; first published 1965), she describes her first attempt at suicide as a desire to return to the father who had been taken away from her in her youth. The imagery of rebirth and emergence from the womb also appears in *The Bell Jar*, where Plath describes the efforts to revive her after she has taken an overdose of sleeping pills.

A consistently high level of symbolism is found throughout all Plath's works. In *The Bell Jar*, for example, the electrocution of convicted spies Julius and Ethel Rosenberg in the summer of 1953 serves the young protagonist as an image for her own electroshock treatments. In many of her poems (such as the title work in *Ariel*), the symbols of speed—figures rushing headlong toward an undefined, distant object—appear. Some critics have interpreted these symbols as Plath's own movement toward her inevitable suicide. Suicide itself appears as a frequent theme in much of Plath's poetry, as in "The Manor Garden" and "Suicide Off Egg Rock," both of which were first published in *The Colossus*. In her late poetry, Plath began to deal with the pain resulting from her father's death, occasionally depicting her father as a Nazi and herself as a Jew. In each of these cases, the symbolism transforms events occurring in Plath's own life into something more universal, a general image in which readers can find their own meaning.

Summary

The period of Sylvia Plath's greatest impact came only after her death. In retrospect, even her earliest poems were seen as providing insight into her troubled personality and the reasons for her eventual suicide. The autobiographical nature of *The Bell Jar* and the introspective glimpses provided by many of her later poems, which were published after her death in *Ariel* (1965) and *Crossing the Water* (1972), gave a new impetus to the "confessional" style of poetry. Leading figures of this literary movement included Robert Lowell, who wrote the introduction to *Ariel*, and May Sarton, the author of *A Private Mythology* (1966).

Plath's writing has also been important in feminist circles. Though Plath herself displayed little interest in feminist causes, her struggles to find a role for herself, reflected through the eyes of Esther Greenwood in *The Bell Jar*, made her works influential to feminists throughout the early 1970's. Furthermore, Plath's negative treatment of male figures in much of her later poetry has caused the poet to be adopted by feminists as a tragic symbol of male oppression.

Bibliography

Broe, Mary Lynn. *Protean Poetic: The Poetry of Sylvia Plath*. Columbia: University of Missouri Press, 1980. Broe traces the development of Plath's literary style and concludes that there is a consistent use of imagery and of "female personae" throughout her works. Contrary to the generally accepted view, Broe argues that even the late poems do not indicate that Plath's suicide was inevitable.

Bundtzen, Lynda K. *Plath's Incarnations: Woman and the Creative Process*. Ann Arbor: University of Michigan Press, 1983. Offering a feminist perspective of Plath's poetry, this analysis explores the ways in which her works were written from a distinctly female perspective. It also includes a feminist interpretation of the symbols in Plath's poetry.

Hall, Caroline King Barnard. *Sylvia Plath*. Boston: Twayne, 1978. Taking a traditional biographical and literary approach, this work places Plath's poetry firmly in the context of the "confessional" school of literature.

Holbrook, David. *Sylvia Plath: Poetry and Existence*. Atlantic Highlands, N.J.: Humanities Press, 1976. This work adopts a psychoanalytical approach to provide a biographical profile of Plath as well as a literary analysis of her novel and poetry. Holbrook is especially interesting in his discussion of how the layer of fiction separating Plath from Esther Greenwood in *The Bell Jar* ultimately breaks down.

Kroll, Judith. *Chapters in a Mythology: The Poetry of Sylvia Plath*. New York: Harper & Row, 1976. Kroll argues that the autobiographical elements of Plath's poetry are always viewed impersonally and are given a larger, symbolic dimension.

Newman, Charles Hamilton, ed. *The Art of Sylvia Plath: A Symposium*. Bloomington: Indiana University Press, 1970. This collection of biographical and literary essays provides an analysis of all the major aspects of Plath's life and poetry. It also includes a useful bibliography and an appendix of Plath's unpublished works.

Wagner-Martin, Linda. *"The Bell Jar": A Novel of the Fifties*. New York: Twayne, 1992. Providing a thorough literary analysis of *The Bell Jar*, this work examines the novel's imagery and literary form, and interprets it in its historical context.

____________, ed. *Sylvia Plath: The Critical Heritage*. New York: Routledge, 1988. This excellent collection of essays includes biographical portraits by individuals who knew Plath and literary analyses by several important critics.

Jeffrey L. Buller

POCAHONTAS

Born: c. 1596; Virginia
Died: March, 1617; Gravesend, Kent, England
Area of Achievement: Diplomacy
Contribution: One of the first women to influence the course of American history, Pocahontas was a critical figure in the survival of the first permanent English settlement.

Early Life

According to estimates by early English settlers in Virginia, Pocahontas was born in 1595 or 1596, but her place of birth is unknown. Her father was Powhatan, the head of a confederation of tribes in Tidewater Virginia. Because he had many wives, it is uncertain which of them was Pocahontas' mother. Although Powhatan named her Matoaca, she was more widely known as Pocahontas, a name that the English understood to mean playful or adventuresome.

In the decade prior to the arrival of English settlers in Virginia, Powhatan was busy consolidating one of the most powerful confederations along the East Coast of North America. It is unclear whether he saw the English as potential allies in this effort or simply as intruders. When, in later 1607, his warriors captured and brought the English leader Captain John Smith to him, Powhatan ordered the staging of an elaborate ceremony. After a feast, Smith found himself being dragged to two large rocks where men with clubs appeared to be ready to execute him. At that moment, a girl, who Smith later learned was Pocahontas, raced to his rescue. She placed her head on his and implored her father to spare the white man's life.

The details of this episode, which elevated Smith and Pocahontas into the pantheon of American mythology, come exclusively from John Smith's pen. Yet according to several scholars who have carefully scrutinized the famed adventurer's writings, there is a ring of truth about it. Powhatan probably put Smith through this mock execution as an initiation or adoption ceremony, a ritual similar to those of other tribes in the region. Whatever Powhatan's rationale, John Smith always credited Pocahontas with his rescue, and whether her actions were spontaneous or staged, from that moment, she became a leading figure in the salvation of the Virginia colony.

Powhatan permitted Pocahontas to visit the English settlement at Jamestown several times over the next year and a half. Her presence made it easier for the English to trade with Indians in the confederation. She advised Smith which tribes to avoid and helped the English negotiate for food. The settlers enjoyed this young teen, who lived up to her playful public name. She delighted the boys at Jamestown by turning cartwheels with them in the marketplace. Pocahontas particularly liked John Smith. Smith also seemed genuinely interested in her culture. He eagerly listened as she instructed him in the Powhatan language and taught her some English in return.

Pocahontas' diplomatic role was even greater than her role in improving trade relations. Four months after Powhatan freed Smith, she participated in the successful negotiations for the release of native prisoners held by the English. Pocahontas also helped an English messenger boy, Richard Wiffin, escape when her father ordered him killed. In December of 1608, while John Smith and several of his men were in Powhatan's village negotiating for corn, Pocahontas warned them of a plot to kill them. After the men escaped, it was almost eight years before John Smith and Pocahontas saw each other.

Life's Work

Relations between the English and the natives rapidly deteriorated when Smith had to return to England in 1609 because of a serious wound he suffered in an accident. Prolonged hostility replaced the cautious peace that had previously characterized Indian-English relations. Because of the warfare, Pocahontas had little contact with the settlers. She did not visit Jamestown for four years, and Powhatan sent her north to live with the Potomacs, the most distant of his subject tribes.

In early 1613, Captain Samuel Argall decided to seize Pocahontas and hold her hostage. Argall hoped to obtain from Powhatan the release of several English prisoners and a substantial supply of corn. On an expedition up the Potomac, Argall persuaded Iapassus, a Potomac chief, to lure Pocahontas aboard his vessel. Argall took his prize to the new settlement of Henrico, about eighty miles upriver from Jamestown, and left her in the care of the Reverend Alexander Whitaker while he awaited Powhatan's response.

Pocahontas now entered the most significant period of her life. Her father, apparently believing that the English would not harm her, released just a few English prisoners and sent only a token amount of corn. Outraged, Deputy-Governor Thomas Dale resolved to hold Pocahontas until Powhatan met his demands. As negotiations continued, the Reverend Whitaker began to instruct his charge in the Christian faith. Joining him in the effort was a widowed planter named John Rolfe.

Rolfe had come to Virginia in spring of 1610 and had already gained notoriety for introducing a successful variety of tobacco into the colony. Because the native plant was too harsh for European tastes, Rolfe had brought the seeds of milder tobacco from Trinidad in 1611. Through careful cultivation, he was able to send a crop to England the next year. He probably met Pocahontas in summer of 1613 while experimenting with tobacco plants in the Henrico area.

Rolfe and Whitaker taught Pocahontas the Lord's Prayer, the Ten Commandments, and the ritual of the Church of England. After several months of indoctrination, the young woman accepted the Christian faith, and the Reverend Whitaker baptized her into the Anglican church, naming her Rebecca.

In the process, Pocahontas gained not only a new faith but also a new suitor. John Rolfe admitted that while instructing the teenager, he had fallen in love with her and wanted to marry her. Acknowledging that he was attempting to bridge an enormous gap between the two very different cultures of Virginia, Rolfe wrote a lengthy letter of explanation to Deputy-Governor Dale. He knew that the church disapproved of marriages with "strange," or heathen, people. Despite Pocahontas' recent instruction in Christianity, Rolfe admitted that he would be marrying a woman "whose education hath been rude, her manners barbarous," and "her generation cursed."

Even as he conceded this problem, however, Rolfe contended that he was presenting Dale with a wonderful opportunity. One of the goals of King James I when he had granted a charter to the Virginia Company of London was the conversion of the peoples they encountered. In the first decade of the colony's existence, it had failed miserably on that score. Now, Rolfe was posing his marriage to Pocahontas as a way to demonstrate to the king that the company could civilize and Christianize natives. This marriage, according to Rolfe, would be for the glory of God, "our Country's good, the benefit of this Plantation, and for the converting [of] an irregenerate to regeneration."

Thomas Dale readily assented to the marriage, but they still needed the permission of Powhatan. Although he likewise agreed, the aging leader decided not to attend the wedding, perhaps wanting to ease the permanent break with his favorite daughter. He sent one of his brothers, Opachisco, to give Pocahontas away at the April 5, 1614, wedding in Jamestown.

The marriage was a momentous event. It inaugurated years of peace between the English and the natives. John Rolfe obviously deserves some of the credit for proposing the match, but Powhatan also played an important role. He may not have wished to jeopardize his daughter with further hostilities, or he may realistically have concluded that the recent warfare had made his confederation too weak to confront the English with superior numbers. Most likely, he was telling the truth when he explained to an English envoy, shortly after the wedding, that he was an old man who wanted to live his remaining days in peace.

Yet it was Pocahontas who was critical in this development. In accepting Christianity and marrying an Englishman, she was renouncing her family and her culture. Given her earlier efforts to ease relations between the Indians and the English, it is not surprising that Pocahontas now would be willing to make such a sacrifice. Since the arrival of white men in her midst, she had always proved willing to act in the interests of peace.

Not wanting to waste the public relations value of the marriage of an Indian princess to an Englishman, the Virginia Company arranged a visit to England for the couple and their infant son, Thomas, in 1616. Accompanied by Deputy-Governor Dale and about a dozen Powhatan Indians, the Rolfes arrived in England in June. Over the next nine months, the Virginia Company worked hard to keep Pocahontas constantly in the public eye. Several appearances at the palace of James I, attendance at a gala staged by the Bishop of London, and a sitting for an engraved portrait ensured that all in the city would know of the famous Pocahontas. By year's end, Londoners could purchase a copy of the only likeness of Pocahontas to be painted in her lifetime. In it, the young woman with dark eyes and high cheekbones is dressed in a beaver hat, a cloth coat, a lace collar, and pearl earrings, and she is holding a three-plumed fan.

Perhaps the most difficult part of the trip for Pocahontas was her reunion with John Smith. It was an awkward meeting for her. She had always adored Smith, but everyone in Virginia had told her that he had died. Only upon her arrival at Plymouth had she learned the truth. Shocked to see him again, Pocahontas initially was silent when she saw him, and then she wept, but finally they talked briefly about their experiences in Virginia. When they parted, she told Smith, "you shall call me child, and so I will be for ever and ever your countryman."

The culmination of Pocahontas' visit to England was her attendance with King James and Queen Anne at the Twelfth Night Masque. The gala event at Whitehall on January 6, 1617, held to celebrate the end of the Christmas season, featured a play by Ben Jonson. Pocahontas enjoyed the masque as well as the rest of her stay in England, but her husband was appointed secretary of the Virginia colony, and they had to return. Shortly after their departure from London in mid-March, she became very ill with a fever. Taken ashore at Gravesend, Pocahontas died and was buried in the parish church there.

Summary

Although Pocahontas' was a short life, it was a truly significant one. Primarily because of John Smith's account of her rescue of him, Pocahontas has been the subject of many novels, biographies, and poems and has become an indelible part of American mythology. More important, she played a role almost always reserved for men in the seventeenth century—that of a diplomat. Undoubtedly, her youth and engaging personality were an advantage. She was her father's favorite, and she captivated the English settlers. Yet Pocahontas demonstrated considerable negotiating skills, which she employed often to improve trade and accomplish prisoner releases for both English and Indian.

Along with Powhatan, John Smith, and John Rolfe, Pocahontas played a pivotal role in early Virginia's history. She gave the English hope that the Indians could be assimilated into their culture, and she demonstrated that it was possible for English and Indian to coexist. The most authoritative assessment of her role in American history came from Captain John Smith, who concluded that she literally was the savior of the first permanent English settlement in North America. In a letter he wrote to Queen Anne in 1616, Smith explained that Pocahontas had been the instrument that had preserved the colony "from death, famine and utter confusion."

Bibliography

Barbour, Philip L. *Pocahontas and Her World*. Boston: Houghton Mifflin, 1970. This is the best comprehensive account of Pocahontas' life and times.

__________. *The Three Worlds of Captain John Smith*. Boston: Houghton Mifflin, 1964. Of the numerous biographies of Smith, this remains the most comprehensive and authoritative.

Davis, Richard Beale. *Intellectual Life in the Colonial South, 1585-1763*. 3 vols. Knoxville: University of Tennessee Press, 1978. Davis provides an excellent analysis of the numerous contemporary writings on Pocahontas and assesses her place in American literature.

Lemay, J. A. Leo. *Did Pocahontas Save Captain John Smith?* Athens: University of Georgia Press, 1992. An interesting study that attempts to discern the truth or falsehood of John Smith's account of his rescue by Pocahontas.

Smith, Bradford. *Captain John Smith: His Life and Legend*. Philadelphia: J. B. Lippincott, 1953. Smith's biography is useful because he makes the best case for the veracity of John Smith's writings. In doing so, he draws on the research of Laura Polanyi Striker into John Smith's years in Europe.

Tyler, Lyon Gardiner, ed. *Narratives of Early Virginia, 1606-1625*. New York: Charles Scribner's Sons, 1907. This collection of primary sources includes John Rolfe's letter to Thomas Dale, John Smith's letter to Queen Anne, and several selections from Smith's *General Historie of Virginia*.

Larry Gragg

KATHERINE ANNE PORTER

Born: May 15, 1890; Indian Creek, Texas
Died: September 18, 1980; Silver Spring, Maryland
Area of Achievement: Literature
Contribution: An important modernist writer, Porter was a fiercely independent and exacting artist whose life and work influenced many writers who followed her.

Early Life

During Katherine Anne Porter's unhappy early life, she received little encouragement to become a creative writer, yet her very misery may have spurred this sensitive and strong-willed young girl to greatness. Born Callie Russell Porter in a log cabin on the Texas frontier, she lost her mother, Mary Alice Jones Porter, when she was only two and struggled through poverty and the humiliation of being a motherless child. Her father, Harrison Boone Porter, seems to have lost his will to provide for himself and his family after his wife's death. Thus, the burden of raising Porter, her brother, and two sisters fell to her father's mother, Catherine Anne Porter, otherwise known as Aunt Cat, who had reared nine children of her own.

Moved to her grandmother's house in Kyle, Texas, Porter was sensitive to the crowded conditions and the fact that neighbors regarded her and her siblings as charity cases. Her biographer, Joan Givner, believes that her father's neglect left Porter with a yearning for affection from men that eventually led to four marriages and innumerable affairs, often with men whose circumstances almost guaranteed instability. Her grandmother's strength of character, however, was a lifelong influence, and Porter eventually adopted her name, with a slight spelling difference, perhaps in an effort to internalize that strength. In later years, when asked about her early life, Porter frequently suppressed painful details and transformed them into more palatable ones. She was furious when researchers discovered her original name. Instead of dirt-poor Callie Russell Porter, she wished to be remembered as Katherine Anne, descendant of a long line of southern aristocrats.

Aunt Cat's death when Porter was eleven deprived her of her only source of stability. After they had lived for a time with Porter's aunt Ellen on a farm near Buda, Texas, which was probably the setting for the short novel "Noon Wine," Porter's father moved the family to San Antonio, where she attended the Thomas School, a private institution that introduced her to drama. Her marriage at age fifteen to John Henry Koontz was partially motivated by a desire to escape from the poverty and unhappiness of her home life. Although she later termed the marriage "preposterous," it lasted nine years, longer than any of her subsequent ones. After she divorced Koontz, she felt liberated from marital restrictions, much as her autobiographical protagonist Miranda Gay felt in "Old Mortality," one of her fine short novels:

> She would have no more bonds that smothered her in love and hatred. She knew now why she had run away to marriage, and she knew that she was going to run away from

marriage, and she was not going to stay in any place, with anyone, that threatened to forbid her making her own discoveries, that said "No" to her.

After a failed attempt to earn a living as an actress in Chicago in 1914, she eventually moved to Dallas seeking office work. There she contracted tuberculosis. In the hospital, she befriended Kitty Barry Crawford, one of the first newspaperwomen in Texas. From her she learned of Jane Anderson, Kitty's college roommate and a war correspondent in Europe. Jane's and Kitty's examples suggested journalism as a career. Consequently, after leaving the sanatorium in 1917, Porter worked for the Fort Worth *Critic* as a society columnist and theater reviewer. When Jane and Kitty moved to Colorado, she went there too and eventually got a job on the Denver *Rocky Mountain News*. In 1918, just two years after her bout with tuberculosis, she was victimized by an influenza epidemic that was sweeping the country. Hospitalized with a temperature of 105 degrees for nine days and with death imminent, she was saved by an experimental dosage of strychnine. The near-death experience caused by the strychnine would eventually be immortalized in the excellent short novel "Pale Horse, Pale Rider." She herself regarded the incident as an important dividing line in her life, after which she devoted herself more purposefully to her writing career.

Life's Work

In 1919, Katherine Anne Porter moved to New York's Greenwich Village, where she was surrounded by artists like herself who were committed to their work. She found work with a magazine promoting Mexico and was soon asked to visit that country as part of her assignment. This began a long relationship with Mexico that influenced several of her works, including her first important story, "Maria Concepcion" (1922). This character study of a strong Indian woman, who is generous despite being oppressed and who is wronged but does something about it, earned her $600 from *Century* magazine and launched Porter's fiction writing career.

She had numerous affairs in New York and Mexico, and in 1926 she was married to Ernest Stock, an Englishman. The marriage lasted only a short time. In 1928, in an episode that was characteristic of her behavior of plunging into love with a man very soon after a breakup with another, she met and had an affair with Matthew Josephson, who was married. Porter was impressed by the fact that his first interest was in her writing: "From a man I surely never had that before." A writer himself, Josephson provided Porter with encouragement and literary guidance that helped her develop confidence in her work.

She began a biography, "The Devil and Cotton Mather," on which she worked periodically for the rest of her life but which she never completed. She was drawn to the subject because of her interest in the phenomenon of mass hysteria as manifested in the revival meetings of her youth, Adolf Hitler's Germany, and Mather's Puritan New England during the witch trials. Another manifestation of mass hysteria and social injustice that attracted her passionate interest was the case of Nicola Sacco and Bartolomeo Vanzetti, Italian immigrants who had been accused of murder. Porter and others believed that the two men were condemned because of their anarchist political beliefs rather than on the basis of legitimate evidence. On the night of their execution in 1927, she took part in a group vigil outside the prison. It would take her many years, but she would eventually publish her account of that event in *The Never-Ending Wrong* (1977).

Porter was exacting in her craft and uncompromising in her artistic vision. She would forgo the large sums of money paid by commercial magazines in order to prevent her works being edited for mass consumption. Thus, many of her finest works were published in "little magazines"; that is, small-circulation journals specializing in experimental writing that would not appeal to the general public. In the company of some of the finest writers of 1920's and 1930's America, Porter published "The Jilting of Granny Weatherall" and "Magic" in *Transition*; "Theft" in *Gyroscope*; "Flowering Judas" in *Hound and Horn*; "Circus," "Old Mortality," and "Pale Horse, Pale Rider" in *Southern Review*; and "The Grave," "That Tree," "Two Plantation Portraits," and "Hacienda" in *Virginia Quarterly*. Most of the books published by Porter consist of collections of these scattered stories. *Flowering Judas and Other Stories* (1930) was published in a limited edition by Harcourt, Brace, then expanded and reissued four years later. Three short novels—"Old Mortality," "Noon Wine," and "Pale Horse, Pale Rider"—were published under the title *Pale Horse, Pale Rider* (1939), and another volume appeared under the title *The Leaning Tower and Other Stories* (1944).

Although her stories featured many themes, one of the major ones was her view that the dark side of human life was an important part of reality even though many of her characters attempted to evade it. She had an interest in evil characters, but she seemed to be more fascinated by the innocent bystander who effectively collaborates with evil by allowing it to perpetuate itself. She attributed the successes of Adolf Hitler, Benito Mussolini, Joseph McCarthy, and Huey Long to the tacit consent of bystanders who had the moral sense to know that these men were wrong. Both "Theft" and "Flowering Judas" exhibit this theme. To complicate matters, as often as not, the evil person is on the "right" side of a particular cause. Her Homer T. Hatch of "Noon Wine," for example, is evil in spite of the ostensible justice of his attempt to reincarcerate a man convicted of criminal conduct; likewise, the men who visit Miranda in "Pale Horse, Pale Rider" to ask why she has not bought liberty bonds are ostensibly working for a good cause, the U.S. war effort, but are clearly portrayed as the basest form of humanity. Porter was convinced that evil, because it was innate in humans, manifested itself everywhere, even in the best of causes or institutions.

Returning to Mexico in 1930 for her health, she met Eugene Dove Pressly, a dozen years her junior, to whom she was eventually married in Paris in 1933. Long wanting to go to Europe, she sailed with him for Germany in 1931. This trip and the diversity of persons aboard the ship provided much of the inspiration for *Ship of Fools* (1962), which would take another thirty years to complete. Her only full-length novel, it attempted to expose the flaws in Western society that had led to two world wars within three decades. Porter was deeply influenced by her visit to 1930's Germany, for during this period Hitler's rise to power had begun. Her impressions of the weakness at the base of Germany's empire-building are recorded in "The Leaning Tower."

Porter loved and needed men, but she was never able to maintain a long-term relationship. According to Givner, she sought two attributes in men: They had to be willing to take care of her and they had to be interested in her work. Whereas Matthew Josephson had satisfied the second but not the first of these criteria, Eugene Pressly satisfied the first but not the second. After several years in Europe, she separated from him. Returning to the United States in 1936, she visited with her father in Indian Creek. As was her pattern, soon after deciding to divorce Pressly, she fell in love with another man, Albert Erskine. A graduate student at Louisiana State University, business manager of the *Southern Review*, and young enough to be her son, he was a friend of her good friends, the writers Allen Tate and Caroline Gordon. After their marriage in 1938, Erskine was horrified to discover that she was nearly fifty years old, while he was in his mid-twenties. She left him just two years later.

Porter had many female friends. From Kitty Barry Crawford and Jane Anderson, early role models, to several younger women who looked up to her, she formed friendships with women who were as committed to their work as she was to hers. Among the most famous of these women were the writers Caroline Gordon, Josephine Herbst, and Eudora Welty. She firmly rejected the advances of lesbians such as Carson McCullers, whose behavior repulsed her. As had been the case with her male friends, personality conflicts often led to permanent breaks in her relations with female friends. She condemned Josephine Herbst for being a dupe of the communists, and, according to Herbst's biographer, even went so far as to denounce her former friend to the Federal Bureau of Investigation (FBI).

Although she leaned toward the Left, Porter rejected involvement with the Communist Party because she did not want to be made a propagandist and lose her artistic freedom. Furthermore, she believed that evil existed in every political movement, even those with which she sympathized: "the mere adoption of a set of ideas, no matter how good the ideas may be, is [no] cure for the innate flaws of the individual." This innate depravity "accounts for the comparative failure of all movements towards human improvement."

Like many artists, Porter struggled to earn enough money to buy the freedom to write what she wanted. In 1940, she spent some time at Yaddo, the writers' colony in New York, took a salaried job in Washington, D.C., assisting Allen Tate at the Library of Congress in 1944, and even went to Hollywood to be a screenwriter at $1,500 a week in 1945. Financial security, however, came only with the increased recognition she received in her later years. The long-awaited publication of *Ship of Fools* in 1962, more than any other event, secured her reputation and ended her financial worries.

After the publication of *Ship of Fools*, Porter increasingly became a public figure. She was a visiting professor at various universities, was awarded several honorary degrees, and was sought after to appear on panels with other literary figures. She even became a guest in the White House of John F. Kennedy and Lyndon Johnson. She did little new writing in her later years, spending most of her time reaping benefits from past work. At the age of seventy-six, for example, she won the Pulitzer Prize and the

National Book Award for the *Collected Stories of Katherine Anne Porter* (1966).

Her spirit did not abate with old age. In her sixties and seventies she had affairs with younger men. As had been the case in her earlier years, when these relationships did not work out, she became as passionate an adversary as she had been a lover. Even in her seventies and eighties, she hired younger men as personal assistants to keep her literary and legal affairs in order, and she carried on at least platonic love affairs with them. She also remained passionate about her artistic independence. At eighty, she was enraged when her publisher wrote an acknowledgment to several of her friends who, in the publisher's view, had helped to collect the works in *The Collected Essays and Occasional Writings of Katherine Anne Porter* (1970). Feeling betrayed, she wrote indignant remarks on copies of this book to the effect that her publisher was impudent for believing that she could not conduct her own affairs and that it was ludicrous to suggest that the men who had been acknowledged were competent to put together a book for her.

A series of strokes paralyzed her writing hand and impaired her speech when she was eighty-seven, and she eventually died in 1980, at ninety years of age. Her body was cremated and buried alongside her mother's grave in Indian Creek.

Summary

Rising from artistic isolation and an unhappy childhood, Katherine Anne Porter became one of the most conscientious of literary craftsmen. Nearly all of her fictional works, despite their relative brevity, took many years to complete. Finely crafted and intensely focused, her small body of writings has been inspiring to other artists, just as her life story has been. Fiercely independent yet also strongly desiring love and care, she vacillated between her role as artist and southern belle. The conflicts that she experienced regarding gender roles are effectively sublimated into much of her fiction and, along with her interests in other aspects of human nature, create a lasting testament to Porter's life and imagination.

Bibliography

Bloom, Harold, ed. *Modern Critical Views: Katherine Anne Porter*. New York: Chelsea House, 1986. This is a book of twelve interpretations of Porter's fiction. It also includes a chronology of her life and a bibliography.

DeMouy, Jane Krause. *Katherine Anne Porter's Women: The Eye of Her Fiction*. Austin: University of Texas Press, 1983. An analysis of feminine psychology in the fiction, particularly the protagonists' conflicting desires for the security of a traditional female role and for the freedom from convention necessary to be an artist.

Givner, Joan. *Katherine Anne Porter: A Life*. Rev. ed. Athens: University of Georgia Press, 1991. The most thorough account of Porter's personal and professional life, this excellent biography often dispels myths propagated by Porter herself.

————, ed. *Katherine Anne Porter: Conversations*. Jackson: University Press of Mississippi, 1987. Porter sometimes fictionalized her life story. This collection of interviews with the author provides her view of her life and art.

Hendrick, Willene, and George Hendrick. *Katherine Anne Porter*. Rev. ed. Boston: Twayne, 1988. An overview of Porter's life and work, this carefully researched book provides a chronology of important dates, a bibliography of works by and about her, and chapters of her life and major works. A good place to begin study.

Porter, Katherine Anne. *The Collected Essays and Occasional Writings of Katherine Anne Porter*. New York: Delacorte, 1970. Reprint. Boston: Houghton Mifflin, 1990. According to Porter, these essays were the opposite of her fiction in that they were limited by time, space, and subject requirements. They range from the personal and biographical to criticism of other writers' works.

Unrue, Darlene Harbour. *Truth and Vision in Katherine Anne Porter's Fiction*. Athens: University of Georgia Press, 1985. An interpretation of Porter's fiction that stresses her exploration of the dark side of life and humankind's vain effort to evade it.

Warren, Robert Penn, ed. *Katherine Anne Porter: A Collection of Critical Essays*. Englewood Cliffs, N.J.: Prentice-Hall, 1979. These essays on Porter's work include contributions from some of the most influential interpreters of twentieth century writing: Warren, Cleanth Brooks, Eudora Welty, V. S. Pritchett, Edmund Wilson, and Mark Schorer, among others.

William L. Howard

MAUD POWELL

Born: August 22, 1867; Peru, Illinois
Died: January 8, 1920; Uniontown, Pennsylvania
Area of Achievement: Music
Contribution: Widely acclaimed as a concert violinist, Powell advanced the cause of women on the concert stage and did much to introduce art music to audiences outside the major urban centers in the United States.

Early Life

Maud Powell was born into a family whose members were noted for their intellectual vigor and personal achievements. Her mother, born Wilhelmina Bengelstraeter, had been adopted by a family named Paul following her parents' death from cholera within months of their immigration from Central Europe; she was herself an accomplished pianist and amateur composer, and she guided Maud's early music studies. William Bramwell Powell, Maud's father, was an educator with innovative ideas who moved his family to Aurora, Illinois, in 1870 to become superintendent of schools and later occupied a similar position in Washington, D.C. Maud's uncle, John Wesley Powell, was the first European to explore the length of the Grand Canyon and gained further recognition as one of the founders of the National Geographic Society. Within this invigorating family circle, Maud emerged as a child prodigy at an early age, and the stimulating environment of her early years may account for the breadth of her own worldview, which characterized her maturity.

Her first studies outside the family were with William Fickensher, a music teacher in Aurora, and with William Lewis in Chicago, a distinguished violinist whose teaching made a lasting impression on Maud. Her early appearances before the public during her childhood years convinced everyone that she was destined for an artistic career. On June 1, 1881, the citizens of Aurora sponsored a concert to raise funds that would enable Maud to study in Europe, a step deemed necessary by many aspiring American musicians in the nineteenth century.

Accompanied by her mother and younger brother, Maud enrolled in the Leipzig Conservatory in October for study with Henri Schradieck, receiving a diploma at the end of the year following her performance of Max Bruch's G minor Concerto with the famous Gewandhaus Orchestra. She next entered the Paris Conservatory to study with Charles Dancla, whom she later regarded as her greatest teacher. In her own view, she learned how to be a musician in Germany, but the French taught her to be an artist. During this period of study, she embarked on a highly successful series of concerts in the British Isles, playing frequently before the royal family. In London, she heard the violinist Wilma Norman-Neruda, later Lady Hallé, a musical figure who later was to become a role model for Maud in her own professional activities. Joseph Joachim, a dominant figure among violinists of the age, heard Maud in England and invited her to become his pupil at the Hochschule für Musik in Berlin. To be instructed by artists such as Schradieck, Dancla, and Joachim was an achievement for any violinist; for a young, female American, such ready recognition and acceptance was extraordinary. Powell's year of study with Joachim led to her debut with the Berlin Philharmonic in 1885, playing Bruch's G minor Concerto once again, with Joachim conducting. Maud Powell was now eighteen years old and ready, by the standards of the day, to embark on a professional career.

Life's Work

Returning to the United States, Maud Powell made her American debut with Theodore Thomas and his orchestra in Chicago on July 30, 1885, playing Bruch's G minor Concerto. The program was a great success, and she repeated it in New York with Thomas and the New York Philharmonic Orchestra at the first concert of that ensemble's season in November. For the next seven years, she made an annual tour of the United States with Thomas, which did much to establish her name with the American public. By her own account, however, these years were difficult. She was still young and missed the camaraderie of the student life to which she had been accustomed. Concert life in the United States was in its infancy; there were few established concert series, very few managers of any real skill or experience, and few performers who could share or appreciate the difficulties facing a young woman who was attempting to establish a reputation as a concert artist. The inner resources she developed during her early family life sustained her as she spent time studying scores, building programs, and expanding her violin technique. In 1887, she signed a three-year managerial contract with L. M. Ruben, an agreement that led to many concerts outside the metropolitan areas along the Atlantic seaboard. She toured with Patrick Gilmore's band in the spring of 1891, and in 1892 she was featured soloist on the European tour of the New York Arion Society, a musical club formed around the tradition of the German *Männerchor* (men's choir). European audiences responded to her playing with extravagant praise, many critics describing the twenty-four-year-old Powell as the greatest living female violinist.

She was invited to perform at the Chicago World's Fair in 1893, and she read a paper titled "Women and the Violin" at one of several musical conventions held as part of the event. The work she presented was but one of many similar papers, speeches, and printed articles written by Powell, all of them articulate testimony to her intellectual vitality and breadth of perspective on musical matters. Reflecting her interest in chamber music, and perhaps following the role model of Norman-Neruda, whom she had heard in London, she established the Maud Powell quartet in 1894 and toured with that group until its dissolution in 1898. Among her most successful tours abroad were those with John Philip Sousa's band in 1903 and 1905. It was with Sousa that she met H. Godfrey "Sunny" Turner, the English manager of Sousa's tour, who in 1904 became Maud's husband and, thereafter, her professional manager.

By the early years of the twentieth century, Maud Powell was well known in both Europe and the United States. Critics and audiences consistently lauded her performances for their complete technical mastery, the varieties of tone she produced on the violin, her complete grasp of musical scores, and her rapport with audiences. Her sense of responsibility to the literature of music was demonstrated by the number of first performances in the United States she gave of works that later became staples of the violinist's repertory, among them the concertos by Peter Ilich Tchaikovsky, Camille Saint-Saëns, Antonín Dvořák, Edouard Lalo (Concerto in F major, Concerto Russe in G minor), Jan Sibelius, and African American composer Samuel Coleridge-Taylor. In 1904, the Victor Talking Machine Company invited Powell to become the first instrumentalist to record on that company's prestigious Red Seal Label (the Celebrity Artist Series). Many of those recordings won prizes for their musical qualities or were included on best-seller lists for their popularity with the public at a time when the recording industry was in its infancy. She was an early member of the Music Service League of America, served on the board of the Brooklyn Music School Settlement, entertained troops in training camps during World War I, and continued her contribution to the musical education of the American public by publishing articles in music journals, giving interviews, and speaking before various groups. In describing her own experiences as student and artist, she consistently emphasized the necessity for discipline, commitment, self-sacrifice, and perseverance in the pursuit of high musical standards; it was obvious that these qualities represented her own philosophy and were guiding principles derived from her own experience. Her enduring goal was to elevate the standards of musical taste among American audiences by sharing with them works of genuine musical substance, performed to uncompromisingly high musical standards.

Rarely has any public figure in any field enjoyed such consistent, unqualified praise for her personal and professional achievements as did Maud Powell. Yet those achievements exacted a toll: She collapsed while on tour and died in a hotel room in Uniontown, Pennsylvania, at the age of fifty-two. Her passing was marked by eloquent testimonials from throughout the musical community. The Maud Powell Foundation of Arlington, Virginia, has been established to preserve the musical legacy of this outstanding violinist and musician.

Summary

In many ways Maud Powell was a pioneer. She triumphed as a female concert artist in a field traditionally dominated by men, but at no time does one encounter any suggestion that her success derived from any deference shown her because of her sex. She was thoroughly American in an era when most classical musicians came from European backgrounds; she did, indeed, study in Europe, but even then she maintained her American identity in her personal and musical demeanor. Through her natural talent and unremitting industry, she established a concert career that was unsurpassed by any violinist of the age, in an environment where there existed no ready format to encourage such endeavors; at the time of her debut, there was little established concert life outside the major urban centers in the East, even though the public demonstrated an enthusiasm for such concerts. She had to build audiences and concert traditions as she progressed. She maintained the highest standards of musical and technical mastery wherever she performed, a quality few people had encountered in an arena of activity that witnessed sensationalism at least as frequently as artistic polish. She was genuinely committed to raising the level of public taste in music, and she demonstrated in all of her activities that she was interested in the musical enlightenment of her audiences as much as in the display of her own virtuosity.

Maud Powell shattered existing taboos and stood as an example for the generations of young musicians, male as well as female, which were to come after her. Aspiring young American artists remain in her debt for the musical paths she laid out for them and the standards she maintained as a hallmark of her career.

Bibliography

Martens, Frederick H. *Violin Mastery: Talks with Master Violinists and Teachers*. New York: Frederick Stokes, 1919. Powell's views on performance, violins, and violin music, all written in first person as though deriving from an interview, and all published while Powell was still alive.

Roth, Henry. *Great Violinists in Performance*. Los Angeles, Calif.: Panjandrum Books, 1986. A review and stylistic analysis of Powell's performances as represented in her recordings, offering a modern perspective on her style of playing.

Schwarz, Boris. *Great Masters of the Violin*. New York: Simon & Schuster, 1983. Contains a summary of the violinist's career, couched largely in the context of her role as an American artist and her efforts in presenting new works of the concert repertory for the violin.

Shaffer, Karen A., and Neva Garner Greenwood. *Maud Powell: Pioneer American Violinist*. Ames: Iowa State University Press, 1988. Neva Greenwood was an ardent champion of Maud Powell whose documentary work was continued and expanded posthumously by Karen Shaffer. Their collaboration produced a biographical study that is by far the most extensive and carefully executed literary monument to Powell's musical legacy as it is represented by her recordings, editions, and arrangements of violin music. The generously illustrated book includes appendices containing a list of premier performances, a chronology of recording sessions, and a detailed discography.

Douglas A. Lee

ANN PRESTON

Born: December 1, 1813; West Grove, Pennsylvania
Died: April 18, 1872; Philadelphia, Pennsylvania
Areas of Achievement: Medicine and women's rights
Contribution: Ann Preston, who became the first woman ever to be appointed dean of an American medical school, was instrumental in securing women's right to study and to practice medicine in the face of heated opposition from the male-dominated medical establishment.

Early Life

On December 1, 1813, Ann Preston, the oldest daughter of Amos and Margaret Preston, was born in the Quaker town of West Grove, Pennsylvania. A minister, Amos Preston wielded personal influence within a community that combined a deep religious commitment with a climate of debate and concern regarding the various social issues of the day. The Preston family had shown particular devotion to the cause of abolition, having become members of a local antislavery society and allowed their home to serve as a refuge for runaway slaves. One of Ann Preston's most notable experiences as a young woman came about when she had heard that slave-catchers were on their way to raid the Preston house. Showing great initiative and courage, Preston saved an escaped slave who had been living at the house by helping her to dress in Quaker clothes, with the traditional heavy veil, and then riding with her directly past the group of approaching hunters. Passing what appeared merely to be two Quaker girls on their way to a meeting, the slave-catchers took no notice of them.

Though this sort of boldness was belied by her slight physical build, Ann Preston repeatedly displayed such signs of character as a young woman. Her commitment to the causes of abolition and temperance led her to write many impassioned articles and petitions in support of societal reform. Preston took such visible and vocal stances despite the fact that she had been forced to leave school prematurely in order to return home to care for her family and was, to a large extent, self-educated. During the time she ran the family household, Preston maintained her connection to the world of letters through an active participation in the small literary association of West Grove. Such was her attraction to this world that in 1849 Ann Preston published a collection of children's nursery rhymes, *Cousin Ann's Stories*.

Central to the early life of Ann Preston was the woeful physical health of the women in her family. The oldest of three daughters, Preston had to bear the deaths of both of her younger sisters during early childhood and then the decline of her mother into invalidism. Ann Preston was the lone daughter left to care for a family that included her six brothers, whose robust vitality stood as a stark counterpoint to the frailty of their sisters. Preston saw in her family's tragedy a cold lesson about the unhealthy upbringing of the girls of her era. Encouraged to learn mundane domestic chores and remain within the confines of the home, women could never hope to attain the physical well-being of their male counterparts, who spent their time outdoors, doing hard work in the fresh air. This early realization would help provide many of Ann Preston's core beliefs about good health, which for Preston had its basis in proper diet and regular exercise.

Life's Work

It was during the early 1840's that Ann Preston began to focus on women's health issues. After having organized and taught several classes on female physiology and good hygiene for women in her community, Preston found that many of her friends and acquaintances from the Quaker community began to encourage her to pursue a career devoted to her new interest. Heeding their advice, Preston applied for and won a place as an apprentice in physician Nathaniel R. Moseley's Philadelphia office in 1847. After two years of working for Moseley, Ann Preston believed herself ready in 1849 to enter medical school, and subsequently she applied to four of the major colleges in the Philadelphia area. Preston was rejected by all four. It was only with the creation in 1850 of the Female Medical College of Pennsylvania by a group of Quakers that Preston was presented with an opportunity to actualize her hopes of gaining a proper medical education. The Quakers who founded the college were headed by a young businessman named William T. Mullen, who had formerly studied medicine and had come to recognize the burgeoning demand being created by women wanting medical training.

In October, 1850, Ann Preston became part of the original entering class at the Female Medical College of Pennsylvania, and on December 31, 1851, she participated along with seven other women in the college's first round of commencement exercises for its new graduates. This groundbreaking commencement did not go unnoticed by the established medical community, which evinced its extreme hostility toward the entrance of women into their once impenetrable fraternity: Fifty Philadelphia police were called on to protect these first eight graduates from a mob of five hundred male medical students who threatened to prevent their graduation. Despite the antagonism that was brought to bear upon these inaugural exercises, the message sent was clear: If rebuffed by the male-dominated establishment, women would resort to building their own institutions. Medical schools had become the first scene of this kind of action, and Ann Preston would later be instrumental in seeing to it that the as yet "closed" city hospitals would be next.

After spending another year at the college doing postgraduate study, Ann Preston joined its faculty in 1853 as a professor of physiology and hygiene, beginning a working relationship with the college that would last the rest of her life. During the 1850's, as a result of the success of the Female Medical College of Pennsylvania as well as colleges such as Penn Medical School, the number of women graduating with medical degrees in Philadelphia rose sharply, with many of these graduates beginning to enjoy successful private practices. In 1858, perhaps in reaction to this growth, the board of censors of the Philadelphia County Medical Society, an all-male organization, recommended to its members that absolutely no advice or support should be given to graduates of women's medical colleges. Then, in 1859, the Pennsylvania

State Medical Society ruled that no member of its fraternity should so much as consult or have any interaction whatsoever with women graduates. At that time, it was impossible for any woman to practice medicine at a Philadelphia hospital, and these resolutions were clear attempts to widen the gap between the established hospitals and the growing number of qualified women physicians.

Having grown extremely frustrated at the hospitals' repeated refusals to grant admission to her students, and now faced with the reactionary dictums of the medical societies, Ann Preston became more determined than ever to establish a teaching hospital connected to the college conducted by women doctors. To bring this goal to fruition, Preston needed to raise huge amounts of financial and political support. That the Civil War loomed on the horizon made the task doubly difficult, in that nearly every spare resource at that time was needed for the war effort. Undaunted, Ann Preston succeeded in creating a board of women managers for a Woman's Hospital and in raising the funds necessary for its establishment. In 1861, although the college was closed on account of the outbreak of war, the Woman's Hospital was founded, and Emeline Horton, a former student of Preston, was instated as its chief resident. In 1862, the college reopened, and in the next year Ann Preston instituted a training school for nurses.

Although Ann Preston had succeeded in founding a hospital that women could call their own, she remained adamant in her drive to gain for her students their rightful entry into the cities' major hospitals. In 1866, after being made dean of the Woman's Medical College—and becoming the first woman to ever hold the office—Preston again took up this struggle with a letter requesting the repeal of the legislation passed by the Pennsylvania State Medical Society in 1859. The letter was ignored. The next year another appeal was made. Again, no action was taken except for the publication of a manifesto that was issued by the society. This was perhaps the classic document marshaling all the arguments against the practice of medicine by women: their physical frailty, the loss of their influence in the home, and the possibility of their attendance upon persons of the opposite sex and the resulting awkwardness.

Ann Preston's reply, published in the *Medical and Surgical Reporter* of May 4, 1867, carefully and patiently rebutted all these arguments. Her response, likely the most eloquent of all her writings, left the society's reasoning in tatters, and it made no further effort to reply. Nevertheless, it was not until 1888 that the first woman was actually admitted to the Philadelphia County Medical Society—nearly forty years after the founding of what then had become the Woman's Medical College. Ann Preston did not live to see that moment. She died on April 18, 1872, having worked and written in the name of the Woman's Medical College until her final day.

Summary

In terms of direct influence upon the generation of women physicians that followed the earliest women graduates of American medical schools, no woman of her era could boast of having greater impact than Ann Preston had. Her name became nearly synonymous with the success and integrity of the Woman's Medical College of

Pennsylvania, an institution that had conferred more than one hundred and thirty medical degrees on women graduates by the time of her death. Ann Preston's brave confrontations with the conservative, fraternal Medical Society of Philadelphia and her extremely eloquent responses to their condemnations of women physicians laid the groundwork for the advances toward equality which her former students would one day enjoy. Although she would not live to see their ultimate fruition, Preston can take credit for labors that eventually gained women physicians admission to the city hospitals of Philadelphia. A woman of patience and determination, Ann Preston repeatedly withstood the hostilities vented upon her gender by the medical establishment and worked tirelessly to provide better opportunities and better training for the women who would follow her into the medical field.

Bibliography

Alsop, Gulielma Fell. *History of the Woman's Medical College, Philadelphia, Pennsylvania, 1850-1950.* Philadelphia: J. B. Lippincott, 1950. Though not a biography of Ann Preston per se, this text provides one of the most thorough portraits of her, devoting eight chapters to the woman whose career and groundbreaking achievements were integral to the Woman's Medical College.

Lerner, Gerda. *The Female Experience: An American Documentary.* Indianapolis: Bobbs-Merrill, 1977. Two documents regarding Ann Preston's battle to gain recognition as a physician are included in this book—the resolution of the Philadelphia CountyMedical Society to discourage women from practicing medicine on the grounds of their unsuitability for the profession and Preston's spirited reply.

Lopate, Carol. *Women in Medicine.* Baltimore: The Johns Hopkins University Press, 1968. In 1966, the Josiah Macy Foundation sponsored a conference that examined why so few women entered the field of medicine in the United States. In her inquiry into this question, Carol Lopate has written a first chapter examining the entrance of women into the medical profession in which she recognizes Ann Preston's contributions.

Morantz-Sanchez, Regina Markell. *Sympathy and Science: Women Physicians in American Medicine.* New York: Oxford University Press, 1985. In this comprehensive history of women in American medicine from the colonial period to the twentieth century, Ann Preston's contributions are woven into the narrative. Morantz-Sanchez explores the role of feminism in this history as well as the unique contributions women made to the field of medicine.

Walsh, Mary Roth. *"Doctors Wanted: No Women Need Apply": Sexual Barriers in the Medical Profession, 1835-1975.* New Haven, Conn.: Yale University Press, 1977. Although it is primarily concerned with Harriot Hunt's and Marie Zakrzewska's contributions to opening up the medical profession to women, this text does make brief mention of Ann Preston's views regarding barriers to women entering the field.

Bonnie L. Ford

LEONTYNE PRICE

Born: February 10, 1927; Laurel, Mississippi

Area of Achievement: Music
Contribution: Internationally acclaimed soprano of the operatic and concert stage, Leontyne Price paved the way for many subsequent black classical performers. The fifth black singer to appear at the Metropolitan Opera, she was the first to sustain a long career there. During her thirty-four-year history at the Met, she became the most sought after prima donna at the opera house.

Early Life

Mary Violet Leontine Price was born to James Anthony and Katherine Baker Price on February 10, 1927, in the city of Laurel, a county seat in southeastern Mississippi. In college, she changed the spelling of her name to Leontyne. The Prices' family life was centered around the church where Leontyne and her brother George spent much of their time. Music was always an integral part of home and church life. Leontyne's father played tuba in the church band, and her mother sang in St. Paul's choir. Leontyne exhibited unusual musical instincts at an early age and her mother immediately sought musical training for her. At three-and-one-half years old, Leontyne began piano lessons with the local music teacher, Mrs. Hattie V. J. McInnis. In school, she sang in choral groups and as school soloist while also excelling in dance and acrobatics. By age eleven, she played regularly for Sunday school and church services.

The first major event that affected Leontyne's future musical career was a trip to Jackson, Mississippi, to hear a concert by the black contralto, Marian Anderson. Impressed by the beauty and power of communication of Anderson's voice, nine-year-old Leontyne at once aspired to a stage career. Her first solo concert was performed on December 17, 1943, in Sandy Gavin School Auditorium, where she played classical piano selections and sang for an audience that demanded several curtain calls.

Leontyne attended Oak Park Vocational High School in Laurel and continued to perform both as a singer and as pianist for the school choirs. Upon graduation, Leontyne won a four-year scholarship to Central State College in Wilberforce, Ohio. She was graduated from Wilberforce in 1948 certified to teach public school music. Recognizing her remarkable gift, however, her teachers had encouraged Leontyne to pursue a performance career. With the advice of her voice teacher, Catherine Van Buren, and the college's president, Dr. Charles Wesley, she obtained a full scholarship to attend the Juilliard School of Music in New York. Additional money for living expenses was contributed by Elizabeth Chisholm, a musician and wealthy white resident of Laurel for whom Leontyne's aunt worked. Mrs. Chisholm had recognized the girl's talent and often paid Leontyne to entertain for occasions in her home. Even when financial support was no longer needed, she remained a lifelong friend and patron. Another important contributor to Price's scholarship fund was celebrated baritone Paul Robeson, who, after hearing Leontyne sing, agreed to perform a benefit concert in Dayton Memorial Hall. She also appeared on this concert program, from which $1,000 was raised for her education.

Life's Work

Leontyne Price entered Juilliard in 1948 and was placed in the voice studio of Florence Page Kimball. Kimball remained a friend, adviser, and voice coach long after her student left Juilliard. It is she whom Price credits for her basic knowledge of vocal technique. Several milestones in Price's career came as a result of her Juilliard work. In 1952, Price was cast in her first major operatic role as Mistress Ford in the Juilliard production of Giuseppe Verdi's *Falstaff*. At these performances, the soprano was heard by numerous important musicians. Virgil Thomson, a noted composer and music critic, was assembling a cast for an International Music Festival production of his opera *Four Saints in Three Acts*. Price was chosen to sing St. Cecilia at the opera's New York opening and later in Paris, marking the beginning of her international appearances. Robert Breen and Blevins Davis were also present at her Juilliard performance in *Falstaff* and immediately offered her a contract as Bess in the 1952 revival of George Gershwin's opera *Porgy and Bess*. *Porgy and Bess* made an international tour sponsored by the U.S. State Department and, in 1953, was produced on Broadway. Price remained with the cast for two years and received wide acclaim for her portrayal of Bess. During the rehearsals for *Porgy and Bess*, Price met baritone William Warfield, who portrayed Porgy. On August 31, 1952, the couple was married. Sadly, professional demands on the two performers overwhelmed the relationship, and they separated physically in 1959, not to separate legally until 1967. They remained friends, however, as well as mutually supportive colleagues.

American composer Nicolas Nabokov, who was also impressed with Price's *Falstaff* performance, introduced her to one of the most influential figures of her professional life—composer and pianist Samuel Barber. Barber heard Price in a performance of *Porgy and Bess* in 1953 when composing his cycle of *Hermit Songs*, and he completed them with Price's voice in mind. He accompanied her when she sang them for the first time at the Library of Congress in Washington, D.C., and later the same year at the Twentieth Century Music Conference in Rome. He then arranged for her to sing his *Prayers of Kierkegaard* in her debut with the Boston Symphony Orchestra. In 1954, Barber was also pianist for the *Hermit Songs* during Price's Town Hall debut recital in New York. This long and valuable association continued throughout their careers.

The year 1955 marked the most radical turning point in Price's career. Upon hearing her in *Porgy and Bess*, Peter Herman Adler cast Price in the role of Floria Tosca in the NBC Opera Company production of *Tosca*, breaking the color barrier in the operatic world, especially in the United States. Although not carried by twelve NBC affiliate stations in the South, the production was still a major success, and the young black soprano was no longer an unknown to the operatic world.

Following *Tosca*, Price's career opportunities multiplied rapidly. She signed a management contract with André Mertens of Columbia Artist Management, who introduced her to conductor Herbert von Karajan. Karajan, then conductor of the Berlin Philharmonic, introduced Price to European opera audiences. After she refused his offer to sing the demanding title role in *Salomé* by Richard Strauss, he presented her instead in a production of Giuseppe Verdi's *Aida* with the Vienna State Opera in 1959, in which she was an enormous success as the Egyptian princess. Just prior to singing Aida, Price made her American operatic stage debut on September 20, 1957, with the San Francisco Opera as Madame Liodine in Francis Poulenc's *Dialogues of the Carmelites*. She continued to appear in San Francisco throughout her career and performances included roles in *Aida* and *Il Trovatore* by Verdi, Carl Orff's *The Wise Maiden*, and as Donna Anna in Wolfgang Amadeus Mozart's *Don Giovanni*. She also appeared in the title role in Jules Massenet's *Thaïs* and as Liù in Giacomo Puccini's *Turandot* at the Lyric Opera of Chicago in 1959.

Leontyne Price was becoming known the world over for her ravishing, warm lyric soprano voice that proved to be the perfect instrument for the works of Verdi and Puccini. She became the most celebrated Verdi singer of her era. The role of Aida, especially, became synonymous with Price, not only for the ethnic heritage that helped make her ideal for the role but also because of the sumptuous quality of her voice, which was able to soar with the drama. When approached by the Metropolitan Opera in 1961, after several previous attempts to schedule a debut performance for her had failed, she chose to portray Leonora in Verdi's *Il Trovatore* so as to avoid making her debut in what the public might interpret as a role for "black sopranos." Her debut, with its forty-five-minute ovation, made sensational headlines. Price sang five major roles with the Metropolitan Opera in her first season—Leonora (*Il Trovatore*), Aida (*Aida*), Donna Anna (*Don Giovanni*), Cio-Cio-San in Puccini's *Madama Butterfly*, and Liù in *Turandot*. Although Price's voice was recognized as lighter in quality than voices of singers often heard in those roles, it had a special quality that projected a highly charged emotional element and adequate power to fill the opera house. In 1962, she had the honor of singing the opening night of a new production of Puccini's *The Golden Girl of the West*. She continued to sing with the Met and in Chicago, San Francisco, Paris, Cologne, Berlin, and the Soviet Union. In 1964, Leontyne Price was doubly honored for her work: She received a Spingarn Medal from the National Association for the Advancement of Colored People (NAACP), and President Lyndon B. Johnson awarded her the Presidential Medal of Freedom.

The highest honor in Leontyne Price's career came in 1966 when she was chosen to star in Samuel Barber's opera, *Antony and Cleopatra*, which had been commissioned for the opening of the new Metropolitan Opera House at Lincoln Center for the Performing Arts in New York. Barber wrote the role of Cleopatra especially for Price, and the music was ideally suited to her voice. Reviews of the performance were mixed as a result of production problems attributed to designer Franco Zeffirelli; nevertheless, references to Price's singing of Cleopatra were glowing. Her repertoire began to include new roles such as Fiordiligi in Mozart's *Cosí fan tutte*, Ariadne in

Richard Strauss's *Ariadne auf Naxos*, and Manon in Puccini's *Manon Lescaut*. In 1985, Price retired from the operatic stage in order to devote more time to concerts, recitals, and master classes while her talent was still at its peak. Appropriately, she chose Aida for her farewell role. Her personal identification with the role focused upon freedom and loyalty to family and country created a special attachment for her to Aida. On January 4, 1985, she had the distinction of singing her last performance as a live telecast from the stage of the Metropolitan Opera.

In addition to opera, oratorio, and recital performances, Price maintained an active recording schedule throughout her career. All of her major roles have been recorded, and more than ten of these recordings earned Grammy Awards.

Summary

Leontyne Price was recognized first for her extraordinary artistry and additionally for the exposure she afforded other African American singers as a result of opening many doors that had previously been closed to them throughout the world. Price was acutely aware of her black heritage and made careful decisions about career issues that she believed would ultimately make life better for minorities. She had friends among the major civil rights leaders of the United States such as Martin Luther King, Jr., and Robert F. Kennedy and supported and worked through organizations such as the American Civil Liberties Union and the NAACP. In 1969, Rust College in Mississippi (where her mother attended school) named a new library in honor of her.

Leontyne Price was the most celebrated American diva of her time. Her presence was demanded on stages internationally. She treated her artistic gift with great respect, using it to communicate messages of love, beauty, and freedom to people all over the world. As an American, as a black woman, and as a consummate artist, she charted new courses and earned the admiration of all who knew her work.

Bibliography

Garland, Phyl. "Leontyne Price: Getting out at the Top." *Ebony* 40 (June, 1985): 31-34. In an intimate interview, Garland explores Price's background, career, and plans following her operatic retirement.

Hughes, Langston, and Milton Meltzer. *Black Magic: A Pictorial History of the Negro in American Entertainment*. Englewood Cliffs, N.J.: Prentice-Hall, 1967. A detailed history, written by noted author Langston Hughes, includes Price among famous African American artists that have made significant contributions to the field of American entertainment.

Jackson, Jacquelyn. "Leontyne Price." In *Epic Lives: One Hundred Black Women Who Made a Difference*, edited by Jessie Carney Smith. Detroit: Visible Ink Press, 1993. This profile, included as part of a select collection on prominent African American women, provides a concise overview of Price's life and accomplishments. Price's appearance in this collection places her within the broader historical context of achievements by women who struggled to overcome unfair limitations placed upon them because of their gender and their race.

Jacobson, Robert. "Collard Greens to Caviar." *Opera News* 50 (July/August, 1985): 18-23, 28-33. Following her farewell appearance at the Metropolitan Opera, Price discusses at length various aspects of her career and personal life, projecting plans for her future.

Lyon, Hugh L. *Leontyne Price: Highlights of a Prima Donna*. New York: Vantage Press, 1973. This thorough biography of Price is filled with personal and professional details which give the reader an understanding of her artistic development as well as a sense of the soprano as a warm, generous personality.

Sargeant, Winthrop. *Divas*. New York: Coward, McCann, & Geoghegan, 1973. Sargeant devotes separate chapters to the lives and professional accomplishments of Leontyne Price, as well as Marilyn Horne, Beverly Sills, Birgit Nilsson, Joan Sutherland, and Eileen Farrell.

Story, Rosalyn M. *And So I Sing: African-American Divas of Opera and Concert*. New York: Warner Books, 1990. A comprehensive historical view of African American divas, this book includes information from research and personal interviews with a separate chapter on Price.

Sandra C. McClain

PEARL PRIMUS

Born: November 29, 1919; Trinidad, West Indies
Died: October 29, 1994; New Rochelle, New York
Areas of Achievement: Dance and anthropology
Contribution: A pioneer in African American dance and an anthropologist specializing in the dances of western and central Africa and the Caribbean, Primus dedicated her life to demonstrating through dance the dignity, beauty, and strength in the heritage of peoples of African ancestry.

Early Life

Pearl Primus was born on November 29, 1919, on the island of Trinidad, the granddaughter of an accomplished Vodoun drummer and the only daughter of Edward and Emily (Jackson) Primus. After moving to New York City with her parents in 1921, Pearl led a sheltered life centered around church, school, the library, and home. She attended Hunter High School and continued her education at Hunter College, where she was an all-around athlete who excelled as a track and field star and set school records in the broad and high jumps.

In 1940, when Primus was graduated from Hunter College with a B.A. in biology and premedical sciences, the thought of becoming a dancer had never crossed her mind; her highest ambition was to become a medical doctor. She was confronted instead by the harsh realities of the Depression-era United States, in which no jobs in the medical field were available to African Americans and employment of any kind was scarce.

While Primus continued her education at night, taking graduate courses in health education at New York University before enrolling in psychology courses at Hunter College the following year, she contacted the National Youth Administration (NYA) in her continuing search for employment. At age twenty-one and with little previous dance training, Primus was placed as an understudy in an NYA-sponsored dance group. Within one year, she auditioned for and won a New Dance Group scholarship and became the first African American to enroll at the school, which had been founded during the Depression for those who wanted to dance but lacked the funds to do so. Under the provisions of this "working" scholarship, Primus cleaned the studio in exchange for dance lessons.

When the NYA dance program was canceled in the summer of 1941, Primus was forced to seek other employment. While simultaneously pursuing her evening graduate studies, taking dance classes at the New Dance Group School (later teaching there herself), and performing with the New Dance Group's resident company, she alternately worked as an artist's model, taught dance classes at a summer camp, worked in a tin factory, was a welder-burner at a shipyard, and operated a switchboard.

It was not until 1942, at age twenty-three, that Primus began to consider seriously dance as a career choice. She sampled dance techniques, taking ballet classes and studying modern dance at the Martha Graham School, the Young Men's Hebrew

Association (YMHA) School, and with modern dancer Charles Weidman. She also studied choreography with modern dancer Doris Humphrey, learning how to explore a movement phrase thoroughly, to discover all of its possible variations before moving on to another phrase. Primus' passion, however, was to explore African culture and to express the dignity of that culture—her cultural heritage—through dance. Primus' twenty-fourth year would mark the professional beginning of her cultural odyssey.

Life's Work

Six months of research went into Pearl Primus' first dance composition, "African Ceremonial." Wishing to choreograph African-based movement, Primus searched through libraries—consulting books, articles, and pictures—and visited museums, seeking out the African sculpture from which she would derive her basic dance positions. After Primus had painstakingly pieced together her dance, based on a legend from the Belgian Congo, she asked her African friends, students at Columbia University who were thoroughly familiar with African traditions, to verify its authenticity. She also consulted with native drummers to validate the rhythms of the dance.

On February 14, 1943, Primus included this solo in her acclaimed professional debut performance at the New York City YMHA in a program shared with four other gifted young dancers. Primus' early performances were praised by John Martin, dance critic for *The New York Times*, who wrote, "Besides strength and speed and elevation, her movement . . . [is] an open channel for her inward power and her pervasive, outgoing honesty." In August of 1943, Primus received Martin's annual award as the most distinguished newcomer of the season, catapulting her into the concert dance world.

The positive critical attention generated by Primus' performing and choreographic gifts led to a ten-month engagement at the New York City nightclub Cafe Society Downtown, her Broadway debut in a ten-day run at the Belasco Theatre, and a subsequent month-long Broadway engagement at the Roxy, for which she rechoreographed her solo "African Ceremonial" into a group piece. In addition to these typical entertainment venues, Primus performed at the first Negro Freedom Rally at Madison Square Garden in 1943 in conjunction with appearances by Paul Robeson and Adam Clayton Powell, Jr.

Primus once described herself as a "dancer of social conditions." Her early work included "modern" pieces in addition to the African-based dances. Termed "dances of protest" by dance reviewer Edith Segal, these compositions were intended to focus attention on the inequities and injustices present in the lives of African Americans; her "message dances" included "Hard Time Blues," protesting sharecropping; "Freedom Train," dealing with segregation; and "Strange Fruit," based on and accompanied by Lewis Allen's poem of the same name, depicting the anguish of a white woman (portrayed by Primus) filled with regret after witnessing a lynching.

In the summer of 1944, Primus made her first trip to the Deep South to seek out African survivals in southern black culture. In order to gain firsthand experience of many subjects she had choreographed through imagination, she visited churches, attended open-air revivals, and lived with sharecroppers, sometimes picking cotton with them in the fields. Although she returned from the South with a vitamin deficiency as a result of existing on a sharecropper's diet, Primus was rewarded with a newfound awareness of race relations in the South. She witnessed black feelings of inferiority, white feelings of fear, and a hunger pervading all: "After travelling through the South I felt licked—I had an absolute hollowness in me for months." Primus revisited the South several times, dancing at schools and churches, gathering new material for dances, and rediscovering the African cultural roots of southern black culture in its rhythms, movement patterns, and songs.

Primus began the year 1946 as the lead dancer in a revival of the musical *Showboat* (1927); choreographer Helen Tamiris had devised choreography specifically suited to Primus' talents. Primus immediately began to question the validity of this musical, observing that black issues were being evaded and that the depiction of black life was dated and shallow. She protested the segregation of blacks from whites on the stage. Although Primus was not able to effect a change in Tamiris' staging at the time, she later was able to restage the dances for the touring company of *Showboat*.

In the spring of 1948, Primus was awarded the last and largest of the Rosenwald Fellowships. The president of the foundation had been impressed by her African-based ceremonial dances and was amazed that she had never been to Africa, that she had pieced together the choreography from books. Her year-long trip, funded by the grant from the Rosenwald Foundation, took her to the Gold Coast, Angola, Cameroon, Liberia, Senegal, and the Belgian Congo. She realized that she needed to travel away from the coast and the urban areas to find the purest dance—dance that retained its original function in village societies, dance that had not been tainted by European culture and commercial influences.

At each village the people would share their dances with her, sometimes she would dance for them, and often they would all dance together. *Dance Magazine* writer Doris Hering related Primus' learning process: "First they explained the meaning of the dance. Then she was obliged to learn by imitation. If she had difficulty ascertaining exactly which muscles to move, a native dancer would hold her body against his or her own so she could literally absorb the movement."

Before leaving Africa in 1949, Primus was decorated for her interpretation of Liberian culture with the Order of the Star of Africa, presented by the president of the Republic of Liberia. Primus was profoundly moved by her first stay in Africa. She would return to the United States spiritually renewed and with the confirmation that the dances she had created from books were remarkably accurate but incomplete. (Reportedly, when Primus danced her Trinidadian ritual, "Shouters of Sobo," for the Eusobo people, "they called the whole tribe together to teach her the dance beginning to end.") Primus eventually returned to Africa several more times: in 1952, to study the effects of urbanization on African culture; in 1959, to serve for two years as the director of the African Center of Performing Arts at the University of Liberia; and in 1962, under the sponsorship of the Rebekah Harkness Foundation.

During a 1953 research trip to Trinidad, Primus met Percival Borde, a native of

Trinidad well schooled in Afro-Caribbean dance. They were married in 1954; their son, Onwin Babajide, was born in 1955. A talented dancer, choreographer, and teacher in his own right, Borde traveled to New York with Primus, codirected her dance company and school, and accompanied Primus on her subsequent African visits. Until his untimely death in 1979, Borde would share Primus' passion for rekindling and passing on the rich heritage of peoples of African ancestry.

Although noted as a gifted performer and choreographer, Primus emerged in later life as an inspirational lecturer and teacher of dance. Primus believed that dance could be used as an educational tool to foster creativity in children and to extend a child's world into that of other cultures. Toward that end, she founded the Pearl Primus Dance Language Institute, served as an acting consultant for the Head Start program, completed a study tour in England focusing on dance education in elementary and secondary level schools, brought dance into cultural enrichment programs in New York City schools, and worked with teenagers in Newark's inner city. Her goal was to pass on the knowledge that dance had instilled in her: "The dance has been my teacher, ever so patiently revealing to me the dignity, beauty, and strength in the cultural heritage of my people as a vital part of the great heritage of *all* mankind."

Her years of anthropological research, complemented by a Ph.D. in anthropology and educational sociology (earned at New York University in 1978) made Primus a sought-after lecturer and teacher at the university level. In the early 1990's, Primus served as artist-in-residence and professor of ethnic studies at the Five Colleges, an educational consortium made up of Amherst, Smith, Hampshire, and Mount Holyoke colleges and the University of Massachusetts.

In addition to lecturing, she also continued to set her choreography on dancers. Her rehearsal style would focus as much on fundamental imagery and accumulated cultural knowledge as on the steps of the dance. Because Primus' African-based dances went beyond mere presentation of dance movements to give the flavor of the basic culture, her rehearsals in 1990 for the Alvin Ailey American Dance Theater's revival of her 1951 piece "Impinyuza" were filled with images of the Watusi she had encountered in Rwanda; repeated head rolls in the piece, she explained, would be used by the Watusi to express "the whole sweep of the universe; the sweep of the clouds . . . the wind sweeping through the poplar trees." Her aim was to elicit not only an expressive performance but also a spiritual one. Pearl Primus has stated, "I present the arts as survival methods." One tends to believe that if the proud heritage of peoples of African ancestry is to survive, it will be thanks to the work of people such as Pearl Primus.

Summary

Pearl Primus dedicated her life to celebrating her African heritage with integrity. She worked tirelessly to accurately represent and honestly express African and African American culture through dance, preferring to present her work on the concert stage so as to avoid the temptation to theatricalize her performances to fill larger entertainment venues. Much of her early work was made up of politically charged, conscience-provoking choreography that focused on the difficult issues confronting African Americans in the 1940's. Her African-based dances, while more pleasant and exciting to watch, were actually cultural lessons emphasizing the strength, beauty, and dignity of the African heritage she embodied. Pearl Primus did not dance to entertain—she danced to enlighten and educate. Although Primus was able to enlighten larger groups through her performances of dances that embody African culture and African American issues, it was through one-on-one contact, teacher to student, dancer to dancer, that her greatest impact was felt. Primus carried on the African traditions of oral history and skilled dancing so that subsequent generations, regardless of race, might know and value African culture.

Bibliography

Dekle, Nicole. "Pearl Primus: Spirit of the People." *Dance Magazine* 64 (December, 1990): 62-65. A brief, information-packed article centered on the Alvin Ailey American Dance Theater's 1990 revival of Primus' "Impinyuza." Brings to life Primus' oral history-based teaching style as well as providing a selective overview of her career. Stimulating reading. Includes photos.

Emery, Lynne Fauley. *Black Dance: From 1619 to Today*. 2d rev. ed. Princeton, N.J.: Princeton Book Company, 1988. A comprehensive study of the dance forms of people of African ancestry. While chapter 8, "Concert Dance Pioneers: 1920-1950," contains only five pages devoted solely to Primus, the remaining material allows the reader to place her role in African American dance in perspective. Chapter 9, "Concert Dance: 1950-Today," contains a brief section on Primus' husband Percival Borde. Contains copious chapter notes, an extensive bibliography, and a brief index.

Gere, David. "Dances of Sorrow, Dances of Hope." *Los Angeles Times*, April 24, 1994, Calendar section, pp. 5, 7. Written on the occasion of the inclusion of Primus' 1943 work "Strange Fruit" in a 1994 program of historic modern dances for women, this two-page article contains anecdotes and detailed descriptions of selected events in Primus' career. Provides insight into her teaching style. Includes two large color photos.

Hering, Doris. "Little Fast Feet." *Dance Magazine* 24 (July, 1950): 21-23. Criticized for its "cute" and patronizing presentation, this three-page article contains one of the most detailed descriptions readily available of Primus' first trip to Africa. Touches on the dance styles of various tribes and describes the changes wrought by outside influences. Includes captioned photos.

Johns, Robert L. "Pearl Primus." In *Notable Black American Women*, edited by Jessie Carney Smith. Detroit: Gale Research, 1992. Provides a concise biographical account of Primus' life and work to 1991. Contains several quotations by and about Primus. Includes an ample reference list.

Wenig, Adele R. *Pearl Primus: An Annotated Bibliography of Sources from 1943 to 1975*. Oakland, Calif.: Wenadance Unlimited, 1983. Contains brief descriptions of a variety of sources beginning with the year of Primus' professional debut and spanning more than three decades. Covers books, periodicals, and newspaper articles and includes summaries of fliers, notices, and taped interviews with Primus. Provides helpful leads on a subject about whom little substantial scholarship exists. Useful for corroborating dates and facts.

Joyce I. Buchea

BONNIE RAITT

Born: November 8, 1949; Burbank, California

Area of Achievement: Music

Contribution: Raitt mingles the techniques of traditional, black country blues with lyrics that illuminate the spirit of her time, putting her gutsy voice and superb slide guitar to the service of issues that reflect her Quaker upbringing.

Early Life

Bonnie Lynn Raitt was born on November 8, 1949, in Burbank, California, to a musical family. Her father, John Raitt, was already well established on Broadway as the leading man in such musicals as *Oklahoma!* and *Carousel*. Her mother, Marjorie Haydock Raitt, enjoyed her own musical career as a pianist and served as her husband's accompanist for many years. Even Raitt's maternal grandfather had been musical; a Methodist missionary, he wrote more than six hundred hymns, which he played on his Hawaiian slide guitar. Bonnie was the second of the couple's three children, and the only girl. She was brought up in the Quaker tradition; Christmas trees always contained room for donations to charity, and service through works was stressed by her parents and their friends, who actively participated in missions to Third World nations.

Raitt got her first guitar, a twenty-five-dollar Stella, as a Christmas present when she was eight years old. Her grandfather taught her a few basic chords, and the counselors at the Quaker camp she attended in the Adirondacks introduced her to protest music by artists such as Pete Seeger. She recalls practicing to recordings of blues musicians Mississippi John Hurt, Son House, and John Koerner. In fact, she learned her unique slide guitar style, with the bottleneck over her middle instead of her ring finger, by teaching herself from records instead of studying with another guitarist.

Throughout Bonnie Raitt's childhood, the family followed John's career between New York City and the Los Angeles area. In 1957, they settled in Hollywood, where she attended University High School. They moved back to the East Coast when Bonnie Raitt was fifteen: She attended a Quaker-run high school in Poughkeepsie, New York, and then began her college years enrolled at Radcliffe College in Cambridge, Massachusetts.

In Cambridge, Raitt met some of the blues musicians she had idolized and imitated for so many years, including Fred McDowell and Skip James. A new boyfriend, manager-promoter Dick Waterman, introduced her to some of the bluesmen whose careers he had helped revive in coffeehouses and small venues around the university. By 1969, her college classes began to take a back seat to performances around New England. Raitt's self-taught techniques, augmented by tips from her new blues friends, proved to be marketable in the expansive 1960's music scene. After a 1970 performance at the Gaslight Club in New York City garnered favorable reviews, Warner

Bros. Records offered her a contract. She gave up college to live the life of a professional musician.

Life's Work

The blues was Bonnie Raitt's music. She began playing dates all over the country, touring with Son House, Fred McDowell, and others. She met Sippie Wallace, a blues singer who cut several records in the 1920's and 1930's and whose song "Woman Be Wise" was one of Raitt's earliest hits. Raitt's interest in the blues and the friendships with various blues artists she developed during these years proved to be more than just a passing fancy; throughout her career, she has insisted on including traditional artists in virtually all of her concert appearances.

Her first album, *Bonnie Raitt*, was recorded in a converted garage near Minneapolis in 1971. Her contract allowed her complete control over her recordings, including advertising copy. She used this freedom to include three Sippie Wallace tunes and to set the direction of her artistic journey, proclaiming through her lyrics a gutsy self-reliance that perfectly suited the burgeoning feminism of the times.

Despite the loose and funky production values of her first effort, it garnered critical acclaim. So did Raitt's second album, *Give It Up* (1972), which mingled blues with contemporary and folk-oriented songs. From that point until the mid-1980's, she managed to record an album nearly every year. One casualty of her prolific schedule was her songwriting career; after "Give It Up," nearly a decade passed before she recorded another original song.

Singing the blues seemed to demand heavy drinking. Raitt has recalled, in various interviews, measuring out drinks for her blues idols when she was nineteen years old, allowing them just enough to get through the evening's performance and stopping them from drinking past the point at which they would forget the words. She soon began drinking with them, knocking back bourbon and gaining a reputation as a hard-driving, hard-drinking blues mama.

Meanwhile, she played concert dates all over the United States, going from folk concerts to college campuses, from night clubs to Carnegie Hall, where she played in 1973. At one point, she estimated that she spent five or six months of every year on the road. She enjoyed the response she got from live audiences, and the spontaneity of her road shows brought her sold-out crowds and critical raves all over the country. Perhaps because of this atmosphere of fun and sharing, which did not translate well onto records, her reputation continued to blossom throughout the 1970's, despite increasingly mediocre record reviews and slow album sales. Raitt got a break in 1977, when her remake of the Del Shannon tune "Runaway" took her to number 57 on the *Billboard* singles charts and propelled her album *Sweet Forgiveness* to number 25.

Raitt had moved to California during the 1970's, where she met and became closely involved with a group of musicians, which included Jackson Browne, Linda Ronstadt, the band Little Feat, and others, whose style was collectively labeled the "L.A. sound." She began to record with these artists, and she used the songs of Eric Kaz extensively on her albums, but the distinctive rough edges that had characterized her earlier style got lost along the way; in the 1980's, her albums tended to be overproduced, while her song selection failed to capitalize on her musical and personal strengths. Critics were not kind, and sales of her records were dismal. After her 1979 disc *The Glow* sold only 200,000 copies, Warner Bros. made little effort to promote Raitt's next album, *Green Light* (1982).

On the political horizon, however, Raitt's activities on behalf of social causes were proving to be consistent and successful. She was a founder, along with Jackson Browne, Graham Nash, and John Hall, of MUSE (Musicians United for Safe Energy), and she recorded two songs on that group's fund-raising record *No Nukes*. She also gave fund-raising concerts for the liberal Christic Institute, the Ocean Sanctuary movement, battered women's shelters, and a group called CoMadres, made up of the mothers and wives of men killed or missing in El Salvador. Although making music is important to Raitt, social activism is what she describes as doing something meaningful.

Raitt's musical life went to pieces in the 1980's. Warner Bros. dropped her in 1983. Raitt had just completed mastering her album *Tongue in Groove* when she got the news; the album, though ready for distribution, was not released. In fact, Warner Bros. told her if she wanted to shop the mastered tapes around to a new label, the price tag would be a steep $500,000, far more than the price for which Raitt believed she could sell them. She reached into her own pocket to keep her band on the road and, in addition to regular concert dates, kept playing benefits for such causes as Farm Aid, Amnesty International, and the antiapartheid movement. Her concerts continued to receive rave reviews, but her recording career appeared to be over. At the same time, her long-term relationship with Rob Fraboni, producer of *Green Light* and *Tongue in Groove* and a member of her road band, fell apart. Raitt said in later years that this was the darkest period of her life.

In 1987, Raitt was uplifted by the chance of a collaboration with the rock star Prince. In interviews, Raitt described this opportunity as a kind of wake-up call; alarmed at the thought of appearing on video with the sensual rocker, she went on a diet. Because alcohol was the primary cause of her weight problem, she was easily convinced to join some friends at a meeting of Alcoholics Anonymous. Although the project with Prince fell through because of scheduling problems, Raitt was on the road to recovery.

Later that year, Raitt signed a new contract with Columbia Records and began working with producer Don Was on her tenth album, *Nick of Time* (1989). She wrote two songs for the album: the title song, which takes a realistic look at aging, and "The Road's My Middle Name." The album garnered immediate critical acclaim. This was partly because of a change in musical tastes; Tracy Chapman and K. D. Lang had repopularized the rawer sound that had long been Raitt's trademark. Partly, however, credit for the album's success must go to Raitt's choice of material and to Was's handling of her smoky blues sound.

In February of 1990, Raitt's twenty-year career finally brought her the acclaim she had long sought but never yet achieved; she won four Grammy awards, three for *Nick of Time*, including Best Album of the Year, Best Female Rock Vocal, and Best Female Pop Vocal, and one for a duet with John Lee Hooker on his album *The Healer* (1989). *Nick of Time* jumped to number three on the charts, selling more than two million copies.

Before the success of the Grammys, knowing even before the awards that she had a hit on her hands, Raitt locked herself away in her tiny oceanside cabin in Northern California for five days to write some new songs. Those songs, released in 1991 on the album *Luck of the Draw*, also drew critical raves as rare and soulful works in the tradition of the blues. The success of this album led to a world and national tour, and Raitt's loyal followers from the 1960's and 1970's were joined by new converts to her musical excellence.

In April of 1991, she married actor Michael O'Keefe in a ceremony in Tarrytown, New York, at which the couple was serenaded by Raitt's father. O'Keefe joined her on parts of her tour, singing on such encore numbers as "Hunk of Love." After twenty years of singing the blues, Raitt seemed finally to have found happiness.

Summary

Bonnie Raitt's commitment to traditional blues music and musicians has helped to keep that peculiarly American form of music alive and in performance. Her own strong vocals, heartfelt lyrics, and superb slide guitar and keyboard playing have earned for her a permanent place in musical history. Beyond the world of music, Raitt's active political stance provides a role model sorely needed by modern society. Raitt demonstrates that it is not enough merely to entertain; one must help to leave the world a better place.

Winning four Grammy awards in 1990 helped guarantee that Raitt's long career in the difficult and competitive field of pop music would not be forgotten. Her longevity as a female musician is unusual; her recent resurrection as a musician of popular appeal proves the value of dedication and perseverance in one's art.

Bibliography

Harris, Sheldon. *Blues Who's Who*. New Rochelle, N.Y.: Arlington House, 1979. This resource book locates Raitt within the blues tradition, gives specifics about her early career and concert dates, and offers information on some Raitt influences, including Sippie Wallace and Son House.

Henke, James. "Bonnie Raitt." *Rolling Stone*, no. 577 (May 3, 1990): 38. This, the most comprehensive interview available, covers Raitt's childhood, her musical influences, and her life both before and after winning the Grammys.

Holden, Stephen. "Bonnie Raitt Captures the Heart of Her Generation." *The New York Times*, March 25, 1990, p. B29. Discusses Raitt's recording history, giving a comprehensive view of her successes and failures, with reasons for each. Includes a discography of all Raitt's solo work.

Palmer, Robert. "A Record Star Who Keeps Her Integrity." *The New York Times*, March 24, 1977, p. C19. A comprehensive view of Raitt's early career, with some pointed questions about alcohol abuse and laudatory descriptions of her commitment to social causes.

Pond, Steve. "Raitt Keeps the Faith." *Rolling Stone*, no. 610 (August 8, 1991): 15-16. An interview that offers Raitt's perspective on her post-Grammy career. She discusses her work on *Luck of the Draw* and her marriage the same year.

Susan E. Keegan

JEANNETTE RANKIN

Born: June 11, 1880; Missoula, Montana

Died: May 18, 1973; Carmel, California

Areas of Achievement: Government and politics and social reform

Contribution: Rankin devoted her life to women's rights and peace. She was the first woman elected to Congress and the only member to vote against the entry of the United States into both world wars.

Early Life

Born in a Missoula, Montana, ranch house on June 11, 1880, Jeannette Rankin was the eldest of seven children. Her father, John Rankin, the son of Scottish immigrants, moved into Montana in the late 1860's. After prospecting for gold, he settled in Missoula, became a builder and contractor, and played a central role in the town's political and economic development. Jeannette's mother, Olive Pickering, migrated from New Hampshire to Missoula in 1878 and served the town as its schoolteacher until her marriage to John Rankin the following year. John developed a lucrative business and purchased a ranch for cattle raising and farming.

The Rankin family was close-knit and loving but fostered each member's individuality. Evenings were often spent in lively discussion and hearing stories of gold prospecting and Indian warfare in the Montana Territory. The family was also very religious, and its beliefs formed the values by which Jeannette lived her entire life.

Although she loved to read, public school bored Jeannette. She found more satisfaction in learning practical skills from her parents. From her mother, Jeannette learned sewing, and she became an expert seamstress. She studied carpentry with her father and constructed a sidewalk in downtown Missoula.

Jeannette entered Montana State University in 1898, but her college experience was as frustrating as her earlier schooling had been. Because the university was located in Missoula, the change of scenery that she desired was impossible, and because the campus was regional, little opportunity existed to meet students from diverse backgrounds. Moreover, she frequently complained that her classes were uninteresting. She completed her studies, was graduated in 1902, and for a short time taught school.

Looking for something more challenging than teaching, Jeannette drifted from one job to another—dressmaker, sawmill supervisor, and furniture builder. In 1904, Jeannette visited her brother at Harvard College in Boston. She found the city exhilarating but was shocked by the slum conditions and the extent of poverty, overcrowded dwellings, and poor health among working-class residents. Repulsed by what she witnessed, Jeannette committed herself to social work.

Life's Work

In 1908, Jeannette Rankin enrolled in the New York School of Philanthropy to study social issues and social work. After completing the program in 1910, she secured employment in a Spokane, Washington, children's home. At that time the state of Washington was considering woman suffrage. Volunteering her services, she distributed leaflets, canvassed voters door-to-door, and delivered speeches in favor of the state suffrage amendment. Washington granted women the right to vote in November, and her participation sparked an enthusiasm that placed Jeannette on a crusade for woman suffrage and social reform.

Rankin returned to Montana in December, 1910, for the Christmas holidays and learned that her home state had scheduled debate on a suffrage amendment for January. She quickly organized the Equal Franchise Society, requested and received an invitation from the state assembly to speak on behalf of the amendment, and presented a well-received argument for woman suffrage. Although the amendment was not passed until 1913, Jeannette was instrumental in its eventual victory.

Having gained a taste for social reform politics, Jeannette Rankin became a member of the National-American Woman Suffrage Association (NAWSA) and joined organizations in several states. By autumn of 1914, she had lobbied and spoken before the legislatures of ten states, marched in rallies in major cities, and petitioned Congress for a national woman suffrage amendment. Rankin was quickly becoming a national personality.

In 1914, war erupted in Europe. Although the United States was not involved, Rankin feared that it might be unable to remain neutral. War, she reasoned, would shift the public's attention from social issues and slow the movement for woman suffrage. While in New York, Rankin helped to form the Women's Peace Party in January, 1915, and lobbied Congress to stay out of the European conflict. Although she spent the next summer in Montana organizing "good government clubs" designed to eliminate corruption and to increase women's rights, she devoted most of her time to speaking and writing against American entry into World War I.

In 1916, the likelihood of war led Jeannette Rankin to take the boldest step of her career. Against the advice of Republican Party leaders, Rankin announced her candidacy for election to the U.S. House of Representatives. Her personal platform reflected her professional goals—an amendment to the U.S. Constitution for woman suffrage, child protection laws, social justice, and good government. She was most demanding regarding continued American neutrality. Her antiwar views, which most Montana voters shared, brought her victory in November. Jeannette Rankin was the only Republican to win office in Montana that year and the first woman in American history to take a seat in the United States Congress.

Jeannette Rankin took the oath of office on April 1, 1917, but the warm welcome she received did not last long. On April 5, the House of Representatives commenced debate on American entry into the Great War. Special attention was focused on Rankin. She symbolically represented all women in the nation. Her vote for or against war would be interpreted as a woman's ability to deal with political crises.

The House debated the war resolution throughout the night. Rankin chose to remain silent but listened intently to the heated arguments. Tensions rose as opponents of war were jeered, hissed, and verbally branded as unpatriotic. When the House voted, Jeannette Rankin rose to her feet. "I want to stand by my country," she said, "but I cannot vote for war. I vote no." She found herself in the minority. Three hundred seventy-four representatives supported the resolution, while only fifty voted against war. On April 7, 1917, President Woodrow Wilson declared war on Germany.

Hannah Josephson stated in her biography *Jeannette Rankin, First Lady in Congress* (1974) that Rankin was warned before the vote that she might lose reelection because of her antiwar stance. Her opposition to war was far more important to her than her concern for reelection. The public's response was swift. Rankin was labeled unpatriotic and a disgrace to women nationwide. Even the National-American Woman Suffrage Association claimed that her vote against war would lose supporters for a constitutional suffrage amendment. Rankin later said that her vote against war was the most significant one she ever made. Women, she believed, had to take the lead to end war.

Once the nation was committed to war, Jeannette Rankin supported American troops, worked in Congress to protect civil liberties, and pushed for social reform. She championed legislation authorizing the government to hire more women workers, to provide financial relief to families of soldiers, to improve conditions for imprisoned women, and to guarantee food, clothing, shelter, and health care for children living in poverty. She participated in congressional debates on a federal amendment for woman suffrage, which Congress finally sent to the states for approval in 1918. As her term in the House of Representatives ended, however, Rankin's antiwar vote resurfaced and caused her defeat for reelection.

During the twenty years which followed, Rankin toured the nation promoting feminist issues. She served the National Consumers' League, which advocated federal child labor laws, better working conditions, and increased women's rights. Most of her energy, however, was directed toward achieving international peace.

The horrors of World War I still vivid in her mind, and aware that social justice could never be attained as long as money was spent on defense and warfare, Rankin helped to form the Women's International League for Peace and Freedom and volunteered her services to numerous other peace organizations. She campaigned against Reserve Officers Training Corps programs on college campuses. She was a central figure at the Conference on the Cause and Cure for War, participated in the Peace March on Chicago, lobbied congressmen to introduce legislation to outlaw war, and advocated the creation of a National Peace Party to challenge both Republicans and Democrats in state and federal elections. As the 1930's drew to a close and the prospect for another world war seemed likely, Rankin intensified her efforts.

In November, 1940, at age sixty, Jeannette Rankin was again elected to Congress on a peace platform. She proposed bills to prevent the sending of American troops abroad and to require a national vote before war could be declared. Neither measure passed, but she persisted throughout 1941. Despite Japan's attack on Pearl Harbor on December 7, Rankin stood for peace regardless of personal consequences. On December 8, Congress voted for war. This time, Rankin cast the only vote in opposition. As before, Rankin received the brunt of public criticism and was not reelected the following year.

Until her death in 1973, Jeannette Rankin traveled the world. The extent of global poverty and injustice she witnessed intensified her belief that only in a peaceful world could social problems be resolved. Based on this view, she condemned America's war in Vietnam throughout the 1960's. In January, 1968, she participated in an antiwar march on Washington. The Jeannette Rankin Brigade, so named by her admirers, petitioned Congress to end the war and "heal a sick society at home."

Summary

Until her death on May 18, 1973, Jeannette Rankin pressed her demands for an end to war, protection of civil liberties, and direct popular vote on critical national issues. She never realized her dream to end war, but she was responsible, directly or indirectly, for the creation of many laws. Her efforts resulted in voting rights for women, support for dependents of servicemen, free postage for members of the armed forces, retention of citizenship for women who marry aliens, child labor and protection laws, and women's rights. Throughout her life she spoke on behalf of labor, for child welfare, for social justice and greater democracy, and against racial prejudice. She further advocated multimember congressional districts, a unicameral Congress, direct election of the president, and the restructuring of the U.S. military into a purely defensive force. Her two elections to Congress opened avenues for women nationally in politics and business. Although she was labeled an idealist and was criticized severely for her antiwar position, Jeannette Rankin possessed the courage to remain true to her convictions and dedicated her life to the betterment of American society and the human race.

Bibliography

Chafe, William H. *The American Woman: Her Changing Social, Economic, and Political Roles, 1920-1970*. New York: Oxford University Press, 1972. Chafe develops a thorough, detailed study of American feminism in the twentieth century, illuminating its development, course, and reception by American society. This work has become a standard in the field and accurately presents Rankin's era.

Dedication of the Statue of Jeannette Rankin. Washington, D.C.: Government Printing Office, 1986. This publication includes a biographical sketch of Rankin and speeches given by prominent political figures in remembrance of her advocacy of women's rights and an end to war. Included is a time line of Jeannette Rankin's life.

Josephson, Hannah. *Jeannette Rankin, First Lady in Congress*. Indianapolis: Bobbs-Merrill, 1974. Although many prominent and influential women with whom Rankin worked receive limited attention and the broad context in which Rankin operated is somewhat vague, Josephson has presented a complete, well-researched biography of Jeannette Rankin. The author's twenty-year personal relationship with Rankin makes the work most insightful and revealing.

Libby, Frederick J. *To End War*. Nyack, N.Y.: Fellowship Publications, 1969. Libby surveys the patterns of antiwar thought and peace organizations in twentieth century America.

Noble, David W. *The Progressive Mind, 1890-1917*. Rev. ed. Minneapolis, Minn.: Burgess, 1981. This work provides an overview of the intellectual foundations of the Progressive Era and the evolution in thought of Progressives themselves. One chapter devoted exclusively to women of the period adequately highlights the feminist movement.

Kenneth W. Townsend

JANET RENO

Born: July 21, 1938; Miami, Florida

Areas of Achievement: Law and government and politics

Contribution: As Florida's first female state attorney, Janet Reno focused on the root causes of criminal behavior, instituting programs to change the social and personal conditions that lead people to commit crimes. As the first woman attorney general of the United States, she declared her intention to reorient the national crime policy in the same way—toward prevention first, and then punishment.

Early Life

Janet Reno was born on July 21, 1938, in the Coconut Grove section of Miami, Florida. Her father, Henry Reno, was a Danish immigrant who worked as a police reporter for the *Miami Herald* for forty-three years until his death in 1967. Her mother, Jane Wood Reno, was an investigative reporter for the *Miami News*. Her maternal grandmother was Daisy Sloan Hunter Wood, a genteel southern lady who instilled in her children and grandchildren a passionate commitment to duty and family.

Janet was the oldest of the Renos' four children, each born a year apart. In 1946, the family bought twenty-one acres on what was then the edge of the Everglades, twenty miles outside Miami. Jane Reno built the family house, where Janet still lives and where she lived with her mother until the latter's death on December 21, 1992. The house became a symbol to Janet that she could do anything she really wanted, if it was right, and if she put her mind to it.

The house had no air conditioning or central heating, and no television. Janet spent much of her time outdoors and developed a love of camping and canoeing. Her family's love of books, poetry, world affairs, and music linked her to the outside world.

While Janet got much of her independent spirit from her mother, who did not tolerate cosmetics, organized religion, or racism, she was also greatly influenced by her father. He was a gentle man who understood protocol. He taught his children compassion and social justice, always treating people with respect and dignity. He told his children stories of police officers, judges, and officials, most of whom were wise, compassionate, and honorable. Janet was drawn to government by the judges and police officers Henry brought home.

Janet attended public schools in Dade County, Florida. In 1960, she graduated from Cornell University with a bachelor's degree in chemistry. At Cornell, she was president of the Women's Student Government and earned her spending money by working as a waitress. She received her LL.B. degree in 1963 from Harvard Law School, where she was one of sixteen women in a class of 500.

Denied a position in one of Miami's large law firms because she was a woman, she took a position in a smaller firm. In 1971, she received her first political appointment as staff director of the Judiciary Committee of the Florida House of Representatives.

In 1972, she ran for a seat in the state legislature and lost, but cheered herself with the knowledge that Abraham Lincoln had also lost his first election.

Life's Work

Janet Reno's career in public service began to flourish when she joined the state attorney's office in Dade County, Florida, in 1973. While there, she was assigned to organize a juvenile division within the prosecutor's office. It was at this time that she began developing views about preventive crime-fighting through services to children and rehabilitating delinquent youths. From 1976 to 1978, she left public service briefly to become a partner in the Miami-based law firm of Steel, Hector and Davis, the same firm that refused to give her a job thirteen years earlier because she was a woman. In 1978 she was appointed by the governor of Florida to serve as Dade County State Attorney, becoming Florida's first female state attorney.

Janet Reno was elected five times to the post of state attorney for Dade County, running as a Democrat in a heavily Republican district. She believed that the first objective of a prosecutor should be to make sure innocent people do not get charged. The second objective should be to convict the guilty according to due process.

Reno took office when racial tension, drug trafficking, and illegal immigration from Cuba, Haiti, and South America were all on the rise. She gained widespread criticism in 1980, when her office failed to convict four white police officers who had been charged with beating to death a black insurance salesman. Miami's black community erupted into three days of rioting and black community leaders called for her resignation.

Reno systematically set out to mend fences with the black community. She attended social functions and meetings, listened to their opinions as well as their anger, and took the time to explain her decisions. She marched in the Martin Luther King, Jr., Day Parade every year following the riots. Her office hired more blacks and Latinos and tackled issues important to minorities. Her policy of pursuing delinquent fathers for child support also helped her gain widespread respect in the black community. When she marched in the Martin Luther King, Jr., Day Parade five years after the Miami riots, she received a standing ovation.

As Dade state attorney she reformed the juvenile justice system, and began aggressively prosecuting child abuse cases. She also instituted a domestic-violence intervention program that relied heavily on counseling for victims and abusers. Beginning in the mid-1980's, she advocated a new approach to the prosecutor's traditional mission, one best described as preventive crime-fighting by trying to get at the root cause of crime. Since most people who go to jail eventually return to their communities, Reno chose to emphasize the importance of rehabilitation. She stated her view that imprisonment cannot serve as the ultimate solution to crime, although she did support life imprisonment sentences for the most violent criminals.

During her term in office, Reno developed a community policing team that helped clean up a crime-ridden Miami housing project. In 1989, she established Miami's innovative drug court, which offered first-time drug offenders a chance to wipe their records clean if they completed a year-long treatment program. Approximately sixty percent of those who start the program finish it, and ninety percent of those who finish remained trouble-free a year later. The court became a model for dozens of others around the country.

In 1990, Reno extended her office's pioneering approach to justice still further, offering young, nonviolent offenders a chance to avoid confinement and a criminal record by undertaking a program of rehabilitation which may include making restitution to their victims.

Reno's accomplishments and support for law and order issues brought her to the attention of the Clinton Administration. On March 12, 1993, Janet Reno was sworn in as the seventy-eighth Attorney General of the United States, the first woman ever to hold that post. Following her swearing-in ceremony, in her first act as attorney general, she told reporters that she intended to protect women who sought abortions from harassment by antiabortion protesters.

She made what may turn out to be the most difficult decision of her career in April, 1993, when she ordered the Federal Bureau of Investigation (FBI) to launch an assault on the Branch Davidian cult compound outside Waco, Texas. The FBI and representatives of the Bureau of Alcohol, Tobacco, and Firearms (ATF) had been locked in a tense confrontation with the cult and its leader, David Koresh, for several weeks; Reno believed the children in the compound were being physically abused. In the end, eighty-six people, including seventeen children, died in the fire that followed. Shortly thereafter, Reno, visibly distraught, took full responsibility for the tragedy. Her earnest manner and the fact that she did not pass blame impressed both Washington officials and ordinary citizens.

As attorney general, Reno hopes to revolutionize how America thinks about law enforcement. She has encouraged government agencies, federal, state, and local, to work together to address the root causes of crime. She wants to start with good prenatal care, continuing to ensure that all children will have adequate health care, education, supervision, jobs and job training. She has advocated flexible workdays so that parents can be home when their children get out of school, and plans to implement flex time at the Justice Department.

She has acknowledged that most of the country's successful crime programs come from local communities, not the federal government, but believes that one of her responsibilities is to keep talking about her crime prevention ideas in order to promote an ongoing, national dialogue. Her enormous influence on the criminal justice debate outside Washington cuts across the political spectrum. She has persuaded the American Bar Association to broaden its criminal studies by examining the needs of children.

Summary

In her years as Florida state attorney for Dade County, Janet Reno gained a reputation as a hard-working prosecutor with a social conscience, and fought for better children's services as a way of preventing crime. In addition, she instituted innovative rehabilitation programs for first-time offenders.

As the first woman attorney general of the United States, Reno brought unquestioned integrity to the office and has been recognized nationally for her strength and honesty. She has become known as a direct, strong-willed, but compassionate politician with a record of attacking the root causes of criminal behavior. In a break with her Republican predecessors, Reno has envisioned her preeminent role as reorienting national crime policy, calling for comprehensive programs that provide a balance between punishment and prevention. Believing society's resources should go toward better education, housing and health care, not more jails, Reno also has stated that she believes hardened criminals should be locked up permanently. As the people's lawyer, she has stated that she wants to be accessible to all citizens and to know what is happening on the streets of America, not just in the Justice Department. By implementing her plans to shift national crime-fighting priorities from punishment of crime to crime prevention, Reno has begun to establish her mark on law enforcement nationwide.

Bibliography

Anderson, Paul. *Janet Reno: Doing the Right Thing*. New York: John Wiley & Sons, 1994. Written by a reporter for the *Miami Herald* who observed Reno for many years, this first book-length biography chronicles Reno's lively family history (her immigrant grandfather discarded his Rasmussen surname in favor of "Reno" upon his arrival), her college and law school years, and her legal career. Emphasizes Reno's integrity, common sense, and strong work ethic.

Gibbs, Nancy. "Truth, Justice and the Reno Way." *Time* 142 (July 12, 1993): 20-27. Provides an in-depth overview of Reno's history and her plans for the Justice Department, specifically focusing on her advocacy for children and cooperation among government agencies as a way to prevent crime.

Laughlin, Meg. "Growing up Reno." *Lear's* 6 (July, 1993): 48-51. Written by a Miami-based writer, the article focuses on Reno's upbringing, yet also includes brief highlights of her career.

Reno, Janet. "A Common-Sense Approach to Justice." *Judicature* 77 (September, 1993): 66-67. An edited transcript of Reno's address to the annual dinner of the American Judicature Society, August 6, 1993. Reno discusses her goals as attorney general and the role of lawyers in society.

____________. "As State Prosecutor: Respected, Abused, Liked and Hated." In *Women Lawyers: Perspectives on Success*, edited by Emily Couric. New York: Law and Business/Harcourt Brace Jovanovich, 1984. Reno discusses her job as Florida state attorney for Dade County, covering the years 1978-1982. Readable, concise explanation of her thoughts and the philosophy behind some of her actions.

Simon, Charnan. *Janet Reno: First Woman Attorney General*. Chicago: Children's Press, 1994. One of the first juvenile biographies about Reno to appear in print, this work provides a useful introduction to Reno's life and career up through her first year as attorney general.

Wood, Chris. "World: America's Top Cop." *Maclean's* 106 (April 5, 1993): 18-20. Discussion of Reno as Florida state attorney for Dade County. Includes information on various programs instituted by Reno to prevent crime, such as Miami's drug court.

Sarah Thomas

ANN RICHARDS

Born: September 1, 1933; Lakeview, Texas

Area of Achievement: Government and politics
Contribution: A longtime activist in Texas Democratic politics, Ann Richards became Texas' second woman governor in 1990 and was the first woman to be elected to that office based on her own merit.

Early Life

Ann Richards was born Dorothy Ann Willis on September 1, 1933, in the rural Texas town of Lakeview, near Waco. Her parents, Cecil Willis and Iona Warren Willis, were children of farmers who had been part of a wave of immigration to Texas during the late nineteenth century. Cecil's family settled on a farm in the Waco area, but Iona moved to Waco (where she met Cecil on a blind date) from Hico—a town just south of Fort Worth—to work in a dry-goods store. The move was not typical for rural Texas women, but Iona was ambitious and independent—qualities that she later instilled in her daughter Ann.

Cecil's salary as delivery truck driver was not large, but both he and Iona valued hard work. Like many people who lived through the Depression, they were also frugal. In order to give Ann all they could, they had no more children. Ann did not experience great hardship or poverty. Nevertheless, Ann was given a rather strict upbringing; she was responsible for much regular work around the house, and she was constantly given special projects to complete. There were also limits placed on the amount of time Ann was allowed to spend socializing. Her parents were active in the community, and they emphasized common-sense notions of decency and fairness in community affairs, sowing the seeds for Ann's later progressive political philosophy.

Ann attended Waco High School, where she was an outgoing student who excelled at debate. She was selected as a delegate to the Girls State mock government in Austin during her junior year, and then as one of two Texas delegates to attend Girls Nation in Washington, D.C., where she shook hands with President Harry Truman. This experience was her first real introduction to both politics and the world outside Waco. While in high school, Ann met her future husband, David Richards.

After her graduation from Waco High in 1950, Ann attended Baylor University on a debate scholarship. David Richards transferred from the University of Texas to Baylor in 1953, and he and Ann were married the same year. They both were graduated in 1954. They then moved to Austin, where David enrolled in the University of Texas Law School and Ann took graduate courses in education and earned her teaching certificate. In 1955, Ann took a job teaching social studies and history at a junior high school in Austin, a post she held until 1956.

Life's Work

It was in Austin as a graduate student that Ann Richards first became involved in

Texas politics. She and her husband became active in the University of Texas chapter of the Young Democrats, and they regularly socialized with other liberal Democrats who supported Lyndon B. Johnson, who was engaged in a power struggle with conservative Allen Shivers for control of the Texas Democratic party. In Austin, Richards made many of the political contacts on which she would later depend during her campaigns for state office.

After his graduation from law school, David Richards began work in a Dallas labor law firm, and, after giving birth at home in Waco, Ann and their new child Cecile Richards joined him there. While the two remained active in the Austin Young Democrats during this period, Ann also spent considerable time volunteering on political campaigns, such as civil rights supporter Henry Gonzalez's 1958 gubernatorial race, progressive Ralph Yarborough's 1952, 1954, and 1956 gubernatorial campaigns, and Yarborough's successful senatorial race in 1957.

It was while Ann Richards was working on the 1960 John F. Kennedy/Lyndon B. Johnson presidential campaign in Dallas that David announced they were to move to Washington, D.C., so that he could begin work as a staff attorney on the national Civil Rights Commission. The two socialized with many transplanted Texas Democrats while in the nation's capital, and they had occasion to meet Johnson while he was vice president. Nevertheless, they soon tired of life in Washington and moved back to Dallas in 1962.

While in Dallas, Ann helped form the North Dallas Democratic Women's group, and she served as its president for a time. She also helped organize the Dallas Committee for Peaceful Integration to fight for the integration of the public schools, a radical view to support in Texas at the time. Ann also continued to spend considerable time rearing her family, giving birth to her sons Clark and Dan.

Though the Richards' lives in Dallas had been rewarding, by 1969 the pull of Austin was too great, and the family moved back. Ann Richards served on the local zoning and planning commission, and, in 1971, she was asked to advise Sarah Weddington about her run for the Texas legislature. Richards devised a way to create a targeted mass mailing for the campaign, and Weddington won the election in 1972. Richards went to work as Weddington's administrative assistant. She also continued to work on other Democratic campaigns during this period, including Wilhemina Delco's successful attempt in 1974 to become the first black woman to be elected to the Texas state legislature.

In 1975, David Richards was asked to run against Johnny Voudouris in the Democratic primary for county commissioner. When David turned down the offer, Ann was asked to step in. The request was particularly unusual because the county commissioner was responsible for overseeing all county road crews, and the position had always been occupied by men. After a shrewd and targeted campaign, Ann beat three-term incumbent Voudouris in the primary and went on to win the general election in the fall.

As county commissioner, and despite initial prejudice, Ann Richards managed to cultivate good relationships with her largely conservative male employees and was able to improve the county road system. She also provided increased funding for support services through her oversight of the county Human Services division.

As a result of Richards' innovations at county Human Services, Lieutenant Governor Bill Hobby appointed her to a special committee to overhaul the delivery of human services statewide. While serving as county commissioner, Richards was asked to serve on President Jimmy Carter's Advisory Committee for Women, where she met many of the most influential women of the time, such as congressional representative Bella Abzug, while they lobbied the president for his support of the Equal Rights Amendment.

Although these years were professionally very good for Ann Richards, her marriage was under increasing stress. As the couple continued to grow apart, Ann's drinking also increased, until it became such a problem that in 1980, at the behest of David and their closest friends, she sought treatment. Although the treatment for alcoholism was successful, the marriage did not improve, and the two were separated. They were divorced in 1984.

During the separation, in 1982, Ann Richards was asked to run in the Democratic primary for state treasurer against Warren Harding. The campaign turned ugly, and Richards' alcoholism became a central issue. She remained forthright and honest about the subject, and the smear tactics backfired. Harding eventually withdrew, and Richards went on to beat Republican Allen Clark by a wide margin in November. She was the first woman to hold a Texas state office in fifty years.

Richards' reforms in the state's revenue system while treasurer—the implementation of up-to-date technology to assist depositing and processing of state money, and reductions in paper work—eventually earned for the state of Texas more than two billion dollars in nontax revenue. She was reelected in 1986.

Her performance as treasurer again brought Richards to the attention of national Democratic leaders, and she was invited to second the nomination of Walter Mondale as the Democratic candidate for president in 1984 and to give the keynote address at the 1988 Democratic National Convention. Her speech at the 1988 convention was an outright, plainspoken assault on Republican nominee George Bush, and it was a smashing success.

In 1990, Richards mounted a gubernatorial campaign to replace retiring Republican Governor William Clements. During the primary, her alcoholism again became an issue, and her reluctance to respond to questions about drug abuse hurt her popularity considerably. Yet, as before, the political mudslinging backfired when it was revealed that her opponent had himself possibly used illegal drugs. Richards won the Democratic nomination.

Her Republican opponent Clayton Williams' marked insensitivity to women's issues and Richards' strong prochoice stance led large numbers of Republican women to vote for her, and on November 6, 1990, Ann Richards was elected governor of Texas. She was the first woman to become governor of Texas in more than fifty years and was the first ever to do so based on her own merits.

As governor, Ann Richards set a progressive agenda for the conservative state and appointed unprecedented numbers of women, Latinos, and African Americans to state offices. She also contributed to the state's economic recovery after several years of recession. In recognition of her achievements both in Texas and on the national political scene, Richards was asked to chair the Democratic National Convention in 1992. In 1994, Richards campaigned for reelection and lost to a Republican candidate whose political connections, wealth, and family name constituted a serious challenge to Richards' bid for another four-year term: George Walker Bush, the forty-eight-year-old son of former President George Bush.

Summary

Ann Richards managed to thrive in the political environment of Texas, a state famous for its conservatism and male-dominated "old-boy" power network. While rewriting the rules of gender and power in Texas, she also managed to implement a decidedly reformist and progressive agenda to a state government woefully bogged down in "cronyism."

A tireless supporter of women's issues and civil rights, she appointed unprecedented numbers of women and minorities to positions of power. A consummate politician, Richards managed both to pierce the "glass ceiling" for women in Texas politics and to develop a power network composed of women, minorities, and liberals that rivaled that of the male-dominated, oil-industry-backed politicians who had been in control in Texas for so long.

Richards also had an impact on national politics. Her plain speaking and firecracker wit launched her into prominence on the national political scene, and, along with several other women Democrats newly elected to major offices, she helped keep the national Democratic Party focused on women's issues while proving to other women that they could succeed in politics in even the most male-dominated of arenas. Richards' forthrightness about her alcoholism and her past marital troubles also set an example for the nation. Ann Richards proved that women could be single and independent and still be successful in the public sphere.

Bibliography

Dow, Bonnie J., and Mari Boor Tonn. "'Feminine Style' and Political Judgment in the Rhetoric of Ann Richards." *The Quarterly Journal of Speech* 79 (August, 1993): 286-302. An in-depth, scholarly treatment of Richards' rhetoric and political oratory, including content analysis and a consideration of the issues of feminism and psychology.

Morris, Celia. *Storming the State House: Running for Governor with Ann Richards and Dianne Feinstein*. New York: Charles Scribner's Sons, 1992. A very detailed narrative account of the campaigns mounted by two women for the governorships of their states. The Ann Richards section does a good job of capturing the flavor of Texas politics. The work argues that Richards' and Feinstein's pursuit of higher office constitute a cultural revolution.

Richards, Ann. *Straight from the Heart*. New York: Simon & Schuster, 1989. An autobiography written in an informal style, this work reflects Richards' personality. It also provides much information about life as a liberal in Texas politics.

Witt, Linda, Karen M. Paget, and Glenna Matthews. *Running as a Woman: Gender and Power in American Politics*. New York: Free Press, 1993. A journalist, a political scientist, and a historian collaborated on this narrative overview of the experiences of women candidates in American politics. Although this work focuses primarily on women candidates at the national level, the authors include Richards' comments on her early campaign work on behalf of Sarah Weddington.

Colin Ramsey

SALLY RIDE

Born: May 26, 1951; Encino, California

Areas of Achievement: Aeronautics and astrophysics
Contribution: An astronaut for the National Aeronautics and Space Administration (NASA) and the first American woman to fly in space.

Early Life

Sally Kristen Ride was born on May 26, 1951, in Encino, a suburb of Los Angeles, California. She was the older of two daughters born to Dale B. Ride, a member of the faculty at Santa Monica Community College, and his wife, Joyce. Sally's parents were active as elders in their Presbyterian church, and Joyce Ride often volunteered her time as an English tutor to foreign-born students and as a counselor at a women's prison.

Sally's parents encouraged her competitive spirit in academics and in athletics. Sally was a born athlete and often played the rough and tumble games of football and baseball with the neighborhood boys. Ride began playing tennis, a less hazardous sport, at the request of her mother. Under the tutelage of tennis great Alice Marble, Sally quickly excelled in this sport and became proficient enough to rank eighteenth nationally. Her excellence in tennis earned her a partial scholarship to Westlake School for Girls, a private preparatory school in Los Angeles. At the preparatory school, Sally became interested in the study of physics through the influence of her science teacher, Elizabeth Mommaerts, and, for the next five years, science and tennis competed for Sally's time and attention.

In 1968, Sally enrolled at Swarthmore College in Pennsylvania as a physics major, but left after three terms to concentrate on her tennis game after winning a national collegiate tennis tournament. Although she was a top-ranked college player, she realized that she did not have the talent to advance to professional tennis. Sally returned to college in 1970 and completed a double major in English literature and physics at Stanford University in California in 1973. After graduation, she briefly considered continuing with Shakespeare in graduate school, but settled on astrophysics to further her dream of working for NASA.

Life's Work

Sally Ride began her path to fame while completing work on her doctoral dissertation at Stanford. One day she read an announcement in the campus newspaper indicating that NASA was seeking young scientists to serve as "mission specialists." Acting on impulse, she applied to join the astronaut program, which had lifted its long-standing ban against women in order to attract additional qualified scientists willing to forgo high salaries in order to work on the new space shuttle program. To Ride's surprise, she made it through the preliminary screening process to become one of the finalists. In 1977, she was flown to the Lyndon B. Johnson Space Center outside

Houston, Texas, for exhausting interviews and fitness and psychiatric evaluation tests. After three months of rigorous testing, Sally Ride officially became an astronaut. In 1978, shortly after earning her Ph.D. degree, she reported to the Johnson Space Center to begin the intensive training required of NASA mission specialists.

In the first year of training, Ride learned parachute jumping and water survival techniques, the latter for the possibility that the shuttle might be ditched in the ocean. She also became acclimated to increased gravity forces, the force encountered during acceleration and deceleration back to earth, as well as to weightlessness. Ride took courses in radio communication and navigation and learned to fly a jet. Piloting a jet proved to be an enjoyable experience for Sally Ride, and she eventually acquired a pilot's license.

Throughout Ride's entire preparation time, NASA maintained its bureaucratic composure regarding its inclusion of women in the space shuttle program. There was no flamboyant talk about one giant step for womankind. Indeed, team player that she was, Ride insisted that her participation in the flight was "no big deal." Whether she liked it or not, news of her flight brought her instant celebrity. Newspapers and television reporters interviewed her again and again, and even President Ronald Reagan gave her an extra share of attention at a White House luncheon. Composer Casse Culver wrote and recorded a song entitled "Ride, Sally, Ride" to celebrate the event, and T-shirts urged the same.

Sally Ride was specifically requested by Navy Captain Robert L. Crippen, a veteran astronaut who had piloted the first shuttle mission in 1981. Crippen said, of his choice of Ride: "She is flying with us because she is the very best person for the job. There is no man I would rather have in her place." Ride, in her unassuming manner, simply stated that she had not become an astronaut to become "a historic figure," and that she believed it was "time that people realized that women in this country can do any job that they want to do." Ride's special virtue was that she was so much like the male astronauts and so utterly and convincingly their equal. She was just as determined, just as disciplined, just as fearless, and just as predictable.

Aboard the *Challenger*, Ride had duties in addition to her scientific work. She was chosen to sit behind mission commander Crippen and copilot Frederick Hauck to act as flight engineer during takeoff and landing. During the ninety-six orbits, she and her fellow mission specialist, John Fabian, worked in weightless conditions with the complex Canadarm—a fifty-foot remote "arm" used to move payloads in and out of the shuttle cargo bay. Ride and Fabian trained for two years on the ground with the computerized arm and became experts in its operation. Another task on the mission was to place Anik-C, a Canadian domestic communications satellite, in a geosynchronous orbit hovering above the equator. This satellite was designed to handle thirty-two color television channels. A second communications satellite, named Palapa-B and owned by Indonesia, was launched into orbit to carry voice, video, and telephone signals to southeast Asia.

Forty other experiments were conducted by the *Challenger* crew. These included studies of metal alloy manufacture, solar cell testing, growth of semiconductor crystals, and glass production. One experiment, devised by high-school students, was a project sending 150 carpenter ants into orbit in the shuttle cargo bay to see how weightlessness affects their social structure. The California Institute of Technology sent an experiment in which radish seedlings were subjected to simulated gravity to find the right gravitational force for best growth. Purdue University's experiment investigated how sunflower seeds germinated in zero gravity. The highlight of the mission was the deployment of a huge free-floating satellite in order to document its position with the first in-space color photographs before recapturing it. The satellite was then released again and snared once more. The crew repeated this procedure for nine and one-half hours before Ride captured the satellite for the last time and stowed it in the cargo bay for the trip home.

Sally's ride (a pun often used by the media) was only one sign of a major change in what could no longer be called the United States manned space program. Much of the daredevil aspect had gone out of space travel. The object was not simply getting into orbit but working there. In fact, Sally Ride recommended that space be used to study the planet Earth to NASA administrator James Fletcher, who made her his special assistant for Long Range and Strategic Planning.

Being a space pioneer was more important to Sally Ride than achieving celebrity as a woman astronaut. Specialists have since been recruited from the ranks of male and female scientists. For all the merits of the scientific and experimental aspects of the Challenger voyage, it was Sally Ride who provoked the world's curiosity. Cool, calm and apparently controlled in any circumstance, Sally Kristen Ride hurtled through space aboard the 100-ton white and blue shuttle *Challenger*. Sally Ride showed that she was certainly made of "the right stuff."

Summary

Although two Soviet women preceded Sally Ride into space, they hardly left their mark on it. About 1963, in the early days of manned spaceflight, a twenty-six-year-old textile mill worker and amateur sky diver named Valentina Tereshkova was put on a rocket by the Soviet Union as a propaganda coup. Reports of that flight say that Tereshkova was sick for most of the three-day flight.

In August of 1982, the Soviets launched the second woman cosmonaut—a thirty-four-year-old test pilot named Svetlana Savitskaya. Her presence, however, was taken lightly by her colleagues.

Ride's mission came to signify the ascendancy of the mission specialist over the pilot. The close-knit brotherhood of test and fighter pilots who made up the original astronaut corps was diluted by those having a new kind of "right stuff"—the ability to do quadratic equations and conduct scientific experiments instead of mere fancy flying. Under these new guidelines, Ride was an ideal candidate not only because of her excellent scientific background but also because she exhibited the ability to learn new skills and solve problems readily. Sally Ride's experiences on the space shuttle earned for her the trust and high regard of her colleagues as well as the admiration of an entire nation.

Bibliography

Begley, Sharon. "Challenger: Ride, Sally Ride." *Newsweek* 101 (June 13, 1983): 20-21. An overview of Sally Ride's life and the results of her crucial decision to join the elite NASA astronaut group in preparation for missions on the space shuttle.

Fox, Mary Virginia. *Women Astronauts Aboard the Shuttle*. Rev. ed. New York: Julian Messner, 1987. Chronicles the experiences of the women who have been selected to participate in the space shuttle program. Aimed at young readers, this work focuses particular attention on Ride's experiences as the first American woman to fly in space while providing equally useful profiles of the various women who followed. Touches on Ride's decision to leave the astronaut program in 1987.

Golden, Frederic. "Sally's Joy Ride into the Sky." *Time* 121 (June 27, 1983): 56-58. In the magazine's "Space" section, Golden tells of Ride's experiences on the second orbiting flight of the space shuttle *Challenger* and includes some of Ride's own observations regarding the public's reaction to her flight.

Otto, Dixon P. *On Orbit: Bringing on the Space Shuttle*. Athens, Ohio: Main Stage Publications, 1986. Aimed at a general audience, this work examines the space shuttle from its design origins through its first twenty-five flights. Contains information about the crew members, payloads, and objectives of each flight as well as many black-and-white illustrations highlighting these missions. Provides a context for understanding Ride's experiences in the space shuttle program.

Ride, Sally, with Susan Okie. *To Space and Back*. New York: Lothrop, Lee & Shepard Books, 1986. Written for a young audience, this book describes the human side of being a member of an astronaut crew. Ride shares her personal experience of space travel on the space shuttle. The book does a fine job of revealing both the remarkable talents and the more ordinary characteristics of those individuals who have chosen to become space pioneers.

Ride, Sally, and Tam O'Shaughnessy. *Voyager: An Adventure to the Edge of the Solar System*. New York: Crown, 1992. Although this work is not specifically related to her shuttle experiences, Ride does draw upon her astrophysics background in order to create this popular account of the two Voyager spacecraft that were launched during the late 1970's in order to explore and transmit images of four of the solar system's most distant planets: Jupiter, Saturn, Uranus, and Neptune.

Jane A. Slezak

ALICE RIVLIN

Born: March 4, 1931; Philadelphia, Pennsylvania

Areas of Achievement: Economics and government and politics
Contributions: A public affairs economist, Rivlin has found herself equally at home in government service, research institutions, and university teaching.

Early Life

Alice Mitchell Rivlin has functioned throughout her professional life on an important seam in American public affairs—the point of intersection between academics and think tanks on the one hand and national government and policy making on the other. Like others who make their home at this juncture, she has worked for a prestigious national institution of policy analysis, engaged in university teaching, and on occasion has accepted appointments in her areas of specialty in the public sector. The background of such people can vary, but the typical career path involves an emphasis on the mainstream of American economic, social, and political thought, and entry into the world of the research institutions almost immediately from graduate school. Alice Rivlin's career illustrates the model well.

Born in Philadelphia in 1931 to Allan and Georgianna Mitchell at nearly the height of the Great Depression, Alice Mitchell received her B.A. degree from Bryn Mawr College in 1952 and a Ph.D. from Radcliffe College six years later. Both schools existed to provide an outstanding education to American women at a time when many of the country's most prestigious private universities were restricted to males, and both offered their graduates demanding training and as good a network into national affairs as was available to American women at the time.

While still working on her doctorate, Alice Mitchell married Lewis Allen Rivlin, with whom she would have three children (Catherine Amy, Allan Mitchell, and Douglas Gray) before their divorce in 1977. In 1957, she took a position as a member of the staff of the Brookings Institution on northwest Massachusetts Avenue in central Washington, D.C. The Brookings Institution has long been one of Washington's most famous institutes of public policy analysis, and Alice Rivlin has essentially lived in Washington and—except for her work in government—has remained affiliated with the Brookings Institution since that time.

Life's Work

Alice Rivlin's initial employment at Brookings lasted for nearly a decade, during which her research focused on education and intergovernmental financial relations, two areas of national interest in the late Eisenhower years and throughout the Kennedy and Johnson administrations. In 1966, she received her first full time appointment to a "political executive" position in the Johnson Administration. Typical of the opportunities normally awarded to academics making the transition to government, the initial post was not an especially lofty one—deputy assistant secretary for program coordination at the Department of Health, Education, and Welfare (HEW), which was later divided into the Department of Education and the Department of Health and Human Services. Before Lyndon B. Johnson left office, however, she had been promoted to assistant secretary for planning and evaluation at HEW. Then, with the inauguration of President Richard M. Nixon in January, 1969, Rivlin returned to Brookings and began researching and publishing in the wide arena involving government policy and social action programs.

Six years later she was once again in the public sector, this time serving the legislative branch as the founding director of the Congressional Budget Office (CBO) from 1975 to 1983. This entity was created by the Congressional Budget and Impoundment Control Act of 1974 in order to provide Congress, in its budgetary negotiations with the president and federal bureaucracies, with an alternative set of technical information on the economy to that provided by the President's budgetary agency, the Office of Management and Budget (OMB). The CBO continues to provide Congress with an analysis of the economic consequences of existing and pending programs as well as alternative budgetary options. Indeed, it is widely considered in the literature to have proven itself to be both more neutral and more accurate in its assessments of the economy than the OMB.

In 1983, Alice Rivlin returned again to the Brookings Institution as a senior fellow, and there she remained for nearly a decade. During this sojourn from government service, she was married to Sidney Graham Winter in 1989, was a MacArthur Fellow from 1983 to 1988, and accepted a post as professor of public policy at George Mason University in nearby Fairfax, Virginia. She also broadened her involvement in the world of applied economics and public affairs, publishing with others such works for Brookings as *Economic Choices 1987* in 1986 and *The Swedish Economy* in 1987. As a widely respected national economist and articulate, frequently cited critic of the large federal budgetary deficits that mushroomed during the Reagan years, Alice Rivlin accepted an appointment during this period as a regularly contributing member of the *Los Angeles Times'* Board of Economists, and also began to serve on the boards of directors of such business organizations as Ryder System, Inc., and UNISYS Corp., and such national groups as the Council on Foreign Relations and the Wilderness Society.

In December of 1992, she was again called upon to accept a post in the government when President-elect Bill Clinton designated her to be his deputy director of the Office of Budget and Management, a department with which she had frequently sparred while heading the Congressional Budget Office. That appointment, as the only woman designated to be a part of President Clinton's economic team and the only member appointed to that team without extensive experience in the wheeling and dealing of policy making, constituted a very high testimony to Alice Rivlin's growing stature among mainstream American economists. At the time of the appointment, she was firmly on record as at variance with the President-elect in some key areas. In one of her last contributions to the *Los Angeles Times* prior to the OMB appointment, she had been candid about the difficulty of using the budget to stimulate the economy, as

President Clinton intended, while simultaneously pursuing the long-term goal of reducing the budgetary deficit. She also advocated such harsh antideficit actions as the gasoline tax which Clinton had rejected on the campaign trail. She was therefore not likely to be a silent observer; quite to the contrary, she was intended to be a creditable voice in the making of the administration's economic policy. Along with the appointments of Lloyd Bentsen as secretary of the Treasury, Lou Panetta as director of the OMB, Robert Rubin as chairman of the National Economic Council, and Robert Altman as deputy secretary of the Treasury, Rivlin's appointment was given much emphasis by Clinton as part of an early effort to steady an American financial market somewhat edgy over the economic implications of his election as president.

In June of 1994, Rivlin was promoted to full director of the OMB after Lou Panetta was named as the new White House chief of staff by President Clinton.

Summary

Whether as a researcher at Brookings or in her work in the public sector, Alice Rivlin has been involved throughout her career in some of the most critical policy issues of the day: education, the intergovernmental financing of social action programs, welfare reform, care for the elderly, and even such foreign policy areas as global partnerships and national security. Still, it is difficult to measure the impact of policy professionals such as Alice Rivlin on the American political process or to quantify their importance to that process. As policy intellectuals operating on the edge of politics, their names are rarely affixed to program outcomes, and even when they are it is usually hard to evaluate the influence they might have had on those programs.

For example, it is not easy to measure Rivlin's impact on the Congressional Budget Office or to measure her influence in the political process in terms of the changing fortunes of that body. The importance of the Congressional Budget Office has diminished since she served as its director, though for largely extraneous reasons. The 1985 reforms resulting from the Balanced Budget and Emergency Deficit Control Act shifted the budgetary procedure from one of Congress restraining the bureaucracies' budgetary demands to one of sequestration and automatic, timetable-based budgetary cuts in the event of a stalemate in budgetary negotiations. In doing so, the act rendered the CBO's inputs much less significant in influencing budgetary outcomes than they had previously been. On the other hand, the reputation for accuracy which the CBO acquired under Rivlin's directorship has continued, and the office consequently remains an important component of the legislative process.

In the broad sense, Rivlin and her fellow policy professionals contribute not so much to the creation of particular programs as to a continual cross-fertilization between the political and academic institutions in American life. In this regard, Alice Rivlin's career has already been a rich one. Unlike most of her peers, she has served in important positions in both the legislative and executive branches of the national government. Nevertheless, she would be unlikely to state her contributions in grander terms. When designated to become deputy director of the OMB by President Clinton, she described herself in a *Washington Post* article of December 11, 1992, as "a fanatical, card-carrying middle-of-the-roader," placing herself clearly in a role as a facilitator in fine-tuning the American policy-making process. Although her impact on the budget and policy in the Clinton Administration will not be measurable for years to come, there is reason to believe that this appointment will not be her last mark on American public affairs.

Bibliography

Bowman, Kathleen. *New Women in Social Sciences*. Mankato, Minn.: Creative Education, 1976. This volume in a biographical series aimed at juvenile readers profiles seven women social scientists. The chapter on Rivlin covers her career up through her work as founding director of the Congressional Budget Office in 1975.

Lampman, R. J., et al. *Income Maintenance and Welfare Reform: Papers and Comments*. Madison: University of Wisconsin Press, 1974. Rivlin's paper on the history of income maintenance proposals and programs forms a central component of this set of discussion papers prepared for the Institute for Research on Poverty. It was published shortly before she began her term as director of the Congressional Budget Office.

Rivlin, Alice M., et al. *Caring for the Disabled Elderly: Who Will Pay?* Washington, D.C.: Brookings Institution, 1988. Rivlin's economics and middle-of-the-road political orientation come through in her contributions to this work on the dimensions and financing of an area of on-going concern in the American political system.

———. *Reviving the American Dream: The Economy, the States, and the Federal Government*. Washington, D.C.: Brookings Institution, 1992. Rivlin's last published book before joining the Clinton Administration, this work offers a powerful study not only of the economic trends in America between 1980 and 1992 but also of the economic bind of the states given the decline in transfer payments from a federal government retrenching in the face of its budgetary deficits.

———. *The Role of the Federal Government in Financing Higher Education*. Washington, D.C.: Brookings Institution, 1961. One of Rivlin's first studies for Brookings, this work provides a good indication of her thinking on a topic of—then and now—great public importance in the United States.

———. *Systematic Thinking for Social Action*. Washington, D.C.: Brookings Institution, 1971. Perhaps the best work in the list for understanding the author. Based on a series of lectures delivered at Berkeley, the work focuses on the twin areas of evaluation research and social action programs.

Rivlin, Alice M., David C. Jones, and Edward C. Meyer. *Beyond Alliances: Global Security Through Focused Partnerships*. Washington, D.C.: Brookings Institution, 1990. This book provides a good example of Alice Rivlin's versatility, with its focus on the area of international relations and national security in a world of ever-increasing interdependency.

Zophy, Angela Howard, and Frances M. Kavenik, eds. *Handbook of American*

Women's History. New York: Garland, 1990. A wide-ranging encyclopedia that includes a brief biographical sketch on Rivlin and her career through the 1980's. Useful in providing a quick summary of her accomplishments.

Joseph R. Rudolph, Jr.

ABBY ALDRICH ROCKEFELLER

Born: October 26, 1874; Providence, Rhode Island
Died: April 5, 1948; New York, New York
Area of Achievement: Patronage of the arts
Contribution: Abby Aldrich Rockefeller's most important contributions were the central role she played in the development of public interest in contemporary art, particularly American art, and the establishment of New York City's Museum of Modern Art. She also influenced family members, particularly her husband, John D. Rockefeller, Jr., and her son, Nelson Aldrich Rockefeller, to aid her in her endeavors.

Early Life

Abby Greene Aldrich was born on October 26, 1874, in Providence, the capital of Rhode Island. She was the third of eight children, three girls and five boys, of Nelson Wilmarth Aldrich and Abby Chapman Aldrich. Her father, who had come to Providence at the age of seventeen from his father's Rhode Island farm, had only a grade-school education. Initially a clerk in a wholesale grocery firm, Aldrich was elected first a member of the Rhode Island Legislature, then a member of the U.S. House of Representatives, and, in 1881, at the age of thirty-nine, a member of the U.S. Senate. From that year until his retirement in 1912, he remained an influential member of the Senate. Largely self-educated, Aldrich had acquired a good library and had developed a keen interest in the arts, including art collecting. His sons and daughters, particularly Abby, were deeply influenced by him in these areas. Abby traveled frequently in the United States and Europe, often accompanied by her father, visiting museums and art galleries. In her early years, she was educated at home by a private tutor; later, she attended and graduated from Miss Abbott's School in Providence in 1893. In was at about that time that Abby Aldrich met John D. Rockefeller, Jr., who was then a student at Brown University in Providence. Following several years of courtship, including frequent visits with her family in Providence and his in New York, the couple were married on October 9, 1901, in the summer coastal home of the Aldrichs at Warwick, Rhode Island. Following a four-week honeymoon at Pocantico Hills, the elder Rockefeller's estate near Tarrytown, New York, they took up residence on West 54th Street in New York City.

Life's Work

In embarking upon her marital career, Abby Aldrich Rockefeller was faced with problems of adjustment, both personal and public. Although she was deeply in love with her husband, they were quite different in personality. He was serious, thoughtful, and reserved, while she was gay, somewhat impulsive, and gregarious. Then there was the matter of possessions. Although Abby Aldrich Rockefeller had been reared in relative luxury, she was now married to a man who was taking on the responsibility of handling one of the great American fortunes. In the years from 1903 to 1915, six children were born to the couple: Abigail (1903), John Davison III (1906), Nelson Aldrich (1908), Laurance Spelman (1910), Winthrop (1912), and David (1915). During these early years, Abby Rockefeller's attention was centered on the care and education of her children, first at day or boarding schools and later at college. In a revealing letter she wrote in 1922, when her six children ranged in age from seven to nineteen, she said, "As I look into the future . . . I see that we shall not have a very quiet or peaceful life for many years to come. Still I am never completely happy, even with all the confusion, unless we are all together under one roof." Her marriage to one of the world's richest men called for much entertaining and numerous social activities. In addition, Abby Rockefeller engaged in many philanthropic activities on her own and in association with her husband. For example, in 1920, she sponsored the building and development of a community center for industrial workers and their families in Bayway, New Jersey. In 1924, she played a prominent role in the design, construction, and furnishing of International House located near Columbia University in New York City. A residential center for foreign students attending universities in New York City, the center was paid for by John D. Rockefeller. Abby Rockefeller also actively participated in the work of a number of religious and charitable organizations. An earlier interest in Providence in the work of the Young Women's Christian Association was followed by service on its national executive board from 1918 to 1936. From 1921 to 1937, she figured prominently in the operation of the Grace Dodge Hotel for women in Washington, D.C. A Congregationalist prior to her marriage, Abby joined her husband's Fifth Avenue Baptist Church, a predecessor of the Riverside Church, where she founded an association in 1922 designed to improve the living conditions of the immigrant and minority groups in New York City's East Side. Besides these and other causes and endeavors, there was also her interest in and support of her husband's numerous philanthropies, such as the Rockefeller Institute for Medical Research (later Rockefeller University) and the Rockefeller Foundation.

Abby Rockefeller was best known, however, for her patronage of the arts. In her early years, she acquired a personal collection of European and Chinese art. Later, she extended her interests to include American artists. With her husband she shared in the planning and restoration of Colonial Williamsburg. She subsequently acquired many items of American folk art, wood carvings of toys, weather vanes of various types, oil portraits, water drawings, and so forth, from which she made extensive donations to Colonial Williamsburg and the Abby Aldrich Rockefeller Folk Art Collection located there. She had also developed a liking for modern art. Her husband did not care for it; he was primarily interested in beautiful products of the past. He did not, however, oppose her interest; in fact, he supplemented her financial means for collecting forays into this area. It is against this background that Abby Rockefeller played a key role in the establishment of New York City's Museum of Modern Art. The first meeting leading to its founding in 1929 was held in her home, and she served in various offices on its board of trustees. In the 1930's and 1940's, she donated to the museum the works of such painters as Henri Matisse, Pablo Picasso, and Diego Rivera, and by the time of her death she had donated some two thousand other paintings, art objects, sculptures, drawings, prints, and other works. In 1938, with her son Nelson, she set up a purchase fund for the museum. She stipulated that there would be no restrictions on the kind of art to be purchased from the Mrs. John D. Rockefeller, Jr., Purchase Fund and that selections would be made solely by an acquisitions committee. In addition, she commissioned works by contemporary American artists such as Ben Shahn and Charles Sheeler, and many of those works she donated to the Museum of Modern Art. During World War II, four of her sons served in the U.S. armed forces and one worked in the State Department. Abby Rockefeller was actively involved in the Museum of Modern Art's programs for raising money to provide military installations with artists' materials and to assist the American Red Cross in securing artists to teach in arts and crafts programs for persons in military hospitals. Late in the war, Abby Rockefeller set up a War Veterans Art Center at the Museum of Modern Art, which provided studios and classes for some fifteen hundred disabled veterans prior to the center's closing in 1948. Although she was in sound health for most of her life, her last years were marred by ill health, and she spent much time at Rockefeller homes in Williamsburg, Virginia, and Tucson, Arizona. On April 5, 1948, she died at home in New York City of a heart attack.

Summary

Abby Aldrich Rockefeller had the responsibilities associated with her marriage to one of the wealthiest men in the world and the rearing of their six children. She was able to successfully unite the carrying out of such responsibilities with a concern for art that made her a pivotal figure in the advancement of American and modern art. Her access to great wealth provided her with a unique opportunity to implement this concern. She led in the creation of an awareness of the beauty and importance of American folk art through the collection and exhibition of such art. Of equal and perhaps greater importance was her role in the establishment and support of the Museum of Modern Art. In addition to serving on its executive board in various capacities, she collected and donated many of the art works that formed its holdings. Through her commissioning of the works of living artists, many of which she later donated to the Museum of Modern Art, she was one of a small number of people who turned that institution into what is called a patronage museum—that is, a museum that justifies the stimulation and collection of the works of living artists—rather than a museum of the traditional type.

Bibliography

Chase, Mary Ellen. *Abby Aldrich Rockefeller*. New York: Macmillan, 1950. A somewhat adulatory early biography. The result of the author's access to members of the Aldrich and Rockefeller families and pertinent documents about them, this brief work provides considerable insight into the background and development of Rockefeller as a person and the factors spurring her interest in art.

Fosdick, Raymond B. *John D. Rockefeller, Jr.: A Portrait*. New York: Harper & Brothers, 1956. The author of this biography was a friend and personal associate of

John D. Rockefeller, Jr., and his wife for forty-five years. For twelve years, he served as president of the Rockefeller Foundation. Devoted primarily to the life and activities of its subject, the book contains many revealing passages about Abby Aldrich Rockefeller, her art interests, and her relationships with her husband and children.

Goodyear, A. Conger. *The Museum of Modern Art: The First Ten Years*. New York: A. Conger Goodyear, 1943. This brief history was written by a man who was present at the organizational meeting of the Museum of Modern Art and served as it president for its first ten years of existence. It is a straightforward account of the establishment and operation of the museum during its first ten years, but it provides a few insights into Abby Rockefeller's and her son Nelson's relationships with the museum.

Kert, Bernice. *Abby Aldrich Rockefeller: The Woman in the Family*. New York: Random House, 1993. Based on nine years of exhaustive research, this 1993 biography of Rockefeller provides thorough coverage of her life and contains pictures of family members and their dwellings. The book emphasizes two aspects of the subject's life: her deep influence on John D. Rockefeller, Jr., and their six children, and her key role in the development of modern art. Her part in the establishment of and championing of New York's Museum of Modern Art is particularly stressed. The author describes Rockefeller's makeup and character in glowing terms. Far less sympathetically portrayed is her husband, who is pictured as being unduly possessive of his wife.

Morris, Joe Alex. *Nelson Rockefeller: A Biography*. New York: Harper & Row, 1960. There are a number of significant passages in this biography of Nelson Rockefeller about his mother. Morris states, for example, that Abby Aldrich Rockefeller was probably the most direct and important influence on Nelson in his youth and early manhood.

Saarinen, Aline B. *The Proud Possessors: The Lives, Times and Tastes of Some Adventurous American Art Collectors*. New York: Random House, 1958. The last chapter in this volume is devoted to the art collecting of the Rockefeller family, including that of Abby Aldrich Rockefeller. The book sheds light on her by way of comparison to other members of her family and to other female art patrons such as Mrs. Potter Palmer, Isabella Stewart Gardner, and Peggy Guggenheim.

Joseph C. Kiger

GINGER ROGERS

Born: July 16, 1911; Independence, Missouri

Areas of Achievement: Film and dance

Contribution: A beloved film actress from Hollywood's classical studio era of the 1930's and 1940's, Rogers is most fondly remembered for her RKO musicals with Fred Astaire.

Early Life

Ginger Rogers was born Virginia Katherine McMath in Independence, Missouri, on July 16, 1911. She received her nickname "Ginger" at an early age. Her parents, William Eddins McMath, an electrical engineer, and mother, Lela Emogene Owens McMath, were separated when she was a child. During the ensuing custody battles, Ginger was abducted several times by her distraught father. Detectives hired by Lela and her parents returned the child from St. Louis, after which father and daughter had little contact.

An aspiring screenwriter, Lela McMath ventured to Hollywood while Ginger stayed in Kansas City with her maternal grandparents. With several credits to her name, Lela next headed to New York City, then the hub of the silent film industry. Ginger joined her mother for a brief stay in Manhattan at the age of six. During her stay, the youngster was tendered a film contract, an offer her mother turned down because of Ginger's age. With America's entry into World War I, Lela McMath headed to Washington, D.C., to work as a publicist for the U.S. Marine Corps. Ginger returned to Kansas City to live with her grandparents.

After the war, Lela returned to Kansas City and accepted a reporting job with the Kansas City *Post*. Soon, mother and daughter moved to Texas, where Lela worked as a drama critic and reporter for the Fort Worth *Record*. Lela also managed the Fort Worth Symphony Orchestra and wrote and directed short historical plays. Sometime in the early 1920's after the death of her former husband, Lela McMath married John Logan Rogers, who formally adopted Ginger, thus accounting for her last name.

In Fort Worth, Ginger fulfilled a childhood dream of performing as a pianist when, at age eleven, she gave a well-received rendition of MacDowell's "To a Wild Rose." Despite this modest success, acting and dancing became her chief pursuits. Her stage debut occurred in 1924, when she was featured in *The Death of St. Denis*, a one-act play by her mother staged at Fort Worth's Central High School. In 1925, her prowess as a dancer was recognized by vaudeville headliner Eddie Foy, who called on her as a last-minute substitute for an ailing regular. Later, Ginger won a statewide Charleston contest and was offered a month-long vaudeville contract. Conscripting two runner-ups, the congenial yet competitive teenager billed her act as "Ginger and Her Redheads."

By now thoroughly fascinated by show business life, Ginger Rogers dropped out of high school for a three-year stint on Midwest and Southern vaudeville circuits chaperoned by her mother. In 1928, Ginger married Edward Culpepper, a fellow dancer known professionally as Jack Pepper. Soon, they were tapping together as "Ginger and Pepper." When the marriage collapsed a year later, Ginger returned to solo bookings.

Life's Work

In 1929, bandleader Paul Ash invited Ginger Rogers to sing with his orchestra at the Paramount Theater in New York. Soon, she appeared in her first Broadway show, *Top Speed* (1929), a debut acclaimed by Brooks Atkinson of *The New York Times*, who described her as "an impudent young thing . . . who carries youth and humor to the point where they are completely charming." Film producer Walter Wanger was also impressed. With the ink hardly dry on a new contract with Paramount Studios, Rogers initiated her feature film debut in *Young Man of Manhattan* (1930) as a brassy jazz-age flapper whose line—"Cigarette me, big boy"—became part of the day's sassy argot.

Another break came that same year when she landed the part of Molly Gray in George and Ira Gershwin's *Girl Crazy* (1930). The production was a talent-packed affair. Touted for her winning ways with such Gershwin tunes as "But Not for Me" and "Embraceable You," Rogers was joined by Ethel Merman making her Broadway debut with "I Got Rhythm" and a pit band that included such future giants of the swing era as Benny Goodman, Jimmy Dorsey, Glenn Miller, and Gene Krupa. No less significant was Rogers' first contact with Fred Astaire, who was on board to help polish *Girl Crazy*'s dance routines. As the hit show sailed into 1931, Rogers continued her daytime treks to Paramount's Astoria studio in Queens, New York, to appear in feature films such as *The Sap from Syracuse* and *Queen High* (both 1930). With the Great Depression taking its toll on Broadway, Rogers' attentions gravitated West where Hollywood was booming thanks to the relative novelty and continuing drawing power of the synchronized sound film.

For all her New York successes on stage and in film, it was Hollywood that made Ginger Rogers a star. During a relatively brief stint as a free-lancer, she appeared in everything from comedies and melodramas to musicals. In 1933, Rogers hit pay dirt at Warner Bros. when she was featured in a scanty, coin-spangled costume singing the ironic "We're in the Money," the opening production number of *Gold Diggers of 1933*. She scored another success at the studio with her portrayal of the cynical, socially ambitious Anytime Annie in *42nd Street* (1933). RKO Studios then partnered her with Fred Astaire for *Flying Down to Rio* (1933). Although they appeared fourth and fifth in the credits after Dolores Del Rio, Gene Raymond, and Raul Roullen, Rogers and Astaire created a sensation with their blithe yet exotic dancing set to Vincent Youmans' "The Carioca."

Critics sang their praises, and the public clamored for more. RKO, constantly at the brink of fiscal collapse during its turbulent economic life, knew a good thing when it danced its way. Indeed, the couple's next project, *The Gay Divorcee* (1934), put Astaire and Rogers at the top of the bill. It also drew on RKO's top talents, producer Pandro S. Berman, director Mark Sandrich, musical director Max Steiner, supporting actors Edward Everett Horton, Alice Brady, Erik Rhodes, and Eric Blore, and art designer Carroll Clark. With a sensuous dance of seduction set to Cole Porter's "Night and Day" and a terpsichorean spectacle woven around "The Continental," the film became RKO's box office champ for 1934, established Rogers and Astaire as bona fide stars. Rogers and Astaire then helped put RKO in the black for the first time since the beginning of the decade with *Roberta* and *Top Hat* (both 1935).

Top Hat, RKO's top money-maker of 1935, is Rogers' and Astaire's most beloved collaboration. George Eells says: "With *Top Hat* they reached the apogee of their power as darlings of the gods, quite untouched by any mundane problems of daily existence." Arlene Croce describes the duo's characters as holdovers from the 1920's, "a faded cartoon of the pre-Crash, pre-Roosevelt Prohibition era." Nevertheless, as Croce implies, it was precisely that rarefied caricature of blasé elegance in the manner of F. Scott Fitzgerald that Depression-era audiences sought in order to escape and dream. With a memorable score of original songs by Irving Berlin, the comedic and bumpy romantic relationship between Fred Astaire's Jerry Travers and Ginger Rogers' Dale Tremont unfolds to the wistful strains of "Isn't This a Lovely Day (To Be Caught in the Rain)" and "Cheek to Cheek," the couple's enduring signature song and dance.

Despite a continuing string of hits such as *Follow the Fleet* (1936), *Swing Time* (1936) and *Shall We Dance* (1937) and their justly earned status as the decade's most famous on-screen couple, Rogers and Astaire bridled at their collective success. It was not a case of personal enmity. Indeed, even though Astaire had virtually functioned as Rogers' mentor as a screen dancer, the actress never begrudged her older colleague his Svengali-like role. Rather, it was a question of pride driven by the desire of each to succeed on his or her own. For Astaire, who had wanted to establish his own identity after sister Adele had retired from their fabled partnership in the 1920's, the issue was especially sensitive, since his sister had received the lion's share of the credit for their success. For Rogers, it was a personal desire to expand into dramatic as well as comedic roles and to emerge on her own from Astaire's debonair shadow. In 1936, Rogers and her mother confronted RKO's moguls with demands for a substantial increase in salary and a genuine opportunity to enlarge her dramatic compass. Bargaining from a position of undeniable strength—her box-office clout—Rogers forced RKO to acquiesce on both accounts.

Her first dramatic star turn under the new RKO arrangement was in the adaptation of the George S. Kaufman-Edna Ferber Broadway hit *Stage Door* (1937), with Katharine Hepburn. In *Vivacious Lady* (1938) opposite Jimmy Stewart and *Bachelor Mother* (1939) with David Niven, Rogers proved an adept comedienne. Her credibility as a dramatic actress was boosted with her sensitive portrayal of a prostitute's daughter in *Primrose Path* (1940). It was *Kitty Foyle* (1940), a poignant yet sentimental romance, that brought Rogers her greatest personal triumph and "happiest moment"—an Academy Award as best actress.

During World War II, Rogers was a tireless worker for the USO, entertaining servicemen at home and abroad. She also appeared at countless war bond rallies. She made a training film called *Safeguarding Military Information* and narrated with Spencer Tracy a film about the role of women in the Coast Guard called *Battle Stations*. Simultaneously, her Hollywood career boomed with such successes as *The Major and the Minor* (1942), *Tender Comrade* (1943), and *Weekend at the Waldorf* (1945). Postwar highlights include *Magnificent Doll* (1946) and *Storm Warning* (1951), a melodramatic indictment of the Ku Klux Klan costarring Ronald Reagan. In the 1950's and 1960's, Rogers ventured into television and returned to Broadway with varying degrees of success. Her autobiography, *Ginger: My Story*, was published in 1991.

Summary

The 1949 reunion of Ginger Rogers and Fred Astaire in *The Barkleys of Broadway*, their last picture together, was a strange art-imitating-life affair focused on a successful yet bickering husband-and-wife musical comedy team. The conflict? Mrs. Barkley wants to "graduate" into serious drama while Mr. Barkley is content to keep on singing and dancing. In real life, Rogers did make the leap while Astaire mostly kept dancing. In the ensuing years, however, it has been the Rogers-Astaire RKO musicals that have continued to live, amazing and delighting contemporary audiences around the world. Though a cliché, there's more than a grain of truth in the proposition that while Rogers gave Astaire sex appeal, he gave her class. As a couple, Rogers and Astaire were (and are) a singular phenomenon, a fact acknowledged by the great Italian director Federico Fellini in his tender yet oblique tribute aptly entitled, *Ginger and Fred* (1986).

Bibliography

Croce, Arlene. *The Fred Astaire and Ginger Rogers Book*. New York: E. P. Dutton, 1972. The definitive source on the Astaire-Rogers partnership, with a thorough production history and analysis of each of the team's ten films. Lavishly illustrated.

Delamater, Jerome. "Astaire and Rogers at RKO." In *Dance in the Hollywood Musical*. Ann Arbor, Mich.: UMI Research Press, 1981. This chapter provides a penetrating analysis of the Astaire-Rogers collaboration during its heyday at RKO Studios. Delamater stresses the Pygmalion-Galatea nature of the pair's professional relationship.

Eells, George. *Ginger, Loretta, and Irene Who?* New York: G. P. Putnam's Sons, 1976. In a chapter entitled "Ginger Rogers: The Survivor," Eells provides a lively account that emphasizes Rogers' professional and personal resiliency and the pivotal role that her mother played in her career.

Jewell, Richard B., with Vernon Harbin. *The RKO Story*. New York: Arlington House, 1982. A valuable and concise year-by-year compendium with brief accounts of every film released by RKO during the period from 1929 to 1960. Includes Rogers' appearances in musicals as well as her comedic and dramatic forays.

Rogers, Ginger. *Ginger: My Story*. New York: HarperCollins, 1991. A genial autobiography that provides useful, although selective, reminiscences on each of

Rogers' seventy-three films as well as the varied phases of her stage career. Illustrated with numerous publicity stills and personal photographs.

Charles Merrell Berg

LINDA RONSTADT

Born: July 15, 1946; Tucson, Arizona

Area of Achievement: Music

Contribution: Linda Ronstadt became a pop-rock superstar in the 1970's, when the industry was primarily dominated by men. She continues to inspire vocalists with her increasingly controlled soprano voice and her commitment to diverse projects.

Early Life

On July 15, 1946, Linda Marie Ronstadt was born, the third of the four children of Ruthmary Copeman and Gilbert Ronstadt. Ruthmary, the daughter of a wealthy German inventor from Michigan, moved to Tucson to attend college. There she met Gilbert, whose family was well established in Tucson from years of cattle ranching and running a local hardware store. Gilbert's Dutch-Mexican father was the leader of a local band, a self-taught guitarist and pianist who showed his children how to play. Gilbert, in turn, taught his children, and Linda learned to harmonize in Spanish with her brothers Mike and Pete, her father, and her grandfather. Linda's aunt, Luisa Ronstadt, was also a successful musician. The year Linda was born, Luisa compiled a book of traditional songs her father sang when she and Gilbert were children. The book was entitled *Canciones de Mi Padre*, and Linda later recorded the music on an album by the same name.

The family was preoccupied with music. Linda remembers listening to records and radio constantly while growing up, including country and western, rock, mariachi, jazz, and light opera. She loved Hank Williams, Elvis Presley, and Lola Beltrán. Her father gave her a duet album featuring Ella Fitzgerald and Louis Armstrong when she was eight; she also listened to Billie Holiday and Django Reinhardt.

When she was fourteen, Linda formed a trio with siblings Mike and Suzi called the New Union Ramblers; they sang Mexican folk music and country songs for local clubs and coffeehouses. One of the trio's musicians, guitarist Bob Kimmel, moved to Los Angeles the year Linda began high school. In 1964, when Linda was eighteen and attending her first semester at the University of Arizona, Kimmel invited her to form a singing group with him in California. She accepted, dropping out of college to speed the process. Together, Kimmel and Ronstadt organized, with keyboardist Ken Edwards, a soft folk rock group called the Stone Poneys, which turned out to be the stepping-stone Ronstadt needed to begin her successful solo career as a performing and recording artist.

Life's Work

Linda Ronstadt's vibrant soprano voice was considered to be the Stone Poneys' strong point, and during a gig at the Troubadour, a club in Los Angeles, she was offered a solo contract by music manager Herb Cohen. Loyal to her group, she turned him down. Cohen eventually introduced the group to a producer at Capitol Records, who produced their first single, "Some of Shelley's Blues"/"Hobo (Morning Glory)," in January of 1965. The group's first album, *The Stone Poneys*, recorded in 1966, featured three Ronstadt solos. They released a second album the following year, *Evergreen Volume II*, which contained the group's only successful single, former Monkee Mike Nesmith's "Different Drum." The song took months to creep up the charts, and the disappointed band members tired of opening for other bands, making barely $100 per month. By the time the song hit number thirteen on the *Billboard* charts in 1968, the Stone Poneys had broken up, so Ronstadt completed the group's seven-year record contract on her own.

The next few years were hard on Ronstadt. She was shy on stage and had therefore resisted a solo career; now she struggled to find her own path in the music industry. Though her third album, *Linda Ronstadt, Stone Poneys, and Friends, Volume 3* (1968), listed her former group, she was backed entirely by studio musicians. *Hand Sown . . . Home Grown* (1969), her first official solo album, had such strong country overtones that Capitol sent her to Nashville to produce her next collection, *Silk Purse*, which enjoyed moderate success. By 1970, the album reached 103 on the charts, and its single, "Long, Long Time," rose to number 25. Ronstadt was nominated for a Grammy Award for Best Female Country Vocal. She made her television debut on *The Johnny Cash Show*, then appeared on a Glen Campbell special. Though she was gaining popularity, Ronstadt refers to the period as bleak. She was constantly on the road opening for bands such as the Doors, Alice Cooper, the Mothers of Invention, and Neil Young; audiences were impatient with her country-folk style, and her self-confidence withered.

In 1971, Ronstadt realized her need for a band and invited Randy Meisner, Glenn Frey, Bernie Leadon, and Don Henley to play for her. They produced *Linda Ronstadt* (1972) together, and then her musicians left to form their own band, the Eagles. Soon after, she signed a contract with Asylum records and began a long, fruitful relationship with manager/producer Peter Asher, who knew how to provide an instrumental setting for Ronstadt's voice. An interpretive singer more than a singer/songwriter, Ronstadt's success is partially the result of her astute ear for which songs to sing, which Asher realized. Together they released *Don't Cry Now* (1973), which included her critically acclaimed version of the Eagles' song "Desperado," and then her first platinum record, *Heart Like a Wheel* (1974). Phil Everly's "When Will I Be Loved?" and Betty Everett's "You're No Good" became top pop singles; Hank Williams' "I Can't Help It If I'm Still in Love with You" made number two on the country and western charts and won the Grammy for Best Female Country Vocal.

Ronstadt's next four albums went platinum, selling more than a million copies each and giving her the reputation of the biggest single female superstar of rock during the 1970's. *Prisoner in Disguise* (1975), *Linda Ronstadt's Greatest Hits* (1976), and *Hasten Down the Wind* (1976) kept her all over the pop charts with songs by J. D. Souther and James Taylor, Smokey Robinson's "Tracks of My Tears," the Holland-Dozier-Holland classic "Heat Wave," and revamped rockabilly tunes. She won a second Grammy in 1976 for Best Female Pop Vocal for *Hasten Down the Wind*. As critics tried to attach a label to Ronstadt's style, however, she eluded them by including a remake of Buddy Holly's "That'll Be the Day," Jamaican reggae folk songs, folk-rock cuts with Karla Bonoff and Wendy Waldman, and a few ballads she wrote herself.

In January of 1977, Ronstadt capped her six-month European and American concert tour with a performance at President Jimmy Carter's inauguration. Then, back in California, she recorded *Simple Dreams* (1977), which included her own versions of Roy Orbison's "Blue Bayou," the Rolling Stones' "Tumbling Dice," Warren Zevon's "Poor, Poor Pitiful Me," and a soulful duet with Dolly Parton, "I Never Will Marry." This last song Ronstadt considers something of a personal theme song. She has been in numerous relationships with various managers, musicians, comedians, and political figures; some of these relationships provided a feast for gossip columnists. The five-foot, two-inch raven-haired singer earned a reputation as a sex symbol during the decade, and even interviewers who were seriously interested in Ronstadt's music wrote about her love life. She has frequently maintained, however, that her career as a singer is her first love and priority, and has vowed to keep it that way.

In 1978, Ronstadt attempted to make a female "superstar" album with Emmy Lou Harris and Dolly Parton, two friends she had long admired; the project was delayed while *Living in the U.S.A.* climbed the charts with the singles "Back in the U.S.A." by Chuck Berry, "Ooh, Baby, Baby" by Smokey Robinson, and "Just One Look." She won the American Music Award that same year and was voted Female Vocalist of the Year by the *Rolling Stone* Readers' Poll. *Mad Love* came out in 1980, featuring new band members Danny Kortchmar and former Little Feat keyboardist Bill Payne. It included songs by Elvis Costello and the Cretones, plus the single "Hurts So Bad."

Ronstadt's career shifted dramatically in the 1980's. Seeking a challenge for her maturing voice and diverse musical tastes, she moved to New York to play Mabel in the 1981 Broadway production of Gilbert and Sullivan's *The Pirates of Penzance*; she later appeared in the film version. While there, she met record producer Jerry Wexler, who encouraged her to sing music from the 1920's, 1930's, and 1940's. Asher was not enthusiastic about the idea, and Ronstadt cut another pop album, *Get Closer* (1982), before she convinced her Asylum manager that she was serious. They contacted orchestra leader Nelson Riddle, who had accompanied Frank Sinatra. Riddle surprised Ronstadt with his desire to record an album instead of a few cuts; they finally produced three albums. *What's New* (1983) features Ronstadt's resonant, beautifully controlled voice on classics such as "Crazy He Calls Me," "What'll I Do," and "Lover Man" with a live studio orchestra. Though her producer originally thought the project a risk, the album turned platinum within three months, becoming the most successful album of Ronstadt's career. *Lush Life* (1984) and *For Sentimental Reasons* (1986) also hit gold, with hits including "Sophisticated Lady," " 'Round Midnight" and "My Funny Valentine." During the same time period, Ronstadt also sang as Mimi in a Broadway production of Puccini's *La Bohème*.

Ronstadt found opera difficult, since she had never received formal training as a vocalist. She moved back to California and, in 1986, fulfilled an old dream by recording and producing *Trio* (1987) with friends Dolly Parton and Emily Lou Harris. The album won a Grammy Award for Best Country Performance by a Group with Vocals. It was also named Album of the Year by the Academy of Country Music and became the first country album in years to climb the pop charts. Then Ronstadt surprised audiences again, recording her Aunt Luisa's collection of Mexican folk music, *Canciones de Mi Padre*, in 1989. The album won a Grammy for Best Mexican/American Performance; Ronstadt also earned an Emmy award for her outstanding televised performance of the songs.

In 1989, Aaron Neville joined Ronstadt to record *Cry Like a Rainstorm, Howl Like the Wind*. The duo won two Grammy Awards for the hit ballads "Don't Know Much" and "All My Life." In 1992, Ronstadt produced Neville's first solo album, *Warm Your Heart*, accompanying him on several cuts. The same year she produced two more albums of Mexican and mariachi music, *Mas Canciones*, and *Frenesí*, which explore Cuban-influenced American pop music of the 1940's and 1950's.

Summary

Linda Ronstadt's rise to superstardom in the 1970's helped bring an end to the male domination of the rock and roll industry. Once she overcame her fear of working alone, Ronstadt tuned in to pop culture, and she has steadily pursued a diverse, prolific, and successful performing and recording career. Though the seductive cover photographs on her early albums and her slow, soulful love ballads lured male fans by the thousands, Ronstadt's music ultimately crossed demographic barriers to thrill fans of all ages, genders, and nationalities.

Her accomplishments as a single female rock star have given Ronstadt the power to open doors for other female performers, including Nicolette Larson and Valerie Carter. Karla Bonoff was first recorded by Ronstadt; Maria Muldaur, Wendy Waldman, Emmy Lou Harris, Dolly Parton, and others have also joined Ronstadt in the recording studio for boosts to their own careers. Together, these women have formed close friendships and a support system that strengthens their status within the music industry.

Bibliography

Bego, Mark. *Linda Ronstadt: It's So Easy!* Austin, Tex.: Eakin Press, 1990. This book strings together interviews without proper citations and seems to have been compiled by an overly devoted fan, but it is still a worthwhile resource for details about Ronstadt's career, her friends, lovers, managers, and accompanists. Includes a discography.

Bloom, Steve. "An Intimate Conversation with Linda Ronstadt." *Down Beat* 52 (July, 1985): 16-19. Ronstadt discusses early and current musical influences, how she became interested in jazz, and what it was like recording with Nelson Riddle.

Helander, Brock. *The Rock Who's Who*. New York: Schirmer Books, 1982. A brief factual account of Ronstadt's career, highlighting songs that became hits and participating musicians.

Herbst, Peter, ed. *The Rolling Stone Interviews*. New York: St. Martin's Press, 1981. Includes the most in-depth interview with Ronstadt available in print during the height of her recording career.

Rosenbaum, Ron. "Melancholy Baby." *Esquire* 104 (October, 1985): 100-108. This intellectually geared interview with Ronstadt reveals her thoughts about the creative process, sexuality, the human response to sadness, and why she continues to produce music about romantic pain and longing.

Mary Pierce Frost

ELEANOR ROOSEVELT

Born: October 11, 1884; New York, New York
Died: November 7, 1962; New York, New York
Area of Achievement: Social reform
Contribution: As First Lady and as a private citizen, Roosevelt worked for civil rights, women's rights, and domestic and international peace and justice.

Early Life

Anna Eleanor Roosevelt, the first child of Elliot and Anna Livingston Ludlow Hall Roosevelt, was born in New York City on October 11, 1884. Her beautiful and aristocratic mother, who was only twenty years old when Eleanor was born, was more involved in the social life of her contemporaries than in the needs of her daughter. Elliot Roosevelt, although handsome and charming, was troubled by problems associated with alcoholism. As a result of her parents' self-absorption, Eleanor's early childhood was lonely and somber despite her family's wealth and social position.

Anna Roosevelt died of diphtheria in 1892, depressed and discouraged by her husband's drinking and irresponsibility. Eleanor idolized her father and imagined that she would live with him and that they would travel to exciting places together. In reality, however, Elliot's attitude toward Eleanor, although expressed in loving words, was characterized by thoughtlessness. Elliot died on August 14, 1894, of complications related to his drinking.

After her father's death, Eleanor lived with her maternal grandmother Mary Livingston Ludlow Hall. A strict disciplinarian, Hall insisted on a regimented life for her grandchildren. Despite her grandmother's insistence that she wear unfashionable clothes and a back brace to improve her posture, and despite the dreary atmosphere of Hall's New York townhouse, Eleanor's childhood was not as miserable as some writers have suggested. She had, for the first time in her life, a stable and orderly home. Her grandmother and aunts were sympathetic and supportive of her academic and athletic activities, and the family's country estate at Tivoli was a pleasant place with spacious grounds for a child to roam.

Eleanor remained in this environment until the age of fifteen, when she was sent to Allenswood, a girls' boarding school in England. Presided over by Mademoiselle Marie Souvestre, Allenswood provided a rigorous academic environment that encouraged young women to think and act independently. Eleanor came into her own at boarding school. She was an outstanding student, was active in sports, was held in the highest esteem by her fellow students, and was a protégée of Mademoiselle Souvestre. She took from Allenswood an intellectual self-possession, an increased sense of tolerance, and a commitment to public activity.

Life's Work

At eighteen, Eleanor Roosevelt returned to New York, at her grandmother's insistence that she make her debut. Although in her own memoirs Eleanor describes herself as shy and awkward at this period of her life, her contemporaries remembered her as attractive and sought-after by the more thoughtful young men. One young man who was particularly interested was Eleanor's fifth cousin once removed, Franklin Delano Roosevelt (FDR), at the time a Harvard student. The two became secretly engaged in November, 1903, and were married in March, 1905, after a courtship during which his rather possessive mother tried to raise obstacles.

During the years before her marriage, Eleanor had become involved in volunteer work in New York City. There she had found a sense of usefulness and satisfaction that social life had never held for her. She worked with the Junior League to teach settlement house children, and she joined the Consumers' League, helping to investigate women's working conditions in factories and department stores. She had first-hand exposure to urban poverty, and Eleanor's commitment to improving the lives of the less fortunate dates from this period of her life.

After their wedding, Eleanor and Franklin settled in New York City in a townhouse adjoining his mother's home. During the next eleven years, Eleanor bore six children: Anna (1906); James (1907); Franklin (1909), who lived only seven months; Elliot (1910); Franklin, Jr. (1914); and John (1916). Her life was filled with domestic responsibilities and with her mother-in-law's interference in the younger Roosevelts' household. Those were years of little personal satisfaction for Eleanor. She had little involvement with friends or work outside her family.

In 1910, Franklin Roosevelt began his political career by winning a seat in the New York state legislature. Eleanor also began her public life. She enjoyed the role of political wife, especially because it brought her into contact with the issues and figures of the day. Contrary to some reports, Eleanor was not opposed to woman suffrage during this period. She had not given the issue much thought until FDR came out in support of votes for women in 1911. Then she realized that "if my husband were a suffragist I probably must be too."

In 1913, the Roosevelts moved to Washington, D.C., where Franklin served as assistant secretary of the Navy under President Woodrow Wilson. There, during World War I, Eleanor organized the Red Cross canteen and the Navy Red Cross. She knitted, entertained troops, and served food to servicemen. She visited soldiers in the hospital and raised money for a recreational center for wounded men. Her work often lasted from 9:00 A.M. until long past midnight. The war years also brought Eleanor heartache and disillusionment when she learned of her husband's affair with her social secretary, Lucy Mercer. Eleanor offered to divorce Franklin at this time, but he refused. Certainly, the Roosevelts' decision to continue their marriage was made partly because divorce was a serious liability in politics in the early twentieth century, but also because Franklin realized that Eleanor's special skills would be invaluable in his career. For Eleanor, the Lucy Mercer episode encouraged her to seek her own fulfillment in the world outside her marriage.

After an unsuccessful run for the vice presidency in 1920, Franklin Roosevelt developed polio in 1921. Spurred by these events, Eleanor became involved in politics both in women's issues and in the Democratic Party. During the 1920's, she became active in the League of Women Voters and the Women's Trade Union League, which supported protective legislation for women. She became acquainted with such activist women as Esther Lape and Elizabeth Read, who introduced Eleanor into a community of independent women. With her friends Marion Dickerman and Nancy Cook, Eleanor built a cottage called Val-Kill on the grounds of the Roosevelt family estate at Hyde Park. There they created a partnership that managed a furniture crafts factory and also published the *Women's Democratic News*. With her friends, Eleanor also purchased Todhunter, a private girls' school in New York City. She taught there three days a week until she became First Lady in 1933. Teaching fulfilled a dream from her days at Allenswood, gave her immense satisfaction, and brought her into contact with the young people she always loved.

With the phenomenal energy that characterized her whole life, Eleanor also entered Democratic politics, first as a representative of her husband during his convalescence and then in her own right as a spokesperson for women and social reform. She organized Democratic women in New York, traveled and spoke for Democratic Party candidates, and advocated the election of women to public office.

When Franklin was elected governor of New York in 1928 and president of the United States in 1932, Eleanor worked with the Women's Division of the Democratic National Committee to involve women in the election process and to ensure that women were appointed to positions in the administration. Among those whom Eleanor brought to her husband's attention was Frances Perkins, the secretary of labor, the first woman ever appointed to a presidential cabinet.

Eleanor had feared that the position of First Lady would mean curtailing her own political and reform activities, but she discovered new opportunities to promote her primary concerns, such as equal rights and the concerns of the poor and dispossessed. She held regular press conferences that were open only to women reporters, gave radio interviews and lectures, and wrote a syndicated newspaper column called "My Day." In addition, she supervised the responses to the thousands of letters she received, sometimes sending a personal note or a check. Eleanor also traveled throughout the country as the president's "eyes and ears," seeing for herself the conditions on farms, in mines and factories, and in the homes of the poor during the Depression. She brought representatives of excluded groups to the White House, frequently seating them next to the president so that he could hear their stories.

A primary commitment of Eleanor Roosevelt's adult life was to civil rights for African Americans. She had grown up in an isolated and prejudiced environment, but living in Washington, D.C., had made her aware of the evils of racism. Her advocacy took the form both of symbolic gestures, as when she insisted on placing her chair in the center of the aisle between black and white sections at a segregated meeting of the Southern Conference on Human Welfare in 1939, and of quiet lobbying, as in her role of messenger between her husband and the National Association for the Advancement of Colored People (NAACP). She supported federal legislation to outlaw lynching and, during World War II, worked to eliminate discrimination in the armed forces.

During the war, Eleanor endeavored to ensure women's participation in all aspects of the mobilization, visited troops in hospitals and in the field, and sought to continue the many New Deal social reforms jeopardized by the country's focus on the international crisis.

Franklin Roosevelt died in April of 1945, during his fourth term as president. Eleanor continued her public life, perhaps feeling freer because she was no longer perceived as a politician's wife. She turned many of her efforts to international matters, an extension of her long-standing interest in building a lasting peace. She had earlier been an advocate of the League of Nations and the World Court, and now President Harry S Truman appointed her as a delegate to the newly formed United Nations, where she served until 1953. She chaired the committee that produced the 1948 Declaration on Human Rights and was nominated four times for the Nobel Peace Prize.

The "First Lady of the World" showed concern for the victims of war and oppression parallel to her continuing domestic interests in civil rights and women's issues. Her last public role was as the chairperson of President John F. Kennedy's Commission on the Status of Women, in which capacity she supported full access by women to economic and political opportunities.

She died in New York City on November 7, 1962, of a rare type of tuberculosis.

Summary

Eleanor Roosevelt's life bore out the advice she had written to women in 1930, "to be ready to go out and try new adventures, create new work for others as well as herself, and strike deep roots in some community where her presence will make a difference in the lives of others."

She defined a new role for women in American public life. Although during much of her life she filled a position as the wife of a prominent politician, her contributions stand on their own. With compassion and a commitment to humanitarian interests, Eleanor helped to place the issues of racial and gender justice on the national agenda. She was an advocate for all excluded groups, using her public visibility as a means to bring their concerns to national attention and using her influence to promote changes in attitudes and in legislation. On the international scene, she reached out to the victims of injustice and poverty, legitimizing and promoting their well-being.

To women of future generations, Eleanor Roosevelt became a model of energy, humanity and courage. Always an example of impeccable courtesy, she could also confront leaders of the Soviet Union or the proponents of segregation and state her case. Eleanor Roosevelt demonstrated the need to redefine power as not only the authority to move armies or to control economic might but also the ability to inspire, to question the status quo, and to work for equality without the expectation of personal gain.

Bibliography

Cook, Blanche Wiesen. *Eleanor Roosevelt*. Vol. 1. New York: Viking, 1992. The first volume of a projected two-volume study, Cook's sensitive biography places

Eleanor Roosevelt in the context of a rich emotional life and emphasizes her lifelong strengths.

Hoff-Wilson, Joan, and Marjorie Lightman, eds. *Without Precedent: The Life and Career of Eleanor Roosevelt.* Bloomington: Indiana University Press, 1984. An excellent collection of articles on Roosevelt's character and contributions. The essays introduce fine scholarship dealing with the major themes in her life.

Lash, Joseph P. *Eleanor and Franklin.* New York: W. W. Norton, 1971.

———. *Eleanor: The Years Alone.* New York: W. W. Norton, 1972. Lash was the first to write a biography of Roosevelt based on full access to her papers. His personal friendship with Roosevelt enabled him to provide a warm and comprehensive picture of her life.

Roosevelt, Eleanor. *The Autobiography of Eleanor Roosevelt.* New York: Harper & Brothers, 1961. Three volumes consolidated into one, this autobiography is indispensable to the student but provides a picture that is too self-effacing.

Youngs, J. William T. *Eleanor Roosevelt: Personal and Public Life.* Edited by Oscar Handlin. Boston: Little, Brown, 1985. Part of the Library of American Biography series, this is an accessible and positive short biography.

Mary Welek Atwell

IDA ROSENTHAL

Born: January 9, 1886; Rakov, Russia
Died: March 28, 1973; New York, New York
Area of Achievement: Business and industry
Contribution: Having created with her partner Enid Bissett in 1922 the first brassiere to give women a natural appearance, Rosenthal cofounded the Maiden Form Brassiere Company. Through sophisticated marketing and advertising, Rosenthal gave the Maidenform brand worldwide recognition and created what remains the largest privately held intimate apparel company in the United States.

Early Life

Born in Rakov near the city of Minsk in Russia in 1886, Ida Kaganovich (changed to Cohen upon arriving in America) was the eldest of seven children. From her father Abraham, a scribe who came from a line of Jewish scholars, Ida inherited a lifelong love of learning. It was from her mother, however, that Ida inherited not only an independent spirit but also a flair for business. As one of the few literate women in the town and the main breadwinner of the family, Sarah Kaganovich applied good business skills to the running of a general store. Sarah encouraged Ida to make something of her life. Before her daughters were even teenagers, Sarah apprenticed both Ida and her sister Ethel to a local dressmaker.

Once having learned to sew, Ida and Ethel were given a machine so that they could set up a dressmaking business in their home. Ida also worked for a period in Warsaw, where she attended the gymnasium, studying Russian and mathematics. The latter subject helped prepare her for a future role as a company treasurer.

While in Warsaw, Ida became involved in the socialist struggle. Upon returning to Rakov, she met and fell in love with William Rosenthal, a young man whose father was a scholar and teacher in Rakov. Both she and William became increasingly involved in the revolutionary movement. When Ida made a speech calling for the overthrow of the government, the local chief of police warned her mother that arrest could follow if Ida continued her revolutionary activities and suggested sending her away. When William was recruited into the Russian army in 1905 to fight against Japan, he chose instead to escape to the United States, where eighteen-year-old Ida joined him a few months later.

Upon her arrival, Ida refused an uncle's offer to live with his family in Hoboken, New Jersey, and would not consider a factory job. To achieve financial independence, she purchased a Singer sewing machine on the installment plan and established her own dressmaking business. In 1906, she married William; with his assistance over the next five years she became Hoboken's preeminent dressmaker. The Rosenthals' first child, Lewis, was born in 1907, and a daughter, Beatrice, was born nine years later.

By 1912, Ida Rosenthal employed six workers and charged from $6.50 to $7.50 for a dress. Among her customers Ida was known for her charm. She was also respected for her integrity and fine workmanship. Through her own hard work she set a high standard for her employees, who appreciated both her fairness and quick grasp of production problems.

Life's Work

In 1918, Ida Rosenthal moved her family and business to 611 West 141st Street in Manhattan, bringing with her a loyal clientele willing to pay $25 for a dress. Among the new customers she gained was the director of her daughter's nursery school, who wore Ida's dresses when she visited Ferlé Heller's fashionable millinery shop at 36 West 57th Street. Enid Bissett, who had her own exclusive dress boutique at Ferlé Heller's, saw the dresses and was so impressed by Ida's ability to interpret a dress style that she hired her as the dressmaker for Enid Frocks. In 1921, Bissett suggested that Rosenthal give up her own clientele and become her partner. Although her family and friends advised against the partnership, Rosenthal weighed the risks and accepted Bissett's offer by investing almost her entire savings of $4,000 to become an equal partner in Enid Frocks.

At Enid Frocks, Bissett and Rosenthal combined their talents to create high quality, fashionable dresses that ranged from $125 to $300. Their goal was not a quick sale, but a satisfied customer who would return because she trusted them to sell her a style that suited her. Rosenthal's belief that the key to a successful business was a repeat customer became the basis on which she built Maidenform in the years that followed.

Despite the fine quality of their dresses, Rosenthal and Bissett believed that the dresses did not fit correctly because women in the early 1920's wore flattening bandeaux that denied the natural curves of the female figure. Bissett experimented by cutting apart a bandeau form and restructuring it so that it had two cups separated by a center piece of elastic. Rosenthal's husband refined Bissett's concept, creating the first uplift brassiere, which was sewn into the dresses as a give-away. As clients who liked the new look returned asking for additional separate brassieres, Ida Rosenthal and Bissett began to sell them for one dollar each. They named their invention the Maiden Form Brassiere because it implied the opposite of the flat "boyish form" look. By 1924, they had registered the Maiden Form name in the United States, and it was only a few years before they had registered the name in Canada, South America, England, Africa, and Indonesia, where they soon began to sell their product.

In 1925, Bissett and the Rosenthals gave up manufacturing dresses in order to market the Maiden Form Brassiere exclusively. Although they kept the showroom in Manhattan, they moved manufacturing to Bayonne, New Jersey. In order to increase production, they pioneered an efficient section-work process whereby a sewing operator no longer produced an entire garment, but performed one specific task. This innovative method continued to be used throughout the intimate apparel industry into the early 1990's.

In 1930, by which time Bissett was no longer active in the operation of the business, the company became the Maiden Form Brassiere Company. Within a few years the manufacturing facility in Bayonne became the world's largest brassiere plant.

In running Maiden Form, the Rosenthals worked as a team: William as president and chief designer, Ida as head of sales and finance. It was Ida who was the personality of the business, using her charisma and femininity to advantage in carefully managing the company she had built. Among the labor innovations for which Ida Rosenthal has been credited was the 1937 decision by Maiden Form to change from paying a worker for the time worked (week work) to paying for the number of pieces produced (piece work). The rate of payment was set by engineering studies of the amount of time needed to perform each operation, a method common to heavy industry but new for apparel companies.

Ida Rosenthal's imagination and ability to see challenges as opportunities led her during World War II to convince the War Department that women wearing brassieres became less fatigued than women who did not. As a result, despite wartime shortages, Maiden Form received priority shipments of fabric to sew brassieres for women engaged in the war effort. Shortages of material for normal production forced the Rosenthals to allocate Maiden Form product, which they did in such an equitable manner that they gained the respect of retailers across the country. During this time, Ida Rosenthal characteristically looked ahead to the postwar era and continued to advertise the Maiden Form brand to keep the name before the public. (The company's name was later changed to Maidenform, Inc.)

Always finding innovative ways to build the company's brand image, the company introduced a bold advertising campaign in 1949 that lasted for twenty years, making Maidenform one of the best known brands of all time: "I dreamed I . . . in my Maidenform bra." The advertisements, which showed women succeeding in fantasy situations outside the home, has been described by Carol Moog as "a kind of emotional road map for the women's lib activities that came to the surface in the seventies."

From the mid-1920's, Ida and William Rosenthal actively supported community organizations in Bayonne and New York. In 1938, the couple donated land for Camp Lewis, a Boy Scout camp for youth from the Bayonne area, in memory of their son, who had died while he was a student at Columbia Law School. By 1953, they had established the Ida and William Rosenthal Foundation, a private charitable foundation that continues to fund the arts, educational institutions, and social service organizations.

When William died in 1958, Ida Rosenthal assumed first the presidency and then the chairmanship of Maidenform, Inc. Significantly, she never allowed Maidenform to become her entire life; she traveled extensively, read, went to the theater and opera, and enjoyed her family and friends. In 1963, Rosenthal returned to Russia as the only woman member of the first American trade delegation invited to view Soviet apparel manufacturing.

Ida Rosenthal never retired. As she herself said, she did not have time to. At the age of eighty in 1966, she suffered a stroke while she was on a business trip to Milwaukee, Wisconsin. This stroke left her incapacitated until her death in 1973.

Summary

Having pioneered the role of a female entrepreneur during the 1920's, Ida Rosenthal also pioneered the role of a woman executive during the 1930's, at a time when most women in the workforce never thought of rising above the level of factory worker or secretary. Her strength as an executive was her ability to grasp all aspects of the business. From her earlier experience in running her own dress business, she understood production, finance, and sales. Most important, she understood what women were thinking and always marketed Maidenform products in response to consumers' needs, never for the sake of a one-time sale.

Unlike many entrepreneurs who live for the moment, Ida Rosenthal built for the future. Her mission was to establish an organization with excellent management that would outlive her. With that aim she invited her daughter Beatrice to join the company upon her graduation from Barnard College in 1938, having impressed upon her from childhood the idea that a woman had to be independent and fulfill her potential. Beatrice's husband, Dr. Joseph A. Coleman, also joined the company in 1946. As a result of the careful planning for succession begun by Ida Rosenthal, the third generation of her family continued to manage the company some twenty years after her death, overseeing a corporation that, as of 1993, made more than $250 million in sales and employed 6,500 people worldwide.

Bibliography

Aqualina, Grace A., and Margaret Dooley Nitka. *Past and Promise: Lives of New Jersey Women*. Metuchen, N.J.: Scarecrow Press, 1990. A comprehensive account of Ida Rosenthal's life, with a detailed description of the Rosenthals' first years in the United States and the development of the Maiden Form Brassiere Company.

Bird, Caroline. "Fashions for Everyone II: Ida Rosenthal, Nell Donnelly." In *Enterprising Women*. New York: W. W. Norton, 1976. Included in an overview of women entrepreneurs compiled in honor of the American bicentennial, this chapter provides a concise summary of the Rosenthals' endeavors in founding Maidenform.

"Maidenform's Mrs. R." *Fortune* 42 (July, 1950): 75-76. A lively account of Rosenthal's charismatic leadership of Maidenform, emphasizing her unflagging concern for efficient production and a quality product.

Moog, Carol. *"Are They Selling Her Lips?": Advertising and Identity*. New York: William Morrow, 1990. A clinical psychologist and advertising consultant, Moog analyzes the psychological strategies behind well-known advertisements. Chapter 1 concentrates mainly on Maidenform's advertising campaigns, beginning with the Dream Campaign that ran for two decades (1949-1969) during Rosenthal's leadership, through the Celebrity Campaign of the late 1980's.

Morris, Michele. "The Mother Figure of Maidenform." *Working Woman* 12 (April, 1987): 82-83. A profile of Beatrice Coleman, daughter of Ida Rosenthal and president of Maidenform from 1968 to 1989. Credit for Coleman's success is attributed to her mother's strong example.

Catherine Coleman Brawer

NELLIE TAYLOE ROSS

Born: November 29, 1876; St. Joseph, Missouri
Died: December 19, 1977; Washington, D.C.
Area of Achievement: Government and politics
Contribution: The first woman governor of a state (Wyoming) in the United States, Ross later served as an officer in the Democratic Party and as a director of the U.S. Mint, one of the first women to head a federal agency.

Early Life

Nellie Davis Tayloe was born on November 29, 1876, in St. Joseph, Missouri. Her father, James Wynn Tayloe, was from a prominent Southern family, one of whose members had built the Octagon House in Washington, D.C., where President James Madison and his wife Dolley lived after the British burned the White House during the War of 1812. Her mother, Elizabeth Blair Green Tayloe, was descended from a family that claimed a distant kinship with George Washington.

Nellie attended public and private schools and had private instruction as well. Her family eventually moved to Omaha, Nebraska, where she completed a two-year program as a kindergarten teacher and taught briefly before her marriage.

While visiting relatives in Tennessee, she met and fell in love with a young lawyer, William Bradford Ross. He moved to Cheyenne, Wyoming, before marrying Nellie in 1902. The Rosses had four sons: the twins, George Tayloe and James Ambrose, born in 1903; Alfred Duff, born in 1905, who died at ten months of age; and William Bradford, born in 1912. Nellie devoted herself to her home and family during her marriage. She was active in the Cheyenne Woman's Club, which concentrated on intellectual self-improvement, and she often presented programs there.

William Ross practiced law and occasionally ran for political office. As a Democrat in a Republican state, however, he had little political success until, to his wife's dismay, he was elected governor of Wyoming in 1922 by a coalition of Democrats and Progressive Republicans. In September of 1924, he became ill and underwent an appendectomy. Complications from the surgery led to his death on October 2, 1924.

Life's Work

Because Governor Ross's death occurred close to the upcoming general election on November 4, 1924, Wyoming law required that his successor be elected then. Democratic Party leaders in Wyoming offered Nellie Tayloe Ross the nomination to fill the remainder of her husband's term. She did not reply and the party took her silence for acquiescence, nominating her on October 14. She had no political experience except for what she had acquired as her husband's confidant and in her tenure as the governor's wife. Although she lived in a state where women had voted since 1869, she had played no role in the woman suffrage campaign. She later indicated that she had accepted the nomination because she wished her husband's programs to continue and believed that she understood what he would have done better than anyone else;

she also expressed the need for some purpose in her own life as she coped with the grief of widowhood. The Republicans nominated Eugene J. Sullivan of Casper, an attorney whose ties to the oil industry may have hurt his campaign since both Wyoming and the nation were immersed in the Teapot Dome scandal involving federal oil lands (including property located in Wyoming).

Nellie Ross did not campaign for office. Friends paid for a few political advertisements, and she wrote two open letters stating her intentions. She probably had two advantages in the election. The first was the sympathy of the voters for her widowhood. She indicated, and many people agreed, that a vote for her was a tribute to her deceased husband. The second advantage was the popular support among citizens for Wyoming to become the first state to elect a woman governor, since it had been first in 1869 to allow women to vote. This election would be the state's only chance to secure this distinction, since Miriam A. ("Ma") Ferguson, wife of impeached former governor James A. Ferguson, was likely to be elected governor of Texas in November. Although Ross won election easily, she did not help other Democrats in Wyoming in what was generally a catastrophic year for Democratic candidates nationwide in the wake of the crushing defeat of the party's presidential candidate by Republican Calvin Coolidge.

Nellie Tayloe Ross was inaugurated as the thirteenth governor of Wyoming on January 5, 1925, still wearing mourning clothes. In her brief address she stated that her administration would not be a new one, but rather a continuation of her husband's. She entered office with much popular sympathy and an administration in place. Since Ferguson was not sworn in as governor of Texas until January 25, Nellie Tayloe Ross was the nation's first woman governor.

When the Wyoming legislature convened in January of 1926, the new governor gave her first major speech, based on her husband's notes on his plans for that legislative session. She called for reductions in both state expenditures and taxes; for state assistance to the economically depressed agricultural industry; and for banking reform, noting the number of recently failed banks. She championed protective legislation for miners and for women and children, and she requested unsuccessfully that Wyoming ratify the federal amendment prohibiting child labor.

Ross recognized that the Republican-dominated legislature had little reason to cooperate with her. On some issues, such as banking reform, she was able to work out compromises with Republican leaders. In a few instances, she used the veto. She believed that her veto of a bill requiring a special election (rather than appointment by the governor) to fill a vacancy in Wyoming's delegation to the United States Senate caused her defeat in 1926. Wyoming's elderly Republican senator had been reelected only a short time earlier, and it was believed that he would not live to complete his term. Republicans did not want their Democratic governor to have the opportunity to appoint a Democrat to the position.

Ross was aware of the public's intense scrutiny of her actions and knew that if she made mistakes as governor, people would use them to claim that women should not hold high elective office. She found curiosity-seekers constantly in her office and on the porch of her home. Although she received invitations to speak all over the country, she declined them all. When she appeared in Calvin Coolidge's Inaugural Parade in Washington, D.C., she got the largest ovation. Many Easterners still thought of Wyoming as an uncivilized place, and its cultured, gracious governor attracted attention simply because she was so different from their expectations.

As an administrator, Ross received mixed reviews. She removed from office some administrators appointed by her husband who were not meeting her expectations. She lamented the difficulties of enforcing Prohibition and advocated better law enforcement. She stood up to the federal government on issues of federal lands and water allocation.

Nellie Ross was nominated by the Democrats for reelection in 1926, but was defeated in a close election by the Republican candidate, Frank C. Emerson. While her veto of the senatorial special election law was one issue, Republicans vaguely alluded to the idea that a man would be a better governor than a woman. Democrats tried unsuccessfully to win women voters by suggesting that a rejection of Ross would be a rejection of woman suffrage. Ultimately she probably was defeated because she was a Democrat in a Republican state and the sympathy issue that had helped her in 1924 was no longer a factor. As it was, she did better than any other statewide Democratic candidate in Wyoming.

Ross never again sought elective public office. Instead, she lectured and wrote articles for magazines. She became involved in national politics, serving as a Wyoming committeewoman to the Democratic National Committee (DNC) and then as vice chairman of the DNC, in charge of activities for women. In 1928, she seconded the presidential nomination of New York Governor Alfred E. Smith. With Eleanor Roosevelt, she headed the campaign drive launched by the party's Women's Division to generate support for Smith. Already a popular speaker, Ross traveled around the country making speeches tirelessly and unsuccessfully for Smith's election. Four years later, Ross was active in the Women's Speakers' Bureau, campaigning for the Democratic presidential nominee, Franklin D. Roosevelt.

With the election of Roosevelt as president in 1932, women became more visible in the federal government. Eleanor Roosevelt acted on her husband's behalf and publicly involved herself in policy issues to an unprecedented degree—one that was not duplicated until Hillary Rodham Clinton became First Lady in 1993.

Franklin D. Roosevelt decided that he wanted to be the first president to appoint a woman to the cabinet. Ross was considered for either secretary of the interior or secretary of labor, but Roosevelt selected Frances Perkins as secretary of labor instead. He appointed a number of women to federal office; among them were Ruth Bryan Owens as minister to Denmark (1933-1936), Josephine Roche as assistant secretary of the Treasury (1934-1937), and Nellie Tayloe Ross as director of the United States Mint.

As director of the Mint, Ross dealt with the American gold and silver bullion reserve and the minting of coins for the United States and several foreign governments. Appointed in 1933, she served as the Mint's first woman director. At that time, huge quantities of gold and silver poured into the U.S. government's coffers. Ross discovered that most of the work was still being done by hand and directed that the process be automated. She emphasized efficiency and was able to reduce the costs of her operation significantly. In 1950, she informed an astonished Congressional Appropriations Committee that she had not needed all of her previous year's appropriation and wanted to return about $1 million of her $4.8 million appropriation. Her efficiency plans reduced the labor needs of the mint and resulted in the discharge of about 3,000 of the Mint's 4,000 employees. She continued as director of the Mint in the Roosevelt and Truman administrations and was not replaced until the Republican administration of President Dwight D. Eisenhower came to power in 1952. Ross continued to make her home in Washington, D.C., until her death on December 19, 1977.

Summary

Nellie Tayloe Ross never intended to have a political career. She believed that women belonged at home and was content there until her husband's death thrust her into politics. Her election was probably attributable to public sympathy generated by her husband's death. She was the first of many women elected to fill out their husbands' unexpired terms in office.

As the nation's first woman governor, she did not have a tremendous impact. She was probably an average governor, although she was regarded more favorably than Texas governor Miriam A. Ferguson. She achieved few of her goals because of Republican control of the legislature. Her defeat for reelection was probably the result of being a Democrat in a predominantly Republican state.

After her defeat, she focused her attention on other political matters by becoming active in the Democratic National Committee and appearing as a popular and effective speaker. Her loyalty and support for Franklin D. Roosevelt led him to consider her for several offices before appointing her the first woman director of the U.S. Mint. She administered the Mint economically and efficiently for almost twenty years. Although she was not the most visible woman in the New Deal, Ross was one of the most durable and effective.

Bibliography

"First U.S. Woman Governor Celebrates Her Centennial During the Bicentennial." *Aging* 268 (February/March, 1977): 13-14. Aimed at a general audience, this biographical sketch provides a concise assessment of Ross's life and career. Discusses her activities after leaving office as governor, when she worked as a lecturer on the Chautauqua circuit and helped organize the women's division of the Democratic Party.

Huch, Ronald K. "Nellie Tayloe Ross of Wyoming Becomes First Female Governor." In *Great Events from History II: Human Rights*, edited by Frank N. Magill. Pasadena, Calif.: Salem Press, 1992. This is a brief, well-written account of her election as governor in 1924, with an analysis of its impact.

Othman, Frederick C. "She Makes Our Money." *Reader's Digest* 57 (November, 1950): 141-144. This condensation of a previously published newspaper article is a rare account of Ross's years as director of the Mint and is especially useful for information on her efforts to automate it.

Ross, Nellie Tayloe. "The Governor Lady." *Good Housekeeping* 85 (August, 1927), 30-31, 118-124; (September, 1927), 36-37, 206-218; (October, 1927), 72-73, 180-197. These articles provide Ross's own account of her years as governor. Except for Barbara Jean Aslakson's thesis, "Nellie Tayloe Ross: First Woman Governor" (University of Wyoming, 1960), these magazine pieces contain the best account of those years.

Ware, Susan. *Beyond Suffrage: Women in the New Deal*. Cambridge, Mass.: Harvard University Press, 1981. This is a well-researched account of influential women in the New Deal. It has information on Ross's activities in the Democratic National Committee, placing them in the context of women's roles in the New Deal.

____________. *Holding Their Own: American Women in the 1930s*. Boston: Twayne, 1982. This well-documented account is useful in placing Ross's activities in the context of her times, but it has only two direct references to her.

Judith A. Parsons

SUSAN ROTHENBERG

Born: January 20, 1945; Buffalo, New York

Area of Achievement: Art
Contribution: As one of America's leading women artists, Rothenberg has pioneered new modes of imagination and vision in painting.

Early Life

Susan Rothenberg was born on January 20, 1945, in Buffalo, New York. Her father, Leonard, was a successful local businessman; her mother, the former Adele Cohen, was a housewife. Both parents were descended from Jewish families that had immigrated to the United States from Eastern Europe. Susan's childhood bears resemblance to the upbringings of most of her generation of American artists. Most of these artists had secure middle-class origins. Their parents worked at more traditional money-making occupations such as law or business, and made enough money to buy a comfortable home and secure a prosperous upbringing for their children. Many of the parents were of immigrant backgrounds. The children went on to fulfill the aesthetic aspirations that the parents had perhaps harbored, but had never been able to fulfill.

Even before she made her first acquaintance with the formal art world by virtue of an adolescent visit to the Albright-Knox Art Gallery in Buffalo, Susan had shown a precocious interest in art. In high school and in college at nearby Cornell University, Susan chose to concentrate on sculpture. Although her teachers discouraged Susan, her sculptural training was later revealed in the tactile, hands-on quality of her painting and in her sensitivity to paint as a physical medium. Susan was initially depressed by her failure at sculpture, but, knowing her own worth, she refused to yield to the criticism of her professors. When she turned from sculpture to painting in her last year of college, it was not in defeat, but in reaffirmation of her inner talent.

Susan entered art school after her graduation from college, but she quickly decided such a formal program of training was not for her. Personal instincts may have contributed less to this decision than did the spirit of the times. Susan became an adult at the time that the counterculture of the 1960's was reaching the height of its popularity. Like many people her age, Susan found this era's ethic of heedless pleasure liberating. Nevertheless, her participation in the counterculture was more than merely a matter of personal gratification. It also was a symptom of the creativity and interest in new modes of perception that would eventually transform her into one of America's leading painters. Susan's youthful drifting eventually led her to New York City, the glittering center of the contemporary art world. In New York, she met fellow artist George Trakas; they were married in 1971, and their daughter, Maggie, was born in 1972.

Life's Work

Since she had switched from sculpture to painting during college, Susan Rothenberg's work had been largely abstract, following in the traditions of the dominant mode of American art since World War II. Up until 1973, Rothenberg's art had proceeded from the standards maintained by the established artists of the day. As Rothenberg began to determine the course her own art would take, however, she became increasingly drawn to a more representative idiom. Chafing against the banishment of images from abstract painting, Rothenberg searched for an emblematic image that would be the hallmark of her painterly craftsmanship. She soon found it in the horse. Rothenberg did not deliberately set out to paint horses. She simply found that one day she had drawn a horse, and that by some subconscious process she had arrived at her first characteristic manner of painting.

Paintings of horses were, to say the least, not the mode in the New York of the mid-1970's. That era's myth of art-historical logic had seen representations of "real" objects such as horses as hopelessly retrograde. Rothenberg's work was, therefore, at best irrelevant. Yet, against all predictions, Rothenberg's series of horse paintings began to earn more and more acclaim as the 1970's proceeded. In part, this reevaluation occurred because the New York art world was itself tired of abstractions, and paintings such as Rothenberg's prompted it to admit this fact. Another factor was that Rothenberg's paintings of the horse were unlike any others yet seen. They were not full-fledged, pictorial representations. They did not portray any realistic background of pasture, stable, or racecourse that situated the horses in a realm familiar to the spectator. They were rigorously drawn, in contour and in form. It was as if Rothenberg was exploring the theoretical idea of the horse as image rather than any palpable portrait of a specific horse or horses.

Because of this seriousness of intention, Rothenberg's horse paintings won her wide recognition in the New York art world. By the time the horse series was well underway, Rothenberg's art had become positively trendy. Late 1970's art critics saw the emergence of a "New Image" school of painters including Bill Jensen and Gary Stephan as well as Rothenberg. All of these artists had been trained in various abstract modes, but had chosen instead to pursue different kinds of representational images.

With the individuality that was to mark her career, however, Rothenberg refused to rest on her laurels. She abruptly halted the horse series in 1979. This was a risky move, as she was undercutting the basis on which her work had become known and praised by critics and collectors. Some observers speculated that Rothenberg's contemporaneous divorce from Trakas was the motivating spur behind her decision, while others concluded that the artist merely wished to stay a step ahead of those who would prematurely classify her.

Rothenberg's work of the 1980's turned to other representational idioms. At first, she focused largely on the human figure. These works were not portraits; they did not refer to recognizable scenes or people. Rather than painting the human figure itself, Rothenberg seemed to be grappling with the challenge of outlining the form of the human being, or even the idea of the human form. Rothenberg's paintings of this era are probably more difficult for the general viewer to appreciate. The horse paintings possessed an immediacy, a wildness, exemplified in the free, bold brushstrokes in which the painting was executed. Rothenberg's human-figure works, by contrast, are more dense, more resistant to easy visual assimilation. In a way, the activity of the paint itself on the canvas is so busy, so rife with formal energy, that it distracts the viewer's attention from the simpler task of "making sense" of the work.

Despite this difficulty, Rothenberg's popularity soared in the 1980's. The art world advanced on a tide of popular interest and economic prosperity not seen before or since. Art became a popular commodity outside the cloistered circles of genteel collectors. The art boom in the avant-garde New York neighborhood of Soho was intimately associated with the contemporaneous surge in stock prices on the Wall Street exchanges a few blocks to the south. As a local television commercial of the day, produced by the Chiat-Day advertising agency for New York Telephone, put it, "Wall Street makes the money, Soho makes the art." Among the most popular artists were those who had just recently made their reputation. Rothenberg was one of these. Rothenberg was often deemed a "Neo-Expressionist." Like the New Image painters, the Neo-Expressionists turned from abstraction to figurative, representative painting. Unlike the cool, detached manner of the New Image painters, though, the Neo-Expressionists were fevered, passionate, and flamboyant. The most typical Neo-Expressionist painters were young, brash white males such as Julian Schnabel, David Salle, and Eric Fischl. Rothenberg's less declarative mode was to some extent strange company for these artists. Yet her work did have expressive and emotional qualities which linked it to that of the Neo-Expressionist painters. It was by dint of this association that Rothenberg achieved national celebrity rare for a living artist.

Nevertheless, there were disquieting aspects to Rothenberg's sudden fame. Rothenberg could not help but notice that she was (sometimes along with Elizabeth Murray) often the only woman included in group shows of the Neo-Expressionist artists. Rothenberg resented being portrayed as "the token woman" and lobbied for greater inclusion of women painters in art shows. Eventually, she refused to participate in any shows in which women were not given an equal opportunity to contribute. Rothenberg also began to believe that being seen as simply another Neo-Expressionist painter reduced her work's aesthetic complexity and individuality. Rothenberg was convinced that the source of her art was something inner and personal. To equate it simplistically with a movement such as Neo-Expressionism obscured the artistic integrity of her work.

After 1985, the decline of Neo-Expressionism left Rothenberg free to pursue her art in a more individual mode. Elements of abstraction and of simpler colors and patterns returned, as Rothenberg sought to make her art at once more personal and more rigorous. As with her shift away from the image of the horse some years earlier, this shift in concentration was paralleled by a change in Rothenberg's personal situation. Rothenberg decided to move from New York to New Mexico. Although New Mexico also was a place where artists tended to congregate, it was a much more remote and serene environment.

Even after the notoriety of contemporary art began to wane in the early 1990's, Rothenberg remained one of America's leading painters. Ironically, although Rothenberg had first come to prominence as part of a reaction against abstraction, her art seemed much more aesthetic when compared to the dominant political tone of the era. Whatever the politics of the art world, Rothenberg's reputation was assured. This was indicated by a large traveling exhibition that began in the fall of 1991. Symbolically, this exhibition opened at the Albright-Knox museum that Rothenberg had visited as a child. Her success had come full circle, and her vision was fully vindicated.

Summary

Before the advent of Susan Rothenberg, there had been many prominent women artists, with Georgia O'Keeffe, Louise Nevelson, Louise Bourgeois, and Helen Frankenthaler as only a few of the most famous. These artists, however, had been seen as powerful exceptions; the male artist was still considered to be the norm. Rothenberg's work had the effect of naturalizing the presence of women in the art world. Rothenberg's work demanded to be accepted on its own terms. Although it was possible to say that certain of Rothenberg's themes and approaches were distinctively female ones, and although Rothenberg was active in espousing the collective cause of women in art, Rothenberg refused to be conveniently bracketed as "merely" a woman artist. Instead, she pursued a rigor and a standard in her art that sought to transcend gender stereotypes and be excellent simply as the art of every talented woman or man can be excellent.

Rothenberg also broke ground in other ways. As the middle-class child of immigrants, she helped mitigate the air of elitism that had always surrounded the American art scene. In her interviews and public appearances, Rothenberg seems to come across as somebody accessible and likable, someone not that much different from other people except for her artistic talent. Rothenberg's combination of ambition and humility, originality and accessibility, has enabled her to have an artistic career less cloistered and more democratic than most.

Bibliography

Basquin, Kit. "Susan Rothenberg: Paint and Form." *School Arts* 92 (February, 1993): 33-36. In this article, Basquin provides a brief biographical sketch on Rothenberg before turning her attention to the formal issues found in Rothenberg's works. Includes a time line of Rothenberg's career.

Hughes, Robert. "Signs of Anxiety." *Time* 141 (March 1, 1993): 60-61. On the occasion of the opening of a traveling exhibition of Rothenberg's work at the Hirshhorn Museum in Washington, D.C., noted critic Robert Hughes assesses what he sees as "the nerviness, durability and occasional brilliance" of Rothenberg's development as an artist and the powerful changes evident in her work since her move to New Mexico.

Levin, Kim. *Beyond Modernism: Essays on Art from the '70s and '80s*. New York: Harper & Row, 1988. This book gives a general overview of the years in which Rothenberg's art came to public notice.

Rothenberg, Susan. *Susan Rothenberg: Paintings and Drawings*. Edited by Michael

Auping. New York: Rizzoli, 1992. This opulent art book, issued to coincide with a traveling exhibition organized by curator Michael Auping, provides the most generous coverage of Rothenberg's paintings available.

Simon, Joan. *Susan Rothenberg*. New York: Harry N. Abrams, 1991. This book, presented in standard art-book format, has plates of most of Rothenberg's major works as well as an excellent introductory essay.

Stevens, Mark. "Brushes with Art." *The New Republic* 208 (May 17, 1993): 36-42. Stevens praises Rothenberg as a practitioner of intrinsic, apolitical art.

Margaret Boe Birns

GREAT LIVES FROM HISTORY

AREAS OF ACHIEVEMENT